ITALIAN
GENEALOGICAL
RECORDS

Amabile Rossi Segato, Age 83, at Her Home in Limena, Padova, Italy

ITALIAN
GENEALOGICAL
RECORDS

How to Use Italian Civil, Ecclesiastical, &
Other Records in Family History Research

By

TRAFFORD R. COLE, Psy.D.

Ancestry®

Cole, Trafford R. (Trafford Robertson), 1951–
    Italian genealogical records : how to use Italian civil, ecclesiastical,
and other records in family history research / by Trafford R. Cole.
    p.   cm.
    Includes bibliographical references and index.
    ISBN 0-916489-58-2
    1. Italian Americans–Genealogy–Research–Handbooks, manuals, etc.
2. Italy–Genealogy–Research–Handbooks, manuals, etc.
I. Title.
E184.I86C615 1995
929' .1'08951073–dc20   95-2042

First printing 1995
10 9 8 7 6 5 4 3

Printed in the United States of America

This book is dedicated to my wife, Fernanda, who has shared with me her life and her passion for Italian history and culture;

and to my mother, Nancy, who inspired a love for family history.

Contents

Tables

Acknowledgements

I would like to thank all of the many clients and friends who, over the last eighteen years, have allowed me to search for their Italian roots in the parishes, town offices, and state archives throughout Italy, where I have gained the knowledge and experience necessary to write this book. In particular, I would like to thank those who have given permission to use their family documents in this book. In alphabetical order they are: Mr. Raymond J. Baccino, Mrs. Anthony Belfiglio, Mrs. A. J. Bergamini, Mrs. Olive Bonato, Mr. Paul Bunnell, Mr. Daniel A. Caliari, Mrs. Fernanda Segato Cole, Dr. Alexander DeVolpi, Mrs. Lisa Ferrante, Mr. Lino Gambarotto, Mr. John R. Gallagher, Mrs. Mary Ann Hellams, Mr. Howard W. Hunter, Mr. Paul Ingram, Mr. Terrance L. Irwin, Ms. Sharon Kent, Mrs. John Luciani, Mr. George Marchelos, Dr. Thomas Militello, Mrs. Mary E. Osborne, Dr. Dennis Packard, Mrs. William Reno, Mrs. Rena Succo, Dr. Vincent A. Transano, Mrs. Ruth Urie, and Mrs. Rosemary Winder.

I also thank the many parish priests, priests in the *curia vescovile* archives, town officials, and staff of the state archives who have assisted me over the years and allowed me to consult the records in their care. In particular, the *l'ufficio di stato civile* of the commune of Vigonza, Padova, has been very helpful in explaining the legal aspects of civil record keeping in Italy. I would also like to acknowledge the assistance of Fernanda Segato Cole, Flora Baldan, and Maria Letizia Cutrona for the maps they contributed to chapters 2 and 5, and of Luigi Mendola, who shared his expertise in heraldry for chapter 4.

Part I

Introduction to Italy and Italian Records

Chapter 1

INTRODUCTION

GENEALOGY IS SAID TO BE ONE OF THE FASTEST-GROWING hobbies in the United States. This fact would surprise no one who has entered the deep waters of family history. Sometimes the waters are murky and sometime crystal clear, but always a submersed world of fascinating people and events invites further investigation.

In a history seminar, the instructor asked each participant to write about the most important events that had occurred during his or her lifetime. To a person, all of the students wrote about events from personal life: marriage, their first children, school, etc. None wrote about the historical events of the time—the election of a president, the opening of Eastern Europe to democracy, new tax proposals. Obviously, the events of most importance to each person are personal experiences and relationships. Genealogy is the study of relationships—of ancestors who are directly related to us. They are our families; they are our role models. To learn more about them is to learn more about ourselves. How did they live? What trials did they endure? How did they overcome the difficulties in their lives? The answers to these questions lead us to investigate ever more our own family histories.

Genealogy is not a new pursuit. The Book of Genesis in the Bible's Old Testament sets forth the genealogy of the Patriarchs, and the New Testament begins with the genealogy of Christ. In the Hebrew culture, lineage has always been very important in determining blessings and the right to priesthood. The Bible is replete with stories of family dramas concerning these birthrights and blessings—from Esau, who sold his rights for a pot of lentils, to Reuben and his brothers, who sold Joseph into captivity in Egypt.

In Biblical tradition, even the modern drama of hostility between Arabs and Jews can be traced back to the family quarrel and animosity between Isaac, the legitimate son and heir of Abraham, and Ishmael, son of the servant woman Hagar, who was cast out of Abraham's tent. From Isaac descended the twelve tribes of Israel, and from Ishmael descended the Arab nations.

Genealogy and the tracing of pedigrees was also important in the Middle Ages under the feudal system. It was according to family line and the rights of the firstborn that titles of nobility were passed from one generation to another. In the sixteenth century, the College of Heralds was formed in England to establish and record family lines, not only in England but throughout Europe.

Not until this century, however, has genealogy become a popular hobby and a passion to people in all walks of life; a pursuit of which the main purpose is not to establish rights to titles and property, but rather to seek knowledge of family and ancestors for personal interest. Historians have proposed several reasons for this new and widespread interest in family history. The most frequently proposed reason is that, following the massive emigration from Europe to new lands, such as the Americas, there has been a breakdown in family bonds and a consequent loss of a sense of belonging among the descendants of the immigrants. Genealogy is the path to discovering our origins and to reestablishing those family bonds.

Another possible motivation is that modern technological society has depersonalized our lives and rendered us so mobile that it has destroyed our sense of identity. Today, fifty percent of families in the United States move every five years (Conger 1981). A family history gives renewed importance to close relationships, reminds us of the human and social aspects of our lives, and reestablishes our personal identities.

A final proposition, especially true for society in the United States, is that, although the American "melting pot" has provided us with an important common social and cultural basis and common objectives, much has been lost in the process. This loss includes the traditions, heritage, and culture of the country of origin—our ethnic-cultural background. The wide success of Alex Haley's book *Roots* and the televised series based on it reflect this search for ethnic pride and for relearning family and ethnic traditions.

Whatever the reasons, there has been an explosion of interest in genealogy and a proliferation of genealogical societies, newsletters, magazines, and publications in the last several years. The 1990–1991 edition of *Genealogical Societies and Historical Societies in the United States* (edited by J. Konrad. Indianapolis: Ye Olde Genealogie Shoppe, 1990) lists 2,900 genealogical and historical societies in the

United States alone. It also lists ninety-six ethnic and sixty-seven religious archives. This number has surely increased since that time.

In 1987, Dr. Thomas E. Militello, of Palos Verdes, California, frustrated by genealogy societies, researchers, and others who expressed little interest in Italian genealogy, created an organization called P.O.I.N.T. (Pursuing Our Italian Names Together). He established a computer database of Italian surnames and a newsletter called *POINTers* to share information about Italy, genealogy, and family histories. The first issue, published in the spring of 1987, was a leaflet of four pages with some information about his initiative. Just two years later, without fanfare or publicity, *POINTers* had grown to fifty pages with 248 regular subscribers in thirty-four states and Canada and a database of 5,445 surnames from 783 submittals. By March 1994, 1,917 people had submitted 13,750 surnames from forty-nine states and several foreign countries. That this initiative, in only seven years, without the support of any well-established genealogical societies and without costly publicity, has made such strides is true indication of growing interest in Italian genealogy. It also demonstrates the need for a concerted and organized effort in pursuing genealogical research.

ITALIAN GENEALOGY

The fascinating search for ancestors and personal roots can be particularly rewarding for Italians. Compared with many other ethnic groups, Italian-Americans and Italian immigrants to other countries have some unique advantages in pursuing their family histories. Among these advantages are the family unity typical of Italian society, the relatively recent period of major Italian emigration to America, the relative immobility of the Italian people within Italy itself, and the record keeping of Catholic priests.

Italian society, even today, is based on the extended family as the most important social unit. Until World War II, Italy remained mainly an agricultural society; approximately sixty percent of the population lived off the land or had jobs directly related to agriculture (Chabod 1961). Large families are typical in this type of society, because male children provide additional hands to till the earth, and all children contribute to the family economy. Another tradition was that of the *famiglia patriarcale*, or "patriarchal family." In this system, the oldest male was the family head; he directed with authority his sons and their families and even his grandchildren. Often the whole extended family lived under one roof, and the family head supervised all work activities. Groups of extended families lived together in small agricultural communities, and most families were interrelated. In this way the family first, and then the community, became the central and most important aspect of social life.

Italy's political system enhanced this kind of family and community authority because the country, until it became politically unified in 1870, was divided into small principalities and foreign-controlled states concerned mainly with their own often-shifting political alliances and laws. As a result, the real authority was the community made up of the family heads. The government was perceived as a distant and usually hostile entity concerned only with taxing and recruiting local military fodder for faraway wars. The Mafia, today seen as illegal, violent, and sinister, grew out of the need for defense of the local families against the tyranny of the government imposed on Sicily by foreign powers. Thus, again, the family was an important element of power and authority.

Even today in Italy, although the country has become industrialized, the importance of the extended family and the community is undeniable. Any Italian, when asked where he or she is from, will always indicate the town of birth first. In fact, few Italians identify themselves as Italian. Rather, they identify themselves as being from a region or town of origin. My wife, Fernanda, is first a Padovana (from the town of Padua), then a Veneta (from the Venetian region); then only reluctantly would she identify herself as an Italian. So this sense of community has not diminished, and there is a conscious effort today to keep alive the separate traditions and language dialects of each region.

Although the patriarchal system has broken down with the decrease in the importance of agriculture, the family remains central in Italian life. Children still stay with the family and live at home until they marry. It is not at all unusual for children of age thirty or more to continue living at home; it is a disgrace to the family if these unmarried adults, particularly women, move away to live on their own, unless it is necessary for work in a faraway city. In the same way it is not uncommon for the elderly to live with their children when they are no longer capable of caring for themselves. The *nonna*, the grandmother, very often cares for the children when both parents have to work. The elderly have a useful function within the family structure and are respected for this. The extended family can always be relied upon to assist the nuclear family. In Veneto in the north, where many residents are bricklayers and carpenters, brothers often take turns helping each other to build houses for their families.

What do these traditions mean for genealogists? What advantages do they offer? It might be expected that, despite a move to a new country, the sense of family would survive and that persons of Italian descent would be among the first to desire to research their genealogy and find out about the community and traditions of their origin.

The family provides the first and best step in compiling a family history. The most essential step in genealogical research is to obtain information from family members—any facts they know about their parents and grandparents, family stories, old letters, information uncovered during visits to the homeland, and so on. These are invaluable sources of information that are enriched by the personal experiences of these relatives—and you could reasonably expect that Italians, because of their sense of family, would have many family stories. Many immigrants continued to write and keep in contact with relatives who stayed behind, and there may be letters and records of such transactions. Some immigrants even returned to the homeland to sell land or to make financial arrangements for those left behind. In New York City's Little Italy and in other areas with a high concentration of Italians, the immigrants were divided according to regional differences, and they maintained their separate dialects, traditions, and even culinary practices. All of this is an essential part of a family history.

ITALIAN EMIGRATION

The first European acknowledged to have discovered the New World was an Italian named Cristoforo Colombo (Christopher Columbus). He opened the way for millions of Europeans to emigrate to new lands of opportunity and freedom. Although Colombo discovered America in 1492, it was another 140 years before an Italian immigrant entered the New World. From the available historical records, it is known that the first immigrant was a young man named Pietro Alberti, who was originally from the isle of Malamocco near Venice. This navigator became a member of the Reformed Church while serving in the Dutch navy, and he immigrated to New Amsterdam on 2 June 1635.

Italian emigration can be divided into three periods: the earliest emigrants were explorers and adventurers; during the mid-1800s, many political refugees left Italy; the final period (after 1870) saw massive emigration for economic reasons. In the earliest period, lasting from 1492 to the mid-1800s, many prominent Italian explorers followed Colombo. One was Amerigo Vespucci, a map maker and explorer whose first name was given to the lands of the New World. The Caboto brothers, Giovanni (known in the United States as John Cabot) and Sebastiano, explored the New England coast and the Hudson Bay area. Giovanni da Verrazzano explored New York Bay, and Henri di Tonti sailed up the Mississippi River, becoming the first Italian to set foot in Michigan. Many of these explorers returned to Europe, but other adventurers and merchants stayed. One of them was Filippo Mazzei, a physician, merchant, and horticulturist who came to America in 1773 to introduce the culture of grapes and olives in the New World. He became a friend of Thomas Jefferson and was prominent in the American Revolution. It is believed that the statement "all men are created equal" in the Declaration of Independence was paraphrased from Mazzei's writings, and Thomas Paine's pamphlet *Common Sense* included many ideas originated by Mazzei.

The first period of Italian immigration to America was quite limited. In 1820, when the first immigration records were made, there were only thirty Italian immigrants. In the period from 1820 to 1855, only 7,185 Italians immigrated to the United States. By 1860 the Italian population in the United States was approximately 10,000 (Konrad 1990). In that year the first Italian newspaper printed in America, *L'Eco d'Italia,* was published in New York, where a small Italian community had been established. Italians took part on both sides of the conflict during the Civil War; the North's Garibaldi Guards, an Italian regiment led by Col. L.W. Tinnelli, fought at Gettysburg.

The second period, lasting from 1848 to 1870, was spurred by political upheaval, revolution, and widespread unrest in Italy as the Italians tried to shake off the bonds of foreign domination to create an independent, unified country. The result was an influx into the New World of people fleeing the unrest and seeking political haven. More than 20,000 Italians emigrated in this period (Konrad 1990). Among them were several noted musicians, the most famous of whom was Francis M. Scala; he became the leader of the U.S. Marine Corps Band and made it nationally famous.

With the unification of Italy in 1870, many festering economic problems came to the fore, initiating the third period of Italian emigration. Unification and the subsequent government met mostly the cultural, military, and economic needs of the north; the south (*il mezzogiorno*), which depended almost entirely on agriculture, benefitted very little. Most of the land in the south was owned by a few families in an almost-feudal system. To maintain their wealth under the new political system, the landowners increased the rent for the land and lowered wages for the tenants. The new government attempted no land reform or redistribution of the lands; the result was that many *mezzadri,* or farm tenants, were forced off their rented farms and had no means of subsistence. At this time, an Italian farm worker was paid anywhere from 16 to 30 cents a day—a yearly wage of about $240—and worked fifty-four hours each week. At the same time in the United States, the wage was about nine times higher (Konrad 1990). The situation was aggravated by a population explosion caused by better childhood health care; natural catastrophes, such as earthquakes, droughts, and epidemics, also worsened living conditions. These circumstances fueled a massive emigration to the United States and South America. Most of those emigrating from southern Italy settled in New York, along the East Coast, and in Chicago.

In northern Italy, along the Alps, the economy was based on the cultivation of the silkworm. When a blight of the mulberry bush, which was raised as food for silkworms, ruined the silk industry and left the entire region destitute, the United States, Brazil, and Argentina became the new meccas of wealth and prosperity for northern Italians. Since many people from the north were skilled carpenters, they often settled in the coal and mineral mining towns of Pennsylvania and Colorado, where they built the wooden supports for tunnels or cut ties for the railroads. Others found the climate of northern California similar to their own and created a large Italian community there, introducing Italian grapes and wines to the region.

Although the last period of immigration to the United States began slowly, with 55,000 immigrants in the decade from 1870 to 1880 and 307,000 from 1880 to 1890, immigration boomed as word spread of the opportunities to be had in the United States and as economic problems worsened in Italy. Immigration reached its peak in the period between 1890 and 1914, when almost 4 million Italians passed through the New York Immigration Office at Ellis Island (Konrad 1990).

Though the destination for many emigrants from European countries was the United States, modern Italian emigration was directed also to much of South America, Australia, and Canada, as shown by the latest statistics. Whereas in the 1990 U.S. census there were approximately 17 million Italian-Americans, making them the seventh-largest ethnic group in the United States, in Argentina people of Italian origin make up about half of the population, and in Toronto, Canada, there are almost as many Italians as live in Rome (Soldani 1994).

That most Italian immigration to America has occurred in this last century is an advantage to anyone pursuing his or her family history and greatly facilitates accomplishing an important objective in preliminary genealogical research—discovering the town of origin of one's ancestors in Italy.

HISTORICAL CONDITIONS AFFECTING ITALIAN GENEALOGICAL RESEARCH

Most Italian-Americans today are third- or fourth-generation Americans. Many of them have parents and relatives who have heard stories of passage to the New World from the homeland, have visited Italy, or immigrated themselves. There may be letters, photographs, family records, family stories, baptismal or marriage certificates, or other documents that relate the story of emigration and identify family members and the town of origin in Italy. All of these sources help to create a sense of family history, and they establish a starting point for genealogical research.

Research in Italy itself brings other advantages. It may seem incredible to people in the United States where, today, as mentioned earlier, half of the population moves every five years, but in Italy families traditionally stay in the same village or town for centuries. There are several reasons for this, some geographical and some historical.

A map of Italy (figure 1-1) shows a long peninsula, in the familiar boot shape, of 301,000 square kilometers—about the size of Arizona. This peninsula contains two major mountain ranges that together occupy approximately two-thirds of the land area: the Apennine range runs north to south, and the Alps run east to west in the north where Italy borders Austria, Switzerland, and France. Flat land is found in Italy's long coastal area, the Apulia plains, and in the Po Valley in the north.

Because, in ancient times, coastal areas were often attacked by marauding pirates and invading navies, most towns were built inland for better protection. Southern and central Italy are occupied by a series of ancient towns built on the tops of hills for defense. As far as can be seen, every hill and mountaintop is capped by a separate town. The populace lived in the towns for protection and tilled the surrounding land. This situation resulted in the agricultural products typical of Italy—grapes, oranges, olives, and meat and dairy products are easily produced in hilly areas. Each of these towns was isolated from the others; sometimes, with horse and donkey transport, it was a whole day's journey to the nearest town. This relative isolation and the varying political rivalries made people suspicious and wary, and any stranger, even one from a nearby town, might be treated as an enemy. The inhabitants of the towns tended to marry people from within the same community or from nearby towns.

In the Middle Ages the economy depended totally on the products of the land. There was very little commerce, and needs were met through bartering. Each town and city had to be self-sufficient. This independence created a strong sense of property. To retain sufficient land for the sustenance of each family, the property was not divided but was always passed on to the firstborn son. Other male children either had to work for the firstborn or find a vocation in the church or military service. Only exceptionally wealthy families could afford to purchase new land for other sons.

Houses, too, were passed from father to firstborn son. Because they were built to last for centuries, families lived in the same ancestral homes for generations. This lack of mobility is a true blessing to the genealogist. Imagine being able to trace all branches of your family for centuries from the same record source. To anyone who has traced ancestors in the United States who moved once or more in each generation and who married not only people from other towns but often from different ethnic backgrounds, Italian genealogy is a dream come true! Although families of the northern plains and the seaside cities were somewhat more mobile, the tendency of immobility is true of most of Italy.

Another advantage for those researching Italian genealogy is the subject of this book: the abundance of records and information that is available in Italy. Italy is a land of history and scholars, so past events have been recorded and passed on for posterity. Every town in Italy has a unique history and usually some unknown treasure to admire: an ancient cathedral, a mural painting by a great master, a castle wall in ruins; one breathes history. Family history has been recorded as well. Each town in Italy has civil records dating back to at least 1870, some dating to 1809. The Catholic parishes situated in every village and town have records from much earlier periods. Most parishes have records dating back to 1595 or at least to the beginning of

FIGURE 1-1. Map of Italy

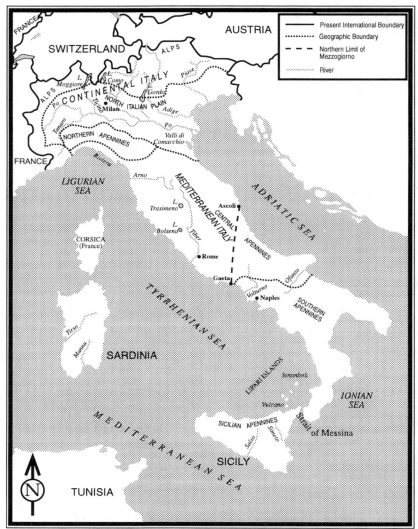

FIGURE 1-2. Geographic Regions

often the inks used were homemade artisan mixtures. Many inks had an acid base that eventually "burned" through the paper, rendering the writing illegible. Some documents crumble in the hands as they are opened; more often the writing has faded and become illegible, particularly when the paper was subjected to humidity. Since most parish records are stored in damp church cellars, faded ink is a constant problem, and the paper too can disintegrate. I found a record that was intact except for the outer inch of paper, which had disintegrated because of humidity. Unfortunately, all of the names had been written in that space, and the record was useless. Fires, floods, human neglect, thieves, and war have taken their toll. In parts of the Trentino region near Austria, all records were lost during World War I when towns were destroyed by artillery fire. Thus, each day that passes and each day that you delay researching your genealogy adds to the risk that some of these record sources will no longer be available.

WHERE TO BEGIN ITALIAN GENEALOGY

The purpose of this book is to assist you in pursuing your own family history by consulting the genealogy record sources in Italy. It will thoroughly discuss not only the existing, available sources but also where to find the records, how to read them, and how to obtain information by mail. To begin research in Italy, however, it is necessary to have some essential information—specifically, the name and approximate birth date of the ancestor who left Italy and the town in which he or she was born. Italy has no central archive for the entire country, nor even regional archives. The most important records, the civil records and Catholic parish records, are kept by the towns and parishes of origin. Thus, it is essential to know from what town the ancestor originated because research often entails writing to local officials or traveling there to personally consult the records.

Although there are methods, using Italian sources, to find an ancestor when the town of origin is unknown, they are time consuming and not always successful, so it is always better to obtain this information before beginning research using Italian sources. Besides direct contact with relatives and the use of family documents, which are always the first steps in research, several other sources available in

the parish. The parish priests of the Catholic church have faithfully recorded the baptisms, marriages, and deaths among their parishioners from these early periods to the present, and these records now form a vital source of genealogical information.

Other sources exist also: university records can date back to the 1200s, and notary records document all property transactions, including wills, dowries, and land sales. There are even census and military records that can supply further details and information about ancestors. Most of these records are found in the archive of each province (similar to a U.S. county) in Italy.

Although Italy has a rich variety of historical records, don't become complacent and delay beginning a family history. These invaluable record sources are unique; often only one copy of each exists. Thus, they are susceptible to damage, destruction, and loss. For example, the older parish records were written on parchment made from goatskin or on very poor quality paper. There were no standardized inks;

the United States can and should be consulted to find out as much as possible about your ancestors. Briefly, some of these are:

Catholic parish records in the United States: ninety-eight percent of Italians are Catholic, and most remained so after immigration. Many married in Catholic parishes in the Americas and baptized their children in them as well. Most parish priests in the United States have been as faithful as their Italian counterparts in recording this information, and the parishes have retained copies of these records. The records may be accessed by writing to the parish in question and asking for copies (though some parishes place restrictions on access). Using these records does, however, require that the researcher know what parish was used by the family.

Federal and state census records: censuses have been taken in the United States since 1790 at ten-year intervals. These are partially indexed and are available, with some restrictions, through the National Archives, some large public libraries, and through the Family History Library (35 North West Temple, Salt Lake City, Utah 84150) of The Church of Jesus Christ of Latter-day Saints. The early census records (1790–1840) provide the name of the head of each household and the number of free white members of the household, both male and female, divided into age groups by category. From 1850 on, the name of every free person whose usual place of abode was the household was listed with age, sex, and color (white, black, or mulatto). Even the profession or trade of every male over age fifteen was listed, as was the birthplace of each family member. Finally, whether the person was able to read and write and whether deaf, blind, dumb, "insane," "idiotic," pauper, or a convict was indicated. This format remained standard through the turn of the century, when more complete statistical information was added. All records also indicate the name of the county and town of residence, information that is essential for locating other important record sources. The more recent census records that date from 1930 to the present must be searched by authorized persons. They are found only at the Bureau of the Census, and there may be other restrictions regarding consultation.

Naturalization records: these records are usually found in the custody of the courts in which they were created. However, because of the large volume of naturalization documents created over the years and space limitations in some courthouses, some older records have been moved from the creating courts to local or state archives. A significant number of federal court naturalizations and a relatively small number of copies of local court naturalizations can be found in the various regional archives of the National Archives. The Family History Library also has a very large collection of microfilmed naturalization indexes and documents.

Naturalization records created after 1906 provide the name of the petitioner, date of filing, country of former allegiance, date and place of naturalization, date and place of birth, age, occupation, a physical description of the person, and the name of a witness (naturalization records created prior to 1906 contain little of genealogical value). Before 1906, individuals could be naturalized in any court of record, and the format of naturalization documents varied widely from one court to another. Post-1906 records can be obtained through the U.S. Immigration and Naturalization Office, 425 Eye St. NW, Washington, D.C., 20536.

Ship passenger lists: available through the National Archives and the Family History Library, most extant passenger lists date from 1800 to the present for Philadelphia, from 1820 for all other East Coast ports, and from 1850 to the present for West Coast ports. These lists are divided into two separate files—customs and immigration lists. The customs passenger lists (available for the period from 1820 to ca. 1891) indicate the name, age, sex, occupation, country emigrated from, and county immigrated to for each passenger. They also provide the name of the vessel, port of embarkation, port and date of arrival, owner of the ship, master of the ship, and number and names of passengers who died during the voyage. The immigration passenger lists (1891–1954) are more informative because, besides the information described above, they also provide the birthplace and last place of residence of each immigrant. They may even show the names and addresses of relatives living in the United States and the name and address of the nearest relative in the country emigrated from. (Access to those lists and related indexes less than fifty years old is restricted.)

Besides these excellent sources, there are many more U.S. records that can provide useful information, such as military records, probate records, tax and assessment records, and vital records. The purpose of a search of American sources is to obtain as much information about your ancestors as possible for your family history, and to identify the town of origin in Italy so that you can continue research using Italian record sources.

For more information about U.S. record sources, you can refer to *The Source: A Guidebook of American Genealogy* (edited by Arlene Eakle and Johni Cerny. Salt Lake City: Ancestry, 1984), among others. Priscilla Grindle DeAngelis' *Italian-American Genealogy: A Source Book* (Rockville, Md.: Noteworthy Enterprises, 1994) is a guide to Italian-American family research in the United States.

There are many different methods of conducting research after an ancestor has been traced to Italy. You can seek information personally by writing to sources in the towns or parishes or by consulting microfilm copies of records that are available in the United States, or even by traveling to Italy to visit the town and parish and consult the records yourself (see chapter 10). You can also delegate research to others—relatives living in Italy, a willing priest, or a professional genealogist—but in all cases it is necessary to know what record sources are available and which should be consulted so that you can personally conduct research in the most efficient manner. The ability to read the documents and understand the important information in them can be very satisfying, whether you are performing your own research or you are reviewing what others have found for you.

This book is divided into three parts. Part I contains a brief history of events and historical figures and discusses how history has influenced Italian genealogical record sources. It also includes a chapter that explains the origin and meaning of Italian surnames and how knowledge of surname variations can facilitate research. Part II deals with the actual records. Separate chapters discuss civil and Napoleonic records; Catholic parish records; other ecclesiastical records; and alternative sources of records, such as military, notary, and university records. Chapters in part III explain how to perform research, including form letters, examples, and practical suggestions. One chapter explains how to read the records, what information is provided in

them, and how this information has changed over the centuries. Appendixes include the addresses of state and diocesan archives.

CONCLUSION

The ultimate objective of this volume is to encourage and enable Italian-Americans and people of Italian descent elsewhere in the world to appreciate Italy's history and culture and to pursue their family histories. I believe that interested persons should research their own genealogy, either by writing to the sources of records or by researching the original sources in Italy or the microfilm copies. Even if you use the services of a professional genealogist, this book should assist you in appreciating the records that were found and in understanding the information included. Certainly each Italian descendant should be proud of his or her rich heritage and impressed by the quantity and quality of the documents that are available in Italy to pursue a family history.

Chapter 2

HISTORY OF ITALY AND ITALIAN RECORD SOURCES

I TALY IS A LAND OF HISTORY. IN EVERY CITY, IN EVERY TOWN, history is expressed through ancient Roman bridges and walls, through medieval churches, through the paintings and statues of the masters. At Padua, near Venice, is an observatory with a telescope that Galileo used for his experiments. In the same city, one of the oldest universities in the Western world dates back to the 1200s. Galileo taught physics there, and a canal that he designed with a system of locks runs through the center of the city. A hospital built in 1210 is still in use, and parts of the old Roman wall still stand. Padua is also the site of the Cathedral of San Antonio. There the saint's body lies embalmed, and masterpieces by Tiziano and Tiepolo adorn the walls.

Well known are Rome and the coliseum, the senate building, and many other sites still intact from the time of the empire's glory, but few know that beneath Rome lie the ruins of an even earlier epoch. Construction of Rome's underground subway system began almost thirty years ago and has yet to be completed because previously undiscovered ruins are frequently encountered. Each discovery requires delays while archaeologists finish uncovering the site or construction deviates in a new direction.

South of Rome, at Pompeii, the ashes of the volcano Vesuvius have preserved the entire ancient city—the Pompeiians' houses, artwork, habits—their way of life. In other areas of Italy are evidence and ruins of even more ancient civilizations. Sicily contains the remains of Greek cities that were established on the island as early as 700 B.C.; the famous Greek amphitheater at Taormina is only one example. The Tuscany region of Italy, known for its Chianti wine and beautiful cities like Florence and Pisa, abounds with archaeological findings of the even earlier Etruscan period, with fine vases, tools, altars to the god Saturn, and entire cemeteries.

Italians live with history. It surrounds them and is part of their everyday lives; many of their traditions and customs are centuries old. Even the modern legal and judiciary system is based largely on Roman and early ecclesiastical laws. It is not possible to understand Italians, their customs, and their way of life without having at least some notion of Italian history. Likewise, understanding why certain record sources exist and why they vary from one area to another requires some understanding of their history. This history is the heritage of Italians everywhere, and it is part of the family history of every person of Italian descent.

ITALIAN HISTORY: THE ANCIENT PERIOD

By around 2000 B.C., Italy was populated by several tribes of Indo-European origin, of which the Italici were one. Each tribe had its own language and culture and occupied a limited territory. These tribes attempted, unsuccessfully, to unite against an invasion by the Etruscans, who appeared in Italy around 900 B.C. The origin of the Etruscans has confounded scholars for centuries. They created a civilization with art, religion, and construction that was unsurpassed in the region. Their language, which used the Greek alphabet but has no affinity with any other language group, has remained undeciphered. The most accepted theory indicates that the Etruscans probably originated in Asia Minor. By the sixth century B.C., the Etruscans had expanded into Latium and Campania and had moved north above the Po River into upper Italy. Their use of writing and their highly developed technical skills in building and engineering helped lead all of Italy out of the Iron Age. Using the Greek system of establishing city-states, the Etruscans formed Etruria, an empire of twelve city-states. Under one monarch, they were united by language, religion, and customs but were often at war with one another.

Contemporary with the Etruscan city-states were several Greek colonies established along the southern shores of Italy and Sicily. Though economically and politically independent from Greece, the colonies of Magna Graecia (Greater Greece, as these towns were named) remained part of the Hellenic world. These colonies were later challenged by the Phoenicians of Carthage, who became allies of the Etruscans and established their own enclaves on Sicily and Sardinia.

The origins of Rome are surrounded by myth and mystery. It is probable that in the seventh century B.C., after the Etruscans had conquered the fortified Palatine Hill overlooking a crossing on the Tiber River, they united the various hamlets of Latins, Sabine, and Etruscans into one city-state. This city was ruled by the Tarquin family, the Etruscan royal house. Legend states that the city's founder was Romulus, descendent of Aeneas of Troy, and that his name was given to the city: Rome.

Around 500 B.C., the Romans overthrew the Etruscan monarch and established their own republic, which lasted for centuries. In the fourth century B.C., the Latin War marked the beginning of Rome's expansion through subjugation and assimilation of neighboring tribes. This expansion was temporarily halted by the Gauls, who defeated the Etruscans in northern Italy and penetrated farther south to sack Rome in 390 B.C. The expansion continued, not as an organized campaign but piecemeal as different Greek colonies were conquered or assimilated. During the Punic Wars, which lasted from 261 to 146 B.C., Rome acquired from defeated Carthage not only Sicily and Sardinia but also Spain and the northern shores of Africa.

From this point on, Rome wielded its new-found power to defeat Greece, annex Macedonia, and dominate Egypt by 168 B.C., creating the basis for an empire that, at its apex in 100 A.D., ruled the known Western world from Britain to the Euphrates River. The empire reached its military height with Julius Ceasar, and the apex of peace and civilization began with Caesar's nephew Augustus. In this period of peace, culture and art reigned, and the transportation network, laws, political institutions, and language formed the basis for a new European civilization.

The immense wealth of the empire was also its downfall, for it created inflation and corruption. The land was taken from the yeomen, who were the backbone of the economic system, and was tilled by slaves; the former landowners were left as beggars. The overextension of the empire and the inability of the military to fulfill its mission with the limited resources provided to it prepared the way for provincial unrest and eventual invasion. By the third century A.D. the empire was shrinking, although it would be another century before Italy itself was invaded. The empire was divided and Rome lost its status as Constantinople became the capital of what was known as the Byzantine Empire. After centuries of persecution by Rome, Christianity was made the official religion of the empire by the emperor Constantine I. Reveling in its wealth but having lost all political and military might, Rome was finally invaded and sacked by the Visigoths in 410 and was easy prey thereafter for marauding Germanic tribes. In 526, Justinian, the Eastern Emperor, revived direct imperial control over Italy. He compiled and introduced into Italy the *corpus juris civilis*, or Roman law, which became the basis for Italian and European law to the present.

Imperial control over all of Italy did not last long. In the sixth century Italy was invaded by the Germanic Lombards, who established their kingdom in the north. Though the Byzantine Empire maintained control in the south and in Rome, Italy was no longer united as a country and would not be united again for almost 1,400 years.

THE MIDDLE AGES

The Middle Ages were dominated by the power struggle between the Roman Catholic church and the Germanic princes. Christianity was first introduced into Italy through the Greek-speaking Jewish communities in the south. As old religious values and customs lost credence in the morally decaying empire, Christianity quickly became popular and spread throughout the peninsula, athough some of the emperors perceived the religion as a challenge to their authority and mounted brutal campaigns to stamp it out.

As the result of divine revelation or through political astuteness, the emperor Constantine proclaimed Christianity the official religion of the empire in 324 A.D. In a time of political disintegration, Christianity became an important unifying element. However, not everyone accepted the religion; as late as the sixth century considerable dissent existed, and pagan gods were still worshiped.

As the Byzantine Empire declined in status, the bishop of Rome became increasingly powerful, asserting authority over the other bishops in the west. The bishop of Rome took the title of pope and had become the head of the Roman Catholic church by the time Rome fell in 476 A.D. As power in the empire shifted from Rome to Constantinople, the resulting power vacuum in the south was gradually filled by the church. The church's leadership became temporal and political as well from 728 A.D., when King Liutprand of the Lombards donated the area of Sutri, Viterbo, to Pope Gregory II. From that holding the church extended its authority over the area of central Italy that became the papal states.

Meanwhile, in the north, the Lombards were finally defeated by Charlemagne in 774. Charlemagne was declared emperor of the Franks and the Lombards on Christmas day, 800 A.D. He united under his rule vast territories of central and southern Europe and created the Holy Roman Empire, which existed for one thousand years.

The relationship between the Holy Roman Empire and the Church was ambiguous; the emperors were chosen by the German princes but were crowned in Rome. The struggle for power first favored the emperor, who, by 1000 A.D., in essence chose the bishops and holders of higher ecclesiastical offices in the church, keeping them subject to his political control. This practice ended when, in the eleventh century, Pope Gregory VII instituted a series of internal reforms in the church, among them enforced celibacy, an end to the selling of church offices, doctrinal rigor, and, above all, reinforced political independence and temporal power for the papacy. The election of the pope (and ultimately all ecclesiastical appointments) was transferred from the emperor to the cardinals and bishops of the Roman territory. The pope retained political control over the papal states, and the bishops became the temporal leaders in their cities.

In the south, as the Byzantine Empire lost its influence, Norman knights who had been hired as mercenaries by the Greeks established claims and began a feudal system. The Norman territories were united under Robert Guiscard in 1053. A central feudal kingdom was created wherein land was granted based on allegiance to the king. The pope legitimized this kingdom, accepting the Normans as his vassals and using them against the enemies of the papal states.

Independent towns, though small, had survived from antiquity in northern and central Italy. With the continuous conflict between the pope and the Holy Roman emperor, many towns gained greater autonomy and, beginning in the twelfth century, became self-governing townships called communes (comuni). Italian nobles and the new class of merchants that was established in the relative political and economic freedom of the communes were the first in Europe to begin using money and to master business procedures. In this period the first investments were made to improve agricultural techniques and, for the first

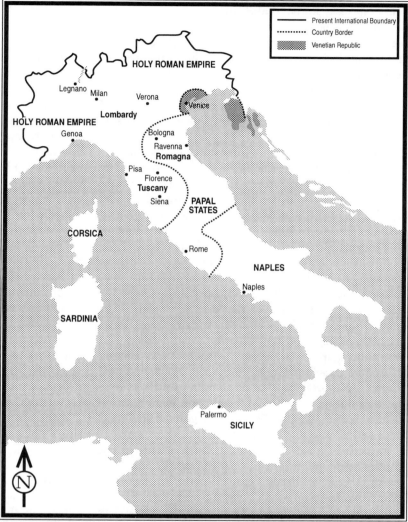

FIGURE 2-1. Italy in the Twelfth Century

time, there was a surplus of food and a subsequent surplus of wealth. This wealth was used to create marketplaces in northern Italy and in the Mediterranean area, around which commerce and industry began to flourish. The plains of the Po Valley became the first industrial region of Europe. Merchants and craftsmen banded together in guilds, becoming a strong political force that ruled the communes and even forced the submission of many of the landed nobility in the area. This led to conflict with the emperor, who sided with the nobility against the communes. The communes then banded together and looked to the pope for protection.

The emperor of the Holy Roman Empire, Frederick II, in the early 1200s inherited the crown of Naples and Sicily from his Norman mother, thus outflanking the pope to control the entire south of Italy and the north and German states as well. The emperor's constant struggle against the pope and against the communes, however, exhausted his resources, and his heirs were unable to maintain control

over the south. Under papal patronage, Naples and Sicily passed to the French house of Anjou, but these rights were contested by the kings of Aragon of Spain. This led to a centuries-long competition between France and Spain for control of southern Italy.

The fourteenth century was one of plagues, war, and famine. The population of Italy at the beginning of the century is estimated to have been about 7 to 9 million (Norwich 1983). Particularly in the south, most inhabitants lived in the towns, placing impossible demands on the land and on agriculture. Farmers still used primitive techniques, and indiscriminate deforestation was common, leading to periodic floods and exhaustion of fertile topsoil. Into this scenario came the "black plague," which first appeared in the early 1300s and then struck with devastating force in 1349. Almost three-quarters of Florence's inhabitants died, and in other urban areas the loss of half the population was common. Many rural areas were hit equally hard, and the deaths, compounded by widespread flight from poorer lands, especially in the south, reduced entire regions that were once inhabited into malarial swamps. The plague was seen as God's punishment of mankind, and many religious groups and factions were formed. In this atmosphere of poverty and fanaticism, nobles, cities, and guilds began to war among themselves for power and, for a century, until the mid-1400s, Italy was rife with internal wars. By the end of the century there were fewer than 4 million inhabitants (Norwich 1983).

The Middle Ages brought three developments that are important for genealogy. The first was the birth of nobility in Italy and the rest of Europe. As the various royal houses were established in Europe, took control of the land, and began to impose taxes, their closest supporters were granted land and special privileges. One of the most important of their supporters' privileges was the right to tax the land and its inhabitants under their jurisdiction, thus assuring the continuation of wealth. On the other hand, they were obligated to provide military and political support to the crown. These supporters of the king or emperor were granted titles that set them apart—such as count, duke, marquee, or lord—and they became the aristocracy. This practice began in Italy as early as the Lombard invasion, and it was an established practice among the Franks and Normans. New titles could be obtained by special service to the king; during the crusades to Palestine, many Norman military leaders who fought well were granted additional lands and titles in southern Italy.

Particularly in Italy, the merchant class, too, found its way to titles and positions of influence through its new-found wealth. A result was the establishment of the *signorie*, whose lordship was based on wealth alone. Among them were many of the powerful families in the towns and cities of Italy. This proliferation of titles, either through support of the crown or through wealth, led to the establishment of numerous noble lines in Italy. Since all rights and titles had to pass from father to son or according to strict rules of heraldry, it became important to establish descent and to investigate family history. Complete pedigree charts for the early noble families can be found in books on heraldry and in public and private archives throughout Italy (see chapter 4).

Since the titled families owned the land and had political, legal, and economic control over their feudal holdings, all records of this early period concern the nobility. They held courts and tried their subjects, collected taxes, and bought and sold property. There are many historical records that deal with these noble families, and information about some of them can be found dating back to 1000 A.D.

The second development from this period of history that is important for genealogy is that of the notary public. This public office was instituted, it seems, by the Franks but was soon employed throughout Italy for collecting taxes. The notary public had the duty of recording all sales and purchases of property, which, at the time of sale, were taxed. The notary public was generally from a noble or well-to-do family and often had studied law. He became a public servant, and, since he also received a commission from the sales transaction, the office of notary public was a path to wealth. The office was often passed from father to son. Throughout this period, land sales were strictly between noble and wealthy families, and few documents remain. Toward the end of the Middle Ages and in the more affluent Renaissance period, however, property transactions became more common, and notary acts can be found in most areas of Italy from the 1400s (see chapter 9). (Notary publics still serve the same basic function in Italy. To become a notary, one must first become a lawyer and then compete for the few available positions. All sales in Italy between private citizens—from cars to businesses to houses—must be registered by a notary public, who is well paid. The transactions are also taxed by the government.)

A third legacy of the Middle Ages emerged during the twelfth and thirteenth centuries: the university. A medieval university was called a *studium generale* and was staffed by professors of the seven arts and of at least one of the higher disciplines of theology, medicine, physics, and law. The first university in Europe was organized in Italy at Bologna, where the masters of ecclesiastical law and the arts joined existing masters of Roman (civil) law to form a secular university. Two guilds were formed: one was for Italians and one was for Europeans, usually Germans. The University of Bologna was soon followed by others in Italy, such as the University of Padua, and in other areas of Europe, such as Paris and Oxford. Most students who attended these universities came from well-to-do families. Records of student enrollment dating to the 1400s or earlier are still extant, and these records form another source available to complete a family history.

The medieval period ended in the late 1400s. Ultimately, the towns were absorbed by the larger commercial city-states, and certain families became the new political powers in the region: the Medici of Florence, the Visconti of Milan, the D'Este of Ferrara, the Scaligeri of Verona, and others. The courts of these families were equal or superior in splendor to those of the royal families of Europe, and the families' interest in scholarship and the arts created the atmosphere necessary for one of the greatest epochs in civilization, the Renaissance.

THE RENAISSANCE TO THE NINETEENTH CENTURY

The Renaissance was an intellectual and cultural revolution without precedent, bringing about a new era for Europe. The commercial revolution had placed vast sums of money in the hands of Italian merchants and bankers, who became the new aristocracy. They then competed with each other in demonstrating their wealth, creating an unprecedented private demand for art. By the mid-fifteenth century, guilds and communal governments were also commissioning works, as was the Catholic church, creating a high demand for skilled artists and craftsmen. The advent of humanism allowed art to portray a fuller range of subjects and images, leaving behind the rigid religious and classical themes of the past. Thus, the works produced in this epoch by such masters as Michelangelo, Leonardo da Vinci, Botticelli, and Raphael are still considered some of the greatest artistic achievements in history.

This cultural revolution went beyond the arts to influence philosophy and science as well; possibly the greatest contribution of the period was the creation of the scientific method. The Renaissance reestablished Italy as the cultural capital of Europe and reinvigorated the idea of Italian nationalism. The seed of Italian unity was planted during the Renaissance, though it would take another four hundred years to flourish.

The Renaissance was a cultural rather than a political revolution. Politically, Italy was still very much divided with a monarchy in the south, the papal states in the middle, and a collection of independent city-states in the north, of which the most important were Florence, Venice, Milan, Modena, and Genoa. In 1455, at the prompting of the pope, a loose alliance among the city-states was formed to prevent internal fighting among the diverse factions. This alliance was maintained for forty years by the great diplomacy of the Medici family of Florence, which guaranteed the peace through a series of pope-statesmen. This forty-year period saw the highest cultural and intellectual achievements of the Renaissance.

With the end of Medici dominance in 1495, the alliance unraveled and internal fighting resumed. Italy was left open to foreign invasion, starting with the French in 1498, who claimed Naples and Milan. French dominance of Naples, however, was brief, as the Spanish intervened in 1499 and occupied the area themselves in 1504. There were further invasions of Italy by Germans and Turks. In 1527 the undisciplined armies of Charles V sacked Rome, looting and burning the city and destroying even churches and convents. Charles V was declared emperor of the Holy Roman Empire and, through a series of political marriages in his family, he consolidated the crowns of Spain, Germany, the Netherlands, and most of Italy, including Naples and Sicily. In exchange for allegiance and money, he guaranteed

FIGURE 2-2. Italy in the Fifteenth Century

protection to the pope and protected the northern city-states from invasion by France or the Ottoman Empire. Through his right to the Spanish crown, he established control in Italy for the Hapsburg house for almost four centuries.

The Spanish dominion, although providing protection from invasion, also resulted in a steady decline in personal freedom, national respect, and economic power in Italy. Even religious and intellectual freedoms were quashed as Italy became subject to the restrictions of the Spanish Inquisition.

In some ways, this foreign domination increased a sense of national unity among Italians. Italian humanism remained alive in the universities and in the arts. For the first time, in the late 1500s, a uniform written language was established for communication among diplomats, clergy, and administrators. This language began to coexist with the local verbal dialects that were used in each region and were incomprehensible from one region to another. The Catholic church, and in particular the papacy, became another focal point of unity, becoming an Italian institution. In this period the church, under pressure from the growing Protestant movements, made several reforms, eliminating the more obvious corruption and abuses of power. It also consolidated and unified basic doctrines of the church during the Council of Trent from 1545 to 1563 and began enforcing them with more vigor. An important edict that was introduced in the Council of Trent in 1563 and then made official by the pope in 1595 was the creation of parish records. Although a few parishes had already begun making regular records of the baptisms and deaths among parishioners as early as 1440, this practice became a general proposal only in 1562 and an official duty of the priests in 1595. The division of the population into parishes was established, and each priest was required to record in separate documents the baptism, marriage, and death or burial of every parishioner. Thus, parish records, one of the most important sources of genealogical information, were begun. The church, having put order in its house, became an integral part of Italian life and a social institution.

The seventeenth century saw a renewal of fighting as the European wars extended into Italy. The expenses of war, the commercial competition of the English and Dutch, and another bout of the plague all but devastated Italy's economy and created a depression that would last another century. Southern Italy was convulsed in a peasant war against the Spaniards and the feudal lords. These rebellions were initially successful, garnering massive popular support and conquering entire provinces, but eventually the lords won, taking terrible revenge on the rebels and their supporters in 1648. As a result, the south remained in a feudal state, exploited by the Spanish and feudal lords and isolated from the economic progress of the rest of Europe. The economic division between northern and southern Italy remains to this day and still creates considerable political and civil friction.

In 1700, the last heir of Charles V died in Spain, and another war for political control broke out in Europe, resulting in more fighting and invasions in Italy. As a result, in 1748, Naples and Sicily were again united under a resident monarch tied to the crown of Spain; however, Spanish control in the north was replaced by an Austrian republic that extended power over Milan and Lombardy all the way to the Tuscany region, where the last Medici had died in 1737. The Duchy of Savoy in the west also increased in size and was elevated to a kingdom with the annexation of Sardinia and expansion into Lombardy.

Under the "enlightened despots" of Austria, in particular Maria Theresa and Joseph II, prosperity and some freedom returned to northern Italy. With the improvement of land and sea routes, such as the first coach route across the Alps in 1771, the region became increasingly integrated with the trade occurring in the rest of Europe. With increased prosperity came an increase in population, which grew from 13 million to 18 million in less than a century. Even rural areas increased in population, and there was a resurgence of agriculture. After the Italian domination of the Renaissance period and later the Baroque, the arts were at a low ebb; nonetheless, it was in this period that Milan became a world center for opera and fashion.

As Italy progressed into the nineteenth century, art again flourished but was characterized by rejection of the classical forms. This became the Romantic Era. Particularly in music, artists like Rossini, Bellini, Donizetti, and Verdi gained worldwide acclaim. Inspired by the French Revolution in 1789, a sense of individual rights and national identity began to form in Italy, particularly among the growing middle class of merchants and craftsmen who had been excluded from politics for centuries.

Into this political scene came a figure called Napoleon Bonaparte. Napoleon's Italian campaigns of 1797 and 1799 shattered the control of the Austrians, drove the Bourbon king from Sicily and the mainland, and ended the Venetian Serenissima Republic that had remained independent for 1,200 years. At first Napoleon was welcomed enthusiastically as a liberator, but soon it became apparent that one tyrant had replaced others. By 1806, Napoleon, now emperor of France, had annexed large parts of Italy, including Rome, Piedmont, and Venice. He also deeded Naples and later Sicily to his brother-in-law, Murat. Finally, he combined the areas of northern and central Italy and proclaimed himself King of Italy. Although a foreign ruler, Napoleon introduced some very important changes for both Italian unity and genealogy.

For the first time since the Roman Empire, all of Italy was united under one centralized administration. The Napoleonic civil code was introduced, providing a uniform political and judicial system and overcoming the provincialism and fragmentation that had characterized Italy for almost a millennium. Social change that had been introduced in most of Europe now arrived in Italy. In this period the feudal system that was still active in most of southern Italy was declared illegal, and the sale of the expropriated estates of the church and the aristocracy gave added impulse to the rise of a middle class. Commercial routes with the rest of Europe were further improved, and northern Italy prospered in the trade of linen, wool, leather, minerals, and construction. The western Po Valley finally reached industrial prominence and became an independent source of prosperity.

In the south, the situation differed considerably. Even though Joseph Bonaparte and then Murat had reorganized and modernized governmental, administrative, and fiscal institutions, social change was slow to develop. The feudal system was officially abolished everywhere, except Sicily, in 1806, but in the absence of major land reforms, the land remained in the hands of a few powerful families, and there was no move toward forming a middle class or an industrial base as was found elsewhere in Italy.

Napoleon had an equally decisive impact on records of genealogical significance. Under the Napoleonic code, people could no longer be buried in church grounds or in private plots within city limits. Cemeteries were created outside of cities' limits for the first time. Napoleon also introduced the notion of civil vital records. Until this time, the only records of the birth or death of anyone outside the noble families were the church parish records that had been instituted by 1595. Napoleon introduced civil acts of birth, marriage, and death that were recorded by town officials in duplicate. This practice was begun throughout Italy under Napoleon but was continued only in the southern regions after his demise. However, it became the prototype for the Italian civil record system after the unification of Italy in 1870.

THE UNIFICATION OF ITALY

Napoleon was defeated in 1815, and Italy was returned to its previous boundaries and foreign rule. Lombardy-Venetia was returned to Austria and, although Modena, Tuscany, and Parma were apparently independent, they too remained under the control and influence of Austria. The Bourbons returned to the south and established the Kingdom of the Two Sicilies, which comprised all of the south below Rome and the island of Sicily. The papal states, too, were returned to the pope.

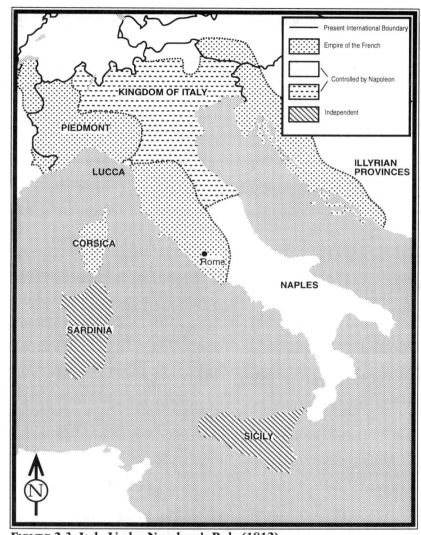

FIGURE 2-3. **Italy Under Napoleon's Rule (1812)**

Some things, however, could not be undone. Italy now had unified fiscal, judicial, and administrative policies. Italians had been working together and interacting and trading freely with one another, thus creating the idea of a united Italy. Even though the abolition of feudalism was extended to Sicily by the new Bourbon king, Ferdinand, there was widespread discontent throughout the area among the millions of peasants, hired out as farmhands, who had hoped to become landowners under a general land reform. Secret societies dedicated to national unity and the overthrow of foreign dominance sprung up, the most famous of them the Carbonari society. They led a rebellion against the king in 1820 and, with the support of the middle class, almost succeeded in defeating him. However, the Austrians intervened in favor of Ferdinand, and brutal repression followed.

The nationalistic wave nevertheless continued to grow and was known as the *risorgimento* (rebirth). Again, artists and intellectuals were major figures in the movement,

concentrating much of their attention on developing a national language and cultural unity. Each region and even each province in Italy had its own language or dialect that was heavily influenced by the prevailing language of local foreign dominance. Thus, in Piedmont the dialect was similar to French, in the south there was a great Spanish influence, and so on. Many regional dialects were incomprehensible to people from neighboring areas, and dialects even varied locally from one town to another.

As late as 1850, Latin was the major written language. Italian, which was derived from the Tuscany dialect, had been developed and was used in diplomatic circles and in some church records from the time of the Medici but was relatively unknown to the general populace. With the open trade and communication among regions that began under Napoleon, the lack of a common language became apparent and gave impetus to a movement to unify the language. Led by Alessandro Manzoni in his novel *I Promessi Sposi* (*The Betrothed*) and the poetry of Giacomo Leopardi, there was

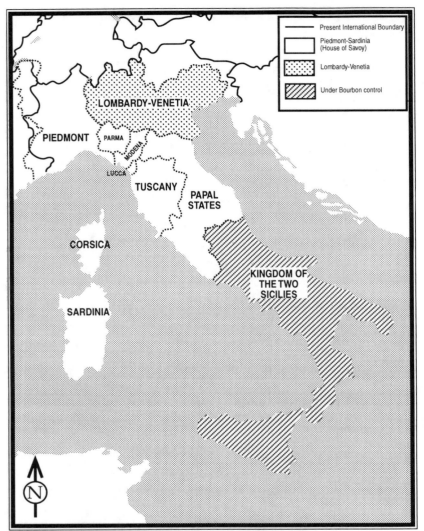

FIGURE 2-4. Italy After Napoleon's Demise (1815)

a great effort to create the basis of an Italian language. Even so, it is estimated that, at the unification of Italy in 1870, only approximately 160,000 out of a population of almost 20 million spoke Italian (Smith 1969). National unity was promoted by other artists as well; in particular, the operas of Antonio Rossini and Giuseppe Verdi, written in Italian, became immensely popular among all classes and throughout Italy.

In 1831, a young man named Giuseppe Mazzini, a former Carbonari, launched the idea of a united Italy as a fulfillment of "national destiny" and created the romantic concept of a society based on democracy and social equality. This idea became very popular among the budding working class in the north and the large peasant population in the south. A series of Mazzinian insurrections from 1832 to 1850 failed miserably, but they paved the way for more practical efforts by two of Mazzini's disciples, Giuseppe Garibaldi and Camillo Benso di Cavour.

The election of a new pope, Pius IX, in 1846 gave hope

to those who believed that the papacy and the church would lead the way to national unity. However, 1848 saw civil unrest in all of Europe, including Italy. At the beginning of that year the pope fled to Rome, and the revolutionaries there set up a temporary republic to be led by Mazzini. Piedmont, having obtained promises of support from the French and other Italian provinces, invaded Lombardy in what is called the First War of Independence against Austria. But with no assistance from the Kingdom of the Two Sicilies or from the other Italian states that had pledged their help, and betrayed by France, which sent troops against Piedmont, this effort was doomed. However, vital lessons were learned from it; the most important of them was that internal disputes and divisions among the Italians caused them to be vulnerable to foreign manipulation. Also, it was realized that the pope and the church not only would not champion the cause of national unity but were actively against it. The only leader who remained a supporter of unity was the King of the Savoy House in Piedmont, Victor Emmanuele II.

The leadership of Piedmont was enhanced during the following years when Cavour became the prime minister of the Piedmont parliament in 1852. Cavour, besides instituting various internal reforms, was able to establish an efficient and functional parliamentary system in Piedmont. He also obtained international recognition and prestige for the House of Savoy through its intervention in the Crimean War in 1855. Then, in 1858, Cavour signed a secret agreement with France in which the French pledged support in a war against Austria. In 1859, the Second War of Independence broke out as Piedmont tried to conquer Lombardy and Venetia. The war did not go as expected; Venetia and the central city-states remained under Austrian control, and Piedmont received Lombardy from the French only in exchange for Nice and Savoy. However, the war later led to the rebellion of the satellite city-states under Austrian control. In fact, in 1860 most of the city-states in central Italy, and even those under the papacy, requested to be part of Piedmont and were annexed by Cavour. Cavour was then criticized by other nationalists because he would not annex the Kingdom of the Two Sicilies as well. Cavour did not want to overextend his resources and doubted that the south, beset by poverty and ignorance, should be part of the new Italy.

Events were taken from his hands by another follower of Mazzini, the soon-to-be-legendary Giuseppe Garibaldi. Garibaldi assembled a ragtag army of enthusiastic patriots, and with these red-shirted "Thousand" he attacked Sicily. Obtaining success more easily than anticipated, he quickly conquered Sicily and moved up the peninsula to Naples. There he deposed the Bourbon monarch and declared the territory part of the House of Savoy. His next objective became Rome and the pope, and he continued his march up Italy. At this point, Cavour, afraid of international repercussions and above all afraid of attacking the French army that still defended Rome, sent Piedmontese troops to stop Garibaldi. Being the romantic and patriot that he was, Garibaldi, rather than fight fellow Italians, turned over the Kingdom of the Two Sicilies and all of the territory conquered to Vittorio Emmanuele II. In 1861, Cavour called a national assembly to establish the Kingdom of Italy and to proclaim Vittorio Emmanuele II the king. At the same time a national parliament was formed and a constitution drawn up.

In the Third War of Independence against Austria in 1866, Italy, siding with Prussia, finally was able to annex Venetia. At this point only Rome was separate from the national unity. Garibaldi had attempted several times to take Rome, but it wasn't until 1870, when

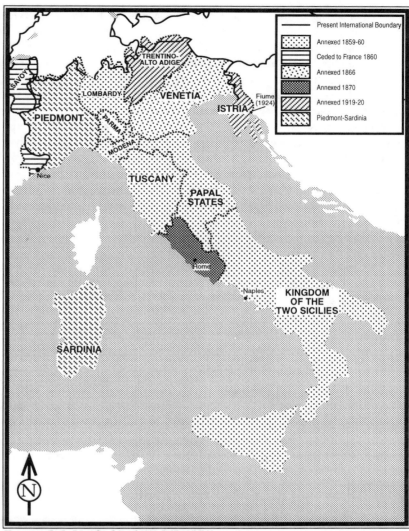

FIGURE 2-5. Unified Italy (1859-1870)

France withdrew its forces from the city to defend against a Prussian invasion, that Rome became part of Italy and the Italian capital was transferred from Turin to Rome. Although Rome was now part of the republic, the division of power between state and church was still an open question and would remain so for another sixty years. As part of the first constitution, Roman Catholicism was declared the national religion, and in 1871 many other concessions were made to appease the pope. Among them, the Vatican was declared a separate and independent state within Rome, and the pope was guaranteed an annual income from the treasury of the state equal to that previously obtained from the papal states. Even so, Pope Pius IX was adamantly against the nationalists; he declared himself a prisoner of the Vatican, appealing to foreign governments for their intervention to save him and his properties. Having declared the doctrine of papal infallibility, Pius IX went on to prohibit all faithful Catholics from participating in the political system, either as candidates or voters.

This situation created a considerable crisis of conscience among the population, who had to decide between the state and the church. This fact is reflected in some genealogical records of this period. From the beginning of the unified republic in 1866, the Napoleonic system of civil vital records was established throughout the republic. Town officials were nominated to record all births, marriages, and deaths among the inhabitants. In some towns where the division between state and church was particularly heated, a power struggle developed between town officials and the church. For almost twenty years, until the state was able to enforce its authority, many people were married by church rite but did not announce their marriage in the town hall according to government rules. Thus, the town would not recognize the marriage and recorded all of the resulting children as illegitimate. Finally, the couple would be forced to remarry by civil rite and to recognize their "illegitimate" children as their own. Examination of the civil records of the period from 1865 to about 1880, in certain areas, will reveal many cases of marriage being recorded after the couple had already had several children. In the parish records, however, the marriage is recorded as having taken place many years before, and there is no question of legitimacy.

Although the tradition of local government was retained superficially, the new political system that emerged in Italy was strongly centralized, with a powerful monarchy and a parliamentary government. The constitution made no clear division of power between the ministers and the monarchy, so, at the death of Cavour, most of the power remained in the hands of the king, and there was a growing division between the population and the government. This division existed mainly because the government, far from the ideas of democracy and social equity espoused by Mazzini, remained a government of the elite. For example, approximately seventy-five percent of the population was illiterate in 1860. Italian was primarily a written language used by intellectuals, and only about one percent of the general population used it. Most still spoke the mutually incomprehensible local dialects, and allegiances were still to local municipal or regional interests. The electoral law, taken from Piedmont, based voting privileges on payment of taxes, which divided the population not only by class but by region as well. In 1870 the electorate was only two percent of the population, or about 500,000, of whom only 300,000 actually voted—one Italian in seventy (Smith 1969)! Thus, the new state was governed by a small political class who were mostly from the north and were elected and supported by the aristocracy and industrial middle class.

KINGDOM OF ITALY TO THE PRESENT

The lack of support for the central government and the regional differences between north and south were exacerbated, in the years following the founding of the kingdom, by excessive taxes and new laws. Cavour had never wanted to accept the south into the new state, but Garibaldi's brilliant military campaign had forced Cavour's hand. The political elites of the north were contemptuous of southerners, considering them intellectually and morally inferior. Cavour himself, speaking of the southern regions, stated: "The purpose is clear . . . to impose unity on the weakest and most corrupt part of Italy." Sicily was the first area to rebel against this "imposition" and against the taxes, and for four years roving bands of peasants and draft evaders waged war against the central government. More than 100,000 soldiers were sent to the region to quell the rebellion, which was mercilessly repressed. As a result, the state remained on a very narrow political base, and frustration over stagnant economic and social conditions created a strong tradition of distrust and extra-parliamentary protest of the government that remains, even today, intrinsic to Italian society.

One of the most unpopular laws that was passed in this period has nonetheless bequeathed an important genealogical resource: the military conscription records. Although military service was obligatory in some areas of Italy before unification, generally it had been required only in times of war or was voluntary. In 1871, however, a general draft was begun that required all Italian males to report before a draft board at age eighteen and be declared eligible or ineligible for military service. Ineligibility was determined primarily by medical evidence of ill health or disability. If this could not be shown, men had to serve from two to three years of military service, depriving their families of the essential added income they provided. Eventually the civil birth records were used to detect draft evaders, and draft evasion became a federal offense. The introduction of the draft was very unpopular, and draft evasion initially was high.

Over the next fifty years, up to World War I, a series of strong prime ministers, from Depretis to Crispi to Giolitti, managed to shift power from the monarchy to the parliament. The political base was broadened, first in 1882, when the vote was extended to craftsmen and store owners, and again in 1912, when almost universal male suffrage was established. In 1904, after a series of compromises, the pope rescinded Pope Pius' edict and allowed Catholics to vote and participate in political activity.

Spurred by European colonization of Africa, Italy initiated a campaign in Ethiopia that ended disastrously with the defeat of Italian soldiers by the native tribes. To avenge this defeat and regain national pride, Italy declared war on the Turks and invaded Libya. Italy was granted Libya by the Turks in 1912 but had to keep an army of 50,000 there to maintain order among the rebellious natives.

These decades saw considerable gains in the construction of railroads, steel mills, seaports, and ships. This effort was part of a general European national movement in which each country competed to create a strong military-industrial base. Northern Italy benefited through close trade contacts with northern Europe and the contribution of massive state subsidies to create a strong industrial base. At the same time, however, the south was virtually de-industrialized as the number of workers declined by one-third between 1881 and 1901.

Agriculture, which was the main source of income for sixty percent of the population nationwide (eighty percent in the south), did not receive the same attention. Whereas the fertile Po Valley in the north was tilled by many small landowners, in central and southern Italy the land was still owned by a few rich landowners who used sharecroppers. Approximately 1.5 million peasants still worked as day laborers, and they often resorted to seasonal migration to make ends meet. Widespread soil erosion, alternating floods and droughts, and the spread of swamp areas with consequent malarial infestations due to wholesale deforestation all combined to worsen agricultural conditions. Land reforms, geared to better distribute the land and to increase land ownership, were manipulated by the middle class and noble families so that the number of people owning land actually decreased from 1861 to 1901. Malaria from the swampy areas and diseases of poverty and filth, such as cholera and tuberculosis, became pandemic. Of almost four thousand Sicilian sulfur miners who reported for the draft between 1881 and 1884, only two hundred were considered physically eligible for military service. The others all showed severe signs of pellagra and tuberculosis (Smith 1969).

With the opening of railroad routes through the Alps in 1885, Italian agriculture became subject to foreign competition, particularly from France, for the first time in centuries. A series of tariff wars to protect Italian agricultural producers, lasting until 1892, not only failed to help agriculture but instead increased the damage by allowing outdated methods to continue and increased the price of food. Again, those who suffered most were the peasants. In 1894, to quell continuous uprisings among Sicilian peasants, a major land reform was proposed by Prime Minister Crispi. The Sicilian landlords furiously battled this reform under the guidance of Marquis Antonio di Rudini. After Crispi's downfall in 1896 due to the Italian defeat in Ethiopia, Rudini became the next prime minister, and all hope of land reform was abandoned. The only solution for many, particularly those in Sicily and the south, became emigration to the Americas, Australia, and other areas of Europe. Because of the open immigration laws in the United States, it was during this period that almost 4 million Italians emigrated there. In all, almost a third of the population of the south emigrated to other countries during this period, although many later returned.

Among those who remained, social unrest provided widespread support of anarchist and socialist philosophies and political parties. To offset these forces, the Catholic church became increasingly active politically, rallying behind the forces of nationalism. As World War I broke out, Italy initially declared neutrality, nullifying the Triple Alliance it had previously signed with Austria and Germany in 1882. The country was divided over whether to maintain neutrality or to intervene. A former socialist and soon-to-become major political figure, Benito Mussolini, became a fervent advocate of military intervention. When the Triple Entente of England, France, and Russia offered Italy the long-sought-after territories of Trentino, South Tyrol, Trieste, Istria, and nearly half of Dalmatia, most of which had long been part of the Venetia republic and were considered Italian territory, Italy could not resist. It signed the Treaty of London and entered the war in May 1915. The war, expected to end quickly, dragged on for more than three years. Again, as with Ethiopia, the political leaders had not consulted with the military, which was woefully ill-prepared for war.

The cost of the war was enormous. Almost 5 million men were called up, most of them peasants or farmers, with southerners heavily over-represented in the front lines. By the end of the war more than 600,000 had died (Smith 1969). Much of the fighting had been on Italian territory, devastating entire regions. The government deficit had increased tenfold and inflation had risen four hundred percent. Italy emerged from the war physically, emotionally, and economically exhausted. During Versailles Treaty negotiations, the Allies, led by the United States, reneged on the Treaty of London, refusing to concede Fiume or Dalmatia to Italy. Gabriel D'Annunzio, a writer and nationalist, led an army of two thousand *legionnaires* into the city of Fiume and occupied it. Finally, in 1920, Trieste was given to Italy, together with Istria and Zara, but most of Dalmatia was ceded to the newly formed Yugoslavia.

Italy was unable to make the shift from a wartime economy to a peacetime one. As the army demobilized, unemployment grew, reaching a peak of 2 million in 1919. By 1920 inflation had increased an additional two hundred percent, and the value of the lire fell three hundred percent. The net effect was to force many businesses into bankruptcy and to wipe out the savings of the middle class. The working class was equally hurt, leading to the formation of militant labor unions. Membership in the socialist unions rose from 250,000 in 1918 to 2 million by 1920. Labor disputes broke out throughout Italy, culminating in a four-week occupation of the factories in September 1920. The government used appeasement and economic compromise to cool the labor unrest but lost the support of the middle class and employers. The government was perceived by them as being in league with the workers to expropriate their property and eliminate capitalism. In the south, too, almost a million unemployed workers occupied and appropriated marshland, mainly in the Latium region (Smith 1969). The government was unable to react, losing the support of the landowners.

The liberal party that had represented the government for decades was soon overcome by a militant socialist party and a conservative Catholic party that, in the 1919 election, came up with 32.4 and 20.5 percent of the vote, respectively (Smith 1976). Into this troubled political scene entered a new group, first created as a movement in 1919, called Fasci di Combattimento (Combat Groups) and later organized as the Partito Nazionale Fascista in 1921. This party was organized and led by Benito Mussolini. To further radicalize the political scene, the Italian Communist Party, partially funded and controlled by the Soviet Union, was formed in 1921. Through a campaign of violence and terror, Mussolini's fascist party took control of many areas of the country and began the "March on Rome." Facing a lack of alternatives, the king, Victor Emmanuele III, legitimized the Fascist Party and prevented an armed coup by appointing Mussolini prime minister in November 1922.

In the beginning, the Fascist government was little different from preceding ones, still using the parliamentary system and seeking support and compromise with other political parties. However, after the party's involvement in the murder of Matteotti, the most outspoken opponent of Fascism, events took a turn for the worse. The opposition parties abandoned parliament in protest, and Mussolini took advantage of this to consolidate his control over the state, silencing the press and creating a dictatorship. By 1927 he had proclaimed himself "il Duce," and he ruled without hindrance until World War II.

The Fascist movement at first was based on capitalism and free trade, but in the worldwide depression of 1929 the government began a gradual process of nationalizing the banking system and industry. This process continued until the most important economic institutions were under the direct control of the government, creating a large bureaucracy and the beginnings of a socialist state. At the same time, small businesses remained in the hands of private owners, enhancing the middle class. Many of the dire effects of the Great Depression felt in the United States were avoided in Italy by this fiscal policy and by stimulating industrial development through a military buildup. As a result, the fascist regime was strongly supported by the middle class and bureaucracy. For the working class, however, strict control of wages was enforced and the trade unions were disbanded. Brutal repression by the secret police of the political opposition, homosexuals, and intellectuals was begun. In a typical week more than 20,000 searches, arrests, and seizures of literature were conducted (Smith 1969).

Fascism became an Italianizing nationalistic force that did much to promote the unified Italy that for so long had escaped the government's efforts. Universal education to the fifth grade became obligatory, Italian was taught in the schools, and local customs and dialects were suppressed. The government even went so far as to require the Italianization of surnames, particularly in the border regions. Thus, for example, family names such as Michlivich became Di Michele, Luttmann became Luttini, and La Pierre became Di Pietro. Mussolini's military exploits, too, were geared to reestablish national pride. In 1935, Ethiopia was again targeted for conquest. By 1936 more than 650,000 troops had been sent there, and Italy was mobilized for war. That year, using modern weapons and even mustard gas, the Italian army defeated the natives and conquered Ethiopia.

This episode, and the increasing alliance between Mussolini and Hitler, began one of the darkest periods of Italian history. The following years saw open persecution of Jews and opposition groups and finally the outbreak of World War II. Although the war was initially supported by the population, after defeat in North Africa by Great Britain and the virtual occupation of Italy by German troops, the popularity of the war dropped sharply. When the Allies landed in Sicily and moved up the peninsula, they were greeted as liberators. In the north, partisan bands headed by communists and socialists began an active resistance that eroded the ability of the German troops to face the Allied advance. Finally, after twenty months of fierce fighting, liberation came. Mussolini, who attempted to flee to Switzerland, was captured and executed by a mob.

After the war, Italians voted against continuing a monarchy. Again, however, there was a division between the north and the south. For example, the inhabitants of Naples, in the south, voted seventy-nine percent in favor of the monarchy (Kogan 1983). A democratic republic was established, and King Vittorio Emmanuele III was exiled. The major party, which until very recently dominated the Italian political scene and was closely tied to the Roman Catholic church, was the Christian Democratic Party. Many other parties, each representing diverse segments of the population, were also formed. The communists, who had created strong local support in north and central Italy through the resistance movement, established a party, as did the socialists, liberals, republicans, and others. This fragmentation of the political scene has led to a postwar history of legislative compromise and stalemate and to the instability of the government, which has fallen fifty-two times in forty-five years.

Italy changed geographically after the war as the areas of Fiume, Istria, and Dalmatia were granted by the Allies to Yugoslavia; part of the alpine region near France was lost as well. Economically, Italy emerged from the war devastated again; it owed a war debt of $400 million to Yugoslavia, Greece, and other nations in reparation. Again, the solution to internal economic woes became emigration. Between 1946 and 1970, approximately 7.5 million people emigrated from Italy. Between 1951 and 1970, 4.5 million emigrated from the south, half of them moving to the industrial north and half emigrating to other countries. Due to stricter immigration laws in the United States, little of this emigration was directed there; however, South America—particularly Argentina and Brazil—and Northern Europe saw a massive influx of Italians in this period. Recently, due to a rapid increase in prosperity during the last twenty years, many of these emigrants have returned to Italy. Even today, however, there is an ongoing process of migration from the hills and mountains of central Italy and Sicily to the industrial plains along the coast and in the north. Thus, small villages and hamlets are being abandoned; often, only a few elderly people, living on government pensions, remain in them. For example, Lucito, near Campobasso, was once a town of seven thousand inhabitants; today its population is less than one thousand. There are more people from Lucito living at Buenos Aires in Argentina today than those still living in the town.

The last forty years have seen the rapid industrialization of Italy and increasing prosperity. Gone are the days of bare subsistence that many in the older generations remember so well. The youth are well educated and skilled for modern employment. Italy has become the fifth most industrialized country in the world and is the center for such industries as fashion, high quality textiles and clothing, shoes, and cinema. Italy is synonymous with high-performance sports cars like Maserati, Lamborghini, Alfa Romeo, and Ferrari as well. Agricultural products, such as olives, grapes, wine, and pasta, are also world renowned. This rapid industrialization has wrought many changes; the society is more mobile now, crowded cities are experiencing problems with crime and drug abuse, and the country is subject to recurrent inflation. Local traditions are still strong, however, and in many ways society is still influenced by the centuries of history that are its heritage. Visitors to Rome can find ancient Roman ruins near medieval churches that are now located next to modern banks and other buildings. Italy's present is built on yesterday's events, and Italian customs are the result of centuries of traditions. These traditions belong to Italians everywhere; they are the core of Italian heritage.

Chapter 3

MEANING AND ORIGIN OF ITALIAN SURNAMES

PART OF EVERY PERSON'S FAMILY HISTORY AND HERITAGE is the family name, or surname. What are its origins, what does it mean, and how was it formed? This chapter, obviously, cannot explore the meanings and origins of all Italian surnames; that task would require a book in itself. Rather, this chapter explains how Italian surnames were formed, classifies their meanings, and describes how the surname can be useful in genealogical research.

There are almost 1 million different surnames in Italy today! However, if we consider the various forms and spellings, the actual roots from which all surnames derive number only a few thousand. To understand why this is true and how family names began, it is necessary to turn to history and examine their earliest origins.

From early history, names were used to identify individuals, but rarely was a family name included. Even Jews, who are believed to have been the first to place emphasis on family lines and genealogy, usually failed to permanently identify a family line by one surname. Thus, Christ has been known as Jesus of Nazareth, Jesus son of Joseph, Jesus the Christ, and Jesus of the lineage of David, but no family name has ever been attributed to him. Often, the name originally given a child was changed during his or her lifetime—for example, when a nickname based on some physical characteristic or life event was acquired. This practice continued from earliest history well into the Middle Ages. Thus, names varied considerably as nicknames were given and new names were created. As new waves of invaders—Turks, Arabs, Greeks, and Franks and other Germanic tribes—penetrated Italy, new names were introduced. Indeed, there was a continuous flux of names throughout this early period.

When the political scene in Europe stabilized under Charlemagne's rule, internal migrations ended, and the Roman Catholic church established its authority and control, names became more standardized and had religious, Germanic, or classical origins. There were religious names from Latin, such as Alessandro, Filippo, Giorgio, Benedetto, Domenico, and Orsola, and from Greek, such as Giovanni, Pietro, Maria, Maddalena, and so on. Common names of Germanic origin were Guido, Rodolfo, and Arduino, and from classical Latin came Augusto, Alba, Laura, Mario, and Silvia.

With the advent of nobility and the need to distinguish family lines and, most importantly, with the beginning use of written documents, it became necessary to identify not only the individual but also his or her family. This practice began simply by including the father's name—for example, Giovanni son of Franco—but, as other generations were added, this method became awkward, so family names were created. Later, in the 1400s, when written documents such as parish records, tax records, and judicial records began to be created—not just for the noble families but for the common people as well—this need became apparent, and family names were established for everyone. When record keeping became more widespread, family names became permanent and remained from one generation to the next.

Although family names have many different origins, they generally belong in one of four major categories: surnames that originate from personal names, from nicknames, from names of localities, and from vocations.

SURNAMES FROM PERSONAL NAMES

The first group of family names includes those that originated from the name of the person who headed the household. Just as the English "Frank son of John" became "Frank Johnson," the same evolution can be found in Italian: Franco figlio di Giovanni became Franco Di Giovanni. As a result, the most commonly used first names of this early period also became the most common roots for family names.

Andrea, a popular name of the Middle Ages, demonstrates how a personal name can become the root for many surnames. Andrea is a Latin variation of the Greek root *andros,* which means "man." This name was common throughout the Holy Roman Empire and Italy based on the prestige of the apostle Andrea (an evangelist and brother of

Simon Peter), who preached Christianity throughout Italy and southern Europe. If the head of the household was named Andrea in the period of initial record keeping, his children might have been called by their given names and Andrei (Latin) or Di Andrea (Italian) to indicate that they were children of Andrea. As the records and the surname became standardized, one of the variations remained the surname or became the root of the surname variation. Andrea is today the root of at least sixty surname variations, among them De Andrea, Andreotti, Andreoni, Andreaccio, Andrat, and Drei. Each of these spelling variations has a specific meaning that depends upon the prefixes or suffixes that are added. For example, in Italian, the endings -otto, -otti, -oni, and -one connote largeness. Therefore, if the Andrea in the village who gave life to the surname was a big man, it is probable that the family name would become Andreotti or Andreone, whereas if he was small or short the surname might be Andreini or Andretti. The ending -accio in Italian has a negative connotation, so, if Andrea had a bad temper or was mean, the name might very well be Andreaccio. "Uccio" is the opposite; it is a term of endearment, so an Andreuccio would be a kind, gentle man.

Another important factor regarding these variations is that they change according to location. While the root Andrei is common throughout Italy, the spelling variations D'Andrea and De Andrea are common in the south; Andreotti, Andreini, and Andreaccio are found predominantly in central Italy; and Andrean, Andreasi, and Andrat belong to the northeast region. Finally, Slavic variations such as Andrich, Andreassich, and Drei are found only in the Friuli region near Yugoslavia. Spelling variations of any surname that are specific to a particular region can be very important to genealogical research, as will be discussed.

The surname was not always based on the male head of the household; there are female name roots as well, the most common being Anna, Agata, Agnese, De Maria, and De Rosa. Some names, such as Ansaldo or Ansuino—mostly those of Germanic origin—were less popular and led to few surname variations, whereas other names, such as Antonio or Giovanni, have hundreds or even thousands of different forms. The surname Giovanni not only has many variations itself but also forms other local roots, such as Vanni, Nanni, and Zanni, due to dialectic changes of the name. These, in turn, are roots for hundreds of other spelling changes in the surname. Thus, for Giovanni, to name only a few forms, there are: Giovanardi, Giovannazzi, Giovannacci, Giovannelli, Giovannetti, Giovannini, Giovannone, Giovagnini, Gianni, Giangrasso, Giannassi, Giannese, Giannetti, Giannini, Giannola, Giannotti, Giannasso, Giambertone, Giambono, Giammaria, Vannone, Vannucci, Vannuzzi, Vannoli, Zangrando, Zambelli, Zambiase, Zambon, Zambonio, Zanelli, Zandonato, Zanata, Zanarini, Zanassi, Zanardo, Zampolli, Zampiero, and many, many others.

The preposition Di, De, Dei, or Del often precedes the group of surnames that originated from personal names.

These translate as "of" and thus mean "son of" (as in Johnson, Hanson, or Williamson). This form is especially common in the south and in the Puglia region in particular, where are found names such as Di Andrea, Di Matteo, Di Pietro, De Cesare, and Del Santo. Although often found in Latin documents in the north, the preposition was usually dropped in the Italian modernization.

An interesting subdivision of this first category is a group of names called *augurale*—that is, of "best wishes." These surnames were most commonly given to children who were orphans, illegitimate, or foundlings. Illegitimate children and foundlings were not uncommon in Italy because of the system of heredity that was intrinsic to the feudal system. Because land was limited and necessary for the subsistence of the family, it could not be divided among the children; otherwise, what remained would soon be insufficient. This situation brought about the right of the firstborn male to inherit the family's land. Other males in the family could work for the firstborn son or enter military service, but rarely would this work support a family. Thus, often only the firstborn son would or could marry. Obviously, this situation created difficulties, and the result was often promiscuity and illegitimate children. The resulting offspring could not be supported and, due to social norms, could not even be recognized, so traditionally the pregnancy was hidden, the newborn often being left on the doorstep of a church to be raised by the church or put in an orphanage. At times this occurred so often that priests kept separate records for the baptisms of foundlings. The infant mortality rate was very high, and, of those foundlings who survived, more often than not the child grew up as a servant working in the house or fields of a wealthy family. To compensate for these grim beginnings, the surname given to the foundling was often intended as one of greetings or good fortune for the child. Common names were Benvenuto (Welcome), Conforte (Comfort), and Bonaventura (Good Fortune). Some names, however, merely explained the child's origin or were even pejorative; the most used were Esposito (Exposed), Trovato (Found), Sventura (Unfortunate), Aflitto (Afflicted), and Brutto (Ugly). Rather than being rare, these names comprise about ten percent of all Italian surnames. Esposito literally means "exposed" or "shown," and as a name derives from the practice among orphanages of displaying the orphans to visitors so that the orphans could be taken into homes as servants. Esposito, in fact, is the most common surname in the city of Naples.

The category of surnames that derive their meaning from a common name includes thirty-eight percent of all Italian surnames and is thus the largest category (De Felice 1978).

SURNAMES FROM NICKNAMES

The second category of surname roots includes those names that take their roots from a personal nickname. These include some of the best known and most common Italian names, such as Rossi, Moro, and Bevilacqua. In the early Middle Ages, before family names appeared, each person was known by his or her name but was often distinguished from others by some personal characteristic and was thus given a nickname. Names like Big John and Frederick Red Beard and George One Eye became common. As written records came into being, the nickname often came to be identified with the family and was transmuted into the family name. These nicknames usually underlined some physical characteristic, such as Biondo (Blond), Rossi (Red), Moro (Dark), Piccolo (Small), Grasso (Fat), Grosso (Big), Sordo (Deaf), Zoppo (Crippled), and so on. In many cases, however, some intellectual or behavioral aspect was emphasized, and these names were not always complimentary. Thus, Astuto (Clever), Bevilacqua (Drinks Water—obviously rare in a wine-drinking country), Fumagalli (Chicken Thief), Tardo (Retarded), and Tontodimamma (Mother's Stupid Boy) are all found.

Other nicknames originated from events that took place in the past, for which we usually have no record. Often, these were the result of some memorable feat performed by the family head. Examples are Magnavacca (Eat a Cow), Maccaferri (Dented Iron), and Squarcialupi (Skinned Wolves). This second group of surnames taken from nicknames makes up an additional fifteen percent of Italian surnames.

It is interesting to note that two of the most common Italian surnames, Rossi and Moro, are in this category. Rossi, which is the most common surname root, is particularly intriguing as a surname when you consider that it means "red," usually referring either to a red beard or red hair. You might wonder why, in a country of relatively dark-skinned, dark-haired Mediterraneans, this name is so widespread—not only in the north, where a Germanic presence was common, but even in Sicily with the root Russo. Many people mistakenly assume that all Italians with the same surname are, or were at one time, related. The surname Rossi, for example, can be found in the Non Valley in the Trentino province, but it is absent in all of the surrounding valleys. It is found again one hundred miles away near Padua and Venice, but it is absent in the lower Po Valley and toward Trieste. It is present in the Canavese Valley, near Turin, but not farther north—and so on. This pattern of local diffusion of a surname in geographically isolated areas, dating back, in each case, to the beginning of the local records in the 1500s, and not being associated with any local noble families, indicates that the surname groupings are independent of one another. Each probably originated with a family head who had a red beard or red hair.

Less surprising as a common surname is Moro, which means "dark" and usually referred to dark hair or a dark complexion. This name was also given to those of presumed Moorish or Islamic origins. Another common surname root in the south is Ricci or Rizzi, which means "curly," probably in reference to curly hair. Then, of course, there is the opposite: Calvi, which means "bald."

SURNAMES FROM ETHNIC OR GEOGRAPHICAL ORIGINS

The third, and very large, category of surname roots denotes the ethnic or geographical origin of the family. This group includes thirty-seven percent of all Italian surnames. Ethnic surnames are found throughout the Italian peninsula and denote immigrants from other countries or regions. Some of the more common such surnames are Greco (Greek), Tedesco (German), Latino, Longobardo, and Siciliano. Even more common, however, are surnames taken from the town, village, or city of origin. This type of surname is found most frequently in northern and central Italy and is the largest category in these areas. Thus, in Genova the most common surname is Parodi, a name originating from a small inland town, Parodi Ligure, that during the Middle Ages was the center of massive emigration to Genova and the coast due to the plague. In the same way, Mantovani, meaning "from Mantova," is the most common surname in Ferrara, and Furlan (from Friuli) is most common in Trieste. Names like Padovan and Trevisan (from Padua and from Treviso) are common throughout northwest Italy.

In most areas of Italy, even until recently, there was very little migration from one village to another. Particularly in the north and central regions, where feudalism never was prevalent, most families owned their homes and land and had little reason to move. In each village, the inhabitants, over generations, knew one another and their families. When someone new moved in, invariably he and his family were regarded as foreigners and referred to as "those foreigners from . . .," indicating the name of their village of origin. This was true even if the village was only a few miles away and often occurred even if the family already had an established surname. Much migration during the Middle Ages was from the countryside to the larger cities and communes, where more work opportunities existed. As a result, it is now common to find geographically-derived surnames in the larger cities and towns.

Another interesting fact about this group of surnames is that they became the family names of many Christianized Jews. During the Middle Ages, and in particular in the epoch of the Holy Inquisition, Jews were severely persecuted throughout Europe. Many, to survive, became "converted" Christians. Jews were not allowed to be landowners in this period or to live in the countryside, so they became merchants and bankers, usually residing in the ghettos of the large cities. To hide their Jewish origins, it was usually necessary to change the surname, so it became common practice to take on the name of the city or town of origin. Thus, they adopted as surnames the names of cities, such as Trieste, Ancona, Ferrara, Genova (Genoa), and so on.

SURNAMES FROM VOCATIONS

The last category of surnames is derived from the work or profession of the family. Family trades and crafts, such as smithing, cobbling, carpentry, and farming, were passed from father to son for generations. Consequently, often the craft or vocation of the family head became the basis of the family name. Therefore, there are numerous surname roots of this type, such as Sartori (Tailor), Fabbro or Ferrari (Smith), Massaro or Masiero (Farmer), Mastro (Teacher), Segato (Carpenter), Guerra, Soldati, or Spada (Soldier), Pane (Baker), and Cardinale (Cardinal). The root Fabbro or Ferri is one of the most common in Italy. It has variations, such as Favero, Faveron, Ferretti, Del Favro, Ferraiolo, Ferrati, Ferrari, Ferrarini, etc. After Rossi, Ferrari is the second most frequent surname in Italy; it is concentrated mainly in north-central Italy. The diffusion of the root *ferri* (iron) attests to the importance in the social structure of the smith's work. That the name is found rarely in the south is not only because less iron ore is located there; it is more evidence of a feudal system that left little room for a middle class there.

Although there are four major surname categories in Italy, not every surname clearly belongs in one specific category. For example, the surname root Marini can be found with the following variations: Marino, Marin, De Marini, De Marinis, La Marina, Marinelli, Marinella, Mariniello, Marinetti, Marinucci, Marinuzzi, Marinolli, Marinotti, Marinotto, Marinoni, Marinacci, Marinazzo, and Marinato. Marinelli is diffused throughout Italy, while Marini is found in the north and in the Tuscany region. Marino is found in the south-central area, Marin is typical of Venice, Mariniello and Marinaccio of Naples, and La Marina is found only in the extreme south. The root Marini has its origin, in some cases, in the Etruscan name Marius (Mario), so it could refer to a family head named Mario or Marius. *Marina* also means "sea," so Marini or its variations may indicate an ancestor who originated from near the ocean. It is also possible that it has been derived from the vocation of sailor (*marinaio*) or someone who made a living from the sea. In some areas of the central south it originates from the names of towns located there, such as Marino and Marini. Thus, as with this name, one surname may have its roots in three or even all four of the name classifications.

A subgroup of names is formed by those whose ancestors worked for noble or wealthy families. Many people mistakenly assume that names based on noble or ecclesiastic titles are evidence of aristocratic roots. Thus, surnames such as Duca (Duke), Conte (Count), Marchese (Marquis), Vescovo (Bishop), Cardinale (Cardinal), and Papa (Pope) are taken as indications of noble origin. Such is not the case, and often just the opposite is true. These names are common in the south and in the Po Valley, where the land was owned by a few wealthy families that had many farmhands working for them. Often, farmhand families worked for the same family for generations or even centuries. If a family worked for centuries for the Rizzi family or any of the other wealthy families that had large amounts of land, it is possible that they were referred to as the workers of Rizzi and subsequently took on the surname Rizzi or Rizzardi or a similar variation. This same process often resulted in the surname of a noble family being taken by its farmhands. Thus, surnames such as Duca or Conte probably are attributable to families that worked for a duke or a count.

Because ecclesiastical leaders were some of the largest landowners, particularly in the papal states, similar origins are true of surnames such as Papa, Cardinale, and Vescovo. They do not denote an ancestral link, born in sin, with a pope or a cardinal. Therefore, although it is easy to assume that a person is of noble lineage because he or she has the same surname as a noble family, it is always necessary first to establish a pedigree chart and genealogy to establish a title.

Another interesting surname variation, which is found throughout what was once the Serenissima Republic (now the Venetian region) and in the Piedmont region near France, is the second family name. Some authors mistakenly refer to these names as family nicknames, as are, on occasion, found in other areas of Italy. However, there are specific differences that render second family names unique. Whereas a family nickname is derived from some personal characteristic of a family member and stays with the individual throughout life, it is not continued from one generation to another. Instead, these second family surnames or, as one author, Vincenzo Tamburin, defines them, "sub-surnames," were acquired through marriage and heredity, were clearly stated in written historical documents, and lasted from one generation to another, sometimes for centuries, with little alteration.

The second family surname was used to distinguish among several branches of the same family line and thus was most frequently used when the family name was very common in one town or area. For example, the surname Zangrando, which means "Big John," is found in the small village of Vodo in the Dolomite Mountains. The Zangrando family is divided into at least six distinct family lines, each of which is distinguished by a separate sub-surname: Del Vecchio, Saccon, Savio, Da Zoppa, Mupitto, and Protor. This division of the family first appears in the parish and historical records of the 1700s and continues even today.

The number of different sub-surnames that were given to a family depended considerably on the prosperity of the family itself. For example, in a nearby village named S. Vito di Cadore, the Belli surname was first divided into nine nuclear family units in the parish records of the early 1600s. As the family prospered and became more numerous in the village, these nine lines were expanded to twenty-one and then to thirty different lines, each with its own distinct sub-surname, during the 1700s. Then many family lines ended after producing no male children, and the family gradually

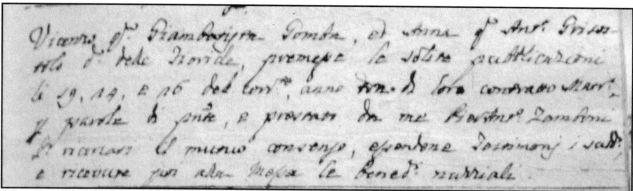

FIGURE 3-1. Marriage Act of Vincenzo Gamba and Anna Crisotolo, Maniago, Pordenone

was reduced in number, so that today there are thirteen different lines, of which seven still have the same original second surname of the nine that began almost four centuries ago.

It is possible that these second family names originated from a nickname of some family member that distinguished him from the rest of the family. Names such as Del Vecchio, which means "Of the Old One," and Da Zoppa, "Son of the Cripple," may be examples of this occurrence. More common, however, is the beginning of a second family name through marriage. In northern Italy, most families owned property. When a family had no sons, the first daughter had rights of inheritance. These women were much sought after because they provided a means for the second- or third-born male in a family to acquire property and have a family. Quite often, when she married, such a woman's surname became the second family name of her husband. This name was kept for their children, thus forming a new family line.

In the Venetian region, the second family name follows the surname in documents, while in the Piedmont region the two surnames are often hyphenated, giving more credence to the idea that they should be considered second surnames. Examples of common surnames found in this area are Corgiat-Bondon, Chiado-Fiorio, Molinaris-Rubat, Troglia-Gamba, and Biima-Besquet. Another difference between the two regions is that, for the most part, the second family name has been dropped from the civil records in the Venetian region, while the hyphenated surnames in the Piedmont region are still used and appear in civil vital records.

This surname variation is emphasized here because it is quite useful in genealogical research for two reasons: first, it gives clear family divisions for many generations, greatly facilitating the determination of the correct family line; and second, in earlier records the two surnames are sometimes switched, the sub-surname is dropped altogether, or the first is dropped and only the second surname is used. For example, for one family in the province of Treviso, the major family name was clearly Bergamin in records dating to the mid-1700s. There were several second surnames for the Bergamins, and this particular family's line was Santin,

giving a composite surname of Bergamin Santin. In a move from one village to another, the surname changed from Bergamin Santin to Santin Bergamin; in the earlier generations, it appeared only as Santin. If you were searching only for the surname Bergamin, the family line would soon be lost.

Another example is from the town of Maniago, Pordenone. In recent records only the family name of Gamba was used, as seen in the marriage record of Vincenzo Gamba (figure 3-1). In the baptismal record of Vincenzo, however, Gamba appears as a second surname and Del Zot as the major surname (figure 3-2). This is true as well for the baptism of Vincenzo's brother, Sebastiano (figure 3-3), but his sister Catterina is identified only by the surname Gamba (figure 3-4). This alternation of the two surnames continues in each preceding generation, with sometimes one and sometimes the other name being omitted. It is essential, then, for the researcher to recognize and search for both names to complete each family group and to establish earlier lines.

A brief examination of how one surname originated and evolved is useful in understanding what has been stated so far. In another example from the town of Vodo, we find in the historical records of 1240 A.D. a certain Bartolomeo Da Gava, who came from the town of Gavas to settle in the area. A record from 1388 mentions one of his descendants named Rizzardo (Richard), who was a *favero*, or "smith." Rizzardo had two sons, both of whom were smiths as well, one named Zambono (Good John) and the other named Rizzardino (Little Richard), which in dialect became Zardino. Zambono went to live in the village of Peaio, and he became the family head of the Del Favero (Son of the Smith) family. Zardino lived at nearby Borca di Cadore and had two sons, Pietro and Antonio. Pietro established the Del Favero surname at Borca, while Antonio and his descendants were known as Zardino. Another descendant of Bartolomeo Da Gava, mentioned in 1416, was named Galleazzo—someone who takes care of the *galli*, or "chickens." His descendants were named Galleazzi. Therefore, from this one ancestor, Bartolomeo, all the following surnames are still found in the area: Da Gava, which derives from a topographical location; Del Favero, which is a vocation surname; Zardino, which comes from a name; and Galleazzi, which comes from a nickname.

The above example also clearly demonstrates the changes that occurred in the surname from its origin. In fact, as stated, the surnames were established with the advent of written documentation and were standardized when vital records of some type were used extensively. As a result, most surnames were formed in the three centuries from the thirteenth to the sixteenth centuries, but new additions or changes have occurred even in very recent periods.

CHANGES IN SURNAMES

When searching parish, notary, or historical records, many researchers are disconcerted to find different forms or spellings of their own surnames. These variations are quite common and are usually due to changes in the language used to write the records, which varies among Latin, dialect, and Italian. Often these variations are very recognizable; for example, the Italian Ferrari may be Ferraris or De Ferraris in Latin and perhaps Ferari in dialect. Other times, however, the variations may differ so radically that it is difficult to discern that they represent the same family name. For example, the surname Rossi may be written in several different forms, such as Rossi, De Roia, Roscia, Rubeis, and De Rubeis, depending on whether the priest was writing in Italian, Venetian dialect, or Latin. Obviously, a researcher who doesn't know that all of these are spelling variations of the same name can be very confused. Often, as a result, the researcher is unable to pursue the family line or complete the family groups. Figures 3-5 and 3-6 are examples of spelling variations of the Rossi surname from the same parish. In the first, from the 1800s (figure 3-5), the surname appears clearly as Rossi. In earlier records, however, some priests wrote in Latin, and the name is present as De Rubeis (figure 3-6). Still earlier acts contained a mixture in the same act of Italian, dialect, and Latin; the names and surnames were in dialect.

Very often, even though the surname remained the same through the centuries, the writing was not standard-

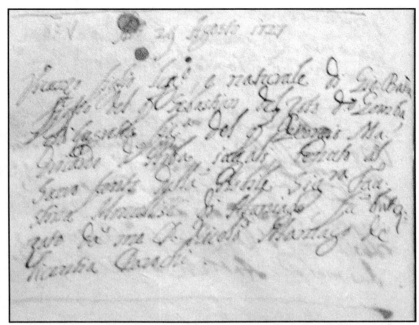

FIGURE 3-2. Baptismal Act of Vincenzo Gamba, 1727, Maniago, Pordenone

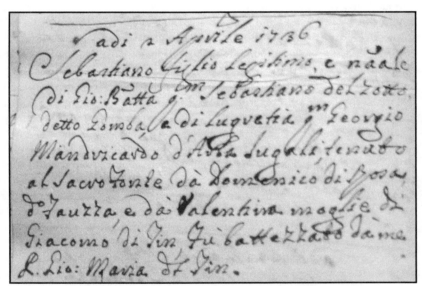

FIGURE 3-3. Baptismal Act of Sebastiano Del Zoto Gamba, 1736, Maniago, Pordenone

ized; thus, spelling variations occurred. The most common of these spelling changes was the addition of double consonants at the end of a name. The surname Zanelli may originally have been written as Zanelo or Zaneli in the records, with an extra "l" then added to form Zanello, Zanella, or Zanelli. Most often the parish priest tried to write the name the way it sounded, and the result was that each priest wrote the name differently. Others tried to Italianize dialectic names, and many seemingly made up the spellings as they wrote. Usually, it was not until the civil vital records were created that a particular spelling of a

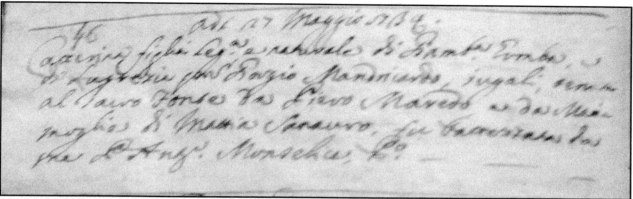

FIGURE 3-4. Baptismal Act of Catterina Gamba, 1734, Maniago, Pordenone

name became permanent. Joseph Colletti, in the Spring 1989 issue of *POINTers*, listed the following spelling variations of his surname: Coleta, Colleta, Colletta, Colete, Collete, Collette, Coleti, Colleti, Colletti, Coleto, Colleto, Colletto—and these are only the Italian variations!

Normally, then, variations in writing the name did not lead to any permanent change in the surname, but this is not always the case. In one town, for example, the surname Preti, which means "priest" in Italian, was also written De Prettis in the parish records when Latin was used. Although this was originally the same family, in the 1600s two family lines were created: one surname continued the Latin spelling and the other became Italianized as Preti; this difference remains today.

Probably the most recent significant change in Italian surnames has been caused by emigration in the last century—particularly by emigration to the United States before World War I. There were several reasons for this change, but the most common was illiteracy. At the height of Italian immigration to the United States between 1880 and 1914, nearly 4 million Italians entered through the port of New York at Ellis Island. There, each was questioned about his or her name, age, place of origin, and so on so that immigration documents could be created. Because neither passports nor personal documents were required for immigrants, and since the vast majority were illiterate, the immigration officials wrote the names and surnames as they understood them. As a result, variations occurred, often rendering a surname unrecognizable. For example, as an acquaintance wrote to me, her grandfather was named Chinice, but at immigration this was changed to Kinish. The relatives who remained in Italy continued to write to Mr. Chinice, and their letters were never delivered.

Another common practice was to Americanize the name, giving a literal translation; thus, Papa became Pope, Moro became Brown, Regis became King, and even a name like Bevilacqua became Drinkwater. This Americanization of the name did not always occur at the moment of immigration. Often the name was changed later to avoid bigotry and discrimination associated with being Italian.

Occasionally, the name was deliberately changed to avoid apprehension by Italian authorities for some offense committed in Italy. The most common offense was draft evasion. As stated, all Italian males were obliged to report for the draft at age eighteen. Emigration was not allowed until after a young man had served his military duty or was exempted. Purposely avoiding the draft or emigrating before completing their military service put the young men at odds with Italian law. Therefore, to avoid being traced, they often deliberately changed their surnames and falsified their birth dates. This practice often renders genealogical research very difficult.

One case clearly illustrates this point. I was searching for information about an ancestor named Nazzaro Reno. This ancestor had always been reluctant to talk about Italy and his personal background, so the only information known was that he had been born on 3 December 1888 at Sondrio, Italy, and that his mother's name was Gioconda. It was also known that he had immigrated to San Francisco, California, in 1905. The first step of research in Italy was to travel to Sondrio and search the civil records there. However, Nazzarro Reno was not found among the birth records from 1870 to 1895. In fact, no one with the surname Reno was found at Sondrio.

A town official stated that the surname Reno is not found anywhere in the region but that Rino is found in the southern portion of the province of Sondrio at Bormio. The records of Bormio and the surrounding towns were searched for a Nazzaro Rino and for any family with a mother named Gioconda, because this is a rare name. All Rino families were searched for a son born in the right period, since Nazzaro might be a second or third name or even a nickname. No one was found with either the name Nazzaro or Gioconda.

A last effort was made by consulting the conscription records for all the military districts in the province of Sondrio for the period 1880 to 1895. These are held at the state archive at Sondrio. There was no one of the Reno or Rino surname who could possibly have been the ancestor but, by chance, the ancestor was found. Born on 30 Novem-

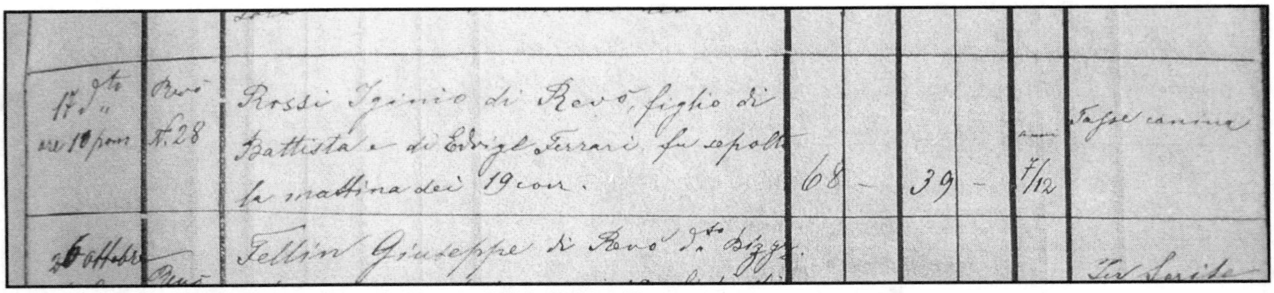

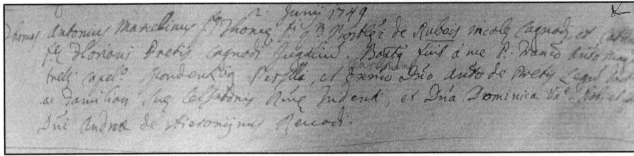

FIGURE 3-5. Baptismal Act of Iginio Rossi, 1892, Revò, Trento

FIGURE 3-6. Baptismal Act of Thomas Antonius Marcellinus De Rubeis, 1749, Revò, Trento

ber and baptized on 3 December 1888 was a young man named Nazzareno Paindelli. His parents were listed as Battista and Gioconda Paindelli. The military record stated that he was a deserter, having emigrated without permission and without having performed military duty. He was listed as living with relatives in San Francisco, California. All information matched, and further investigation established that he had divided his first name, Nazzareno, into Nazzaro Reno, leaving off his surname to avoid possible legal prosecution.

Another major change in surnames occurred from 1922 to 1945 during the Fascist period in Italy under Mussolini. In this period there was a deliberate exaltation of Italian traditions from imperial Rome to the twentieth century, and a political and cultural isolation from the rest of the world was imposed. This isolation was engineered so that Italians could not compare themselves with people of other European countries and thus be "contaminated" by new and dangerous ideas and customs. It is no coincidence that during this period Italian emigration was drastically reduced—except to Libya, Ethiopia, and Somalia, which were parts of the Italian empire. As part of the effort to glorify all things Italian, foreign words, even those in common use, such as "garage," "bar," and "sport," were banned from use and Italian forms, often much more awkward to use, were substituted. This practice was applied as well to foreign or foreign-sounding surnames, particularly along the northern borders of Italy, where there is considerable influence and exchange through language and dialect with the bordering countries of France, Switzerland, Austria, and Yugoslavia (now Slovenia and Croatia). Thus, all surnames with Slavic endings, such as Andreich or Kucel, Germanized names,

such as Widmann and Luttmann, and French names, such as Pouls or Fleury, had to be changed to Italian spellings. Thus, Kucel became Cucelli, Luttmann became Luttini, and Pourls became Puli, to name a few. In recent years, some families have gone through the long process of changing the surname to its original form, but for the most part the Italianized forms have remained.

USING SURNAME VARIATION IN GENEALOGICAL RESEARCH

It should be apparent that, although some surname forms can be found throughout Italy, most spelling variations have specific geographical origins. As stated for the root Marini, Marini and Marinelli are found throughout Italy, but Mariniello and Marinaccio are peculiar to Naples, and Marin is found only in the Venetian region. Sometimes, not only will the family name be found in just one region, but it is confined to one town, one mountain valley, or some other restricted geographical area. For example, while the surnames Negri, Negroni, Negrotto, and De Negri are found throughout the north of Italy, the form Negrinotti originated in one mountain village of the Bergamo province and is found, even today, only in that valley. The fact that some spellings of a surname may have very specific origins in Italy can be of great assistance in research, when no other information is available.

Even first names tend to vary from one region to another and can help narrow the search. Some given names that are frequently found in southern Italy and Sicily (seldom in the north) are Salvatore, Antonino, Carmelo, Pasquale, Rosario, and Gennaro for males; and Rosaria,

Concetta, Assunta, Giuseppina, Annunziata, Santa, and Filomena for females. Some given names most often found in the north are Pietro, Antonio, Giovanni Battista, Lorenzo, and Osvaldo for males; and Antonia, Barbara, Antonietta, Laura, and Cristina for females. None of these is absolutely unique to one region or another, but if no other information is available, such a name may provide a clue as to where an ancestor originated.

One researcher knew only that his grandfather, Giuseppe Avondoglio, was born somewhere in the north of Italy, not far from Switzerland. Since there was no record source left in the United States or Italy that could establish the family's place of origin, telephone books for each of the northern provinces of Italy were searched. The surname, fortunately, was specific to a small area in the province of Torino. By writing to sources in several towns that had a high concentration of the family name in the telephone book, the family's exact place of origin was found and research could be pursued.

Research is not always so successful; another project had less fruitful results. A researcher wrote from England requesting that an ancestor named Giovanni Baccino be found; she had no idea where he came from. The telephone books of all the major cities in Italy were searched first. The surname Baccino was found in only two cities, Genoa and Savona, but the variation Baccini was found in several cities from Sicily to Venice. Research was pursued on Baccino, and it was found to originate on the coast near Savona in about ten different towns, starting in the coastal mountains and descending along specific roads all the way to Savona. Sources in these towns were contacted, but the family still was not located. The question remains: is the ancestor, Giovanni Baccino, from a town near Savona, or was there a change in the spelling of the surname on immigration? Perhaps the root is Baccini or something similar.

From this brief discussion it should be apparent that each surname has its own history and meaning. To find the meaning and origin of your family name is to discover an important part of your family history and Italian heritage, and should certainly be part of genealogical research. Though this survey cannot discuss every name, it should provide insight into how names were formed and how many different meanings they may have.

Chapter 4

NOBLE FAMILIES

LTHOUGH THE VAST MAJORITY OF "ITALO-AMERICANI"—descendants of Italians who emigrated to the Americas—are descended from common agricultural families, there is considerable interest among Americans regarding coats of arms and the possibility of descent from nobility. This interest may be because there has never been a royal family or a recognized aristocracy in the United States; it may simply stem from curiosity or the desire to find an exotic heritage. Whatever the reason, many people spend inordinate amounts of money trying to establish noble lines that do not exist, and they are sometimes misled by heraldry companies that fabricate coats of arms for their families.

The Italian word *nobile* is derived from the Latin *nobilis*, referring to high birth or rank or meaning "well known by the public." Italy has a proliferation of noble families because, unlike in France and England, there was more than one royal court in Italy; at one time the country was made up of many principalities and duchies, each with its own court and aristocracy. Because there were many noble titles, some people are, in fact, related to noble families and should be aware of the excellent genealogical sources that exist for these lines.

HISTORY OF NOBILITY AND NOBLE TITLES

In a general sense, heraldry refers to the art, history, inheritance, and regulation of coats of arms and the use of titles of nobility and knighthood. Heraldry entails all the work of heralds. Today, heralds are court officials in the service of monarchs in England, Spain, and elsewhere. In medieval times, the herald was responsible for recording and controlling the noble titles and the coats of arms for the monarch. The herald's duties also consisted of scorekeeping at tournaments, counting and identifying the dead and wounded after battles, and serving as a messenger for the king.

Coats of arms began as insignia on knights' armor for very practical reasons. Clad in helmets and armor, mounted knights of the eleventh and twelfth centuries were difficult to identify in battle or during tournaments. Only the colorful insignia on their shields and surcoats (cloaks used to protect the knight and his metal armor from rain and wind) identified them. Thus, much like numbers on players' uniforms in modern sports, each knight had a different insignia and crest. From the arms (shield) and surcoat came

the term "coat of arms." The crest was originally a wooden carving attached to the top of the helmet to deflect direct blows to the head, but it became merely ornamental with time. By the end of the crusades in the late 1200s, warfare had progressed beyond the encounters of armored knights, and tournaments became less frequent. The original purpose of these knightly symbols ended, but their use continued.

Widespread illiteracy and different dialects and languages led to the use of coats of arms in lieu of signatures, not only by the knights but by feudal lords, craftsmen, and guilds as well. The signet ring with seal came to identify the person or business on correspondence and documents. As the original generation of "armigers," or arms bearers, died, their sons began to use the same coats of arms. Thus, the seals were established as hereditary property of a particular family, ensuring the continued use of the armorial insignia for centuries to come. The knights who had served in the crusades or in military-religious orders, and who usually had received large tracts of land in return for their services, became the feudal lords or military class from which evolved the nobility. Knighthood itself became a codified rank that was reserved for this emergent class, and the sons continued using the same titles and ruling the same feudal lands. Nobility may therefore be described as a hereditary status derived from land ownership, royal service, or military service for the church or a monarch.

Although these practices began at the time of the crusades with knights who dedicated their services to the church, very few of Italy's, or even Europe's, existing noble families can trace their titles or lines back to these thirteenth-century armigers. In most cases their ennoblement took place much later, but the process was the same: nobility was granted for military or economic service to the king or ruling sovereign. The origin of Italian knighthood and titles parallels that of the rest of Europe. Because Italy consisted of a series of states and principalities, many noble titles were conferred by each court, and there is some variation in titles from one area to another. For example, the title *patrizio*, used for holders of large amounts of land even in the Roman era, was used in some city-states in the north, while the hereditary title of knight was used mainly in Sicily and Sardinia.

Some of the more common noble titles follow: *principe*, or "prince," comes from the Latin *princeps*, a term for a supreme leader, reflecting its military origin. The area under the reign of the prince was the *principato*, or "principality." This title was often used interchangeably with the title *duca* (duke), which comes from a word for a military leader, *dux*. The *duca*, too, ruled large areas of land that, like the principalities, were practically independent sovereign states. Thus, the Ducato (Duchy) of Savoy was ruled by a duke (who later became the king of Italy when Italy became a kingdom), and the Granducato of Tuscany was ruled for decades by the famous Medici family. These titles were bestowed directly by the emperor or reigning sovereign or by the church, and there was a precise hierarchy. Prince was the highest title, followed by duke, *marchese*, count, viscount, and baron. In 1395, for example, Gian Galeazzo Visconti received the title of *duca* for the Duchy of Lombardy directly from the emperor Venceslao. Though the family had been the feudal lords over most of the same territory since 1277, it previously had had no noble title.

The title *marchese* originated with those called *marches*, who guarded and protected the border regions of the empire. This was not a common title in Italy, but the city of Treviso, for example, was ruled by a *marchese* because it was considered a border region. The title of *conte* (count) was widespread in Italy. There are two explanations for the origin of this title: one states that it originated from the Latin word *comes*, which means "companion" and indicated a loyal companion of a monarch. More probably it comes from the word *comites*. In Roman times the *comites* were government functionaries who had jurisdiction over the different provinces (*comites provinciarum*) and cities (*comites civitatum*). After the fall of the empire this usage disappeared, but it was revived by the Franks, who divided their territory into "counties," in the eighth century. The head of each county was the *comites*, or "count." Later, as a noble title, it was awarded not for military service but for feudal land holdings, indicating that it had the same roots as the *comites*. *Visconte*, or "viscount," means vice count or assistant to the count. The word "baron" has Germanic origins. Originally it referred to all the subjects of the king of the Longobards, but later it was used as a feudal title to indicate those who had full power and legal jurisdiction over their land holdings.

A title was given to a specific person, and only the firstborn male son was allowed to inherit the title. If he died before his father it was passed to the next son, and so on. The other brothers and sisters were considered to be nobles but had no titles. All of the descendants of the various branches of a titled family were considered noble and were usually well off, but only one descending line held the title. Therefore, if the term *nobilis*, often abbreviated *Nob.* or *N.H.* (abbreviation for *nobil homo*, or "noble man"), precedes the name of an ancestor in parish or civil documents, it indicates that the person belonged to a noble family but may have had no other title. Such a status is fortunate for the researcher because there are likely to be additional genealogical sources that describe the family. Another title of note is that of knighthood. As an institution, knighthood is very old but, unlike hereditary titles, knighthood, or *cavaliere*, was an individual title given for outstanding merit.

Those who directly descend on the firstborn line from an ancestor who held a title have a right to the title. Almost always, however, particularly for the noble titles mentioned above, the direct line of descent is well known and the title is already established. More often, you may find in the parish or civil records the title *nobilis* or *illustrus* before the name of an ancestor. In such a case either the family was of titled nobility, being one of the many collateral lines without the title, or the family was not titled at all. Often the term *nobilis* was used lightly for any well-to-do family. In the north, for example, were "rural" or "gentry" nobles—families that were granted extensive land holdings and local feudal rulings but to which no title was given. In the Val di Non in the Trentino region, each town had one or more of these *nobilis gentili*, who owned much of the land, often became notaries, and were often the political leaders but had no official titles. Often the town was named for the noble family, as originally the families who lived there may all have worked for that family. In this valley, the main town, Cles, was named for the noble Cles family. This family had no official title other than *nobile*, but it produced many illustrious historical figures, including Bernardo Cles, the Bishop of Trent, who helped organize the Council of Trent. Scattered throughout this mountain valley are more than thirty noble families, none of which has a specific title other than *nobile* but each of which has its own coat of arms and seal. More important to the genealogist, there are historical records, notary and university records, and sometimes even established genealogies for these non-titled families.

The two most comprehensive sources of Italian coats of arms, and important historical sources as well, are G.B. Di Crollalanza's *Dizionario Storico Blasonico* (Milan, Italy: Hoepli, 1906) and Vittorio Spreti's *Enciclopedia Storico-Nobiliare Italiana* (Milan, Italy: Grafiche Carettani, 1932). Both are multi-volume works that contain the coats of arms of thousands of families. Figure 4-1 is a page from Spreti's work regarding a noble but non-titled family, the Schipani. While some works list only the various coats of arms, Spreti's work includes the shield and provides a history of each family. So for each family listed in the "Elenco

SCHIPANI.

ARMA: D'azzurro al braccio di carnagione movente dalla destra dello scudo e tenente una spiga di grano d'oro.

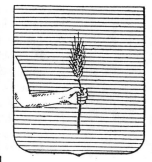

DIMORA: Napoli.

Nelle concessioni nobiliari trascritte nei Registri Privilegiorum del collaterale, detti « Nuovi », il magnifico Filippo Schipani della città di Taverna, il 17 febbraio 1497, aveva conferma di privilegio di familiarità ed esenzioni fiscali con i suoi eredi e successori da re Ferdinando II d'Aragona (vol. I, fol. 39, a t. a fol. 42).

Di origine calabrese, godette nobiltà in Taverna e fu ascritta al primo Ordine civico della città di Monteleone. Fu ricevuta, per giustizia, nel S. M. O. di Malta nel 1795, in persona del cav. Vincenzo Schipani.

Fu riconosciuta di antica nobiltà nelle prove di ammissione delle RR. Guardie del Corpo, nel 1856 (v. Verbali R. Commissione dei Titoli, vol. X, pag. 262) ed ascritta al Registro dei Cavalieri di Malta per giustizia.

Per successione della famiglia Calà, non legalmente riconosciuta, avrebbe avuto diritto al titolo di duca di Diano (Principato Citra) con l'anzianità della concessione ottenuto da Carlo Calà Ossorio, con diploma dato a Madrid il 7 luglio 1654, esecutoriato in Napoli il 20 novembre dello stesso anno. (Archivio di Simancas Segreterias Provinciales, vol. 54, fol. 211 a t.; Archivio di

Stato Napoli, Rep. Quinternioni, n. 248 (108), fol. 340-343. Registrato in *Titulorum*, 7 fol. 30).

La famiglia è iscritta nell'El. Uff. Nob. Ital. del 1922 col titolo di nobile (mf.) pei discendenti da Riccardo, aspirante a Regia Guardia del Corpo nel 1858, in persona di GUGIELMO, n. Sala Consilina 19 maggio 1832, di Ignazio (n. 1801, † 1866) e della nob. Maria Moncada dei duchi di S. Giovanni († 1855), succeduto al fratello Vincenzo (n. 30 luglio 1830, † 24 settembre 1867); spos. a Napoli 20 gennaio 1860 con Luisa Ragozzini († 26 gennaio 1872).

Figlie: 1) Giulia, n. 18 giugno 1862; 2) Matilde, n. 26 maggio 1863; 3) Maria, n. 18 dicembre 1865; 4) Ottavia, n. 1° marzo 1869.

Fratelli: Concetta, n. 2 agosto 1834, sp. 24 gennaio 1866 al nob. Tommaso *Schipani;* RICCARDO, già R. Guardia del Corpo, n. 25 settembre 1836, † 9 dicembre 1903, spos. 13 maggio 1868 con la nob. Caterina Lancellotti.

f. f. p. di s.

SCHIPANI.

ARMA: D'azzurro al braccio di carnagione, movente dalla destra dello scudo, tenente una spiga di frumento di oro.

Famiglia siciliana dichiarata nobile per delibera della Commissione dei Titoli di Nobiltà il 9 marzo 1858.

La famiglia è iscritta genericamente nell'El. Uff. Nob. Ital. del 1922 col titolo di nobile (mf.).

v. s.

FIGURE 4-1. Excerpt From Spreti's "Enciclopedia Storico-Nobiliare Italiana" Regarding the Noble Schipani Family

Ufficiale dei Nobili," the official list of noble families recognized by the monarchy until Italy was made a republic in 1946, Spreti provides a wealth of data. Each section begins with the description of the coat of arms (*arma*). It then indicates the home (*dimora*) of the family, in this case Napoli (Naples), and then provides the family history. Even though the Schipani family was not officially titled or "nobilized" until 1858, it had a long history of feudal holdings and illustrious members who are noted in this history. This was true of many families that were nobilized in the nineteenth and twentieth centuries. When making a request for noble status, it was necessary to demonstrate a

family history of illustrious deeds and land holdings. In this case, the family had already received special recognition, land holdings at Taverna in Calabria, and tax exemptions as early as 1497 from King Ferdinando II d'Aragona. Another member of the family, Vincenzo Schipani, was made a knight in the Order of Malta in 1795, and Gugielmo Schipani was a member of the Royal Body Guards and Knights of Malta when he requested a noble title in 1856.

The family history then delineates the genealogy of the family that received the noble title. Thus we learn that Gugielmo was born at Sala Consilina on 19 May 1832; he

FIGURE 4-2. A Page From Maspoli's "Stemmario Quattrocentesco delle Famiglie Nobili della Citta' e Antica Diocesi di Como," Including the Coat of Arms of the Marcello Family

libraries and some state archives keep copies of the works.

Besides these monumental works, which list all the coats of arms and families found in the "Elenco Ufficiale dei Nobili" of 1922, there are many other works that list only coats of arms, such as Carlo Maspoli's book on the coats of arms of the noble families of the city of Como, titled *Stemmario Quattrocentesco delle Famiglie Nobili della Citta' e Antica Diocesi di Como* (figure 4-2), or that list the history and coats of arms of local nobility, illustrious families of the area, and contain discussions of local history. These works can be very important in pursuing the genealogy and family history of illustrious families.

Because shared surnames do not necessarily indicate a common ancestry, it is not sufficient to have a surname that appears in Spreti's work to claim the coat of arms and history of that family. For example, there are several Rossi families in Spreti's work, including that of Count Rossi of Florence. While Rossi is the most common surname in Italy, being found in almost every province in north and central Italy, its bearers are seldom related to a noble family. It usually originated with a person who had red hair or a red complexion. Also, surnames that denote a noble title, such as Conte or Barone, more likely originated with servants or feudal workers who worked for a count or baron and thus took that surname (see discussion in chapter 3).

How do you discover if there is, indeed, a noble line in your heritage? In ecclesiastical records there is almost

was the son of Ignazio, who was born in 1801 and died in 1866, and of Maria Moncada, daughter of the duke of S. Giovanni. It gives the date of Gugielmo's marriage to Luisa Ragozzini of Naples (20 January 1860), and the names and birth dates of his children and his siblings. Thus, considerable genealogical information is contained in a few paragraphs of an easily-consulted book. More-detailed histories are present for some families, and for many there is less information than is provided in this example, but usually the geographical origin and some history of the family are included. Also, the genealogy of the first noble family member is included, as is the coat of arms. Spreti's and Crollalanza's works can be found in many university and city libraries in the United States, and, in Italy, most large

always a clear indication of nobility in the titles, such as *don* or *dominus*, or *donna*, meaning "lord" or "lady," that precede the name of the person. Other titles of respect are *ill.* or *illustrus*, or *magnifico*, or even *signore*, all of which indicate some degree of wealth or eminence. An official noble title, such as *cavaliere*, *nobile*, or *barone*, may also be included. Even offices, such as that of notary, may be mentioned. If only titles of respect are used, but there is no official noble title, those referred to may well be of a wealthy or important family that had no title of nobility. Nevertheless, there may be a written history of the family, or it could be mentioned in local histories. Other titles used in the records, such as *maestro* or *villico*, indicate that the person was a craftsman or landholder and may not have much significance, especially if they are used repeatedly in the records.

Usually, in a particular town or village, only one or two families were referred to in the records with titles—a sure indication of importance. For example, in the rather large town of Maniago in Pordenone province, only one family was described with the title *illustrus nobile*: the Maniago family, for which the town had been named. A castle and private chapel in the town belonged to the family—usually in a small town there are physical indications of who the important families were. For example, statues, the name of the town square, street names, palaces, estates, etc., often derive their names from the nobles or wealthy members of the community.

What is true of ecclesiastical records is certainly true of notary, civil, and other sources as well. There is inevitably indication of title or illustrious standing in acts and documents that refer to noble families. If you find no such evidence in the acts you have consulted, you are probably one of millions who came from hard-working agricultural families. Some noble families had to flee Italy, either because they fell out of favor or as a result of conflict with other, more powerful, families, and some of them emigrated to France, England, and America. For example, a Farnes family in the United States was originally called Farnese. They fled to England in the sixteenth century after a plot to assassinate the pope failed, and later they emigrated to the United States. However, the people who were most likely to emigrate to other lands were those who had no property, wealth, or anything else to lose in Italy. Thus, heraldry or research on a noble title must be pursued using the same genealogical tools and sources as any other research. It is necessary to search the civil, Napoleonic, and ecclesiastical records until direct patrilineal descent (father to first son or legal right of inheritance) can be established. Once this is accomplished, other sources, such as armories, local histories, and family genealogies, can be consulted.

Some genealogy and heraldry companies in Italy and the United States will provide a history of one's family and a coat of arms for a fee. Some of them are reputable, but many find this an easy way to make money without conducting any real research. These companies have thousands of family histories and coats of arms. For a person with the surname Rizzi, for example, the company will send the coat of arms of the Rizzi family and will provide a detailed history and genealogy of the family, often taken from Spreti's *Enciclopedia* and other historical sources. They may charge several hundred dollars for what amounts to little more than office work, and the person might be led to believe that this family line is somehow related to his or her own when, in fact, there may be no connection whatsoever. What's more, often the company will offer to provide the history for that surname or for any of the surname roots. Thus, not only will this be done for

someone with the surname Rizzi, of which there is mention in the armories, but for any similar surname derivation, such as Risso, Rizzati, Rizzuli, Ricca, Ricciulli, Ricci, Rizzini, or Riccetti, just to name a few! Therefore, any surname can be inserted into a prepared family history and added to a coat of arms, leading someone to believe that complete research of a family's history has been performed. These practices have nothing to do with genealogy or heraldry research!

In 1946, Italy became a democratic republic. The king, Umberto II of Savoy, was exiled and the monarchy and aristocracy were abolished. In the absence of a governmental heraldic authority, the Collegio Araldico was created by Prince Vittorio Emanuele. This body publishes its *Libro d'Oro della Nobiltà Italiana* (*Golden Book of Italian Nobility*) every three or four years. Not properly an armory but rather a peerage register, it lists the names and titles of most of Italy's existing noble families. Those who submit to the Collegio Araldico proof of patrilineal descendence of noble lineage through a well-documented genealogical search may request to be included in the book.

Most of the early armories (representations and written descriptions of coats of arms) and many of the genealogies of the aristocratic families are found in the private archives of those families and are not available for consultation. These families are very protective of these ancient manuscripts and documents, and they do not permit outside consultation, even by professional researchers. In any case, there are many records that do contain historical and genealogical information about these families, and they become an important source of information.

RESEARCHING NOBILITY

If you have found that an ancestor came from a noble or otherwise illustrious family, several record sources are available for continuing the research. As will be discussed in chapter 9, notary and university records are particularly useful for researching wealthy, land-holding families. Also, local histories and family genealogies can be found in local libraries or state archives. For families of a certain standing there may be published family histories, and there are often handwritten documents and genealogies. Before examining these sources of information, however, be aware that researching a noble family is not always easy.

Most families in Italy remained in the same town or village for generations, even centuries, and their entire genealogy can be obtained from the records of one parish. Even the maternal lines often originated from the same town or neighboring towns and can be pursued without much difficulty. This is because the family's property was conserved for each new generation; rarely was there any change of possession. For the wealthy families, however, that was not necessarily the case. Very often they had extensive land holdings that were not limited to one town

FIGURE 4-3. A Page From Maspoli's Work Showing the Coat of Arms of the Noble Volpi or De Vulpis Family (upper right)

Noble families often had private chapels on their property. Although, normally, baptisms, marriages, and funerals were performed in the town's main church or cathedral and were recorded in the parish records, often the noble families counted priests, archpriests, monsignors, and bishops among their members; these ecclesiastical officers performed private ceremonies and kept private records for the family. These records can still be found in the private archives of some families but are not available for consultation. Therefore, even if you have wealthy or noble ancestors and thus more record sources are available, the research itself may be more complicated and difficult to accomplish than for the common farmer!

The Volpi family, discussed in chapter 9, is a case in point. In each generation there was a major move of the family. The family history began at Venice, and it was only through the examination of university records that it was traced to Trento. From there, all trace of the family was lost. Searches were made at Mantova and Verona, where it was known that the family had estates, but nothing was found in any of the many parishes of those cities. Another search was made at Como, where historical records revealed that the noble Volpi family had originated there. Although a wealth of information about the Volpi family was found, the branch of the family in question was not mentioned. Only through the university records was the family located at Pavia. There, seemingly, the family records were kept at a small church called S. Maria Maggiore, but it no longer represents a parish and, despite intense research efforts at the *curia* and state archive, no trace of the records has been found. There are notary records concerning the family, but, in the mid-1700s, all mention of the surname disappeared again. So, while a "normal" family can usually be traced with relatively little effort back to the 1600s through parish records, this family line ends in the late 1700s and has been researched only with great effort and expense.

This example is not meant to discourage the potential researcher but rather to caution that having a noble line can be a mixed blessing. The genealogy for the branch of the Volpis of Como back to the 1400s, in contrast, is easily

or even one province, and the family moved from one place of residence to another. The main line of a family may have remained in the town of origin, while other branches of the family moved away to take care of other estates. The duties of notaries often required them to move from one town to another. In each of these cases, it is often very difficult to follow the movements of the family. Also, the wealthy customarily married into other noble or wealthy families, so the wives almost invariably came from other towns or cities, often located far away. Thus, research quickly spreads to many different towns and parishes. Since marriage took place in the bride's parish, it is often difficult to locate the origin of the maternal lines.

available. Examining some of the documentation regarding the Volpi family should give you an idea of the information that can be found. The first example (figure 4-3) is from Maspoli's *Stemmario Quattrocentesco delle Famiglie Nobili della Citta' e Antica Diocesi di Como.* It contains copies of coats of arms taken from parchments of the 1400s. There is an explanation of each blazon and each variation. It is interesting to compare the stem De Vulpis from the parchment (figure 4-3, upper right corner) with the complete coat of arms of the Volpi family from Trent (figure 4-4).

Another handwritten work on parchment found in the state archive at Como, published in the 1700s, gives the history of the Volpi family at Como based on notary records, beginning with the will of Gio Pietro Volpi to his son Difendente and continuing for eight more generations. A list of the wills is shown in figure 4-5, and the complete genealogy of the principal branch of the family is also shown (figure 4-6). The parchment also gives the genealogy of lateral lines and contains each will and a history of the family. It is interesting to note that Gio Antonio, the son of Gio Pietro, was a bishop of the city of Como and that the family had many relatives among the ecclesiastical officers at Como, Milan, and other cities. In fact, in every generation there was at least one priest and often more, as shown on the genealogy. The third generation provides an interesting example of the law of the firstborn: Antonio, husband of Emilia Tridi, inherited everything from his father Ippolito. His sister Benedetta married with a dowry, but all three of his brothers, having no inheritance, became priests. Gio Pietro became the bishop of Novara. In the Middle Ages a bishop had vast powers and essentially ruled over the territory of his diocese—so even when a wealthy family could not divide property among all the children, usually the other sons were able to exercise power and authority by becoming ecclesiastical leaders, soldiers, or notaries.

Many other books in the state archive at Como and the city library also contained historical information regarding the Volpi family, but the genealogical material there was scarce. It can readily be seen, however, that a wealth of information exists. Not only is there a complete genealogy for several generations that could not be found in parish records, but the history of the family and of each major figure in the family is included.

It is common to find in the state archives and civil libraries books, both old and recent, regarding local histories of a town or valley and histories of important families. These are often families that would never appear in the *Libro d'Oro della Nobiltà Italiana* but that were important

FIGURE 4-4. Coat of Arms of the Noble Volpi Family of Trent (courtesy of Alexander De Volpi)

in the history of the province or city. In the case of the Volpi family, even though all family members were mentioned in the genealogy, no dates were included. In other cases, however, even more complete genealogies may be presented.

The last example is a family history, included in a manuscript on famous Venetian families, of the Marcello family. Found in the state archive at Venice, some fifty pages of the manuscript are dedicated to the history and genealogy of this family. The family history begins with Petrus Marcello, a judge in the Serenissima Republic in 890 A.D. The complete family genealogy begins in 1215 and brings all branches of the family, with birth, marriage, and death dates, up to the early 1800s, when the manuscript was completed. The first page (figure 4-7) describes the early history of the family, and the next (figure 4-8) depicts the genealogy of one branch of the family from 1354 to 1594. The family, besides many statesmen, bishops, merchants, and military officers, also included Benedetto Marcello, born in 1686, a famous musician and contemporary of Antonio Vivaldi.

FIGURE 4-5. List of Wills of Members of the Volpi Family of Como, Including Eight Generations Over 250 Years; From the State Archive, Como

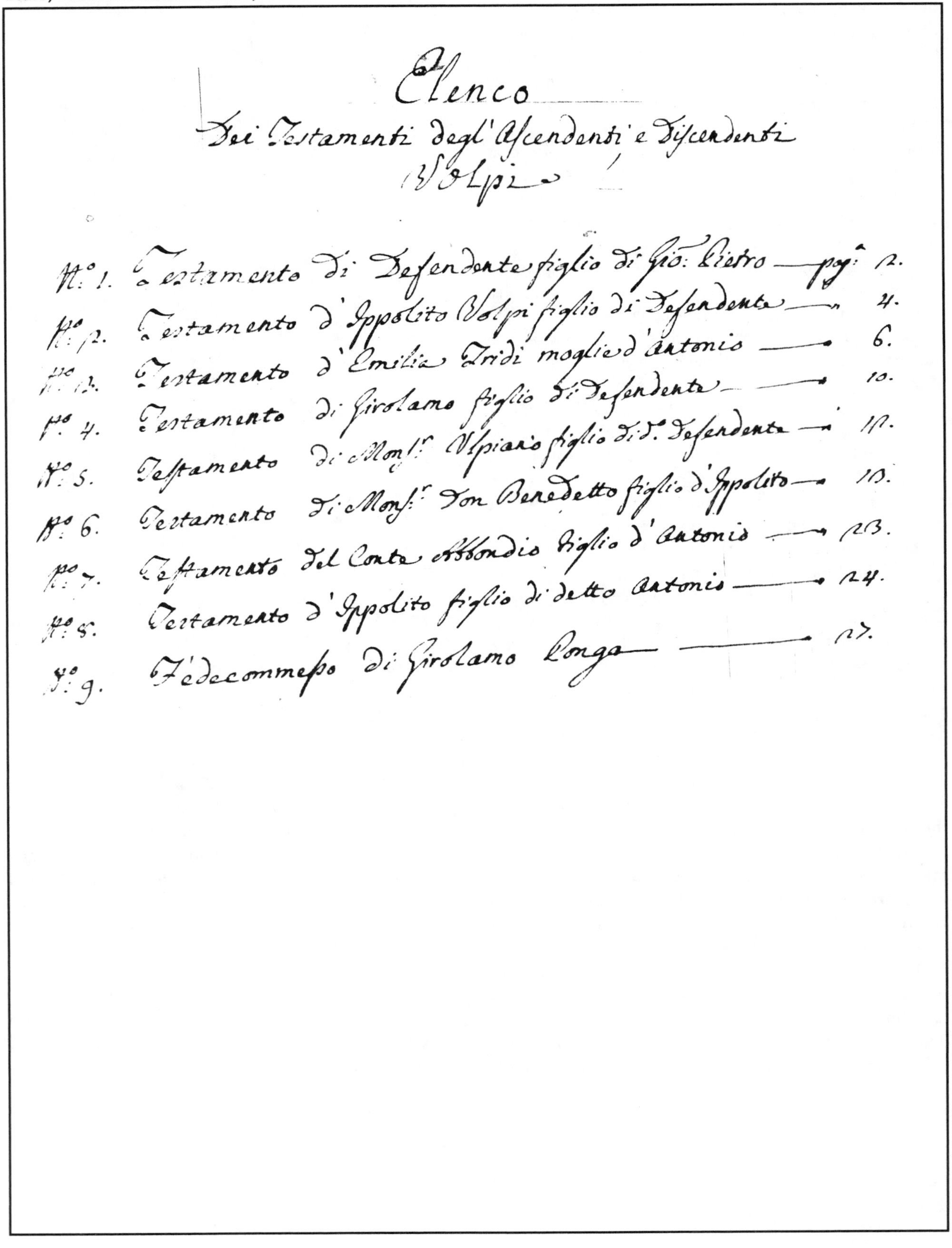
Elenco

Dei Testamenti degl'Ascendenti e Discendenti

Volpi

N.o 1. Testamento di Defendente figlio di Gio: Pietro — pag: 2.

N.o 2. Testamento d'Ippolito Volpi figlio di Defendente — 4.

N.o 3. Testamento d'Emilia Tridi moglie d'Antonio — 6.

N.o 4. Testamento di Girolamo figlio di Defendente — 10.

N.o 5. Testamento di Mons.r Volpiano figlio di d.o Defendente — 12.

N.o 6. Testamento di Mons.r Don Benedetto figlio d'Ippolito — 13.

N.o 7. Testamento del Conte Abbondio figlio d'Antonio — 23.

N.o 8. Testamento d'Ippolito figlio di detto Antonio — 24.

N.o 9. Fedecommesso di Girolamo Longa — 27.

FIGURE 4-6. A Branch of the Noble Volpi Family of Como, Beginning With Gio Pietro in the Fifteenth Century; From the State Archive, Como

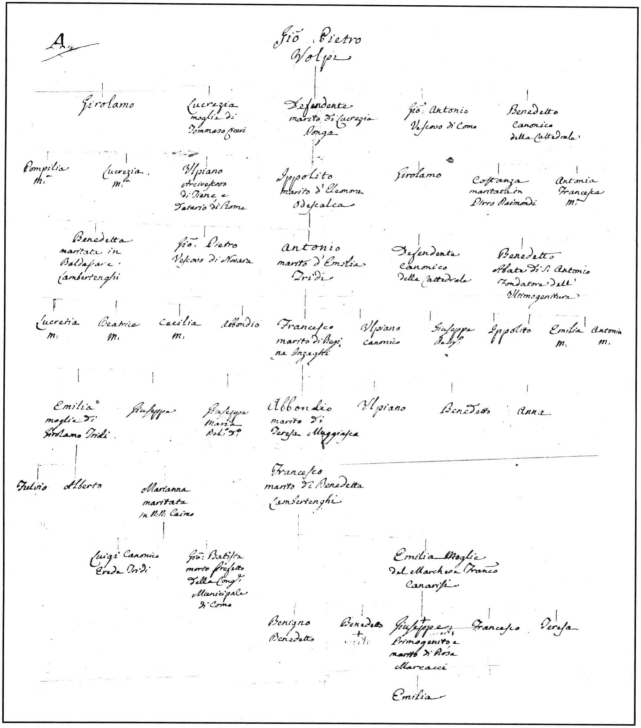

FIGURE 4-7. A History of the Marcello Family of Venice, Beginning With Petrus Marcello, Who Died in 890 A.D.

FIGURE 4-8. A Branch of the Family Pedigree of the Marcello Family

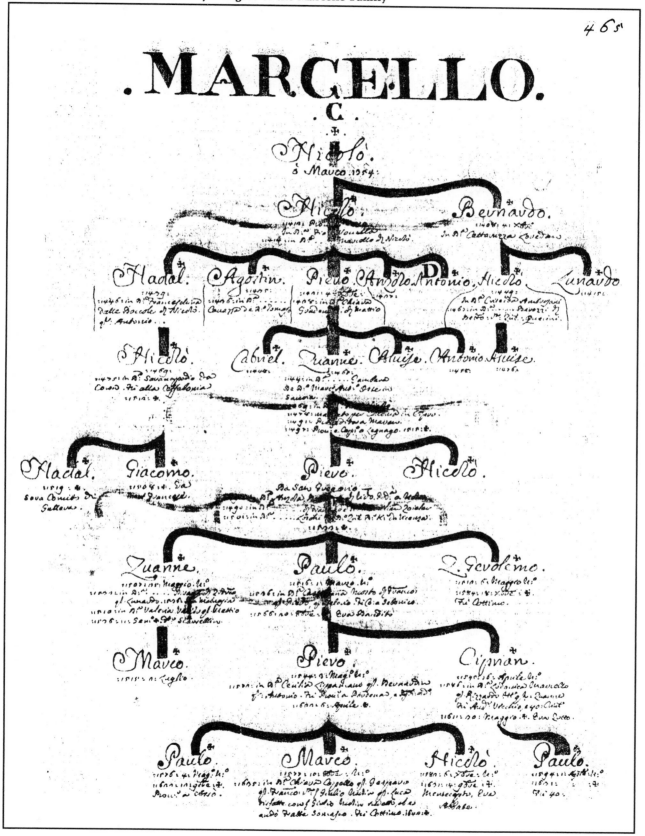

Part II

The Records

Chapter 5

CIVIL VITAL RECORDS

THERE ARE MANY POSSIBLE MEANS OF OBTAINING INFORMATION about your ancestors. Most family histories start with memories of relatives, old letters, perhaps the family Bible, and so on. Other sources of information include passports, immigration records, naturalization records, military and census documents, parish records, etc. Frequently, as these various sources are investigated, differences and discrepancies arise in the dates and information provided.

Two examples from my family illustrate this point. My mother's mother had always celebrated her birthday on the first of April. None of her children, including my mother, had any reason to doubt that she had been born on that day. Only at her death, on examination of her birth certificate, was it discovered that she was actually born on 31 March. From her sister, we learned that she had celebrated her birthday on the first of April since she was a young girl because all her older sisters had their birthdays in March, and she wanted to be different.

The birth date of my father's mother was listed as the year 1896 in all of her official documents—naturalization documents, marriage certificate, passport, death certificate, and so on. It was not until after her death, in pursuing her genealogy, that we learned from her English birth certificate that she was several years older. In fact, she had lied about her age since meeting my grandfather during World War I. She was several years older than he and was afraid that she would lose him!

The question arises: Which document is most accurate—which source should you believe? A primary source is a record created at or very close to the time an event took place and is therefore considered to be the most reliable (though not necessarily error-free). If there are discrepancies in names or dates among various records, the birth certificate is generally considered the most reliable document because it presumably was created at the time of birth with information supplied by a reliable witness.

To understand how the civil vital records are organized and where to find them, it is first necessary to understand the political organization of Italy. As the United States is separated into states, counties, and cities, Italy is divided similarly. Italy is divided into twenty regions, which correspond to U.S. states, and 103 provinces, which are similar to counties. Figure 5-1 shows the regions and provinces of Italy as it is organized today (1994). Although most regions and provinces have remained the same over the last 150 years, several new provinces have been created in recent years in response to population growth, including six that were approved in 1993. These are Biella and Verbano-Cusio-Ossola in Piedmont, Lecco and Lodi in Lombardy, Rimini in Emilia-Romagna, Prato in Tuscany, and Crotone and Vibo Valentia in Calabria. In 1993, Italy's government proposed to reduce the number of regions from twenty to twelve and to increase the regions' autonomy from the central government. Since this movement seems to be a priority of the recently formed government, a map showing the proposed changes is also included (figure 5-2). As the population changes in the future, there will probably be more changes in this political breakdown.

Within each province are the communes (*comuni*), which are townships that may include several *frazioni*. A *frazione* is a village or hamlet that often has existed for centuries. Most *frazioni* have separate parishes but are too small to support all the services that a township has to offer. Rather than abolish the village and its name, which usually has historical roots, several *frazioni* are grouped under the political jurisdiction of a larger town; together they form a commune (*comune*). For example, I live in the commune of Albignasego, which includes the town of Albignasego and the *frazioni* of Mandriola, Lion, S. Giacomo, S. Agostino, Carpanedo, and S. Lorenzo. There is no limit to the population of a commune; Albignasego has 28,000 inhabitants, but Rome, which is still one commune, has approximately 3 million. Most communes have only a few *frazioni*, but some have many; Capannori, in Tuscany, has thirty-one *frazioni* covering a land area larger than Rome, and Acquasanta, in the Marche region, has twenty-three.

The initial division of Italy into provinces, communes, and *frazioni* was part of the important administrative changes that Napoleon introduced in Italy during his brief reign in the early 1800s. During that time the streets were named and street numbers were given to each house. No two streets within a commune, even if in two separate

FIGURE 5-1. The Regions and Provinces of Italy

The Regions and Provinces of Italy

Piemonte–Piedmont Region
1. Alessandria   AL
2. Asti   AS
3. Biella   BI
4. Cuneo   CN
5. Novara   NO
6. Torino (Turin)   TO
7. Verbano-Cusio-Ossola   VB
8. Vercelli   VC

Valle D'Aosta–Aosta Valley Region
9. Aosta   AO

Liguria–Ligury Region
10. Genova (Genoa)   GE
11. Imperia   IM
12. La Spezia   SP
13. Savona   SV

Lombardia–Lombardy Region
14. Bergamo   BG
15. Brescia   BS
16. Como   CO
17. Cremona   CR
18. Lecco   LC
19. Lodi   LO
20. Mantova   MN
21. Milano (Milan)   MI
22. Pavia   PV
23. Sondrio   SO
24. Varese   VA

Trentino-Alto Adige–Trento-South Tyrol Region
25. Bolzano (Bozen) BZ
26. Trento (Trent)   TN

Veneto–Venetian Region
27. Belluno   BL
28. Padova (Padua)   PD
29. Rovigo   RO
30. Treviso   TV
31. Venezia (Venice) VE
32. Verona   VR
33. Vicenza   VI

Friuli-Venezia-Giulia–Friuli Region
34. Gorizia   GO

35. Pordenone   PN
36. Trieste (Triest) TS
37. Udine   UD

Emilia-Romagna–Emilia-Romagna Region
38. Bologna   BO
39. Ferrara   FE
40. Forli'   FO
41. Modena   MO
42. Parma   PR
43. Piacenza   PC
44. Ravenna   RA
45. Reggio Emilia   RE
46. Rimini   RN

Toscana–Tuscany Region
47. Arezzo   AR
48. Firenze (Florence)   FI
49. Grosseto   GR
50. Livorno   LI
51. Lucca   LU
52. Massa Carrara   MS
53. Pisa   PI
54. Pistoia   PT
55. Prato   PO
56. Siena   SI

Umbria–Umbria Region
57. Perugia   PG
58. Terni   TR

Marche–Marche Region
59. Ancona   AN
60. Ascoli Piceno   AP
61. Macerata   MC
62. Pesaro   PS

Lazio–Latium Region
63. Frosinone   FR
64. Latina   LT
65. Rieti   RI
66. Roma (Rome)   Roma
67. Viterbo   VT

Abruzzo–Abruzzi Region
68. Chieti   CH
69. L'Aquila   AQ

70. Pescara   PE
71. Teramo   TE

Molise–Molise Region
72. Campobasso   CB
73. Isernia   IS

Campania–Campania Region
74. Avellino   AV
75. Benevento   BN
76. Caserta   CE
77. Napoli (Naples) NA
78. Salerno   SA

Puglia–Apulia Region
79. Bari   BA
80. Brindisi   BR
81. Foggia   FG
82. Lecce   LE
83. Taranto   TA

Basilicata–Basilicata Region
84. Matera   MT
85. Potenza   PZ

Calabria–Calabria Region
86. Catanzaro   CZ
87. Cosenza   CS
88. Crotone   KR
89. Reggio Calabria RC
90. Vibo Valentia   VV

Sicilia–Sicily Region
91. Agrigento   AG
92. Caltanissetta   CL
93. Catania   CT
94. Enna   EN
95. Messina   ME
96. Palermo   PA
97. Ragusa   RG
98. Siracusa   SR
99. Trapani   TP

Sardegna–Sardinia Region
100. Cagliari   CA
101. Nuoro   NU
102. Oristano   OR
103. Sassari   SS

FIGURE 5-2. Proposed Changes in the Regions of Italy

are you?) or *Da dove viene?* (From where do you come?). The first Italian phrase means "Where were you born?"; the second means "What was the last place you came from?" Since the latter is more similar to the English phrase, an Italian would state the port of *emigrazione* or the last town that he or she visited, or just "Italy," rather than the birthplace. Consequently, there was some confusion, and often the wrong place is listed as the town of origin.

It is necessary to understand how the civil vital records are created in Italy and where they can be found. Civil vital records were introduced in Italy by Napoleon, and, although they were not continued throughout Italy after his demise, their form remains in use for the Italian civil vital records today. Each original record of birth, marriage, and death is made in duplicate. One copy remains at the commune, and one is sent to the *procura della repubblica* of the province. The *procura della repubblica* is similar to a U.S. county court and is found in the seat of each province—the major city for which the province is named. The *procura della repubblica* is presided over by the *procuratore*, whose function is similar to that of a U.S. district attorney. Because the civil vital records are legal records and are necessary for legal affairs of the government, such as military conscription, the duplicate is held by the *tribunale* (county court) under the jurisdiction of the *procuratore*. There is no national archive, nor are there archives at a regional level (except at Florence, where the provinces of the Tuscany region have created a regional archive for older documents). Thus, all civil records are found at either the commune or the provincial seat.

Laws regulate the use and consultation of these records. One is a law of privacy that protects these records from outside consultation or reproduction. It states that, for all civil acts occurring within the last seventy-five years, only the subject himself or herself or a family member may request an original certificate. Even so, the birth certificate will normally not mention the names of the parents or the family member.

frazioni, can have the same street name. Houses, too, were divided into categories from rural to luxurious for tax purposes, and farmland was measured and registered for the same reasons. The communes were given jurisdiction for all administrative duties within their areas, including the registration of all births, marriages, and deaths.

Often, confusion arises in the search for an ancestor's place of origin because, in immigration records or family lore, the place indicated is a *frazione*—not the commune; because most gazetteers do not list the *frazioni*, research becomes more difficult. Therefore, it is important, when beginning research with family documents, to search not only for the name of the village of your ancestors but for the commune or, at least, the province or region so that the correct *frazione* can be identified.

Another potential source of confusion regarding immigrant ancestors arose from language differences that sometimes occurred at the point of immigration or naturalization. The English "Where are you from?" can be translated into Italian in two distinct forms: *Di dov'è?* (Of where

All requests for documents must be made directly to the commune of origin—not to the *tribunale.* The records held by the *tribunale* are not open for consultation; they serve for legal purposes of the state only. For example, they are used to establish the draft call of all males at age eighteen. After the seventy-five-year period of privacy has ended, the copies of the records from the *tribunale* may be turned over to the state archive of each province for open consultation. Unfortunately, however, in many cases the state archive does not have sufficient space to accommodate these records, so they remain unavailable for consultation. In a few provinces, those records that precede the privacy period are being microfilmed by the archives and will become available. In most cases, however, the most accessible or the only source for these records is the town's *ufficio di stato civile* (civil vital records office). In provinces where the earlier records have been turned over to the state archive—for example, in Tuscany and parts of the south of Italy—the Utah Genealogical Society is microfilming the civil records (see chapter 10). These may become available for consultation in the local family history centers operated by the LDS Church's Family History Library.

There is a distinction in Italy, in each commune, between the *anagrafe* office and the *ufficio di stato civile*. The first is concerned only with people who are currently alive and residing in the commune. It releases documents for daily use for purposes such as school enrollment, passport application, driver's licenses, etc. Thus, the *anagrafe* office keeps track of all the important data on each resident, including birth, marriage, family unit, death, emigration from the commune, and so on. It would be a simple matter to gather all necessary genealogical data for living residents from this one source, but it is of little use as a family history source for those who have died or relocated.

The *ufficio di stato civile* is the repository where all vital information regarding anyone who was born, married, or died in the town is registered and stored. Thus, for an Italian who was born in Venice but is living in Padua, the *anagrafe* of Padua can supply a birth certificate that serves for most official purposes, but the extract of the original birth act will always be kept at Venice, where he or she was born. The *ufficio di stato civile* there would need to be contacted for a copy of the original document. If the person then marries at Padua, this act will be registered in that city, and the original will be kept there. Likewise, if the person dies in Rome, the death act will be found there. Therefore, in the town of residence, all vital information is noted and a certificate can be released, but the original act and the complete extract of birth, marriage, or death can be found only in the commune where the event took place. Thus, to obtain extracts of the original acts, it is necessary to know in which commune each vital event took place. As will be made clear by examining the documents, there is a major difference between a certificate and the extract of the original act, and another difference still between the extract and the original act itself.

STATE CIVIL VITAL RECORDS

The keeping of civil vital records began officially in Italy with the unification of the country between 1860 and 1870. In most areas of the south, they were begun in 1866 and continued to the present. In the Piedmont region (the old Duchy of Savoy), they were begun in 1839, and in what was the Serenissima Republic (under Venice) they were not begun until 1870 or 1871. (As previously mentioned, in many areas the keeping of civil vital records began under Napoleon's rule in the early 1800s. These records are discussed separately in chapter 6).

The civil vital records of the Italian state are held at the commune level. Commune officials are the only persons who are authorized to consult these records and release certificates. If you supply the name of the person and the exact date, there is normally a fee of L1,000 for each certificate. However, if you supply a name only, requiring the staff to search a range of dates, the fee can be up to L10,000 (about eight dollars at the present exchange rate) for each name and date found. Since town officials are usually very busy, some requests may be ignored or delayed for months before reply. Rarely will officials conduct extensive research.

Personal consultation of the civil records of the commune is allowed for those records that precede the seventy-five-year privacy period. First, however, permission must be obtained from the *procura della repubblica* of the province by making a written request that states the reasons for consulting the records. Sometimes permission is granted to direct relatives who are able to properly consult records within a few days of the request. In some smaller communes, the mayor of the town may grant permission in response to a written request, but this is the exception rather than the rule. In any case, only the town officials can make out the civil certificate of the act. (See chapter 11 for more information about writing for permission and obtaining records through correspondence.)

For each type of act—birth, marriage, or death—there are three types of documents: the original (*la copia integrale dell'atto*), the certificate (*il certificato*), and the extract of the act (*estratto dell'atto*). Unless you specify otherwise, the town office will normally send the certificate in response to a request; however, it contains little information other than the pertinent name and date. The extract, instead, provides more useful details, including the names of parents; it can be obtained upon request. Original acts cannot be transcribed or copied; you can view them only by personally consulting the original records or microfilm copies. Each of these variations will be discussed for each type of act. Because almost all civil vital records in Italy follow the same format and contain similar information, each document discussed will be completely transcribed and translated so that you can view all information provided in any given act.

Birth Certificates

The first document examined is the *certificato di nascita*—the birth certificate (figure 5-3). First, as in this example, all documents list the name of the township, or commune, and the province (*provincia*). Although each province may have a different format for the certificate (and formats tend to change every few years), the information supplied remains essentially the same. The certificate shown is titled "Certificato di Nascita." It begins:

L'Ufficiale dello Stato Civile in base alle risultanze degli atti esistenti in questo Ufficio Certifica che

Or:

The Civil Vital Records Officer, based on the examination of the existing Acts, certifies that:

At this point, the person's name appears. In most cases, the surname appears first, followed by the given name, as in this example. Often, the surname appears in all-capital letters and the given names in lowercase letters. On some certificates there is a separate line for each; *cognome* would indicate the surname and *nome* the given names.

In Italy today there is a difference between a person's full name and the "administrative" name used by the *anagrafe* office. Usually, the administrative name is the person's first (given) name, or the first two if they go together as one name—for example, Maria Rosa or Gian Paolo—whereas the full name may include several names. Only the administrative name is shown on a certificate of birth, so it is necessary to have the extract of the original document to obtain the person's full, legal name. My son's administrative name is Jeffrey Cole, but his full name is Jeffrey Sandro Robertson Cole. (Some European countries, Italy among them, have laws regarding the naming of children. The English tradition of passing the same name from father to son, with the use of "senior" and "junior" to distinguish them, is prohibited in Italy; so, in Italy, a man's first name may not be the same as his father's because this would give them the same administrative name. Since my first name is Trafford, I could not give my son the first name Trafford, but it could be given as a second or third name. Therefore, my first son is named Joel Matteo Trafford Cole; I could not call him Trafford Matteo Joel Cole. Even in earlier periods, a father's name was normally given to his son only if the father died before the son's birth. Instead, Italians traditionally name their children after the children's grandparents.)

The certificate's next entry is *e' nato in*, or "born at." Here is indicated the name of the town of birth. In all cases, on both the certificate and the extract, the name of the commune only, not the *frazione*, will be indicated. Only in the copy of the original act—*copia integrale dell'atto di nascita* (integral copy of the birth act)—will you find the

exact address and/or the *frazione* mentioned. This distinction can be very important. Often, a researcher will have a birth certificate which states that an ancestor was born in a specific town or city; however, when research has to extend before 1865 to the parish records, evidence of the ancestor may not be found in the indicated town. Therefore, it becomes necessary to search in all of the *frazioni* of the township—and there may be ten, twenty, or more hamlets, each with its own parish, to search for the family. A city the size of Rome may have more than three hundred parishes. The integral copy of the birth act is made out only when requested for a marriage, so, normally, this act will not be released unless you explain the need for this information.

The next entries indicate the date of birth: *il giorno* the day, *del mese di* or *il mese* the month, and *dell'anno* or *l'anno* the year. Normally, these were written out to avoid any confusion. (Numbers, months, and years and their translations are listed in chapter 12.) In this case the date is *primo aprile milleottocentonovantasette*—the first of April, 1897. (Note that when dates are written as numbers only, the day and month are reversed from American practice—the day is always written first. Thus, below, 5.12.1990 refers to the fifth day of the twelfth month—December 5th—not the twelfth day of the fifth month, as in American practice. And don't be misled by the fact that the months of the year and most titles and designations, such as the English Mr. and Mrs., are not capitalized in Italian, as they are in English.

The next lines usually indicate where the act is found. In this case it is

come risulta dal registro degli atti di nascita di questo Comune per l'anno 1897 al N. 29 Parte I Serie =

Or:

as results from the record of the birth acts of this Commune for the year 1897 at Number 29, Part I, Series [none]

Civil vital records are divided into separate volumes for each year and are standardized. While, for most towns, there is only one volume per year, in large cities there may be many volumes for each year. Naples, for example, is divided into twelve districts with separate records for each district. There are five to ten volumes for each year for each district, making almost one hundred volumes per year of birth records only. The number stated here (29) is the number of the act; they are placed in chronological order. Normally, each act comprises one page, so the act number is the same as the page number. *Parte* and *serie* refer to the volume number and the series or district. For most towns the volume is volume I, with no series number.

State civil records (and Napoleonic civil records, discussed in chapter 6) are indexed in two different ways. Each record volume contains an index of surnames, and

FIGURE 5-3. Civil Birth Certificate of Rosa Ermelinda Maccagnan, 1897, Molvena, Vicenza

Cod. 12.0087.00

COMUNE DI ....MOLVENA..

PROVINCIA DI ....VICENZA..

CERTIFICATO DI NASCITA

L'UFFICIALE DELLO STATO CIVILE

in base alle risultanze degli atti esistenti in questo Ufficio

CERTIFICA

che ....MACCAGNAN ROSA ERMELINDA..

è nato in ....MOLVENA..

il giorno ....PRIMO..

del mese di ....APRILE..

dell'anno ........MILLEOTTOCENTONOVANTASETTE..

come risulta dal registro degli atti di nascita di questo Comune

per l'anno ....1897.... al N. ....29.... Parte ..I.. Serie ..=..

Si rilascia in carta ~~libera~~ per l'uso a lato indicato
~~xresaxlegalex~~

li ....5.12.1990..

L'UFFICIALE DELLO STATO CIVILE

ICA SpA Pd - RG - 11-88

RILASCIATO IN

☐ CARTA RESA LEGALE
☐ CARTA LIBERA

(all. B - D.P.R. 26-10-72 n. 642, o di altre vigenti disposizioni di legge).

per uso:

☐ elettorale e ruoli giudici popolari
☐ leva militare
☐ imposte, tributi e tasse successione
☐ operazioni del debito pubblico
☐ assistenza sanitaria e beneficenza
☐ assicurazioni sociali obbligatorie, pensioni e assegni familiari
☐ iscrizione nelle liste di collocamento
☐ scuola materna e dell'obbligo
☐ presalari e borse di studio
☐ tutela minori ed interdetti, affidamento, adozione speciale, affiliazione
☐ rilascio certificato casellario giudiziario (domanda, certif. nascita)
☐ rilascio passaporto per emigrazione a scopo di lavoro
☐ edilizia agevolata
☐ agevolazioni in favore dell'agricoltura
☐ espropriazione per causa di pubblica utilità
☐ gratuito patrocinio legale
☐ amministrativo a richiesta

☐ ....

usually there are ten-year indexes called *indici decennali* in separate volumes for all recorded births, marriages, and deaths. Usually these are by decade—one from 1870 to 1879, another from 1880 to 1889, and so on. (Some begin in the year that the civil records were begun and continue in ten-year increments.) All indexes are arranged alphabetically by surname, and they sometimes include the name of each child's father, in addition to a reference to the year of the record volume and the *parte* and *serie* number. (Some Napoleonic records lack the ten-year indexes, but most are indexed by volume.)

The last line of the certificate is *Si rilascia in carta libera per l'uso a lato indicato*. This sentence literally translates as: "This is released in free paper for all the uses indicated at the side." Note that at the right side is a list of official and administrative uses for the document. Often this list is not found on the certificate. Instead, it will state "released for all administrative purposes" (*rilasciato per uso amministrativo*) or "for all purposes consented by the law" (*per ogni uso consentito dalla legge*). All three statements have essentially the same meaning. In Italy, there is a distinction between a free certificate, such as this one, and an official certificate needed, for example, to marry or to retire. A *bollo*, or "stamp," presently of L15,000, is placed on an official document to legalize it. This is nothing more than an indirect tax paid for the legalized document. The stamp has no value in the United States or anywhere outside Italy, unless perhaps the document is being used to apply for Italian citizenship. (Thus, it is wise, when writing to a town source, to specify that you want the certificate *in carta libera*—"on free paper." See chapter 11.) Finally, the date on which the certificate was created and the name of the civil vital records officer (*ufficiale di stato civile*) are indicated and are stamped with the town seal.

Birth Extracts

Figure 5-4 is an extract of a birth act, or *estratto per riassunto dell'atto di nascita*. This document is similar to the birth certificate but provides additional information. In most cases, this document is preferable for genealogical purposes. Note that, besides differing from the birth certificate in format, the extract has important additions. Not only is the date of birth given, but the time of birth is also stated. The phrase *le ore* refers to the hour and *e minuti* to the minute. In this case, the child was born at 20:09. (Italians use a twenty-four-hour clock, so 20:09 indicates nine minutes after eight o'clock in the evening; 8:09 would indicate nine minutes after eight o'clock in the morning.)

Another addition to the extract is the clear indication of the child's sex as male (*di sesso maschile*) or female (*di sesso femminile*). In the birth certificate, the sex is implied by the way the name is written, which might not be obvious to anyone who does not know Italian well. This extract also includes a separate line for the surname, and all of the

person's names are included—not just the first name and surname. In this case, note that the child had just one given name: Antonio. Most important for genealogical purposes, only on the extract—not on the certificate—are the names of the parents listed. This practice results from the privacy act. Since for most administrative purposes in Italy only the birth certificate is used, no one can learn from the certificate alone if a person was illegitimate or a foundling, or any information about the parents. This information is considered confidential.

In the extract, the father is indicated by his first name only; his surname is understood to be that of the child. The mother, however, is identified by both her given name and maiden name. Here, *pat.* (paternal) *Luigi* and *mat.* (maternal) *SENORE Teresa* indicate the father and mother. More commonly, the document would simply state *PUTTERO Antonio di Luigi e di SENORE Teresa* (*di* means "of").

Note that, in Italy, as in most of Europe, a woman retains her maiden name throughout life as her legal name; she does not take on her husband's surname, although it may be acknowledged by appending it to her legal name with the word *in*. For example, my wife is listed in commune records still as *Fernanda Segato*, but she can sign her name as *Fernanda Segato in Cole*. Thus, the maiden name of Teresa in this example is Senore. If the wife were to appear with the same surname as her husband, in this case Puttero, it would indicate that she was from a different branch of the Puttero family and that that was her maiden name.

The final difference between these documents is the entry for *annotazioni marginali*—"marginal notes." Normally, when the person marries, or sometimes when he or she dies or emigrates, the event is noted in the original birth act and written in the margin. On the extract of the birth act this additional information is included; on the birth certificate it is not. To marry, it is necessary to have a copy of the original birth act as part of the nuptial documents. Thus, at the time the request is made, information about the marriage is written into the original birth act. In this case, it is written *nel di' 2.10.1910 atto n.22 ha contratto matrimonio in questo Comune con CASTAGNO Carola*: "on the day 2 October 1910 he was married in this town with CASTAGNO Carola." Annotations such as this can be crucial in genealogical research because it is Italian custom to marry in the town and parish of the bride; because the baptismal and birth records do not indicate the wife's town of origin or where the couple was married, a similar annotation in the birth record of the groom can make all the difference in locating and following the maternal line.

The original birth act provides all of the above information, and it indicates the family's place of residence, usually including a full address. Often, it also indicates when and in what parish the person was baptized and the name of the celebrating priest. It often indicates the vocations of the father and mother as well. Since, in most families, the same vocation was passed from father to son for generations, this

FIGURE 5-4. Extract of the Civil Birth Act of Antonio Puttero, 1888, Avigliana, Torino

COMUNE DI AVIGLIANA

PROVINCIA DI TORINO

UFFICIO DELLO STATO CIVILE

ESTRATTO PER RIASSUNTO DELL'ATTO DI NASCITA

Anno *1888*   Atto n. *116*   Parte *I*   Serie *2*

Si certifica che dai Registri degli atti di Nascita esistenti presso questo Comune, anno, parte, serie e numero sopraindicati, risulta che

l'anno *1888*

il giorno *VENTISEI*   del mese di *OTTOBRE*

alle ore *20*   e minuti *9*

in AVIGLIANA è nato un bambino di sesso *maschile*

col cognome *PUTTERO*

al quale venne   dat il nome: *ANTONIO*

pad. Luigi   mat. SENORE Terese

Annotazioni marginali: *nel dì 2.10.1910 atto n. 22 ha contratto matrimonio in questo Comune con CASTAGNO Carola.*

Si rilascia il presente estratto per uso   USI PER I QUALI NON E' PREVISTO IL BOLLO

Avigliana, li *29 7 1987*

L'UFFICIALE DELLO STATO CIVILE

Riilasciata ai sensi art. 3 del
D.P.R. n. 432 del 2.5.1957.

P. Manillo - Torino

item provides considerable information about the family. Normally, however, as mentioned earlier, the entire contents of the original act will not be released by the town office. This information can only be found through personal research of the original records or microfilm copies.

Marriage Certificates

The distinction between the marriage certificate and the extract of the marriage act is similar to that between the birth certificate and extract. Like all acts, the act of marriage is registered in the town where the ceremony took place. It has been and still is traditional in Italy for the marriage to take place in the parish church of the bride. The bride's family is responsible for the marriage, the flowers, the reception, and the *pranzo nuziale,* or "wedding dinner." It is customary to wed on a Saturday morning. Usually, the bride's family and guests are invited to her home and the groom's guests to his home for refreshments. They then accompany the bride or groom to the church for the wedding ceremony. After the wedding, the family and special guests attend a banquet that starts at noon and continues all afternoon and evening with seemingly endless courses of *hors d'oeuvres,* pasta, and meat, intermixed with drinking of wine, *spumante,* and dancing. Such celebrations still occur in most of Italy, but changing customs and rising costs now dictate that both families split the expense, and the meal is limited to a long lunch with four or five main courses. In the south, however, these traditions remain stronger, and families sometimes spend tens of thousands of dollars for the wedding ceremony and dinner.

Like the birth certificate, the marriage certificate can be obtained from the *anagrafe* office of the town of residence. The *ufficio di stato civile* will also send the certificate on inquiry but, because it does not contain as much information as the extract of the act, you should specify the *estratto dell'atto di matrimonio* when writing and address the request to the *ufficio di stato civile.*

The marriage certificate (figure 5-5) begins with the same format as does the birth certificate: the name of the commune and province; the title, *certificato di matrimonio,* or "marriage certificate"; and the statement

Il sottoscritto Ufficiale dello Stato Civile, sulle risultanze dei registri di questo ufficio, Certifica

Or:

the undersigned Civil Vital Records Officer, based on the examination of the records of this township, Certifies:

Obviously, formats vary somewhat from one part of Italy to another and depending on when a certificate was created, but the essential information remains the same.

The form goes on to state the date and place of the marriage:

che nel giorno _____ del mese di _____ dell'anno mille _____ nel Comune di _____

Or:

on the day _____ of the month _____ in the year one thousand and _____ in the Commune of _____

And *Si sono uniti in matrimonio*—"They were united in marriage."

Next, the certificate provides information first about the groom (*sposo*) and the bride (*sposa*). The information for both is the same and so can be considered together. Note that words that are masculine or that refer to a male normally end in "o"; words that are feminine or refer to a female end in "a." Thus, for example, *sposo* refers to the male and *sposa* to the female; *nato* means "born" in reference to a male and *nata* means "born" in reference to a female.

First is the bride's or groom's name. Usually, the given name appears in lowercase and the surname in all-capital letters; otherwise, the surname appears first. *Stato civile* indicates the marriage status of each, whether single (*singolo* or *celibe* for a male, *singola* or *nubile* for a female), divorced, (*divorziato/a*), or widower/widow (*vedovo/a*). (A law allowing divorce has existed in Italy only since 1970 and in its present form since 1978, so divorce is noted only on the most recent certificates.) *Nato/nata in* indicates the place of birth and *il* the date of birth. This is a modern format for the certificate; earlier forms, similar to the extract that follows, do not list the exact date of birth but rather the person's age (*d'anni*). Next is the profession or vocation of the bride and groom: *di professione.* (For a list of common vocations, see chapter 12).

The last indications for bride and groom are the current place of residence (*residente in*) and citizenship (*cittadino/a*). Usually, because Italians were not very mobile until after World War II, the residence is the same town in which each was born. The citizenship is almost always Italian—*Italiano/a*—except near border regions.

Finally, the certificate ends with a reference to act and number and indicates whether it is a legalized document or is written on "free paper."

Come risulta dall'atto inscritto nel registro degli atti di matrimonio di questo Comune per l'anno _____ al N. _____ Parte _____ Serie _____

Or:

As results from the act written in the record of the marriage acts of this Commune for the year _____, at Number _____, Part _____, Series _____

FIGURE 5-5. A Typical Marriage Certificate

Cat. 154 - XII

COMUNE DI_____

PROVINCIA DI _____
_____

CERTIFICATO DI MATRIMONIO

Il sottoscritto Ufficiale dello Stato Civile, sulle risultanze dei registri di questo Ufficio,

CERTIFICA

che nel giorno _____ del mese di _____

dell'anno mille _____

nel Comune di _____

si sono uniti in matrimonio

Sposo _____ | Sposa _____
_____ | _____
_____ | _____
stato civile _____ | stato civile _____
nato in _____ | nata in _____
il _____ | il _____
di professione _____ | di professione _____
residente in _____ | residente in _____
Cittadino _____ | Cittadina _____
_____ | _____

come risulta dall'atto inscritto nel registro degli atti di matrimonio di questo Comune per l'anno _____ al N. _____

Parte _____ Serie _____

Si rilascia in carta libera/resa legale per l'uso a lato indicato.

Dalla residenza municipale, li _____

L'Ufficiale dello Stato Civile

_____

RILASCIATO IN

☐ CARTA RESA LEGALE

☐ CARTA LIBERA

(all. B - D.P.R. 26-10-72 n. 642, o di altre vigenti disposizioni di legge).

per uso:

☐ elettorale e ruoli giudici popolari
☐ leva militare
☐ imposte, tributi e tasse successione
☐ operazioni del debito pubblico
☐ assistenza sanitaria e beneficenza
☐ assicurazioni sociali obbligatorie, pensioni o assegni familiari
☐ iscrizione nelle liste di collocamento
☐ scuola materna e dell'obbligo
☐ presalari e borse di studio
☐ tutela minori ed interdetti, affidamento, adozione speciale, affiliazione
☐ rilascio certificato casellario giudiziario (domanda, certif. nascita)
☐ rilascio passaporto per emigrazione a scopo di lavoro
☐ edilizia agevolata
☐ agevolazioni in favore dell'agricoltura
☐ espropriazione per causa di pubblica utilità
☐ gratuito patrocinio legale
☐ amministrativo a richiesta

_____
_____
☐ _____
_____
_____

This information is exactly the same as found in the birth certificate; in fact, it is found either at the beginning or the end of all certificates. The last line is similar to the birth act: *Si rilascia in carta libera/resa legale per l'uso a lato indicato,* or "this is released on free/legalized paper for the uses indicated at the side." Again, in the margin there is a list of uses from which the town clerk must choose one or more.

All certificates must be signed by the civil vital records officer, with the official stamp of the town and the date. Otherwise, the certificate is not valid.

Marriage Extracts

Figure 5-6 is an extract of a marriage act from Torre Pellice in the province of Torino. Note that there are few differences from the marriage certificate. The format does differ in that the reference to the number of the act is at the top of the record and the information about the groom and bride is presented consecutively rather than side-by-side in columns. However, the major difference is that, in the extract, the birth dates of the bride and groom are not indicated—only their ages. More importantly, the names of the parents of the bride and groom are provided.

Note the form used in providing the names, as it is very common in all records. The groom's name appears as *RAJNAUD Luigi Tommaso fu Giuseppe e di LIONARDO Delfina.* The surname is indicated by all-capital letters, and the father's surname is not stated because it is assumed to be the same as that of the son. However, both the given name and maiden surname of the mother are given. In this case, the preposition *fu* is used in reference to the father of Luigi Tommaso, while below the preposition *di* is used in reference to the father of Maria Ottavia. Obviously, this is not a gender difference; rather, *fu* indicates that the father of Luigi is deceased, whereas *di* is stated for living relatives. This one word provides additional information that can be important for research.

In addition to all of the above information, the original marriage act includes the names of the presiding priest or town official and of the witnesses and details of the legal aspects of the marriage. However, this additional data was not always provided in earlier acts, so some original acts differ little from an extract of the act. In any case, a copy of an original act will not be created unless there is a legal reason for it.

Death Records

Death records are distinct in that they can be more difficult to locate than others. Since the advent of the hospital in the last century as a place to go for the cure of disorders—even those of old age—many more people now die in hospitals than in the past, when they were cared for at home. Most hospitals are located in large towns and cities, and not every town has a hospital. Even though someone may have lived his whole life in one village, being born, christened, married,

and buried there, quite often he or she will have died in a hospital in a nearby city; if so, the official death act is held among the town records of that city. It will have been transcribed in the *anagrafe* office of the deceased's town of residence, so a certificate can be made out there, but the extract of the death act will not be available there. Since there may be many hospitals in a given area, and because people sometimes travel far to specialized clinics, sometimes it can be very difficult to find where the death took place. It may be mentioned in the annotations of the birth act or in the parish records, but otherwise it may be impossible to locate. The town office usually has no burial record; it will be found at the cemetery or the parish. Even though the ancestor may be buried in his or her village, the death will not be recorded there if he or she died elsewhere in a hospital.

Death Certificates

Death records follow much the same format as do the previously described birth and marriage documents. The differences between the death certificate and the extract of the act are much the same as well. Figure 5-7 is a death certificate—*certificato di morte*—from the city of Milan. Because Milan is the seat of the province, the name of the province is not given. The date of the certificate's release is shown at the top of the certificate rather than the bottom, as is more common. In this case the name and surname are both written in all-capital letters, making reading more difficult, but the certificate follows the convention of placing the surname—Berasi—first. No mention is made of the deceased's profession, but his residence (*residente*) was in Milan.

Next, *nato in,* or "born at," is a good example of the disadvantages of a certificate versus an extract—a clerk decides how much information to include on the certificate. In this case it is indicated that the person was born at Bleggio Superiore, but it is not mentioned that this is an entirely different province that is in another region. In fact, at the time of this person's birth it was in another nation, being under the jurisdiction of Austria.

The following line provides space for stating either the exact birth date, with space for the date, act number (*atto n.*), record number (*Reg.*), and page number (*P.*) of the birth act, or the approximate age (*di anni*). The word "approximate" should be emphasized because, often, if exact information about the person was lacking, the age was determined based on the memories of relatives or on how old the person seemed to have been; errors were often made. Thus, the difference between the given age and the actual year of birth can often be five or even ten years.

Stato civile refers to the person's marital status. *Celibe* refers to a single male and *nubile* to a single female, *vedovo/a* refers to a widower or widow, *marito* means "husband," and *moglie* means "wife." In most cases, the death certificate will include the name of the husband or wife of the deceased and may even include the name of a deceased partner, too, if the person was a widow or wid-

FIGURE 5-6. Extract of the Civil Marriage Act of Luigi Tommaso Rajnaud and Delfina Lionardo, 1895, Torre Pellice, Torino

PROVINCIA DI **TORINO**

COMUNE DI TORRE PELLICE

UFFICIO DELLO STATO CIVILE

ESTRATTO ATTO DI MATRIMONIO

Anno 1895 Atto N. 32 Parte 1^ Serie = = =

Si certifica che dai Registri per gli Atti di Matrimonio esistenti presso questo Comune, anno, parte, serie e numero sopraindicati, risulta che il giorno CINQUE del mese di NOVEMBRE dell'anno MILLEOTTOCENTONOVANTACINQUE in TORRE PELLICE è stato contratto matrimonio

TRA

1o RAJNAUD Luigi Tommaso fu Giuseppe e di LIONARDO Delfina

nato in Porte di Pinerolo (Prov. di Torino)

di anni ventiquattro

di professione scalpellino cittadino italiano

residente in Torre Pellice (Prov. di Torino)

2o CUSINATO Maria Ottavia di Bartolomeo e di DREZZA Celesta

nata in Mozzecane (Prov. di Verona)

di anni venti

di professione casalinga cittadina italiana

residente in Torre Pellice (Prov. di Torino)

Si rilascia il presente certificato per uso amministrativo ed ai sensi dell' art 3 DPR 2.5.57 n 432 completo di generalita'.

lì 22 giugno 1965

L'Ufficiale dello Stato Civile (Rosien Francesco)

L'Ufficiale dello Stato Civile

Francesco Antony

REC'D JUN 24 1965

FIGURE 5-7. Civil Death Certificate of Romano Berasi, 1940, Milan

COMUNE DI MILANO

UFFICIO STATO CIVILE

Certificato di Morte

Milano, 22·11-1991

BERASI

ROMANO

professione ——————————— residente in Milano

nato in Beffio Superiore

di anni settantuno (atto n. ——— Reg. ——— P. ———)

Stato Civile Marito di: Ferrieri Clementine

è morto nel giorno 11· dicembre

mille novecentoquaranta in Milano.

come risulta dal Registro degli Atti di Morte dell'anno 1940.

al progressivo N. 1813 Registro 1 Parte 1 Serie /

In carta libera per gli usi per i quali la legge non prescrive il bollo.

L'UFFICIALE DELLO STATO CIVILE

43655

ower. Here it is indicated that Romano was the husband of Clementina Ferrieri.

Next are indicated the date and place of death: *e' morto nel giorno* means "he died on the day"; the day and year are indicated. *In* translates to "at" in English, and the city of Milan is indicated. Finally, a reference to the act number is given: taken from the record of the death acts of the year 1940 at number 1813, record 1, part 1, series [none]. Again, the certificate is signed and stamped.

Death Extracts

The extract of the death act (figure 5-8) provides additional information. There are differences from one form to the other; for example, in this extract, the person's name, Amabile Rossi, and the number of the act are shown in the right margin, and the town and province—Saonara, Padova—are at the top. Normally, the information provided in death act extracts is always the same. The additions to be found in the extract are the hour of death, the address of the deceased, and, in some cases, the names of the deceased's parents. In this example, after the date, *il giorno quindici* (on the fifteenth day), *del mese di Aprile* (of the month of April), *dell'anno Millenovecentosessantasei* (in the year 1966), the exact time of death appears: *alle ore dodici e minuti zero*—"at the hour twelve and zero minutes" (noon).

The deceased's address is stated as well: *nella casa posta in Via Rizzo N.31,* "in the house in Via Rizzo number 31." On this extract the names of the parents are not indicated, but usually they are, particularly when the deceased was a child. The extract further states that Amabile Rossi's profession (*di professione*) was that of *casalinga,* or "housewife." The date and place of her birth are also indicated: *nata in Limena il 06.03.1880*—"born at Limena on 6 March 1880." (Often, in older records, only the age of the deceased, not the exact birth date, was included.) She was the widow (*vedova*) of Giuseppe Segato.

As shown, the extract contains much valuable information for identifying the deceased. Therefore, it is always better to request the extract of the death act rather than the certificate.

Figure 5-9 is an original death act. Additional information found on it includes the names of the town mayor and the two people who testified to him that, indeed, Gaetano De Lorenzo died. Other information, including name, age, and profession, is given about the two who testified and two persons who actually witnessed the death, but the information regarding the deceased is the same as that contained in the extract of the act. Again, the town office normally does not allow the viewing or copying of any original act, so it is necessary to request the extract.

Family Certificate

Another civil record of great interest is the *stato di famiglia* (state of the family) certificate. The *anagrafe* office of each

town keeps a record of all the people living in a place of residence. This record is updated as children are born, marry, and move away, and as deaths occur. Thus, it shows who is living together in a place of residence at any given time.

Even more important for genealogical purposes is the *stato di famiglia originario* (original state of the family) certificate, also called the *stato di famiglia storico* (historical state of the family) certificate, two examples of which are shown here (figures 5-10 and 5-11). It is kept not at the *anagrafe* office but at the *ufficio di stato civile,* and it documents not those present in a household at a given time but all members of the family, past and present, including those who moved away or died. Therefore, for the genealogist, the *stato di famiglia originario* certificate is a valuable source for documenting an entire family unit.

A census was taken from the beginning of the Kingdom of Italy in 1871. However, the original purpose of this census was to identify potential taxpayers, who were usually the heads of households. Consequently, the only name that appeared was that of the household patriarch. The number of people living in the home, which sometimes included several families, was also included. This census varied somewhat from region to region, and those censuses taken during the first fifty years do not provide very accurate documents for genealogical purposes. Not until 1911 did the first nationwide census include the names of all people living in each household and provide accurate vital statistics about each. The *stato di famiglia originario* is based on this census material. Therefore, in most areas of Italy, it exists as a document only from 1911 onward. The same information can be obtained for earlier periods if the *ufficio di stato civile* staff are willing to reconstruct the information from original birth, marriage, and death records. The staff of most towns' vital record offices are very busy and usually will not conduct such research. Nevertheless, it is certainly worth requesting. For the example shown in figure 5-10, the town office staff did perform the research and charged only L55,000—less than $40—for the certificate.

The certificate first indicates the town and the province—in this case, Sulmona in the province of L'Aquila. Then it states *riscontrati gli atti anagrafici di questo comune, certifica che la famiglia originaria di MARCONE Giacinto, qui residente era cosi' composta.* This statement indicates that the source of the information is the *anagrafe* records and that this is the certificate for the original family of Giacinto Marcone (the head of the household), who had been a resident. In many cases, the certificate provides not only the name of the head of the household but also the exact address of residence.

Next are the column headings: *N. d' Ord.* simply refers to the order in which the family members are presented in the document. *Cognome e nome* refers to the surname and given name of each family member. *Relazione di parentela* indicates for each person on the certificate his or her relationship to the family; here the relationships appear as

FIGURE 5-8. Extract of the Civil Death Act of Amabile Rossi, 1966, Saonara, Padova

COMUNE DI   S A O N A R A

PADOVA

PROVINCIA DI ....

_____

UFFICIO DELLO STATO CIVILE

_____

ESTRATTO per riassunto dal Registro degli Atti di MORTE dell'anno 19 __92__

Davanti all'Ufficiale dello Stato Civile del Comune

di   S A O N A R A .... viene dichiarato

che il giorno __Quindici__ del mese di __Aprile__

dell'anno __Millenovecentosessantasei__

alle ore __dodici__ e minuti __zero__

nella casa posta in Via __Rizzo__ N. __31__

è mort a __ROSSI AMABILE__

residente in __Saonara__

di professione __casalinga__

che era nat a in __Limena__

il __06.03.1880__ stato civile __vedova Segato Giuseppe —__

Per estratto conforme all'originale rilasciato in carta __libera, art.__

7 Legge 29.12.1990 n. 405 – – – –

li __23.07.1992__

Registro parte __I^__

Serie __===__

N. __6__

ROSSI

AMABILE

L'UFFICIALE DELLO STATO CIVILE

L'Ufficiale dello Stato Civile

Mariano Daniele

FIGURE 5-9. Reproduction of the Original Death Act of Gaetano De Lorenzo, 1886, Rosolì, Reggio Calabria

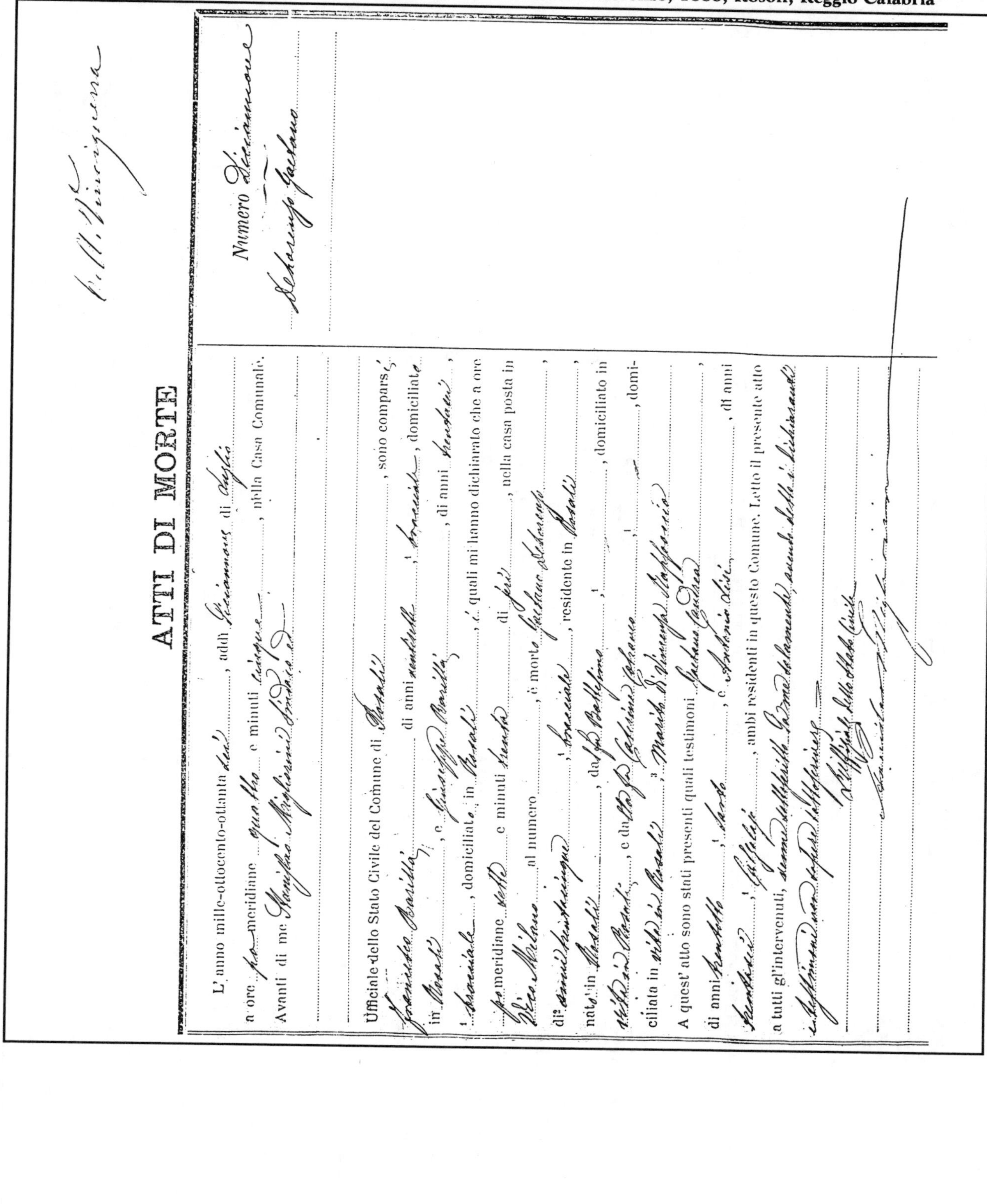
ATTI DI MORTE

Numero

L' anno mille-ottocento-ottanta ..., addì ... di ...
a ore ... meridiane ... e minuti ..., nella Casa Comunale.
Avanti di me ...
Ufficiale dello Stato Civile del Comune di ..., sono compars...
di anni ..., ..., domiciliato in ..., e ..., di anni ..., ..., domiciliato in ..., i quali mi hanno dichiarato che a ore ... meridiane ... e minuti ... di ..., nella casa posta in ... al numero ..., è morto ...
di ..., ..., residente in ..., nato in ..., da ..., ..., domiciliato in ..., e da ..., ..., domiciliata in ..., ... domi-
A quest' atto sono stati presenti quali testimoni ..., di anni ..., ..., e ..., di anni ..., ..., ambi residenti in questo Comune. Letto il presente atto a tutti gl' intervenuti, ...

FIGURE 5-10. Certificate of the State of the Family Act of Giacinto Marcone, 1911, Sulmona, L'Aquila

Mod. 3 AN - 01

N. .... REGISTRO

DIRITTI RISCOSSI

Segreteria L. ....

L'IMPIEGATO

COMUNE DI SULMONA

PROVINCIA DI L'AQUILA

Ripartizione III · Servizi Demografici

L'UFFICIALE DI ANAGRAFE

riscontrati gli atti anagrafici di questo Comune, certifica che la famiglia di ORIGINARIA DI MARCONE GIACINTO *qui residente,* ~~*è*~~ ERA *così composta :*

N. d'ord.	COGNOME E NOME	Relazione di parentela	Luogo di nascita	Data di nascita	Stato Civile	Annotazioni
1	MARCONE GIACINTO	CAPO	SULMONA	22.08.1872	CONIUG.	
2	SPERA ELVIRA	MOGLIE	POPOLI	24.01.1873	CONIUG.	
3	MARCONE FILIPPO	FIGLIO	ROMA	19.04.1899	CELIBE	
4	MARCONE FRANCESCO	FIGLIO	SULMONA	23.10.1900	CELIBE	
5	MARCONE DOLORES	FIGLIA	SULMONA	21.01.1902	NUBILE	
6	MARCONE VIOLA	FIGLIA	SULMONA	05.09.1903	NUBILE	
7	MARCONE ALESSANDRO	FIGLIO	SULMONA	06.04.1909	CELIBE	
	================================					

NOTA BENE: La qualifica di capo - famiglia è attribuita solo ai fini anagrafici e, pertanto, è irrilevante a tutti gli altri effetti.

In carta libera per uso

Sulmona, lì 14.02.1989

Il Compilatore

COMUNE DI SULMONA - UFFICIO ANAGRAFE

L'UFFICIALE DI ANAGRAFE

L'UFFICIALE D'ANAGRAFE

(Anna Maria De Collibus)

Anna Maria De Collibus

Stab. Tip. « ANGELETTI » - Sulmona

FIGURE 5-11. Certificate of the State of the Family Act of Rosa Maccagnan, Salcedo, Vicenza

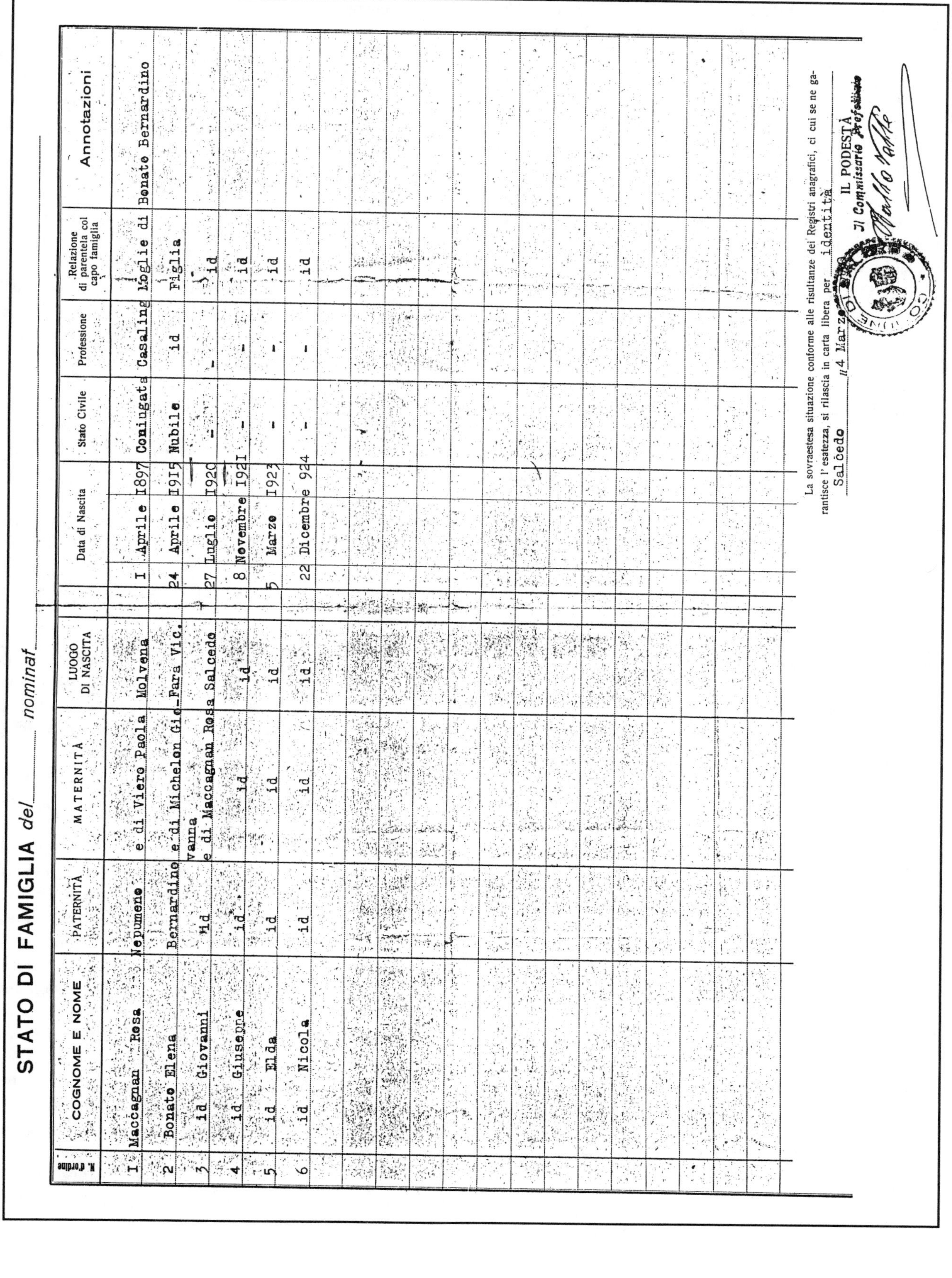

STATO DI FAMIGLIA del _____ nominat_____

N. d'ordine	COGNOME E NOME	PATERNITÀ	MATERNITÀ	LUOGO DI NASCITA	Data di Nascita	Stato Civile	Professione	Relazione di parentela col capo famiglia	Annotazioni
1	Maccagnan Rosa	Nepumene	e di Viero Paola	Molvena	I Aprile 1897	Coniugata	Casaling	Moglie di	Bonato Bernardino
2	Bonato Elena	Bernardino e di Michelon Gio-vanna	Fara Vic.	24 Aprile 1919	Nubile	id	Figlia	
3	id Giovanni	id	e di Maccagnan Rosa Salcedo	27 Luglio 1920	-	-	id	
4	id Giuseppe	id	id	id	8 Novembre 1921	-	-	id
5	id Elda	id	id	id	5 Marzo 1923	-	-	id
6	id Nicola	id	id	id	22 Dicembre 924	-	-	id

La sovraestesa situazione conforme alle risultanze dei Registri anagrafici, ci cui se ne garantisce l'esattezza, si rilascia in carta libera per identità

Salcedo ____ 4 Marzo ____

IL PODESTÀ
Il Commissario Prefettizio

capo (family head), *moglie* (wife), and *figlio* or *figlia* (son or daughter). (Often these are abbreviated: *CF* stands for *capofamiglia* [family head], *MG* for *moglie*, and *FG* for *figlio/a*.) Note that, in the same column (*relazione di parentela col capo famiglia*) of the second example (figure 5-11), after the first child, *id* appears for *idem*, or "the same."

Most document forms, such as shown in figure 5-11, include columns for *paternità* and *maternità*, in which the names of the father and mother of each person listed appear. Therefore, this column provides the names of the parents of the head of the household and of his wife, which can be very important in continuing research. In the first example (figure 5-10), however, this information does not appear. The next columns, *luogo di nascita* and *data di nascita*, indicate place of birth and birth date. Sometimes another column, *atto di nascita*, indicates the number, part, and series of the birth act.

As indicated on the certificate, most members of the family documented in the first example were born at Sulmona, but the wife is from Popoli, another large town not far away. It is probable that the marriage act of the couple would be found at Popoli; had the wife's birthplace not appeared on the certificate, the marriage act might not be found at all. Even more importantly, the certificate reveals that one of the children was born in Rome; undoubtedly, research at Sulmona would have revealed no trace of this child in the birth records, and his existence would never have been known. The second example also indicates that the parents are from different towns. Thus, the researcher learns from one certificate where the paternal and maternal lines may be pursued.

Also found on both certificates is the exact birth date (*data di nascita*) for each family member. The birth date is usually given, but sometimes the age is given instead, particularly for the parents. (Note again that the numbers in the date are inverted from the American system; for example, 05/09/1903 is the fifth of September and not the ninth of May.) *Stato civile*, again, refers to marital status; *coniugato/a* (sometimes abbreviated CGT) means "married," *nubile* or *Nbl* refers to a single woman, *celibe* or *Clb* a single man. *Vd* is short for *vedovo/a* and indicates a widower or widow. Note that the first example (figure 5-10) contains only one more column—*annotazioni*. Most certificates, as in the second example, include *professione* (vocation); in this case, Rosa was a *casalinga*, or, "housewife." (Note that all of her children, even the males, are mistakenly listed as the same.) Usually, the profession is indicated for each family member who arrived at adulthood. The last column, *annotazioni* (annotations), has been left blank. Many certificates also list the death date or emigration date for each person. As always, the certificate is signed, dated, and stamped.

The family certificates are the last of the civil vital records that are available from the *ufficio di stato civile* of any commune in Italy. However, earlier Napoleonic civil records can be found at the state archives of each province (see chapter 6).

PARISH CIVIL VITAL RECORDS

Napoleon introduced civil vital records (separate from ecclesiastical or parish records) into Italy as early as 1804 in some regions and by 1809 in most of Italy. In Austria, however, parish records have always been considered civil vital records as well, so no separate civil records were kept. As a result, a curious duplication of records began in parishes of regions of northeast Italy that, after the fall of Napoleon, became part of the Austrian Empire. In 1816, when the area was ceded to Austria, civil vital records were continued—not by town officials but by the parish priests, who were given responsibility for keeping the civil records. The dioceses required the priests to make out separate civil records with a format that differed from that of the normal parish records and the previous Napoleonic civil records. Thus, starting from the eastern part of the Lombardy region and including the Venetian, Trento, and Friuli regions, much of Slovenia, and parts of Croatia, separate parish civil and ecclesiastical records can be found. These records generally exist for the period from 1816 until unification with the Italian state in 1870. In the Trento region, which did not become a part of Italy until World War I, these were continued until after the war's end in 1918.

During this period, the parish ecclesiastical records were continued using the traditional format (see chapter 7), but the parish civil records had a unique format that was uniform throughout the area. Figure 5-12 is an example from Plautz in Croatia. The records occupy facing pages of the volume; the pages are divided into columns. This birth record is in German, but the columns are the same as those found in similar Italian-language records (figure 5-13), demonstrating the widespread use of this format. The more recent records (after 1865) were usually written on preprinted forms, as seen in these two examples. Previous volumes were laid out by hand. These records exist in the form of birth, marriage, and death records. There were no family group records comparable to the *stato di famiglia* civil record during this period.

Parish civil records are distinguished here both because the format used, which is so different from normal parish records, can be confusing, and because, for certain regions, these records are the more useful source because they usually contain complete information. For example, both the birth date and the baptismal date are included, and information such as the names of the child's grandparents, the name of the midwife, and, occasionally, the vocations of the parents is included. In death records, an important detail is the cause of death. These details do not normally appear in parish baptismal records.

FIGURE 5-12. Parish Civil Birth Acts, 1861, Plautz, Croatia

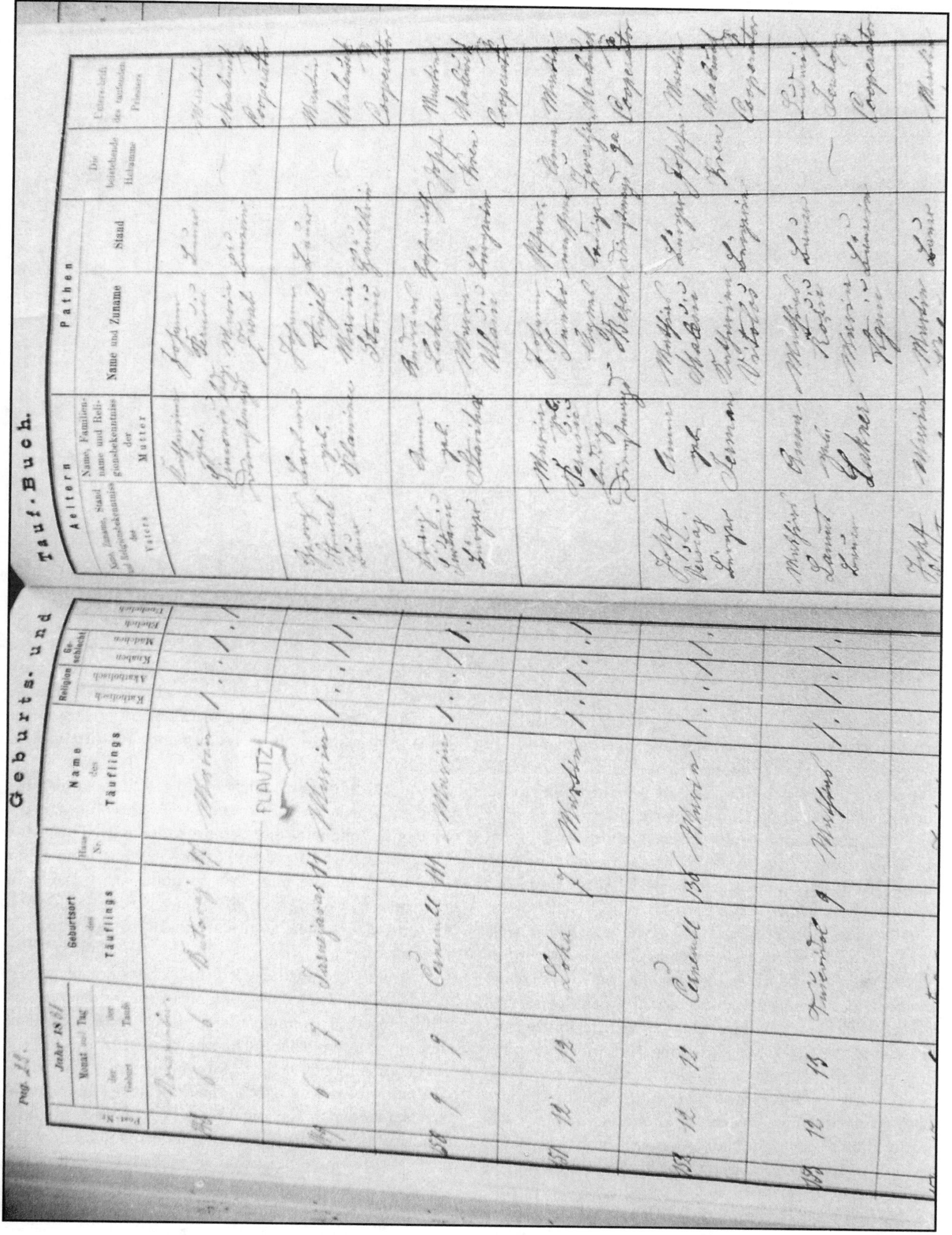

Geburts- und Tauf-Buch.

Pag. 22. Jahr 1861

Post-Nr. | Monat und Tag der Geburt / der Taufe | Geburtsort des Täuflings | Haus Nr. | Name des Täuflings | Religion: Katholisch, Akatholisch | Geschlecht: Knaben, Mädchen | Ehelich, Unehelich | Aeltern: Name, Zuname, Stand und Religionsbekenntniss des Vaters; Name, Familienname und Religionsbekenntniss der Mutter | Pathen: Name und Zuname, Stand | Die beistehende Hebamme | Unterschrift des taufenden Priesters

PLAUTZ

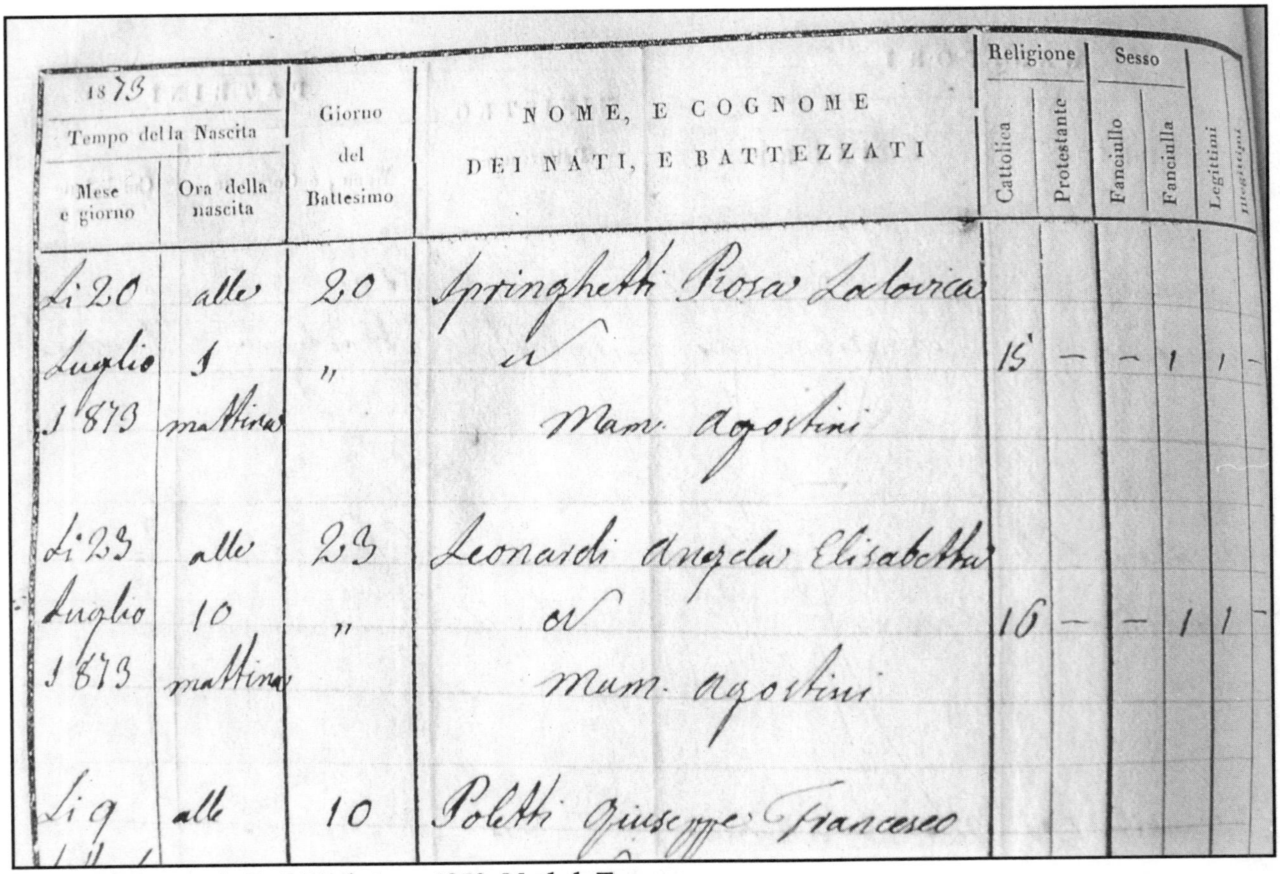

1873 Tempo della Nascita: Mese e giorno	Ora della nascita	Giorno del Battesimo	NOME, E COGNOME DEI NATI, E BATTEZZATI	Religione: Cattolica	Protestante	Sesso: Fanciullo	Fanciulla	Legittimi	Illegittimi
Li 20 Luglio 1873	alle 3 mattina	20 "	Springhetti Rosa Ludovica a Mam. Agostini	15	—	—	1	1	—
Li 23 Luglio 1873	alle 10 mattina	23 "	Leonardi Angela Elisabetta a Mam. Agostini	16	—	—	1	1	—
Li 9	alle	10	Poletti Giuseppe Francesco						

FIGURE 5-13. Parish Civil Birth Acts, 1873, Mechel, Trento

Birth Records

Although there were slight variations from one place to another, the birth documents usually were arranged as shown in the example from the Trento region (figure 5-13). The record begins with the year (*anno*) in the top left-hand corner. Next, *tempo della nascita* (time of birth) is divided into two sub-columns: *mese e giorno* (month and day) and *ora della nascita* (hour of the birth). *Giorno del battesimo* (day of baptism) and *nome, e cognome dei nati, e battezzati* (name and surname of the born and christened) follow. The left-hand page ends with the columns *religione* (religion), divided into *Cattolica* (Catholic) and *Protestante* (Protestant); *sesso* (sex), divided into *fanciullo* (young boy) and *fanciulla* (young girl); and *legittimi* (legitimate) and *illegittimi* (illegitimate). (Most children were legitimate, and almost all were Catholic.) The facing page (not shown but similar to the German-language example–figure 5-12) usually begins with *paternità* (paternity) or *padre* (father), followed by *maternità* (maternity) or *madre* (mother). The next column refers to the godparents; it may state *patrini* or *padrini* (godparents), or it may specify *patrino* or *padrino* (godfather) and *matrina* or *madrina* (godmother). The final column is normally titled *condizione* but sometimes is titled *professione* (profession); it lists the professions or vocations not of the parents but, rather, of the godparents. Some birth records may have a separate column, titled *sacerdote* (priest), for the name of the priest who performed the baptism. Often, however, this information is written under the child's name.

Another addition, which may be written under the name but which does not create a separate column, is the name of the midwife (*ostetrica* or *mammana*). This is the case in figure 5-13, where *Mam*–an abbreviation for *mammana*–and the midwife's surname are written. In small villages, usually only one or two women performed this service, and their names are found in almost all the annotations.

Figure 5-14 is a birth record from a considerably earlier period (1820s). The information presented is similar to that in the preceding example, but there are some variations. There is only one column for the date of birth, and the precise time is not given. More important, there is no column for the date of baptism, so this can be found only in the separate parish baptismal records. Also, instead of the number of the act, there is a column for the number of the house (*casa*) where the family lived. Two of the columns are on the left-hand rather than the right-hand page as in the previous example, but otherwise the same information is given. Thus, it is obvious that, for different time periods and in different regions, the same general format is used and the same information is provided.

Marriage Records

A similar division into columns on two facing pages is true for marriage records as well. As seen in the facing pages of figure 5-15, the date of the marriage (*data del matrimonio*) comes first, followed by the number of the act (*numero dell'atto*). The next column (*sposo* or *nome dello sposo*) contains the name of the groom, the names of his parents, information about when the banns were announced, and the name of the priest who officiated at the marriage. The left-hand page ends with columns for the religion (*religione*), age (*età*), and marital status (*stato civile*) of the groom. On the facing (right-hand) page, the same columns are repeated for the bride (*sposa* or *nome della sposa*), providing her name and those of her parents. As may be seen, the professions of both the groom and the bride are listed in these respective columns. For example, in the center of the page, Antonio Agostini is indicated to have been a *villico* and his bride, Elisabetta Emerentian, a *villica*. Thus, they were both farmers who owned their land. In some cases, the profession does not appear at all; in other parishes, not only are the professions of the groom and bride given, but those of their parents are indicated as well. Next, information about the bride's religion (*religione* or just *Cattolica*) and her age (*età*) appears. (Note that, in this example, since almost everyone was Catholic, the *religione* column simply contains the number of each entry.) Then, columns for the witnesses (*testimoni*) and their professions (*condizione* or *professione*) appear. The fact that there is a separate column for the professions of the witnesses, but not for the parents, indicates the importance of the witnesses.

Death Records

The death acts (figures 5-16 and 5-17) are similarly divided, but usually they occupy only one page of the document (rather than facing pages), as less information is supplied. The information provided begins with *tempo della morte* (time of death), where both the date and the hour of death are noted. Next, a column for the number of the house of residence, *n.o casa* (not found in the other records) appears. The name of the deceased is given in the next column, *nome e cognome del defunto*, together with the names of the parents (if the deceased was a child or never married) or the name of the deceased's spouse. The next columns are

similar in indicating religion, sex, and age: *religione, maschio* (male), *femmina* (female), *età* (age). The last column can be quite interesting: it concerns the cause of death and is labeled, in this case, *malattia e qualità della morte*, or, "sickness and quality of death." In some records it is more appropriately labeled *causa della morte*, or "cause of death."

In these records, causes like *marasmus* (stomach disorders), *infiamazione* or *convulsione* (inflammation, fever, and convulsions), or, similarly, *apoplessia* (apoplexy) are found frequently. Diseases such as *tifo* or *diarrea* (both indicate typhus), *dissenteria, cholera*, and *consunzione* or *tisi* (both indicate tuberculosis) are often mentioned as well. These examples indicate that two died from worms (*vermi*), one from "unnatural" childbirth (*parto non naturale*), and one from ulcers (*ulcera*). Illnesses obviously were not classified then as they are now so, often, it is difficult to identify what the exact cause of death may have been. In this column the sacraments that were administered at death, such as *estrema unzione* (extreme unction) or *confessione*, may also be indicated. More commonly, however, a separate column titled *sacramenti* is included. In some cases, as seen in figure 5-17, information is given about the burial. In this case, burial information is limited to *sepolta nel cimitero*, or "buried in the cemetery," but some records also specify the burial date or indicate which cemetery if the burial was in a large city.

It should be possible, using the examples provided in this chapter, to understand and translate all civil vital acts found anywhere in Italy, since the format and information are widely used. In summary:

Civil vital records should always be consulted if possible, as they are an important source of information and can normally be found in the commune back to around 1867. Earlier civil records continued from Napoleonic records can be found in the state (provincial) archives for most of south and central Italy, and in the parishes for regions near Austria.

It is always necessary to identify the ancestor's township or commune of origin, rather than just the *frazione*, to conduct research using the civil records.

Civil documents can be obtained for any town or *frazione* by writing to the *ufficio di stato civile* of the commune where the act took place (see chapter 11).

Always seek the extract of the act rather than the certificate. Only in the extract will the parents of the ancestor and other valuable information be included.

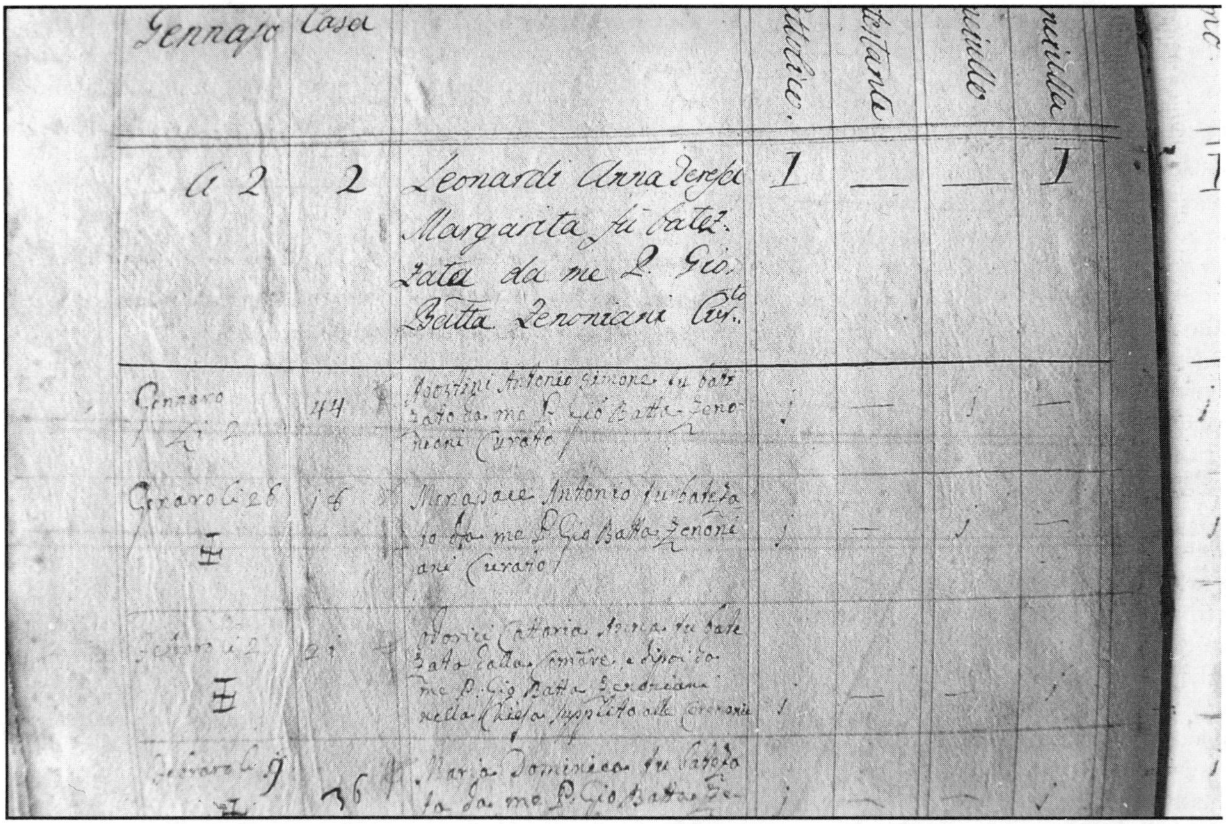

Gennajo Casa

a 2 2 Leonardi Anna Teresa Margarita fu battezzata da me D. Gio. Batta Zenoniani Curato

Gennaro li 2 44 Agostini Antonio Simone fu battezato da me D. Gio Batta Zenoniani Curato

Gennaro li 28 16 Menapace Antonio fu battezato da me D. Gio Batta Zenoniani Curato

Maria Dominica fu battezata da me D. Gio Batta Ze-

FIGURE 5-14. Parish Civil Birth Acts, Mechel, Trento; Left-Hand (above) and Right-Hand (right) Facing Pages

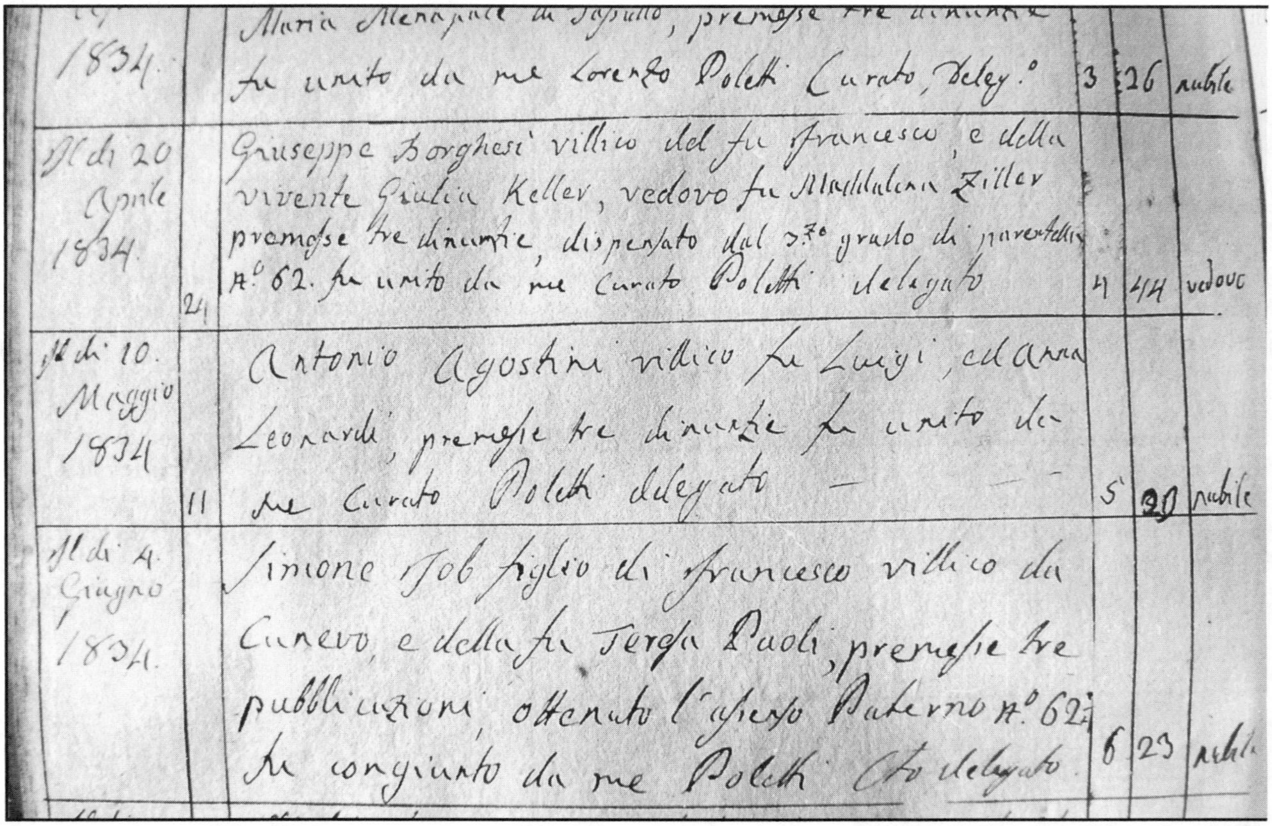

1834. fu unito da me Lorenzo Poletti Curato, Deleg.° 3 26 nubile

Il di 20 Aprile 1834. 24 Giuseppe Borghesi villico del fu Francesco, e della vivente Giulia Keller, vedovo fu Maddalena Ziller premesse tre dinunzie, dispensato dal 3.zo grado di parentella N.° 62. fu unito da me Curato Poletti delegato 4 44 vedova

Il di 10. Maggio 1834 11 Antonio Agostini villico fu Luigi, ed Anna Leonardi, premesse tre dinunzie fu unito da me Curato Poletti delegato — 5 20 nubile

Il di 4. Giugno 1834. Simone Job figlio di Francesco villico da Cunevo, e della fu Teresa Paoli, premesse tre pubblicazioni, ottenuto l'assenso Paterno N.° 62. fu congiunto da me Poletti C.to delegato 6 23 nubile

FIGURE 5-15. Parish Civil Marriage Acts, Mechel, Trento; Left-Hand (above) and Right-Hand (right) Facing Pages

		Padre	Madre	Nome	Condizione
1	—	Antonio f.° di Antonio Leonardi di Mechel	Rosa f.° di Giovanni Leonardi di Mechel	Giacomo Leonardi Margarita Ved. Odorici	Contadino. Vicina.
	—	Luigi q.m Gio: Stefano Sagorini alias	Anna figlia di Antonio Leonardi Mechel	Simon Borghesi f.a Elena Borghesi	Contadino Signora
		Antonio q.m Iacopo Fenaza figlio	Vittoria vidua q.m Giacomo Barbi	Lorenzo Borghesi Maria moglie di Giuseppe....	Contadini
		figlio di q.m Marco Odorici	Lucia figlia q.m Gio: Agostini di Mechel	Nicolo di Agnese Anna moglie di Lorenzo Leonardi	Contadini
		Nicolo figlio q.m Valentini di Igmedi	Domenica figlia di Gio: Ronca Sagorini di Mechel	Pedrigo Leonardi q.m ....moglie Maria	Contadini

	Maria Agostini.			3	25	nubile	Poletti Giuseppe Poletti	
Con Anna Poletti vidua fu Michele, e Barbera Romedi, vedova fu Giacomo Leonardi				4	44	ved.a	Giovani Zambias Antonio Poletti	vedova... vig.°
Con Elisabeta Cenerentian vidua fu Bartolommeo, e della vivente Elisabeta Poletti				5	24	nubile	Antonio Poletti Giuseppe Poletti	vig.°
Con Margarita vidua Leonardi figlia di federico, è fu Catenina Romedi, avuto l'ispenso Paterno n.° 63				6	20	nubile	Giuseppe Nicoledi Nicolo Odorici	fato ... valtvijo

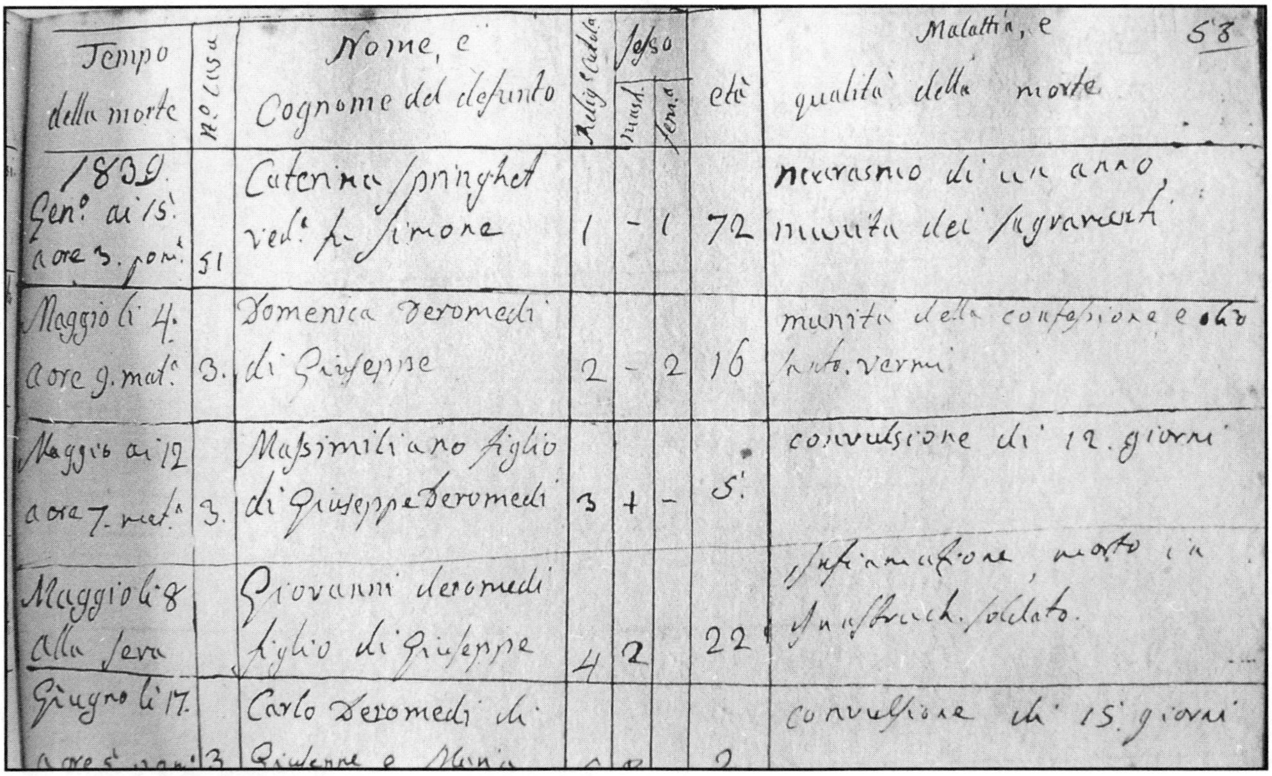

Tempo della morte	N.° d'Ordine	Nome, e Cognome del defunto	Relig. Cattol.	Sesso Masch.	Sesso Femin.	età	Malattia, e qualità della morte	58
1839 Gen.° ai 15. a ore 3. pom.	51	Caterina Springhet ved.a fu Simone	1	-	1	72	marasmo di un anno, munita dei sagramenti	
Maggio li 4. a ore 9. mat.°	3	Domenica Deromedi di Giuseppe	2	-	2	16	munita della confessione e olio S.to. vermi	
Maggio ai 12 a ore 7. mat.°	3	Massimiliano figlio di Giuseppe Deromedi	3	+	-	5.	convulsione di 12. giorni	
Maggio li 8 alla sera		Giovanni Deromedi figlio di Giuseppe	4	2		22	Infiamazione, morto in Inspruch. soldato.	
Giugno li 17. a ore 5. pom.	3	Carlo Deromedi di Giuseppe e Maria			2		convulsione di 15. giorni	

FIGURE 5-16. Parish Civil Death Acts, Mechel, Trento

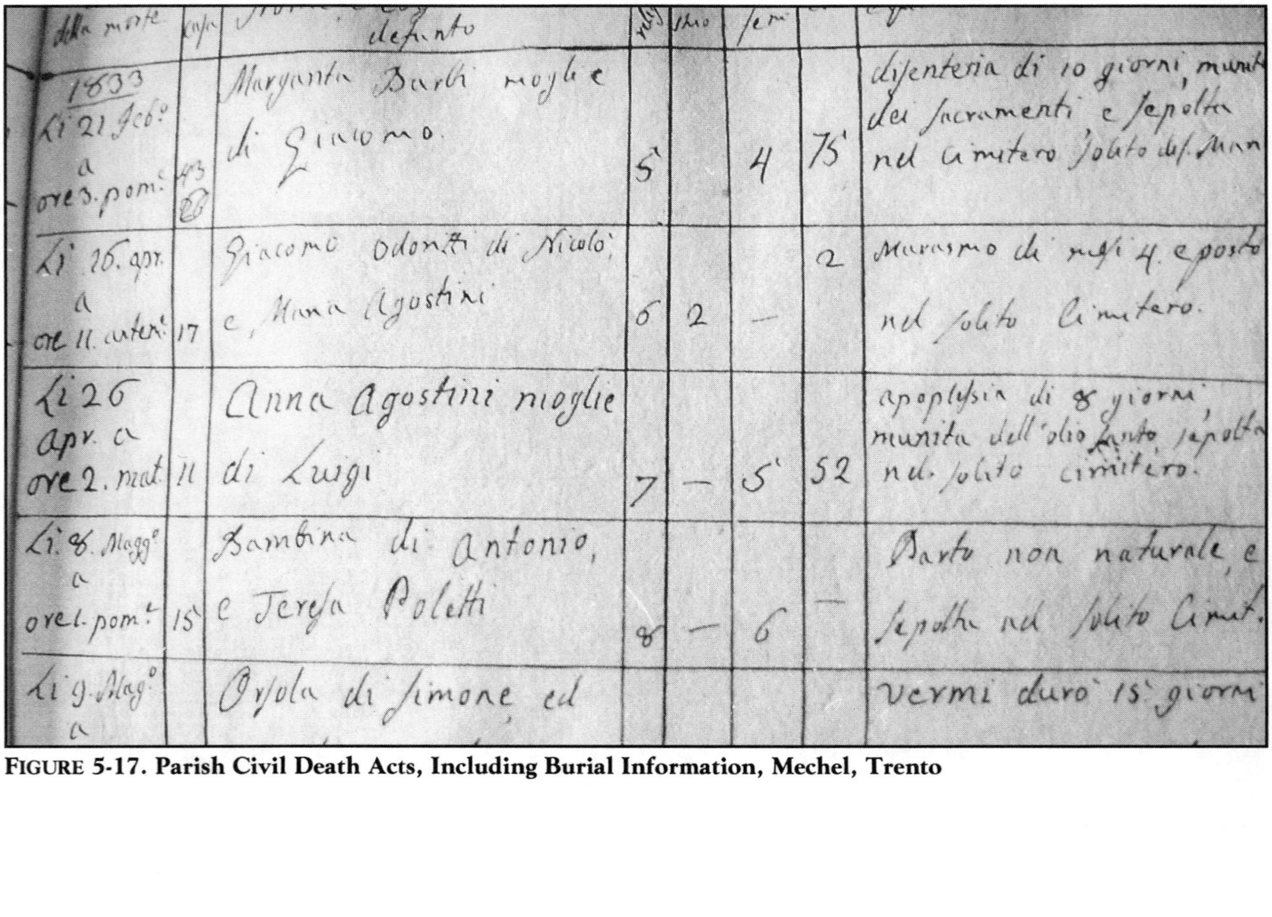

della morte		Nome ... defunto	Relig	Masch.	Fem.		Malattia ...
1833 Li 21 Feb.° a ore 5. pom.	43	Margarita Barli moglie di Giacomo.	5		4	75	disenteria di 10 giorni, munita dei sacramenti, e sepolta nel cimitero solito def. Man
Li 26. apr. a ore 11. anter.°	17	Giacomo Odorizzi di Nicolò e Maria Agostini	6	2	-	2	Marasmo di mesi 4. e posto nel solito cimitero.
Li 26 apr. a ore 2. mat.°	11	Anna Agostini moglie di Luigi	7	-	5.	52	apoplesia di 8 giorni, munita dell'olio santo, sepolta nel solito cimitero.
Li 8. Magg.° a ore 1. pom.°	15	Bambina di Antonio, e Teresa Poletti	8	-	6	-	Parto non naturale, e sepolta nel solito Cimit.
Li 9. Mag.° a		Orsola di Simone, ed					vermi durò 15. giorni

FIGURE 5-17. Parish Civil Death Acts, Including Burial Information, Mechel, Trento

Chapter 6

NAPOLEONIC CIVIL RECORDS

N APOLEON CONDUCTED CAMPAIGNS IN ITALY IN 1797 AND 1799. By 1806, as emperor of France, he had annexed large parts of Italy, including Rome, Piedmont, and Venice. Napoleon was the first to enact administrative reforms, to divide Italy into distinct regions, provinces, and townships, and to begin civil record keeping. As he gradually took control of all of Italy, more towns began to keep civil records. After Napoleon lost power in 1815, however, these records were discontinued in many regions.

Napoleonic records were continued in the Kingdom of the Two Sicilies—comprising most of southern Italy from Naples and Campania down to Sicily and controlled by the Bourbon House of France—the Grand Duchy of Tuscany, and the Abruzzo region. Even in these areas there was some variation. In Sicily, Napoleonic records exist for the period from 1820 to 1865, when Italian civil records were begun. Throughout the rest of the south and in Tuscany and Abruzzo, they date from 1809 to 1865. In the former papal states, which extended from what are now Molise, Latium, Umbria, and Marche to Emilia-Romagna, they exist only for the period from 1810 to 1814. In the north, they were begun in 1804 in Piedmont and in 1806 in Veneto and Lombardy, usually ending in 1814 or 1816 at the latest. They were never introduced in Sardinia, nor were they in the Trentino and South Tyrol areas, which never came under Napoleon's rule. In Piedmont, where the Napoleonic records date only from 1804 to 1814, the Duchy of Savoy began keeping civil records in 1839. In the areas controlled by the Austrian empire, such as Veneto, Lombardy, and Trentino, parish priests became the civil vital records officers and kept separate civil records in the parishes (see chapter 5).

Most of the extant Napoleonic records for southern and central Italy have been microfilmed by The Church of Jesus Christ of Latter-day Saints (LDS church), and these reproductions are available at the church's family history centers throughout the United States and Canada (see chapter 10). In Italy, the Napoleonic records are held by the archive of each separate province. The archive is normally found in the province's major city and contains these records and many alternative sources (discussed in chapter 9). The records are organized by commune, and they can be voluminous, depending on the size of the commune.

There are separate records for birth, marriage, and death acts. Two copies of each act were created; one copy went to

the *pretura della repubblica* and one copy remained in the town. (The *pretura della repubblica* is the provincial seat—the major city in each Italian province—where the *pretore*, or federal district judge, presides. The *pretore* is the highest authority for all civil matters in the province. Before the creation of the Italian state, the *pretore* was responsible for all civil acts in the province. After the unification of Italy this responsibility passed to the *procuratore*, or district attorney.) The town copies have since been removed from the separate towns and deposited in the provincial (state) archives.

Unlike post-Napoleonic civil vital records, which are almost always legible and in good condition, many of the Napoleonic records have deteriorated from the effects of long storage in humid cellars. Most can be read, though often with considerable difficulty. Because the Italian civil records were modeled on the Napoleonic records, the format of most of the Napoleonic records is similar to that of the Italian civil records discussed in chapter 5. The exception, as will be seen, is the marriage act, which is much more complex in the Napoleonic form. Since the same basic format is found throughout Italy, a careful examination of each act will provide a clear guide to read and interpret Napoleonic records that originated anywhere in Italy.

BIRTH RECORDS

The birth act documents held by the state archives are the original birth acts. No certificates or extracts are officially available, but usually a photocopy can be made of the act. There were two formats for the birth act according to who declared the birth to the town official. The first example (figure 6-1) is an act for which the father made the declaration. For this format, a full translation is provided below. The second format (figure 6-2) was used when a midwife

FIGURE 6-1. Napoleonic Birth Act of Angela Lorenzo, 1832, Rosolì, Reggio Calabria

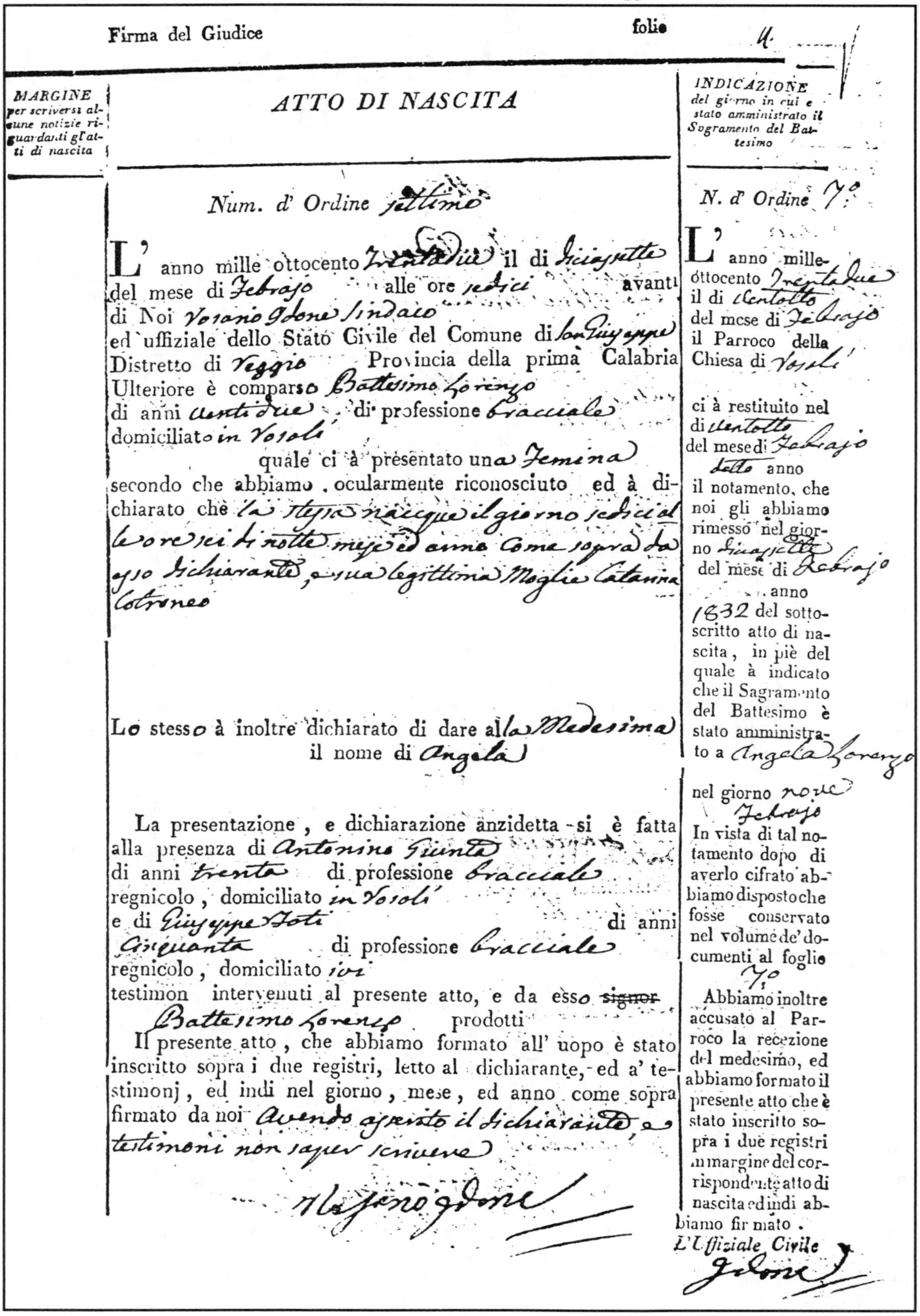

FIGURE 6-2. Napoleonic Birth Act of Anna Carmela Scolastica Caldarelli, 1820, S. Stefano, L'Aquila

ATTO DI NASCITA.

NUM. *dodici* D' ORDINE. *12*

L'anno mille ottocento venti, il *dì ventinove* del mese di *Marzo* — alle ore *quindici* avanti di noi *Gregorio Cocci Sindaco* — ed Uffiziale dello Stato Civile del Comune di *Santo Stefano* — Distretto di *Aquila* Provincia di Aquila, è comparsa *Maria Antonacci* di anni *sessanta* — di professione *Ostetrica* domiciliato in *questo Comune, Strada la villa* quale ci ha presentato una *Femmina* secondocchè abbiamo riconosciuto, ed ha dichiarato che la stessa è nata da *Conjugi Anna Antonucci Cocci* di anni *venticinque* domiciliata in *questo Comune, Strada Braspe, da Emiddio Cal davella* di anni *trentuno* di professione *pastore* domiciliato in *questo Comune, Strada Federale nel* giorno *vent'otto* del mese di *Marzo* — anno corrente alle ore *sei di notte* nella casa di *abitazione dei conjugi suddetti* La stessa ha inoltre dichiarato di dare alla *figlia* il nome di *Anna Carmela Scolastica*

La presentazione, e dichiarazione anzidetta si è fatta alla presenza di *Giacomo Cocci* — di anni *cinquanta* di professione *braccicale* regnicolo domiciliato in *questo comune, Strada la Torre* e di *Donato S. Innocenzo* di anni *trentatre* di professione *braccicale* — regnicolo, domiciliato in *questo Comune, Strada la Chiesa* Testimonj intervenuti al presente atto, e da esso Sig.r *Maria Antonacci* prodotti.

Il presente atto, che abbiamo formato all' uopo, è stato inscritto sopra i due Registri, letto al dichiarante, ed ai testimonj ed indi, nel giorno mese, ed anno come sopra, firmato da noi. *Il vendersi detto la dichiarante di non saper firmare, e da Ostetrico registro dichiarante Gregorio Cocci Sindaco Giacomo Cocci testimonio ..... Di Innocenzo testimonio*

Cifra del Giudice delegato dal Presidente del Tribunale Civile.

INDICAZIONE
Del giorno, in cui è stato amministrato il Sacramento del Battesimo.

NUM. *dodici* D' ORDINE. *12*

L'anno mille ottocento venti il dì *trentuno* del mese di *Marzo* Il Parroco di *Santo Stefano* ci ha restituito nel dì *trenta* del mese di *Marzo* anno corrente il notamento, che noi gli abbiamo rimesso nel giorno *ventinove* del mese di *Marzo* anno corrente del controscritto atto di nascita in piè del quale ha indicato, che il Sacramento del Battesimo è stato amministrato a *Anna Carmela Scolastica* nel giorno *ventinove dett'mese*

In vista di un tale notamento dopo di averlo cifrato abbiamo disposto, che fosse conservato nel volume dei documenti al foglio *dodici*. Abbiamo inoltre accusato al Parroco la ricezione del medesimo, ed abbiamo formato il presente atto, ch'è stato inscritto sopra i due Registri in margine del corrispondente atto di nascita, ed indi lo abbiamo firmato.

L' Uffiziale dello Stato Civile,
Gregorio Cocci Sindaco

made the declaration. For this example, only the differences from the example in figure 6-1 will be noted.

Firma del giudice is for a judge's signature. This item is not always present, and I have found few certificates that were actually countersigned by a judge. The judge signed only the copy that was sent to the Pretura, not the town's copy, which is usually found at the state archive. *Folio* (or *foglio*) is the page number of the record—not the act number; in older records, one page was considered as being both sides of a sheet.

Margine per scriversi alcune notizie riguardanti gl'atti di nascita translates as "margin to write notes regarding the birth act." This space was sometimes used to note whether a child died at birth or whether there was a question of legitimacy. *Atto di nascita* means "birth act," and *Indicazione del giorno in cui è stato amministrato il Sagramento del Battesimo* means, literally, "Indication of the day in which the sacrament of Baptism is Administered." Thus, this act serves as both a birth act and a baptismal act.

Num. d'Ordine indicates the number of the act—in this case *settimo* (seventh). The following item is often misleading to those who do not know Italian well or who are performing research hurriedly, without proper care: an exact date and hour are indicated, but they do *not* represent the time of the child's birth. Rather, this item indicates when a witness appeared before the town mayor, who was also the civil vital records officer, to formally declare that a child had been born. (Because this date is at the beginning and is prominent, whereas the actual birth date is handwritten later in the document, many researchers mistakenly focus on it as the actual birth date of the child.) The procedure, still used today, required a witness, usually the father but often also the midwife who assisted in the birth, to state before the mayor or town official that a child had been born. This procedure was required to occur within three days from the time of the child's birth and was also the declaration of the child's name.

The first paragraph of this act is written as follows:

L'anno mille ottocento *trentadue* il dì *diciasette* del mese di *Febraio* alle ore *sedici* avanti di Noi *Rosario Idone Sindaco* ed uffiziale dello Stato Civile del Comune di *San Giuseppe* Distretto di *Reggio* Provincia della prima Calabria Ulteriore e' comparso *Battesimo Lorenzo* di anni *ventidue* di professione *bracciale* domiciliato *in Rosolì*

quale ci a' presentato un *a Femina* secondo che abbiamo ocularmente riconosciuto ed a' dichiarato che *la stessa nacque il giorno sedici alle ore sei di notte mese ed anno come sopra da esso dichiarante e sua legittima moglie Catarina Cotroneo.*

This translates as:

In the year one thousand eight hundred and *thirty-two*, on the *seventeenth* day of the month of *February* at the hour *sixteen hundred* [4 p.m.], before us, *Rosario IDONE, Mayor* and officer of Civil Vital Records for the commune of *San Giuseppe* in the District of *Reggio* in the Province of the First Calabria, appeared *Battesimo LORENZO*, age *twenty two*, vocation farm worker, living at Rosolì

who presented us a *Female* that we visibly witnessed, and he declared that *the same was born on the sixteenth day at six at night on the month and year stated above, and child of the same person making the declaration and his wife, Catarina COTRONEO.*

In this act, the father was declaring the birth of his daughter. Note that it was necessary for the child to be personally presented to the mayor for identification. If the child was sickly the officer might visit the home—but he had to personally see the child. (Today, it is still necessary for the father to declare a child to the town office within three days. However, the child need not be personally presented; a declaration from a hospital or doctor is sufficient.)

Note that there was a further division of the province into districts; usually there were two or three districts per province. This political division no longer exists, but there are districts for the courts and military districts for the draft. It is also noteworthy that the province now called Reggio Calabria was named the Prima Calabria Ulteriore at the time this act was created, and that the town of Rosolì today is a *frazione*, part of another commune.

The second birth act example (figure 6-2) is from the province of L'Aquila, hundreds of miles from Rosolì, Calabria, where the first act originated. Nevertheless, these examples share almost exactly the same format, again demonstrating the unifying effect of Napoleon's rule in Italy. This second act differs in the fact that a midwife (*ostetrica*), Maria Antonucci, declared the birth and presented the child to the town mayor. Thus, the format differs to include the names of both parents of the child, citing first the mother, in this case Annantonia Cicci, age twenty-five (*venticinque*), and then the father, Emiddeo Caldarelli, age thirty-five and a shepherd (*pastore*). Here the actual date of birth is part of the form with space provided for the day (*giorno*), month (*mese*), year (*anno*), and hour (*ore*). The house in which the birth took place is also noted. In this example it was "the house of the above stated husband and wife." Note that birth in a hospital was not a consideration, telling us much of how customs have changed!

The remainder of the second example is identical to the first, so the translation provided below for the first example differs only in its particulars from the second. The next line to be considered provides the name of the child: *Lo stesso a' inoltre dichiarato di dare alla medesima il nome di Angela* Literally translated, this means: "The same [referring to the father] has also declared to give to the same [referring to the child] the name of Angela." In this certificate only the given name is included. In the second, the name of the child is given as Anna Carmela Scolastica. The child's surname is always assumed to be the family name of the father and so is not specified on the act declared by the father. Only an illegitimate child would have the mother's family name, and the fact would be noted: in place of the father's name would be written *di padre ignoto*—"of unknown father." It would also be indicated that the child was *illegittimo*, and the surname of the mother would be written in. In the case of a foundling, not only would the father be unknown, but the mother would be indicated as unknown too—*di madre ignota*—or it might simply be stated *di genitori ignoti*: "of unknown parents." In this situation a midwife would present the child, and the name and surname would be decided by the town official or by those who would raise the child—often the parish priest. Usually, for a foundling, there is also a note in the margin explaining the circumstance in which the child was found. (Often these children were left on the steps of a church.)

Both the illegitimate child and the foundling present a problem to the genealogist pursuing a family line. If, on both the civil birth act and the baptismal act, *di padre ignoto* or *di genitori ignoti* is stated, there are no other records that will provide more information about the family line. In the case of an illegitimate child the paternal line ceases; in the case of a foundling, both lines cease. Usually, the foundling was placed in an orphanage to be cared for by the church. Rarely were foundlings formally or legally adopted. Rather, they were taken in by families as soon as possible and worked as servants for their "keep." Sometimes foundlings appear in the census records, but more commonly they appear in the parish *status animarum* records (discussed in chapter 7). This is not an uncommon genealogical problem. Illegitimacy was widespread, but social pressure against it was strong, so many of these children were left to the church.

The last part of the birth act (figure 6-1) contains information about the witnesses to the act. Two witnesses (who were usually not relatives of the child) were required. This part is written:

La presentazione, e dichiarazione anzidetta si e' fatta alla presenza di *Antonio Giunta* di anni *trenta* di professione *bracciale* regnicolo, domiciliato in *Rosali'* e di *Giuseppe Toti* di anni *cinquanta* di professione *bracciale* regnicolo, domiciliato *ivi* testimoni intervenuti al presente atto, e da esso signor *Battesimo Lorenzo* prodotti

Il presente atto, che abbiamo formato all'uopo e' stato inscritto sopra i due registri, letto al dichiarante, ed a' testimoni, ed indi nel giorno, mese, ed anno come sopra firmato da noi *Avendo asserito il dichiarante, e testimoni non saper scrivere*

Rosario Idone

This means, literally:

The presentation and declaration just made was done in the presence of *Antonio GIUNTA*, age *thirty*, by vocation *a farmhand*, citizen residing at *Rosolì* and of *Giuseppe TOTI*, age *fifty*, and by vocation *a farmhand*, citizen residing *at the same place*, witnesses who intervened for this act and were brought by *Battesimo LORENZO*

The present act, which we have written according to the laws, was written on the two records, read to the declaring father and the witnesses, on the day, month and year stated above, and signed by us, *the declaring party and the witnesses having affirmed to not know how to write.*

Rosario IDONE

Quite often, as above, it is stated that the father or witnesses cannot write. In such a case, the only signature would be the mayor's. Sometimes, however, the illiterate parties signed with an X. The requirement for the father or midwife to provide two witnesses was true for all acts and is still true today. Note that both birth acts are identical in this second part.

The last part of the birth act is the baptismal statement in the right margin. This information was added by the civil vital records officer on the basis of a note from the parish priest. It does not constitute a baptismal act; that was created by the priest himself. However, the information here constitutes a second copy and can be used. By providing the name of the parish in which the act was performed, this section provides a very valuable clue for continued research. In a large city, such as Rome, where there are hundreds of parishes, knowing the parish of origin is crucial to continuing genealogical research. Even in smaller towns the parish of a *frazione* may be noted, indicating where further research can be pursued.

There is a separate order number for the baptism (*N. d' Ordine*) because not every child was baptized. In this example, the two correspond as number seven. The act then reads:

L'anno milleottocento *trentadue* il dì *ventotto* del mese di *Febbraio*, il Parroco della Chiesa di Rosolì ci a' restituito nel *ventotto* del mese di *Febraio detto anno* il notamento che noi gli abbiamo rimesso nel giorno *diciasette* del mese di *Febraio* anno *1832* del sottoscritto atto di nascita, in pie' del quale a' indicato che il Sagramento del Battesimo e' stato amministrato a *Angela Lorenzo* nel giorno *nove Febraio*

This portion gives all the essential information and is translated as follows:

In the year eighteen *thirty-two,* on the *twenty-eighth* day of the month of *February,* the Parish of the Church of Rosolì returned to us on the *twenty-eighth* of the month of *February* of *said year* the copy that we gave to him on the *seventeenth* of *February* of *1832,* of the below-signed birth act, at the foot of which he indicated that the Sacrament of Baptism was administered to *Angela* LORENZO on the day *nine February.*

The procedure here is rather fascinating. After the mayor had written and signed the birth act, he provided a copy of the act for the family's parish priest. The priest then wrote in and signed when the baptism took place, returning the act to the town vital records office to be transcribed into the civil record. This is an indication of the importance and consideration that was accorded these procedures. Even so, it is interesting to note that the wrong baptismal date is given here. It states that Angela was baptized on the ninth of February—seven days before she was born! Undoubtedly this was an error of transcription; the nineteenth is correct. This example illustrates why it is always better to consult original records. When transcription occurs, errors are often made.

Another point regards the family surname. The father's name is indicated in the birth act as Battesimo Lorenzo. Neither name is in capital letters, and Battesimo is listed first, which, in modern practice, implies that it is the surname. Because Lorenzo is a common first name and Battesimo, which means "baptism," is very unusual, the tendency would be to cite this name as Lorenzo Battesimo. The surname is not mentioned again in the birth act, and only in the baptismal annotation do we find that the surname is, in fact, Lorenzo and not Battesimo—another indication that it is always better to pursue research with care, reading all available information.

The rest of the baptismal annotation concerns bureaucratic procedure and can be read as follows:

In vista di tal notamento dopo averlo cifrato abbiamo disposto che fosse conservato nel volume de' documenti al foglio — 7. Abbiamo inoltre accusato al Parroco la

ricezione del medesimo ed abbiamo formato il presente atto che e' stato iscritto sopra i due registri in margine del corrispondente atto di nascita ed indi abbiamo firmato.
    L'Uffiziale Civile
    Idone

This may be understood as:

Having seen said annotation, and after having transcribed it, we dispose it to be conserved in the volume of the documents at page 7. We also have provided a receipt for the parish priest for having received the same, and have made out the present act, which has been written on both records, in the margin of the corresponding birth act, and we have signed the same.
    Civil vital records officer
    IDONE

Again, note that all Napoleonic civil records were made out in two original copies: one for the town vital records office, now kept at the state archive of each province, and one for the *pretura della repubblica,* which is not available for consultation.

MARRIAGE RECORDS

The state archives usually have two separate volumes for marriage records, though sometimes they are combined. One set of records deals only with the marriage act, called the *atti di matrimonio;* the other set of records, which can be very valuable for genealogical research, includes all the documents that were required by law before the marriage could be performed. These records are usually called *pubblicazioni.* The marriage ceremony was actually the last step in a long bureaucratic process. It was first necessary to make out a document in which the couple declared their intent to be married; it was called the *atto di solenne promessa di celebrare il matrimonio.* Then the bann, called *notificazione,* was written. Finally, several weeks later, the actual marriage was performed. These documents will be examined in detail in the order in which they were created.

Marriage is considered a very important sacrament by the Catholic church and the Italian state. Therefore, it is not taken lightly, even in the bureaucratic sense. To be married the couple has to provide, today, just as they did 150 years ago, a birth or baptismal certificate for each partner. Before the unification of Italy in 1870, it was also necessary to obtain the consent of both fathers of the couple. If a father was dead, his death certificate was also included in the documentation, and it was the duty of the paternal grandfather to give consent. If the grandfather was also deceased, the mother was responsible, and if she was dead another male relative could give permission. In each case the death certificates of the deceased were included in the documents.

The first act, the promise of marriage—*atto di solenne promessa di celebrare il matrimonio*—was made so that all the documents could be checked and the bann made out. Banns, called either *le notificazioni* or *le pubblicazioni*, are a Catholic tradition in which a couple's declaration to marry was posted on the church door and, after the state took control, at city hall for all to see. If one spouse was from another town or parish, the bann was posted in both towns and/or parishes so that both populations could see them. The bann was posted so that, if one of a couple had been promised to someone else or if the man had gotten another woman pregnant, there was time for the families to protest the coming marriage and to stop it before it was performed. It also gave the couple a last moment to reconsider, although very rarely was the promise not followed by a wedding. After a marriage was celebrated, there was no legal recourse, nor was there divorce. Banns are still used in Italy; it is necessary to wait two Sundays and the following Thursday from the posting of the bann outside the city hall before the wedding can take place. In the last century, two Sundays was the normal waiting period, though, as can be seen in the first example (figure 6-3), it could be months.

The first marriage document examined is the *atto di solenne promessa di celebrare il matrimonio*. This translates directly as "the solemn promise to marry act." These acts were numbered in separate chronological order, which does not necessarily correspond to the numbering of the marriage acts. This act is number 1. It begins with the date and the place:

L'anno mille ottocento trentanove il di' *quindici* del mese di *Febbraio* alle ore *venti* avanti di noi *Antonio Ciarrocca* Sindaco ed uffiziale dello Stato Civile del Comune di *Santo Stefano* Distretto di *Aquila* Provincia di Aquila sono comparsi nella casa comunale . . .

This act follows the basic format of the civil records, which should now be familiar. It translates as:

In the year one thousand eight hundred and thirty-nine, on the day *fifteen* of the month *February* at *twenty hundred hours [8 p.m.]* in front of myself, *Antonio CIARROCCA*, mayor and civil vital record officer of the town of *Santo Stefano* in the district of *Aquila* in the province of L'Aquila, in the city hall appeared . . .

The record next provides the names and information about each of the betrothed couple, starting with the name of the groom-to-be.

Antonio Battistone di anni *ventisei* nato in *questo comune* figlio di *Isidoro Battistone* di professione *bifolco* domiciliato in *questo comune* e di *Domenica Gallina* di professione *filatrice* domiciliata in *questo comune*; E *Carmina Pasquale* di anni *ventidue compiuti* nata in *questo comune* domiciliata in *questo comune* figlia di *fu Stefano Pasquale* di professione *bifolco* domiciliato in *questo comune* e di *fu Grazia Ranieri* di professione *filatrice* domiciliata in *questo comune medesimo di santo Stefano*.

This section provides considerable valuable genealogical information about both the couple and their parents. The age, place of birth, and vocation of each is given, as are the names of their parents and the parents' professions. A direct translation is:

Antonio BATTISTONE, of age *twenty-six*, born in *this town*, son of *Isidoro* BATTISTONE, by vocation *farmer*, living in *this town*, and of *Domenica* GALLINA, by vocation *weaver*, living in *this town*; And *Carmina* PASQUALE, of age *twenty-two*, born in *this town* and living in *this town*, daughter of *the deceased Stefano* PASQUALE, by vocation *farmer*, who lived in *this town*, and of the *deceased Grazia* RANIERI, by vocation *weaver*, living in *this same town of Santo Stefano*.

Note that the given name is written before the surname in all of these documents. It is up to the reader to distinguish one from the other. The next part of the document is standardized and concerns the witnesses and the consent of the parents. It reads as follows:

I quali alla presenza de testimoni, che saranno qui' appresso indicati, e da essi prodotti, ci hanno richiesto di ricevere la loro solenne promessa di celebrare avanti alla Chiesa secondo le forme prescritte dal Sacro Concilio di Trento, il matrimonio tra essi loro progettato *coll'assistenza e presenza del padre e madre dello sposo e dando verbalmente avanti de' qui sottoscritti testimoni il di loro pieno consenso, senza assistenza e presenza de genitori e dell'avo paterno della sposa per essere morti.*

This part of the document provides insight into the proceedings necessary for marriage. It was necessary for the couple to appear before a town official with their parents and at least four witnesses who would testify of the promise of marriage and that the parents had given their consent. Today, the presence of the parents is necessary only if the person is under the legal age of eighteen, but it is necessary to have seven witnesses. This section translates as:

The same appeared with their own witnesses, who will be specified hereunder, and have requested for us to

FIGURE 6-3. Napoleonic Solemn Promise to Marry Act of Antonio Battistone and Domenica Gallina, 1839, S. Stefano, L'Aquila

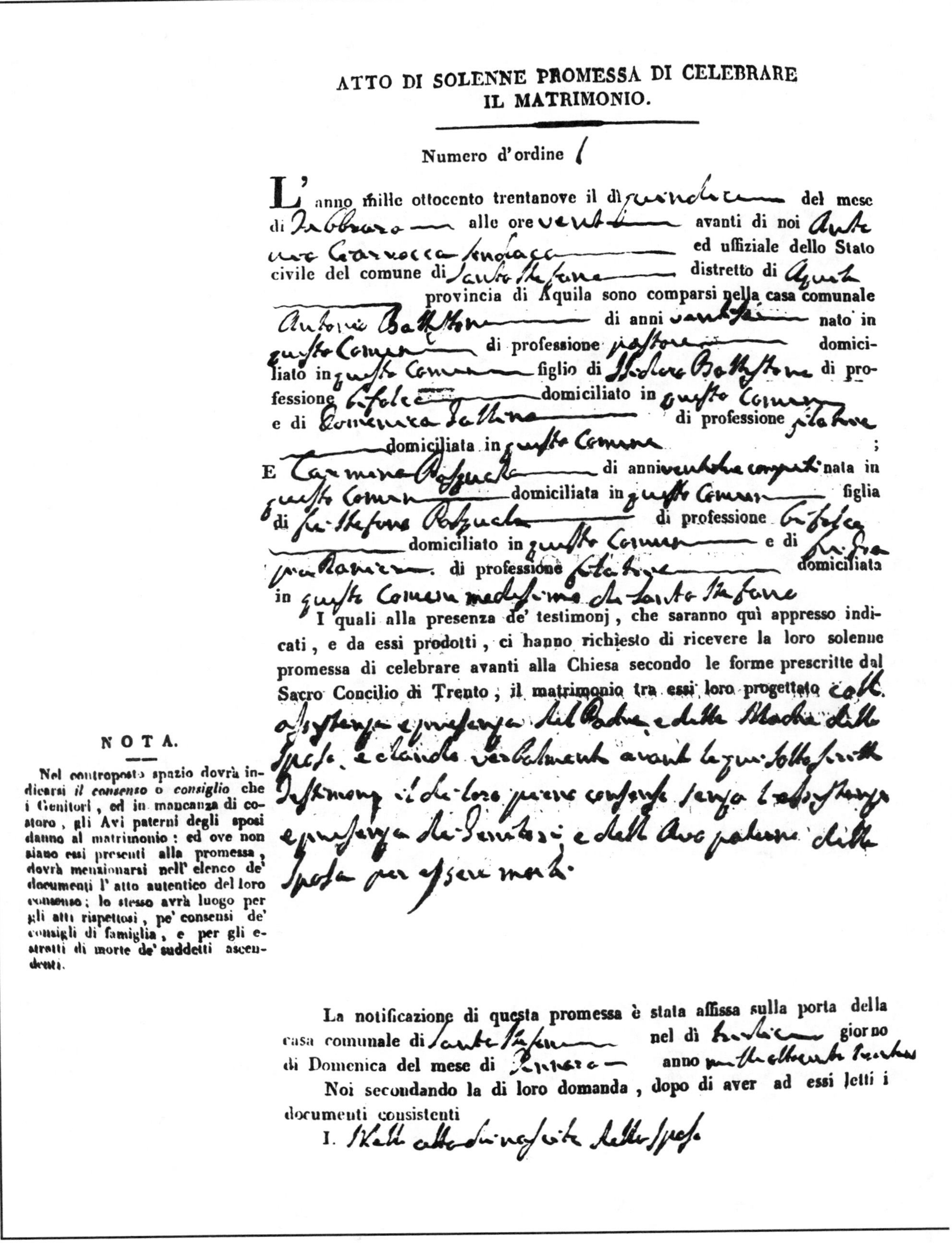

ATTO DI SOLENNE PROMESSA DI CELEBRARE IL MATRIMONIO.

Numero d'ordine *1*

L'anno mille ottocento trentanove il dì *[quindici]* del mese di *[Febbraro]* alle ore *[venti]* avanti di noi *[Antonio Cararocca sindaco]* ed uffiziale dello Stato civile del comune di *[Santo Stefano]* distretto di *[Aquila]* provincia di Aquila sono comparsi nella casa comunale *[Antonio Battistone]* di anni *[ventisei]* nato in *[questo Comune]* di professione *[pastore]* domiciliato in *[questo Comune]* figlio di *[Isidoro Battistone]* di professione *[bifolco]* domiciliato in *[questo Comune]* e di *[Domenica Gallina]* di professione *[filatore]* domiciliata in *[questo Comune]* ;

E *[Carmina Pozzuoli]* di anni *[ventidue compiti]* nata in *[questo Comune]* domiciliata in *[questo Comune]* figlia di *[fu Stefano Pozzuoli]* di professione *[bifolco]* domiciliato in *[questo Comune]* e di *[Maria]* *[Ramieri]* di professione *[filatore]* domiciliata in *[questo Comune medesimo di Santo Stefano]*

I quali alla presenza de' testimonj, che saranno qui appresso indicati, e da essi prodotti, ci hanno richiesto di ricevere la loro solenne promessa di celebrare avanti alla Chiesa secondo le forme prescritte dal Sacro Concilio di Trento; il matrimonio tra essi loro progettato *coll'* *[assistenza e presenza del Padre, e della Madre dello Sposo, e essendo verbalmente avanti li qui sottoscritti testimonj il di loro pieno consenso senza l'assistenza e presenza dei Genitori e della Ava paterna della Sposa per essere morti.]*

La notificazione di questa promessa è stata affissa sulla porta della casa comunale di *[Santo Stefano]* nel dì *[undici]* giorno di Domenica del mese di *[Gennaro]* anno *[mille ottocento trentanove]*

Noi secondando la di loro domanda, dopo di aver ad essi letti i documenti consistenti

I. *[l'atto di nascita della Sposa]*

2 nell'atto di nascita della Sposa

3 Nell'atto di morte del Padre della Sposa

4 Nell'atti di morte della Madre della Sposa

5 Nell'atto di morte dell'Avo paterno della Sposa

6 Nell'atto di notificazione fatta in questo Comune di non essersi state opposizione alcuna al detto matrimonio

7 Nell'atto del seguito matrimonio

ed il capitolo VI del titolo del matrimonio delle leggi civili intorno ai dritti ed obblighi rispettivi degli sposi, abbiamo ricercato da ciascuna delle parti una dopo l'altra la dichiarazione che elleno solennemente promettono di celebrare il matrimonio innanzi alla Chiesa, secondo le forme prescritte dal Sacro Concilio di trento. Di tutto ciò ne abbiamo formato il presente atto in presenza dei quattro testimonj intervenuti alla solenne promessa, cioè:

di *Giuseppe Antonucci* di anni *trentatre* di professione *bracciale* regnicolo, domiciliato in *questo Comune*, di *Giuseppe Perella* di anni *ventisette* di professione *bracciale* regnicolo, domiciliato in *questo Comune*, di *Pietro Ciarrocca* di anni *trentatre* di professione *bracciale* regnicolo, domiciliato in *questo Comune*, e di *Michele Perella* di anni *cinquanta* di professione *bracciale* regnicolo, domiciliato in *questo Comune*

Di questo atto, che è stato iscritto sopra i due registri, abbiamo dato lettura a' testimonj, ed ai futuri sposi, ai quali ne abbiamo altresì date due copie uniformi da noi sottoscritte per essere presentate al Parroco, cui la celebrazione del matrimonio si appartiene, ed indi si è firmato da *per noi dallo sposo, dal Padre dello sposo, da testimonj per aver detto, tanto la sposa che la Madre dello sposo di non saper firmare*

Antonio Ciarrocca sindaco

antonio battistone sposo
isidoro battistone
Giuseppe Antonucci Testimonio
Giuseppo Ricciotelli Testimonio
Io pietro ciarrocca testimonio
morrone dello Sposo Testimonio

receive their solemn promise to be joined together in Church according to the prescribed forms of the Holy Council of Trent, in their planned marriage — *The groom being accompanied by his father and his mother, who have here verbally given their full consent in front of the undersigned witnesses. The bride is not accompanied by the presence of her father or mother or paternal grandfather because they are deceased.*

The note in the left margin is rarely found in these records. It was to remind the town official that the empty space was to be filled in with the consent of the betrothed couple's parents, and it states that if they are dead the grandfather's consent is required; and that in case of the death of any of them, the death certificate was to be included. It also states that if the parents did not appear before the town official when the document was drawn up, a written statement of their consent was to be included with the other acts.

The end of the first page and the beginning of the second list the documents that are included with this act:

La notificazione di questa promessa e' stata affissa sulla porta della casa comunale di *Santo Stefano* nel di' *Tredici giorno* di Domenica del mese di *Gennaio* anno *milleottocentotrentanove*

Noi secondando la di loro domanda, dopo di aver ad essi letti i documenti consistenti
1. nell'atto di nascita dello sposo
2. nell'atto di nascita della sposa
3. nell'atto di morte del padre della sposa
4. nell'atto di morte della madre della sposa
5. nell'atto di morte dell'avo paterno della sposa
6. nell'atto di notificazione fatta in questo comune di esservi stata opposizione alcuna al detto matrimonio
7. nell'atto del seguito matrimonio

The English meaning is:

The notification of this promise [the bann] has been fixed on the door of the city hall of the town of *Santo Stefano* on the day *Thirteen*, a Sunday in the month of *January*, in the year *eighteen thirty-nine*

We have received the request of the same after having read them the following documents
1. birth act of the groom
2. birth act of the bride
3. death act of the bride's father
4. death act of the bride's mother
5. death act of the bride's paternal grandfather
6. The act of the bann made in this township showing that no one was opposed to this marriage
7. The future marriage act

This list of documents outlines the wealth of genealogical information that can be gathered about each family. There are the birth or baptismal acts of both spouses, which provide exact dates. In this case there are also the death records of both parents of the bride and even her paternal grandfather, providing information on three generations of the family. Each of these birth and death documents is found with the marriage acts.

The document continues with the procedures for the marriage, which were read to the engaged couple, and the statement of the witnesses:

ed il capitolo VI del titolo del matrimonio delle leggi civili intorno ai diritti ed obblighi rispettivi degli sposi, abbiamo ricercato da ciascuna delle parti una dopo l'altra la dichiarazione che elleno solennemente promettono di celebrare il matrimonio innanzi alla Chiesa, secondo le forme prescritte dal Sacro Concilio di Trento. Di tutto cio' ne abbiamo formato il presente atto in presenza dei quattro testimoni intervenuti alla solenne promessa, cioe':
di *Giuseppe Antoniacci di anni trentatre di professione falegname regnicolo, domiciliato in questo comune*
di *Giuseppe Rusciolelli di anni ventisette di professione bifolco regnicolo, domiciliato in questo comune*
di *Pietro Ciarrocca di anni trentatre di professione bracciante regnicolo domiciliato in questo comune*
e di *Marco Rusciolelli di anni -cinquanta di professione vaticale regnicolo, domiciliato in questo comune*
Di questo atto, che e' stato iscritto sopra i due registri, abbiamo dato lettura a testimoni, ed ai futuri sposi, ai quali ne abbiamo altresi' date due copie uniformi da noi sottoscritte per essere presentate al Parroco, cui la celebrazione del matrimonio si appartiene, ed indi si e' firmato da *per noi dallo sposo, dal padre dello sposo, da testimoni per aver detto, tanto la sposa che la madre della sposa, di non saper firmare.*

Translated:

(having read to those present the documents) and chapter VI of the marriage civil laws regarding the rights and obligations of both bride and groom, and having obtained from each of the couple a solemn declaration that they intend to be united in marriage in the Church, according to the prescribed format of the Holy Council of Trent; from all of this we have created the present act in the presence of the four witnesses who have taken part of this solemn promise, that is:
Giuseppe ANTONIACCI, *age thirty-three and by vocation a carpenter, a citizen living in this commune*
Giuseppe RUSCIOLELLI, *age twenty-seven and by vocation a farmer, citizen and living in this commune*

Pietro CIARROCCA, *age thirty-three and by vocation a farm hand, citizen and living in this commune*
Marco RUSCIOLELLI, *age fifty and by vocation a water carrier, citizen and living in this commune*
This act has been written on two separate records, all parts read to the witnesses and to the future spouses, to whom we have also given two exact copies, written by us, to be presented to the parish priest, who will perform the marriage, and the same has been signed by *us for the groom, the father of the groom, the witnesses, the bride and the mother of the bride, as all declared to not know how to sign their names.*

[Underneath is the signature of each, written by the mayor.]

Aside from valuable genealogical information concerning the two spouses and their families, this act also provides insight into the proceedings surrounding the marriage and the relationship between the state and the church. The rite of marriage belonged to the church but, for the first time, the state, under Napoleon, interceded in what had been a religious matter, enacting laws that regulated both the marriage itself and the rights and responsibilities of each spouse within the marriage. Marriage had become a civil affair. Before the marriage could be performed in a religious ceremony, it also had to be performed by the mayor for the state. These requirements were revolutionary and again demonstrate the great changes wrought by Napoleon. Note also that the Italian language was used in all of these documents, even though it was not the spoken language of the people and only a few knew how to read and write it. The use of Italian was a strong factor in the eventual unification of Italy.

Napoleon respected the power of the Roman Catholic church, and civil law was based mostly on existing ecclesiastical law. However, the church did not always placidly accept or recognize this new civil power. Considerable protest arose within the church, especially after the Italian state was formed in 1865 and assumed the right to regulate the conduct and recording of births, marriages, and deaths. Particularly in the south, where the new government was never popular, this protest took the form of actual boycotting of these civil powers. For example, marriage acts for many married couples will not be found among the civil vital records of the expected time period; however, often the same marriages were recorded in the civil records years after children were born. In these cases the couple had married in the church but never performed the civil procedures for marriage. Consequently, the state would declare the marriage illegal, all resulting children being considered illegitimate. In the end the state won the struggle because illegitimate children could not inherit, and the state controlled the notaries and property transactions. The state could exercise other civil powers as well. As a result, these couples eventually registered their marriages with the state and had to legally recognize their children as their own to legitimize them. Thus, among records for the period from 1865 to around 1885, it is not uncommon to find records of these civil marriages, including documentation about each child, when they were born, and the parental recognition to legitimize them. In the parish records the same marriages may be recorded as having taken place years before, and in them all of the resulting children are recognized as legitimate.

It is fitting, then, that the last part of this document (the column on the right side) concerns the annotation of the wedding performed in the church, demonstrating the coordination between the state and the church. As stated in the last paragraph of the document above, two copies of the solemn promise to marry act were sent to the parish priest, together with a certificate authorizing the priest to perform the marriage. In turn, the parish priest made out a declaration of the actual wedding ceremony on one of the copies that he had received from the town office. This, then, was presented to the mayor and transcribed onto this act in this space. This column reads as follows:

INDICAZIONE
Della seguita celebrazione Canonica del matrimonio
Num. d'ordine 1
L'anno mille ottocento trentanove il di' *cinque* del mese di *Aprile* il Parroco di *Santo Stefano* ci ha rimessa una delle copie della controscritta promessa, in pie' della quale ha certificato, che la celebrazione del matrimonio e' seguita nel giorno *cinque* del mese di *Aprile* anno Mille ottocento trentanove alla presenza de' testimoni *Domenico Colajezzi, Luca Antoniacci*
In vista di essa noi abbiamo disteso il presente notamento, e dopo di averla cifrata abbiamo disposto, che fosse la copia anzidetta conservata nel volume dei documenti al foglio 7
Abbiamo inoltre accusato al Parroco la ricezione del medesimo, ed abbiamo sottoscritto il presente atto ch'e' stato iscritto su i due registri.
L'uffiziale dello stato civile.
Antonio Ciarrocca

This section provides the date of the marriage in the parish and is translated as:

NOTICE
of the celebration of the Canonical marriage
Order number 1
In the year eighteen thirty-nine on day *five* of the month of *April*, the Parish Priest of *Santo Stefano* has sent us a copy of the here-written promise, at the bottom of which he has certified that the celebration of the marriage took place on day *five* of the month of *April*, in the year one thousand eight hundred and thirty-nine, In the presence of the witnesses, *Domenico*

COLAJEZZI, *Luca* ANTONIACCI
Considering this, we have written the present note, and after having done so, we disposed the copy from the parish to be conserved in the volume of documents as page 7.
We have also acknowledged to the parish priest to have received his copy, and we have written the present act on both the records.
Town civil record officer.
Antonio CIARROCCA

Noteworthy is the use of the first person plural by the mayor in referring to himself. This was a common practice among all civil officers; the "we" or "us" refer to him as an officer of the state. It is also fascinating to regard how each step of the process was carefully documented with written copies of every document, each of which had to be acknowledged and preserved.

The next document shown (figure 6-4) is an example of the certificate that the mayor filled out and sent to the parish priest, accompanied by the two copies of the solemn promise to marry act. This certificate indicated that the betrothed couple had made the promise and presented all necessary documentation required for marriage, and it constituted the official civil permission that allowed the priest to proceed with the marriage. (Because no genealogical information is provided, it has not been translated.)

Next are shown two examples of banns that were made out by the town office (figures 6-5 and 6-6). Because very few people knew how to read, the bann normally was read aloud and then were posted on the door of the town hall. The normal practice was to read the bann aloud after mass on Sunday; this was why at least two Sundays had to pass after the promise before the marriage could take place. The second format illustrated (figure 6-6) is that most often found in the marriage documents, so it will be examined in detail and translated. This example concerns the proposed marriage of Isidoro Battistone, the father of Antonio Battistone, whose marriage promise was examined earlier (figure 6-3). (The marriage act of Isidoro will also be examined to demonstrate that the procedures and forms used were the same throughout this period, which spanned two generations.) The first part of this act reads:

Atto di pubblicazione del Matrimonio.

Provincia *di Aquila*   Distretto *di Aquila*
Comune *di Santo Stefano*   Quartiere *della Piazza*

Oggi giorno di Domenica, che *sono le sette* del mese *di Aprile* corrente dell'anno mille ottocento *undici* ad ore *quattordici*
Io qui sottoscritto Cancelliere (usciere) di questa municipalita', per esecuzione dell'articolo 63 del Codice

Civile, mi sono portato avanti la porta principale della residenza della municipalita', ed ho fatta la *seconda* pubblicazione del matrimonio, che vogliono contrarre

Or:

Marriage Bann

Province *L'Aquila*   District *L'Aquila*
Township *Santo Stefano*   Neighborhood *Town Square*

Today, on a Sunday on the *seventh* of the month of *April* of the year eighteen *eleven* at the hour *fourteen hundred* [2 p.m.]
I, the here undersigned Clerk (usher) of this municipality, in execution of article 63 of the Civil Code of laws, went before the main door of the town hall, and administered the second bann of marriage that they desire to contract between

As can be seen, it was standard in all towns to read the bann on a Sunday. Only the hour was left up to the town official. Also, it can be deduced that this procedure, as every other step in the wedding process, was dictated by law. The bann was read before the main door of the town hall, which in most towns was directly in front of the town square. The parish church was usually on the opposite side of the square.

The next part restates information about the spouses:

Isidoro Battistone
di professione bifolco
di anni dicianove non compiuti, minore
assistito dal di lui Padre Leonardo Battistone di professione bifolco, di anni sessantadue e dalla di lui Madre Domenica Leone, di professione tessitrice di anni cinquantasei domicilianti in questo comune di Santo Stefano, quartiere della Piazza
e'
Domenica Maria Orazia Gallina
di professione tessitrice
di anni ventitre, non compiuti, Maggiore assistita anche dal di lei Padre Pasqualantonio Gallina di professione vaticale di anni sessanta e dalla di lei Madre Lucia Chiarelli, di professione tessitrice di anni cinquantanove domicilianti in questo comune di Santo Stefano quartiere della Villa.

Here is interesting personal information that is rarely found in other records.

Isidoro BATTISTONE
by vocation a farmer
of age nineteen not yet achieved, a minor

FIGURE 6-4. Certificate From the Civil Vital Records Officer Authorizing the Parish Priest to Perform the Ecclesiastical Marriage Ceremony

CERTIFICATO

39.

DELL' UFFIZIALE DELLO STATO CIVILE.

Da presentarsi al Parroco per la celebrazione del Matrimonio.

L'uffiziale dello Stato Civile del Comune di *Santo Stefano* certifica, che gli sposi *Michelangelo ...* ... *di questo Comune, e Maria Francesca Colajazzo ...* ...

hanno adempito a tutte le solennità prescritte dal Codice Civile, per la contrazione del di loro matrimonio, nei termini del Real Decreto dei 16 Giugno 1815, e che se n'è formato l'atto corrispondente nella casa comunale, in data de' *vent uno Ottobre*   In conseguenza essi sono rinviati innanzi al Paroco, conformemente alle disposizioni dello stesso decreto, per essere congiunti in Matrimonio, secondo le forme prescritte dal Concilio di Trento.

Dato in *S. Stefano li 21 Ottobre 1817*

Firma dell' Uffiziale

Luogo del Sugello Comunale

FIGURE 6-5. First Marriage Bann, S. Stefano, L'Aquila

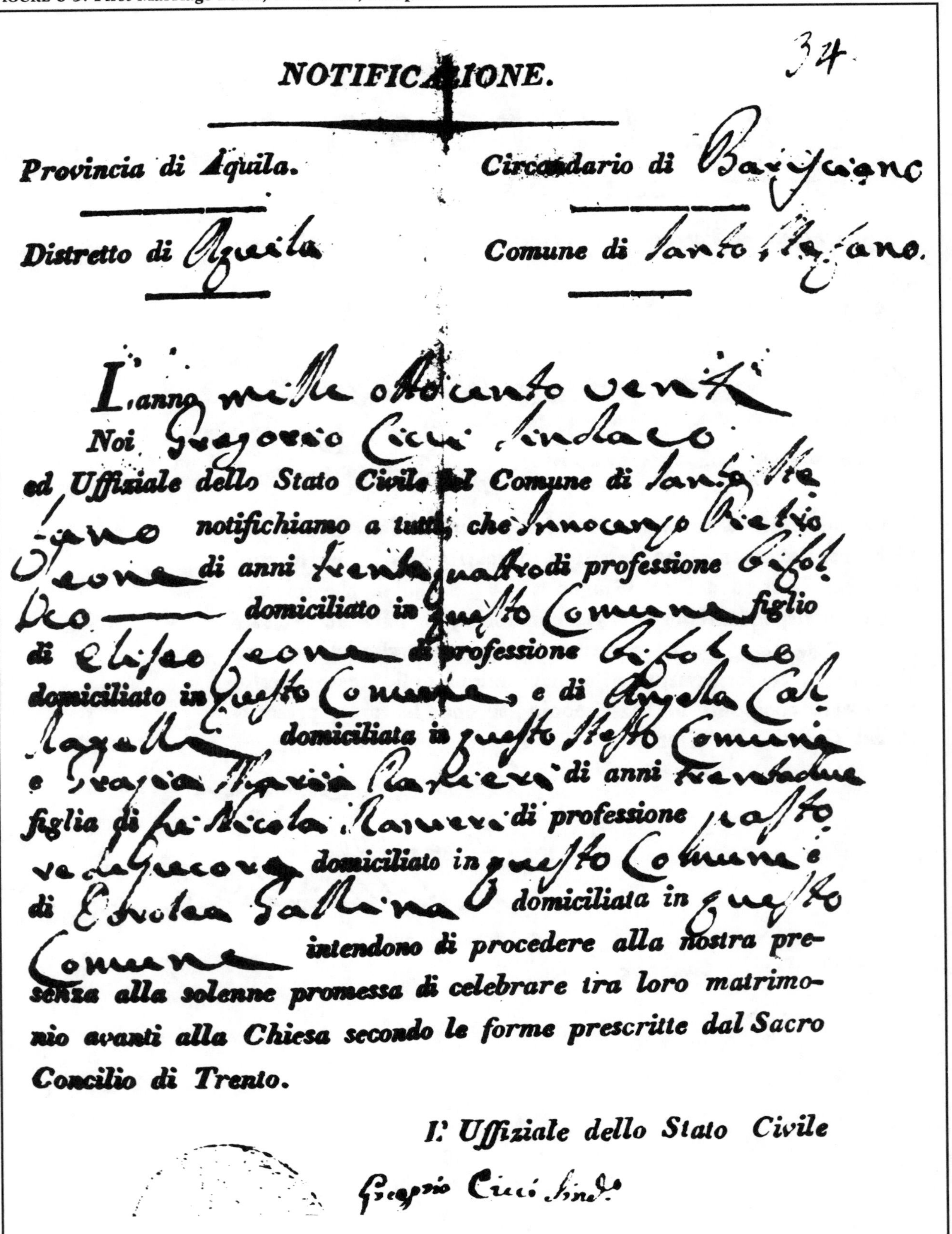

NOTIFICAZIONE.

34.

Provincia di Aquila.   Circondario di *Barisciano*

Distretto di *Aquila*   Comune di *Santo Stefano*

L'anno *mille ottocento venti*
Noi *Gregorio Cicci Sindaco*
ed Uffiziale dello Stato Civile *del* Comune di *Santo Ste-*
fano notifichiamo a tutti, che *Innocenzo Pietro*
Leone di anni *trentaquattro* di professione *Bifol-*
co domiciliato in *questo Comune* figlio
di *Eliseo Leone* di professione *Bifolco*
domiciliato in *questo Comune*, e di *Angela Cal-*
lagalli domiciliata in *questo stesso Comune*
e *Grazia Maria Barbieri* di anni *trentadue*
figlia di *fu Nicola Barbieri* di professione *pasto-*
re di Greco domiciliato in *questo Comune* e
di *Ercolea Gallina* domiciliata in *questo*
Comune intendono di procedere alla nostra presenza alla solenne promessa di celebrare tra loro matrimonio avanti alla Chiesa secondo le forme prescritte dal Sacro
Concilio di Trento.

I.° Uffiziale dello Stato Civile

Gregorio Cicci Sindaco

FIGURE 6-6. Second Marriage Bann, S. Stefano, L'Aquila

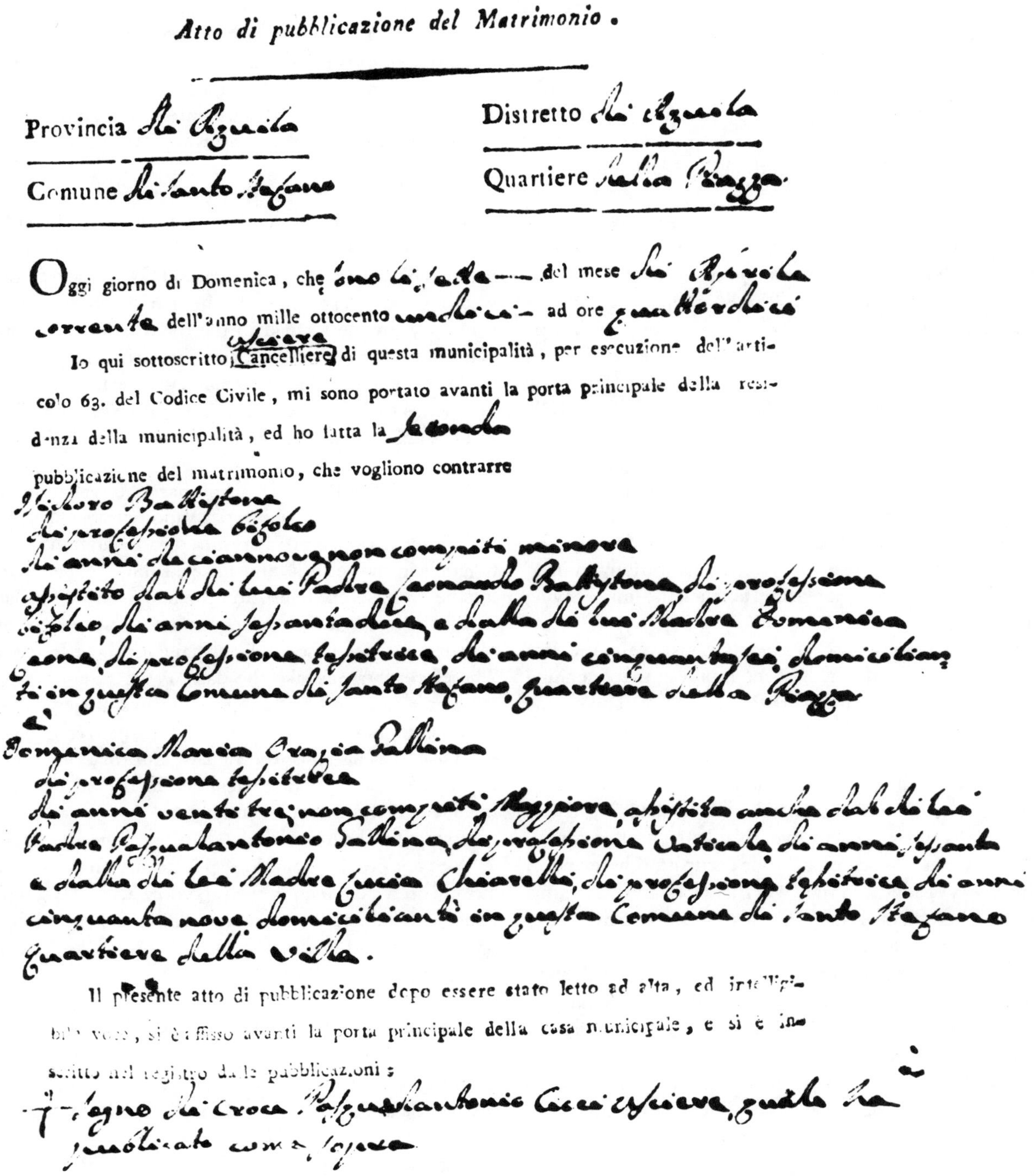

Atto di pubblicazione del Matrimonio.

Provincia *di Aquila*   Distretto *di Aquila*

Comune *di Santo Stefano*   Quartiere *della Piazza*

Oggi giorno di Domenica, che *sono le sette* — del mese *di Aprile*
corrente dell'anno mille ottocento *undici* — ad ore *quattordici*
Io qui sottoscritto Cancelliere di questa municipalità, per esecuzione dell'articolo 63. del Codice Civile, mi sono portato avanti la porta principale della residenza della municipalità, ed ho fatta la *seconda*
pubblicazione del matrimonio, che vogliono contrarre

Isidoro Battistone
di professione bifolco
di anni diciannove non compiti minore
assistito dal di lui Padre Fernando Battistone di professione
bifolco, di anni sessantadieci, e dalla di lui Madre Domenica
Sona, di professione tessitrice, di anni cinquantasei, domiciliati
ti in questa Comune di Santo Stefano, quartiere della Piazza

e
Domenica Maria Grazia Salbina
di professione tessitrice
di anni venti tre non compiti Maggiore, assistita anche dal di lei
Padre Pasqualantonio Salbina, di professione articale, di anni sessanta
e dalla di lei Madre Grazia Chiavelli, di professione tessitrice, di anni
cinquanta nove domiciliati in questa Comune di Santo Stefano
Quartiere della Villa.

Il presente atto di pubblicazione dopo essere stato letto ad alta, ed intelligibile voce, si è affisso avanti la porta principale della casa municipale, e si è inscritto nel registro delle pubblicazioni:

+ segno di croce Pasqualantonio Cicci Esquiere, quale ha
pubblicato come sopra

assisted by his Father, Leonardo BATTISTONE, by voca-tion a farmer, age sixty-two, and by his Mother, Domenica LEONE, by vocation a weaver, age fifty-six, living in this town of Santo Stefano in the Town Square neighborhood.
and
Domenica Maria Orazia GALLINA
by vocation a weaver,
of age twenty-three not yet achieved, of legal age, assisted by her Father, Pasqualantonio GALLINA, by vocation a water carrier, age sixty, and by her Mother, Lucia CHIARELLI, by vocation a weaver, age fifty-nine, living in this town of Santo Stefano in the Villa neighborhood.

There are several interesting points to note in this informa-tion. Isidoro's age is given as "nineteen not yet achieved," even though he is still eighteen and his birthday is several months away. Although not often, sometimes the age was stated based on the age the person would become during the year, though the birthday might have been much later in the year. The same is true for his betrothed, Domenica. (The legal age for marriage in Italy, even from the Middle Ages, has been twenty-one; only in the 1970s was it changed to eighteen. Today, an individual cannot marry if still a minor without the written consent of at least one parent.) During the time of this example, parental or family consent was required for a marriage to be performed. Marriage was an important social and economic institution; in fact, marriages were often arranged by families, the union having little to do with love.

Santo Stefano is a rocky, mountainous area at the base of the Gran Sasso, the highest mountain in the Apennine range in central Italy; it towers to 10,000 feet. The people there have traditionally subsisted mainly by farming and raising sheep. Even those who were farmers usually had some sheep and goats, and all the women worked as weavers. The Abruzzo region, where L'Aquila is located, is still famous today for its woven blankets and bed covers. Because water was scarce, a major occupation here and in other areas of southern Italy was that of water carrier; this person would fill huge vats with fresh spring water each day and sell it in a village.

This document also provides the name of the neighbor-hood in which the family lived; it is the only act among these examples that does so. It indicates that one family was from the main square, while the other lived near a small castle called the Villa. For a small town like Santo Stefano such information might make little difference but, in a large city like Naples or Rome, these could be clues that encour-age further research.

The bann ends with its reading:

Il presente atto di pubblicazione dopo essere letto ad alta, ed intelligibile voce, si e' affisso avanti la porta principale della casa municipale, e si e' iscritto nel

registro delle pubblicazioni:
† segno di croce Pasqualantonio Cicci usciere quale ha pubblicato come sopra

Or:

The present act of publication, after having been read aloud with an understandable voice, was affixed on the main door of the town hall, and the same was written in the record book of the banns:
† sign of the cross for Pasqualantonio CICCI, the usher who communicated the above bann

This statement confirms that the bann was read to the population and then posted outside for all to see for at least two weeks before the marriage, all necessary procedures before the marriage could take place. Though the traditional wedding was performed in the parish church, a civil ceremony was performed in the town hall by the mayor. Naturally, the church wedding was recognized by the Catholic church, while the marriage performed by the mayor was the official civil act. This procedure is still true in Italy, and the two ceremonies are usually performed the same morning.

Finally comes the actual act of marriage, which provides the exact date of the civil marriage and repeats much of the same information. Since all of this documentation is found together in the records, and since a similar format is used for the promise, the bann, and the marriage act, the latter usually being the last document found, unwary or hurried researchers often mistake the promise for the marriage act. Therefore, they mistake the date of the promise for the marriage date and fail to properly examine all of the documents. Besides coming away with the wrong date of marriage, they also miss the valuable information provided in the other acts, among them the birth and death acts included with the documentation.

Except for the marriage date, the marriage act (figure 6-7) does not provide genealogical information that has not already been examined in the preceding acts. The complete document does, however, provide additional insight into the laws and procedures that surround this act, so it will be examined in detail. The act begins:

Num. 1 Atto della celebrazione del Matrimonio

Provincia *di Aquila*   Distretto *di Aquila*
Comune *di Santo Stefano*   Quartiere *della Piazza*

Oggi che *sono le quattordici* del mese di *Aprile* del anno mille ottocento *undici* ad ore *diciannove*
Nella casa municipale, avanti di noi incaricato degli atti dello stato civile ed alla presenza di quattro testimoni richiesti dal presente atto dell'articolo 75 del Codice Civile sono comparsi:

Isidoro Battistone
> *di professione bifolco*
> *di anni diciannove non compiuti minore*
> *nativo di questo comune di Santo Stefano assistito dal di lui Padre Leonardo Battistone di professione bifolco di anni sessanta due e dalla di lui Madre Domenica Leone di professione tessitrice di anni cinquanta sei domicilianti in questo comune di Santo Stefano quartiere della Piazza, e*

Domenica Maria Orazia Gallina
> *di professione tessitrice*
> *di anni venti tre non compiuti, maggiore*
> *nativa di questo comune di Santo Stefano assistita anche dal di lei Padre Pasqualantonio Gallina, di professione vaticale di anni sessanta, e dalla di lei Madre Lucia Chiarelli tessitrice d'anni cinquantanove, domicilianti in questo comune quartiere della villa e che loro rispettivi genitori hanno prestato il di loro consenso a norma degli articoli 148,149,150,159 e 160 del Codice Civile*

The first part is very similar to the bann, and the personal information is exactly the same:

Number 1 Act of the celebration of Marriage

Province *L'Aquila*	District *L'Aquila*
Commune *Santo Stefano*	Neighborhood *Town Square*

Today, *the fourteenth* of the month of *April* of the year eighteen-*eleven*, at the hour *nineteen-hundred* [7 p.m.] In the town hall in front of us, the civil vital records officer, and in the presence of four witnesses needed for the present act, as stated in article 75 of the Civil Code, appeared:

Isidoro BATTISTONE
> *by vocation a farmer*
> *of age 19 not yet reached, a minor*
> *native to the town of Santo Stefano, assisted by his Father, Leonardo* BATTISTONE, *by vocation a farmer, age sixty-two, and by his Mother, Domenica* LEONE, *by vocation a weaver, age fifty-six, all living in this town of Santo Stefano in the Town Square neighborhood, and*

Domenica Maria Orazia GALLINA
> *by vocation a weaver*
> *of age twenty-three not yet reached, of legal age,*
> *native to this town of Santo Stefano, assisted also by her Father, Pasqualantonio* GALLINA, *by vocation a water carrier, age sixty, and by her Mother, Lucia* CHIARELLI, *a weaver, age fifty-nine, all living in this town of Santo Stefano in the Villa neighborhood, and that their respective parents have all given formal consent according to the norms of the articles 148, 149, 150, 159 and 160 of the Civil Code*

Not always was all of this information provided on the form. Much of the content was left up to the town official, but normally there was little variation. An item found in some marriage documents is *stato civile*—the civil status of the person as single or previously married. If either of the spouses was a widow or widower from an earlier marriage, this fact was noted in all of these documents, along with the name of the previous spouse. The death certificate of the first spouse would probably be included among the documentation as well. Otherwise, this is the standard format for the marriage certificate.

The remainder of the marriage act reads:

Essi sposi ci hanno richiesto di procedere alla celebrazione del matrimonio tra loro progettato, essendosene gia' fatte le pubblicazioni, ordinate coll'articolo 63 del Codice Civile: la prima nel di trent'uno del Mese del marzo dell'anno mille ottocento undici alle ore quattordici giorno di domenica, e la seconda nel di' sette Aprile di detto anno mille ottocento undici alle ore quattordici anche giorno di domenica.
Non essendovi opposizioni al detto Matrimonio, annuendo alle loro domande, si e' fatta la lettura dei documenti presentati, e richiesti dalla legge relativamente al loro stato, ed alla formalità del matrimonio, egualmente che del esposto del titolo del matrimonio intorno a' diritti, e doveri de rispettivi sposi.
Abbiamo ricevuto da ciascuna delle parti contraenti l'una dopo l'altra la dichiarazione, che elleno si vogliono prendere rispettivamente per marito, e moglie:
In nome della legge perciò abbiamo pronunciato e pronunciamo, che i sopradetti *Isidoro Battistone e Domenica Maria Orazia Gallina*
sono uniti in matrimonio.

This part, which documents the actual marriage ceremony, is translated as:

The couple has requested that we proceed with the marriage ceremony that they have planned, having already published the bann, ordered by article 63 of the Civil Code, the first of which
on the day thirty-one of the month of March of the year eighteen-eleven, at fourteen-hundred hours [2 p.m.] on a Sunday, and the second on the day seven April of the same year, eighteen-eleven, at fourteen-hundred [2 p.m.], also on a Sunday.
There not being any opposition to said Marriage from the bann, accepting their request and reading all the documents that have been presented, and the requirements of the law relative to their new civil status, the formalities of marriage, and reading from the text the marital rights and duties of each spouse.
We received from each of the contracting partners, one after the other, their declaration that they desire to take

FIGURE 6-7. Marriage Act of Isidoro Battistone and Domenica Maria Orazia Gallina, 1811, S. Stefano, L'Aquila

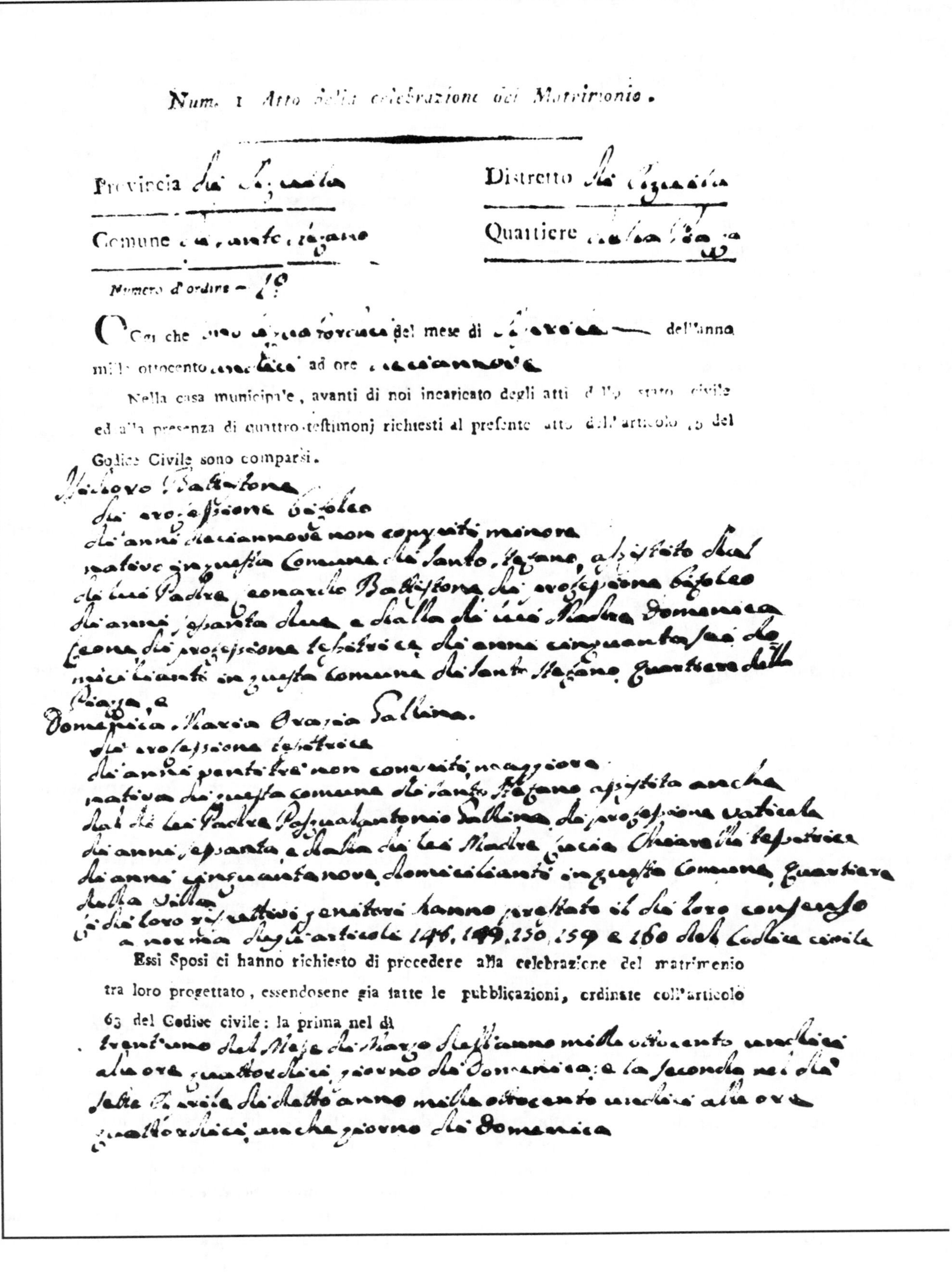

Non essendovi opposizioni al detto Matrimonio, annunziato alle loro Domicilie, nè _____ fatta la lettura de'documenti presentati, e richiesti dalla legge relativamente al loro stato, ed alla formalità del matrimonio, egualmente che del *capo presente del titolo del matrimonio intorno a' dritti, e doveri de' rispettivi sposi.*

Abbiamo ricevuto da ciascuna delle parti contraenti, l'una dopo l'altra la dichiarazione, che elleno si vogliono prendere rispettivamente per marito, e moglie:

In nome della legge perciò abbiamo pronunziato e pronunziamo, che i sopradetti

Teodoro Battistone, e Domenica Maria Grazia Salvina

sono uniti in matrimonio.

Le persone intervenute nel presente atto per testimonj sono:

_____ Salvina
_____
_____ professione Chierico
domiciliante in questa Concezione, quartiere _____ in _____
che ha dichiarato _____ esser parente _____ grazia, ma _____
_____ ventuno
_____ professione Sartore
domiciliante in questa Concezione, quartiere Borgno
che ha dichiarato non esser parente.
_____ Colavincenzo
_____ quaranta
_____ professione sartore
domiciliante in questa Concezione, quartiere della Pi____
che ha dichiarato non esser parente. _____
Donato Macca
_____ trenta
_____ professione Sartore
domiciliante in questa Concezione, quartiere Borgno
che ha dichiarato non esser parente.

Dopo essersene fatta del presente atto la lettura agli Sposi, ed a testimonj, l'hanno con noi sottoscritto.

+ Segno di croce di Teodoro Battistone _____
+ Segno di Croce di Domenica Grazia Maria Salvina sposa.
_____ testimonio presente.
Vincenzo _____ Felice _____ testimonio presente
Donato Colavincenzo _____ testimonio presente
+ Segno di Croce di Donato _____ testimonio presente
_____
_____

each other for husband and wife.

In the name of the law, therefore, we pronounced, and do here pronounce, that the above stated *Isidoro BATTISTONE and Domenica Maria Orazia GALLINA* are united in marriage.

The document continues with a list of the four witnesses and personal information about each, then the signatures of the newlyweds and the witnesses.

This examination of the marriage process demonstrates the social, legal, and religious importance given to marriage. Divorce became legal in Italy only in 1970, and in the period of these documents it was unheard of. The secular tradition of the bride's dowry and the groom's providing a home and usually land also made marriage an important economic and social institution.

The marriage documents represent one of the most important genealogical resources. The wealth of information found in them for at least two generations of ancestors is unequaled in any other act, except the *certificato della famiglia storico* of the commune (see chapter 5). Unfortunately, in the Napoleonic era there was no equivalent to this last certificate, so the final document to be examined is the death act.

DEATH RECORDS

In the Napoleonic records, the death act is very similar to the equivalent act in the Italian civil records, which has already been discussed (chapter 5). No civil burial records were kept; these were left to the parishes, but Napoleon did institute some fundamental changes in the laws concerning burial. Until the early 1800s, when Napoleon took control, cemeteries were usually next to the parish churches in the middle of the towns and cities. Members of some of the more illustrious families were buried in the basement of the church itself, and some families, particularly the nobles and large landowners, had family burial plots on their own land. Napoleon halted these practices, deeming them unhygienic, and required that all cemeteries be outside the city limits and that every person be buried in the cemetery within two days of death. This rule is still valid for new cemeteries, but many of the older ones that had been outside city limits have since been incorporated into the cities with the expansion and growth of the larger communities.

The death act provides the least amount of new information about an ancestor. Nevertheless, no good research is complete without the death records of ancestors to help confirm the family line. (For example, I saw a project for which generations of research had been compiled starting from an ancestor who, it was eventually found, had actually died in infancy and thus was of the wrong family line.) The Napoleonic death records can also provide information about the generation that was born and married before the

beginning of civil records. Thus, one or even two generations of ancestors who were born before 1809 but who died in this period can be identified through these records. When there are no earlier parish records, or for those who are interested in data that wouldn't appear in the parish records, such as the deceased's vocation, death records are vital. Thus, a proper study of the Napoleonic civil death acts is useful when researching a family history.

The first document shown (figure 6-8) is a typical example of a death act. Different formats can be found, as in the second death act included (figure 6-9), but the information provided is essentially the same. Both of these examples are from the town of Santo Stefano, but the form is the same throughout Italy.

ATTO DI MORTE

Num. *ventuno* D'Ordine *21*

L'anno mille ottocento ventuno il dì *tredici* del mese di *Agosto* alle ore *venti* avanti di noi *Pietro Santavicca Sindaco* ed uffiziale dello Stato Civile del Comune di *Santo Stefano* Provincia di Aquila sono comparsi *Simone Cicci* di anni *cinquant'otto,* di professione *Vaticale,* Regnicolo domiciliato in *questo Comune nella Piazza* e *Giuseppe Angelo Cataldo* di anni *quarantanove* di professione *chirurgo,* Regnicolo domiciliato in *questo Comune nella Torre,* i quali hanno dichiarato che nel giorno *tredici* del mese di *Agosto* anno *corrente* alle ore *sedici* è morta *nella propria sua casa Innocenza Chiarelli vedova del fu Sabato Colajezzi, di anni sessanta* nata in *questo comune* di professione *filatrice* domiciliata in *questo Comune* figlia di *fu Severino Chiarelli* di professione *pastore* domiciliato in *questo comune* e di *fu Maria Leone* di professione *filatrice* domiciliata in *questo medesimo Comune di Santo Stefano*

Per esecuzione della legge ci siamo trasferiti insieme co' detti testimoni presso la persona defunta, e ne abbiamo riconosciuta la sua effettiva morte. Abbiamo indi formato il presente atto, e abbiamo iscritto sopra i due registri, e datane lettura ai dichiaranti, si' e' nel giorno, mese ed anno come sopra segnato da noi, *e da dichiaranti giurati.*

Santavicca

Simone Cicci dichiara come sopra

Giuseppe Cataldo dichiara come sopra

   Cifra del Giudice Delegato,

As with the civil birth record, some researchers, not familiar with this act and working hurriedly, mistake the first date for the death date and a witness for the deceased ancestor. Both the death date and the name of the deceased always appear in the middle of the act. This is apparent with the translation of the act:

FIGURE 6-8. Death Act of Innocenza Chiarelli, 1821, S. Stefano, L'Aquila

ATTO DI MORTE.

NUM.*ventiuno* D'ORDINE. *28*

L'anno mille ottocento ventuno *il dì tredici* del mese di *Agosto* alle ore *venti* avanti di noi *Pietro Santavicca Sindaco* ed Uffiziale dello Stato Civile del Comune di *Santo Stefano* Provincia di Aquila sono comparsi *Simone Cicci* di anni *cinquantotto* di professione *vaticalaio* Regnicolo, domiciliato in *questo Comune nella Rapa* e *Giuseppe Angelo Cato Rob* di anni *quarantanove* di professione *Chirurgo* Regnicolo, domicilia to in *questo Comune nella Torra* i quali han dichiarato, che nel giorno *tredici* del mese di *Agosto* anno corrente alle ore *sedici* è morta nella propria sua Casa *Innocenza Chiarelli vedova del fu Sabato Colajezzi de anni sessanta* nata in *questo Comune* di professione *filatrice* domiciliata in *questo Comune* figlia di *fu Severino Chiarelli* di professione *pastore* domiciliato in *questo Comune* e di *fu Maria Leone* di professione *filatrice* domiciliata in *questo medesimo Comune di Santo Stefano.*

Per esecuzione della legge ci siamo trasferiti insieme co' detti testimonj presso la persona defunta, e ne abbiamo riconosciuta la sua effettiva mor- te. Abbiamo indi formato il presente atto, che abbiamo inscritto sopra i due Registri, e datane lettura ai dichiaranti, si è nel giorno, mese, ed anno come sopra segnato da noi. *e la dei quaranti verbanti*

Santavicca

Simone Cicci dichiaro come sopra

Cifra del Giudice Delegato,

DEATH ACT

Number *twenty-one* in order *21*

In the year eighteen twenty-one on the day *thirteen* of the month of *August* at the hour *twenty [8 p.m.]* before us, *Pietro* SANTAVICCA, *Mayor* and Vital Records Officer for the commune of *Santo Stefano*, Province of L'Aquila, appeared *Simone* CICCI, age *fifty-eight*, by vocation *Water Carrier*, citizen living in *this commune at the Town Square*, and *Giuseppe Angelo* CATALDO, age *forty-nine*, by vocation *surgeon*, citizen living in *this commune at the Tower*, both of whom declared that on the day *thirteen* of the month of *August* of the *current year at the hour sixteen [4 p.m.] Innocenza* CHIARELLI, *widow of Sabato* COLAJEZZI, *age sixty, died in her own home*, born *in this commune*, by vocation *a spinner* and living *in this commune*, daughter of *the deceased Severino* CHIARELLI, by vocation *a shepherd* living in *this commune* and of *the deceased Maria* LEONE, by vocation *a spinner* living in *this same commune of Santo Stefano*

To obey the law we visited together with the witnesses the deceased person, and we witnessed that she was in all effects dead. We therefore have formed the present act, which has been written in both records and, having read the same to the witnesses, yes, on the same day, month, and year as written above by us, *and signed by the witnesses declaring.*

SANTAVICCA,
Simone CICCI *declares as above*
Giuseppe CATALDO *declares as above*
Signature of the Delegated Judge

The next example of the death act (figure 6-9), from just three years earlier, has a different format, but the procedure was essentially the same. Two witnesses testified before the mayor regarding the death, and the mayor personally visited the home to witness the death. (It was rare for someone to die in a hospital. Hospitals did not have good reputations and were often created as places to segregate the ill and dying during the plagues. Thus, they had a reputation as places to be avoided—not in which to be cured!) In this example, it was left to the town official to write appropriate information about the deceased rather than just fill in blanks. As a result, much less information is provided. On this form is stated, after the date, the name Elisabetta Florio, widow of Marco Santavicca and daughter of the deceased Giovanni Florio and Lucia Ruscitti. Unfortunately, her age and the vocations of all three persons are not indicated; this information is usually found in the civil records but not in the parish records. Possibly for that reason, in this area—the Abruzzi region—the format of the act was changed to include greater detail.

This concludes the discussion of Napoleonic records and civil vital records in general. These records are a principal source of genealogical information in Italy. In many areas of southern and central Italy, research can be pursued from 1915 back to 1809 by personally consulting the microfilm copies of these records available at family history centers of the LDS church throughout the United States and Canada (see chapter 10). These detailed examples should aid the researcher in personally conducting this research using microfilm records or in Italy itself, or at least in checking the work of other researchers.

FIGURE 6-9. Death Act of Elizabetta Florio, 1818, S. Stefano, L'Aquila

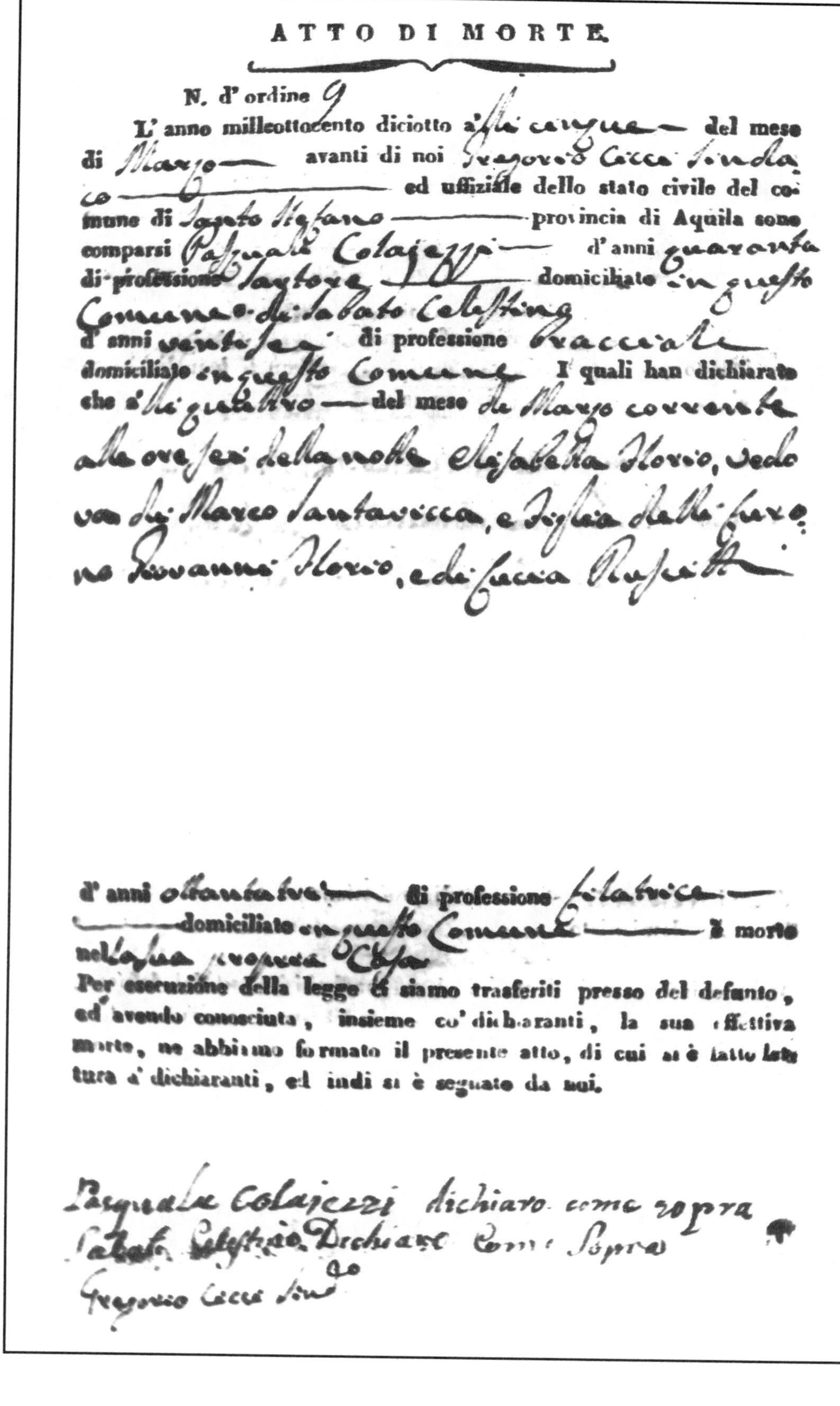

ATTO DI MORTE

N. d' ordine 9

L' anno milleottocento diciotto a' dì cinque del mese di Marzo avanti di noi Gregorio Cecca Sindaco ed uffiziale dello stato civile del comune di Santo Stefano provincia di Aquila sono comparsi Pasquale Colajezzi d' anni quaranta di professione Sartore domiciliato in questo Comune, e di Sabato Celestino d' anni ventisei di professione bracciale domiciliato in questo Comune I quali han dichiarato che a' dì quattro del mese di Marzo corrente alle ore sei della notte Elisabetta Florio, vedova di Marco Santavicca, e figlia delli furono Giovanni Florio, e di Lucia Rufitti

d' anni ottantatre di professione filatrice domiciliato in questo Comune è morto nella sua propria Casa

Per esecuzione della legge ci siamo trasferiti presso del defunto, ed avendo conosciuta, insieme co' dichiaranti, la sua effettiva morte, ne abbiamo formato il presente atto, di cui si è fatto lettura a' dichiaranti, ed indi si è segnato da noi.

Pasquale Colajezzi dichiaro come sopra
Sabato Celestino Dichiaro come Sopra
Gregorio Cecca Sindaco

Chapter 7

PARISH RECORDS

THOUGH THE CIVIL RECORDS CONSTITUTE A PRIMARY SOURCE of information (as discussed in chapters 5 and 6), the Catholic parish records are certainly the most complete and probably the most valuable genealogical source in Italy. These records, in most parishes, provide complete information on christenings, marriages, and deaths of almost all Italians dating from the late 1500s to today. For the period before the advent of civil records with Napoleon in the early nineteenth century, the parish records are the main source for all genealogical information. Given the importance of this source, it is necessary to understand the origins of the records and to know what information they contain.

The Roman Catholic church is headed by the pope and the Council of Cardinals, who regulate church affairs worldwide. On a local level, the church is divided into dioceses that are presided over by bishops. Within each diocese there are many parishes (*parrocchie*), each with its own parish priest (*parroco*). The parish is the basic organizational unit of the church; the parish priest cares for the spiritual and often the physical needs of the people living in the parish. The parish is a territorial division of varying size. Sometimes several parishes are grouped together in a *pieve*, which is presided over by an archpriest (*arciprete*). Most towns have their own parishes, but often a small village is part of the parish of a nearby town. Larger towns and cities have several parishes.

When Martin Luther nailed ninety-nine protests against the Roman Catholic church to the door of the Cathedral of Wittenberg in 1525, he started a powerful Protestant movement that swept through most of Europe. The need for reforms was spurred not only by the widespread corruption and greed of the clergy and the lack of a coherent doctrine within the church itself, but also by strong political interests and conflicts. In this epoch there was a long-standing conflict between the church and local princes and dukes over who would choose the clergy—particularly the bishops, because bishops exercised extensive political power and owned vast estates of land. The church reserved this power of choice for itself, but the kings and princes, particularly in Germany, resisted control from Rome. They insisted that the choice of bishops be theirs, often choosing from their own noble families. When the Protestant Reform began, it represented an excellent means for the German princes, among others, to liberate themselves from Rome by sustaining a religion that was more subject to their rule.

There were various reactions within the hierarchy of the church itself to the Protestant Reform. Some, like Cardinal Contarini of Venice, wished to compromise with the reformers and to incorporate some of their demands into Catholic doctrine, such as allowing the populace to read the Bible. Others, however, led first by Pope Clemente VII and later by Cardinal Carafa, believed only in the total repression of these heretical ideas. Those who favored repression prevailed, and all Protestants were excommunicated from the church. In Italy, a court of inquisition based on the Spanish model prohibited every contact with the heretics. The inquisition then used every method, including torture, to identify people whose beliefs were contrary to those of the church.

After the death of Pope Clemente, church leaders realized that there was a need to reform certain practices and doctrines of Catholicism. As a result, a council of all the leaders of the church, including the cardinals and all the bishops from each diocese in Europe, was begun in the city of Trent on 13 December 1545. The Council of Trent was a failure, mostly due to resistance from the Germans and open conflicts between the French and the Spanish; of the 500 or more dioceses in Europe, only 237 sent representatives. In 1547, the council was moved to Bologna and soon after was suspended; it was revived in 1551 but again abandoned. In 1555, Cardinal Carafa became Pope Paul IV and, rather than seek conciliation and internal reform through the council, he gave more power to the inquisition. The ecclesiastical court could now try and imprison nearly anyone for offenses ranging from swearing to immorality and not observing the Sabbath. There was strict censorship, and books that did not meet the approval of the inquisition were publicly burned.

Not until after Paul IV's death and after the treaty between France and Spain in 1561 was Paul's successor, Pope Pius IV, able to reunite the Council of Trent. The important reforms of the council were finally concluded in December 1563. This council established some of the basic procedures, doctrines, and practices that were to regulate the church for the next several centuries, and it stands as one of the most important historical agreements of the epoch. Several internal reforms were enacted, such as the enforcement of clerical celibacy and the requirement for bishops and priests to reside in the diocese and parish of their jurisdiction. The "indulgences" that had inspired Luther's revolt were also eliminated. Doctrines such as justification and purgatory were defined, and the procedures for celebrating baptism, marriage, Eucharist, and the Mass were all specified. It was decided that the basic doctrine had to be preached to all faithful members; therefore, a formal catechism was begun. All clergy members had to attend special seminaries to qualify for their callings, and they were no longer allowed to accumulate earthly wealth.

Most important for genealogy, the Council of Trent established that every parish priest would maintain written records of the baptisms, marriages, and deaths of all parishioners and outlined the procedures for each of these sacraments. The procedures for creating these records were based on the practice of the church in Spain, which had begun written records as early as 1442.

The sweeping reforms of the Council of Trent, though proclaimed as law for all of the church on 26 January 1564 by Pope Pius IV, were not received warmly, particularly by the clergy, and were not immediately enacted everywhere. A gradual process was started whereby each diocese had to ratify and implement the reforms of the council. They were not universally accepted until a new papal proclamation was declared in 1595.

As a result of these events, some parish documents in Italy were begun as early as 1545, but most commenced during the period from 1563 to 1595. When a new parish was established after this period, the records began with the creation of the parish.

When searching for early parish records in the town of origin of your ancestors, remember that one parish may, at a time when it had fewer inhabitants, have included what are now several widely separated villages. Later, as the villages grew in population and built churches of their own, new parishes were formed. For example, S. Vito di Cadore, in the Alpine region of northern Italy, was the *pieve,* or main parish, where the ordinances were performed, and the records began there in 1563. In the beginning it included what are today four other parishes in the towns of S. Vito, Borca, Venas, and Vodo di Cadore, besides several other nearby hamlets. In 1635, Vodo became a separate parish with its own records, and in the 1700s Borca and Venas became separate parishes as well. The gradual process of

dividing large parishes into smaller parishes as the towns grew took place throughout Italy. In some areas, such as the Trento region, the mother parish (*pieve*) still holds the records for all of the surrounding villages and hamlets, even though each has its own church and priest. Thus, Sanzeno in the Non Valley in Trento still keeps records for Sanzeno, Banco, Piano, Casez, and Dambel, all of which are large villages with their own churches and priests.

This becomes an important consideration when you are searching for the records of ancestors. If the parish church of the family's town of origin has no records or, more likely, if the records date back only to the eighteenth or nineteenth century, it is possible that in an earlier period the town was under the jurisdiction of another, larger, parish. In such a case it is necessary to search nearby parishes for earlier records that include the family's town of origin. The growth of towns has not always followed their historical importance, so it may be that a large town today once was in the parish of a nearby hamlet.

Whereas civil record keeping, both during Napoleon's rule and after the creation of the Italian state, was based in part on the ecclesiastic format created by the Council of Trent for the parishes, there are some very important differences. Two in particular are worth mentioning. First, as has been discussed, the civil records began with an established format that was uniform throughout Italy and contained all the essential information necessary for the act. This became true of parish records only after the civil records were begun, when the church decided that it was a good policy. Thus, after 1810 (and differing widely in date from region to region), preprinted forms with space to write the appropriate information came to be used for parish records. Before this period, however, all records were handwritten, and the form and language differed from one town and priest to another and over time. Some essential information specified by the Council of Trent was usually included but, otherwise, each priest could include what he wanted (usually as little as possible). Also, each priest wrote in the language he desired. The preferred language was Latin, but Italian and dialect were often used as well. The Latin used often was pig-Latin mixed with dialect; it is therefore rather difficult to decipher.

To accommodate these variations, this chapter examines several acts for each ordinance—baptism, marriage, and death—from different locations in Italy and from various time periods to better illustrate the many styles that can be encountered. (See chapter 12 for more information on how to read these documents and the handwriting in them.)

The second major difference between the parish and civil records is that the first are unique; there are no copies. As discussed in previous chapters, every civil act, beginning with the Napoleonic records, was made out in two separate copies that were stored in two different locations: one at the town office and one at the *pretura della repubblica* (Napoleonic) or the *procura della repubblica* (post-Napoleonic).

They were created in duplicate not only because each copy served a different purpose, but also to protect the records from loss, theft, or damage. As a result, few of these records have been lost. (One exception is Monte Cassino. During World War II, the town was heavily bombed by the Allies in their drive up the Italian peninsula. The parish records had been stored in a monastery overlooking the city that became the epicenter of the battle, and all of the parish documents were lost. The civil records were destroyed with the town hall and the district court, so all documents in the area were lost. After the war, residents contributed documents in their possession and made notarized statements regarding their personal statistics and those of relatives and friends. These were then cross referenced to eliminate discrepancies and became the new civil records. A similar situation occurred at Civitavecchia, a city on the coast below Rome. However, with few exceptions, the civil records have remained remarkably intact because there have always been two copies stored in separate facilities.) This practice was not followed for the older parish records.

The church learned from the state the usefulness of separate, duplicate records, and many dioceses began to require that a second copy of the parish records be sent to the *curia vescovile* (bishop's office) of each diocese. This practice did not become widespread, however, until the 1900s. As a result, usually there is only one unique copy of any of the parish records.

Through the centuries, war, bandits, fire, humidity, and simple neglect have contributed to the loss, destruction, and damage of many parish records. These effects were not confined to the past; I have found records mingled with firewood or dumped in humid cellars, where they have rapidly deteriorated. Priests have kindly lent their records to students or friends or unscrupulous researchers, only to have them lost or vandalized with pages cut or torn out.

Usually the damage is not deliberate, but time itself has taken a toll. The parish records, particularly those of several centuries ago, were made on parchment of goat skin or on very low quality paper, as little else was available. Ink was normally homemade by the priest with varying results. Often the ink was too liquid, soaking into the poorly bonded paper, blurring the writing and rendering it illegible. Most forms of ink smudged with humidity, and these flaws are present in almost all the parish records. Even when a whole volume has not been compromised, there will be pages or acts that are illegible. Usually the worst enemy of the records is humidity, which fades the ink and causes the paper to deteriorate, starting along the edges, where names are often written. Often, too, the ink base was too acid, and would, with time, "burn" through the paper. Some records actually crumble in the hand due to this process. Also, termites and other insects may attack the paper, leaving holes in the documents.

In Benevento, a priest told me that all of the parish records and an extensive historical library of the parish were lost after World War II when local peasants stole anything that would burn to warm themselves and cook their food. Another priest in the Tuscany area told of parishioners burning the parish archives in spite because the town council, with the approval of the new parish priest, approved the construction of a new parish church in a newer part of town to replace the old church, which had been damaged during an earthquake and was traditionally near the old town square.

Incidences of loss, theft, damage, or destruction of parish records have been numerous. There are no duplicates of these unique and valuable documents, and more are lost as time goes by. This fact should motivate all those who are interested in their Italian heritage to begin the search for their ancestors today. Tomorrow could be too late!

As with civil records, there are no national or regional archives of parish records. For the most recent records, copies are kept at the Curia Vescovile of each diocese. Officials in a few dioceses, such as Arezzo and Pordenone, concerned about damage and loss of the records, have gathered all parish records predating 1900 in the *curie* to be stored, restored, and rebound. To consult the vast majority of parish records, however, it is necessary to travel to the individual parishes. The records there are under the supervision of the parish priests, and access is controlled by them. With increasing frequency, the *curie* have instructed priests to allow no consultation of these records, fearing theft or vandalism. Usually, too, parish priests are very busy; unless they have a special interest in ancient documents, they are reluctant to "waste their time" with persons who want to consult the records or with people who write for information. In all fairness to the priests, most of them are overworked and have very little competence in reading old handwriting, so it is usually only a bother for them. Records are often left unattended in old, humid churches, and it is very difficult to find a priest who will take the time to allow research among them.

This problem has been exacerbated in recent years, as there are fewer and fewer priests, and the average age of those who remain is increasing. Particularly in the Apennine area, throughout central Italy, there has been a massive emigration of the population to the coastal areas and to the north, where work is more available. As a result, many towns have been reduced to a few inhabitants and their churches closed. Often, one priest travels to five or six different villages on a Sunday to say Mass and is responsible for all the parishioners of the villages. Apella, for example, a village that once had several hundred inhabitants, has been reduced to a dozen or more retired couples; the last birth in the village took place more than twenty-five years ago. The priest comes once a week from a town about fifteen miles away. He is responsible for six other similar hamlets, but during the week he also teaches philosophy at a high school.

To personally consult parish records, the best way to proceed is usually to go first to the *curia* and obtain written permission for research directly from the bishop or vicar. The *curia* may assist the interested researcher in finding out whether the parish is still open, where the records are held, and who the presiding priest is. Often, the *curia* staff will want to know the purpose of the research and to have a personal reference. In any case, even with permission from the *curia*, the last word is with the parish priest. Thus, prior notification by telephone or by letter and a modest offering for the parish are in order. The priest is not obliged to permit research, and it is through his courtesy that consultation of the records is allowed. This same procedure must be followed by any professional researcher in Italy, and permission to view and research the records is not always granted.

Unfortunately, the parish records have not been systematically microfilmed, so few are available in the United States. Some exceptions are the records of the Waldensian parishes in the Turin province (see chapter 8) and the dioceses of Trent, Bolzano, Vercelli, and Ivrea. In some areas, such as Campobasso and Isernia, where some parish records were held in the state archives, these records have been microfilmed, as have civil records. Elsewhere in Italy, however, the records must be personally consulted at the parish or, in some cases, at the *curia*.

After the parish has been located and permission obtained from the *curia* or the parish priest, actual consultation of the records can begin. Three basic parish documents, found throughout Italy, are useful for genealogy: baptismal or christening records, marriage records, and death records. Also found in central Italy, where the papal states once existed, are the *status animarum* or *stato delle anime* (state of the souls) records. Examples of each of these acts are examined and translated below.

BAPTISMAL RECORDS

The first sacrament in the life of any Roman Catholic is baptism. Church doctrine declares that individuals must purify themselves from the original sin of Adam and Eve through baptism. Without baptism, a person cannot achieve paradise, and if a baby dies soon after birth without baptism, it must remain in a state of "limbo" for eternity. As a result, the practice in the church for centuries has been to baptize children as soon after birth as possible. In earlier centuries, due to the high risk of infant mortality, baptism was usually performed on the day of or the day after birth. It was rare when two or more days passed between birth and baptism. After a difficult birth, if a child seemed likely to die before the priest could arrive, the midwife was sanctioned by the church to perform the sacrament herself. If the child died, this baptism was considered sufficient; if the child lived, the ceremony was repeated by the priest. In the last century, medical advances have allowed delays of a week or longer

between birth and baptism.

During the 1800s, most dioceses in Italy introduced preprinted volumes for the various documents, including baptismal records, with standardized information given. The first act examined (figure 7-1) is from Alpette in the Piedmont region and was created in 1881. The act begins with the title, *atti di battesimo*, or "baptismal act," and then provides both the christening date and the birth date of the child and the names of the parents:

N. 7 *Ceretto Gianone Filippo* [left margin]
L'anno del Signore mille ottocento ottanta *uno* il *primo* del mese di *maggio* è stato presentato alla Chiesa un fanciullo nato il *primo* del mese di *maggio* alle ore *dieci anti meridiane*, figlio di *Pietro* del *fu Domenico* nativo di *Alpette* e della *Goglio Clara* del *vivo Tommaso* nativa di *Alpette* coniugi *Ceretto Gianone* domiciliati in *Alpette* . . .

This translates as:

N. 7 *Ceretto Gianone Filippo*
In the year of our Lord one thousand eight-hundred eighty-*one* on *the first* of the month of *May* was presented to the Church an infant [male], born *the first* of the month of *May* at the hour *ten anti-meridiane* [a.m.], son of *Pietro* of the *deceased Domenico*, native of *Alpette*, and of GOGLIO *Clara*, daughter of the *living Tommaso*, native of *Alpette* of the family CERETTO GIANONE, living at *Alpette* . . .

There are several items of note in this first section. First, each separate act is numbered, but the pages are not. In this case there are only two acts per page, and the acts are numbered yearly, beginning at "one" again each year. Parish records contain nearly every possible variation of numbering. Sometimes both the pages and the acts are numbered, other times the pages only or the acts only. Sometimes the numbering is by year, as in this case, but often the act numbering continues throughout each record volume. Often, in older records, the pages are numbered with one number for the front and back of each sheet, as this was considered one page. Most common in records from before the 1700s is the total lack of numbering or indexes in any of the volumes.

In this case, to aid in finding the right act, the given name and surname of the child are in the margin of each act, as often found in parish records, particularly in this region of Italy. If there are no indexes to the records and it is necessary to examine every page and act of a volume, this greatly hastens the search, allowing the researcher to scan the page and find the desired surnames. On occasion, however, the name or surname in the margin does not correspond with that in the act; thus, an act can be missed when using this reference only.

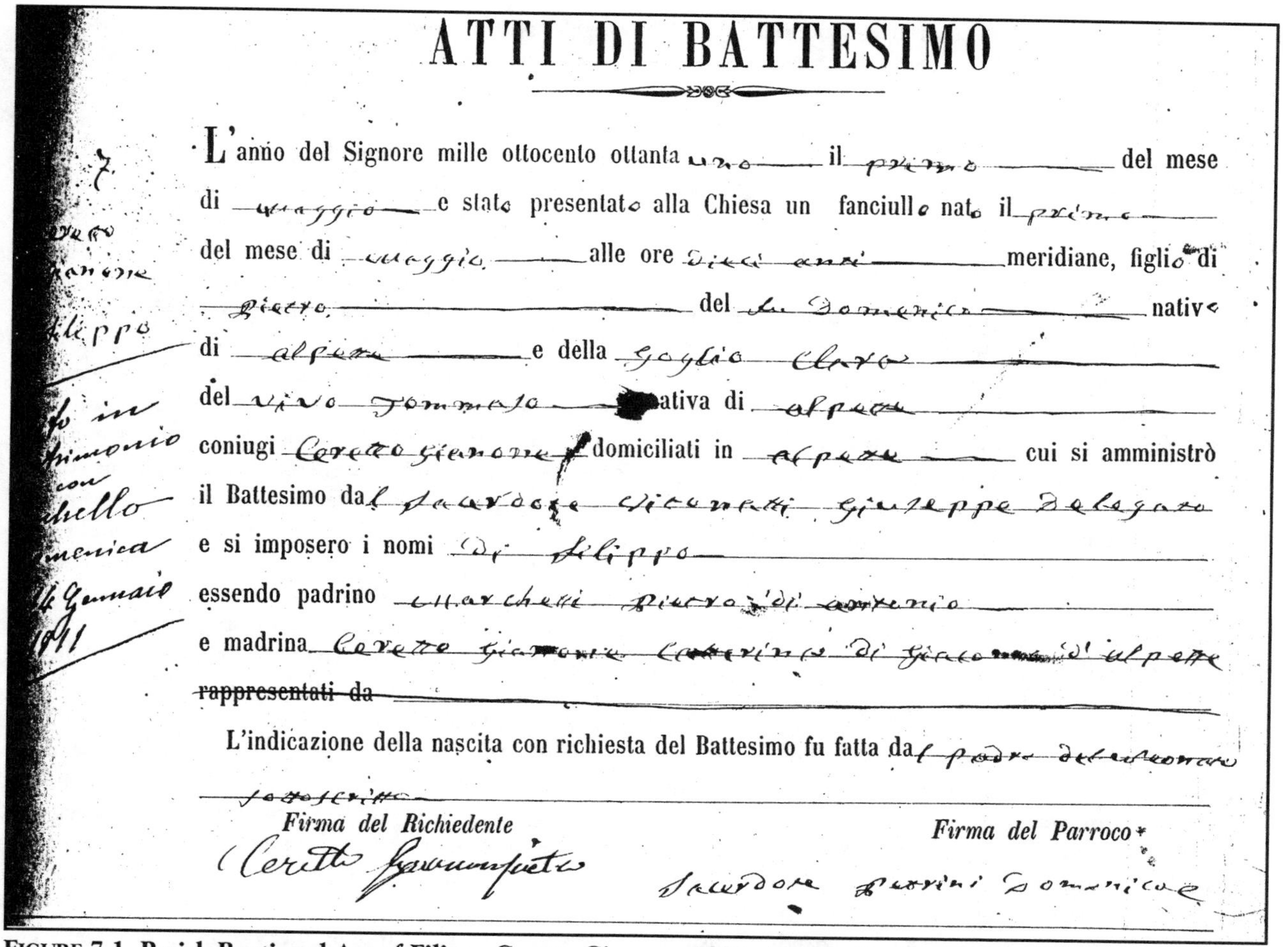

ATTI DI BATTESIMO

L'anno del Signore mille ottocento ottanta *uno* il *primo* del mese di *maggio* e stato presentato alla Chiesa un fanciullo nato il *primo* del mese di *maggio* alle ore *dieci anti* meridiane, figlio di *Pietro* del *fu Domenico* nativo di *Alpette* e della *Gaglio Chiara* del *vivo Tommaso* nativa di *Alpette* coniugi *Ceretto Gianone* domiciliati in *Alpette* cui si amministrò il Battesimo dal *sacerdote Vitonetti Giuseppe delegato* e si imposero i nomi *di Filippo* essendo padrino *Marchetti Pietro di Antonio* e madrina *Ceretto Gianone Caterina di Giacomo d'Alpette* ~~rappresentati da~~

L'indicazione della nascita con richiesta del Battesimo fu fatta da *padre dichiarante sottoscritto*

Firma del Richiedente
Ceretto Giovambatista

Firma del Parroco
Sacerdote Perrini Domenico

FIGURE 7-1. Parish Baptismal Act of Filippo Ceretto-Gianone, 1881, Alpette, Torino

The act begins by stating the child's baptismal date and then provides the exact birth date as well, as do most documents dating back to the mid-1800s. In earlier records, however, there is great variety in the information provided. In the usual form, the act states the exact baptismal date followed by some reference to the birth, such as *nato oggi* (born today) or *nata ieri* (born yesterday) or *nato stanotte* (born last night). Sometimes there is no reference to the birth at all, and occasionally only the birth date is given.

This act also gives the names of both parents—which is common—and the name of the father of each spouse—which is uncommon. In general, the older the act, the less information is included. Thus, acts from the 1500s and 1600s may contain only the full name of the father and the first name of the wife; rarely are grandparents included. As in some of the civil vital records discussed earlier (chapter 5), *fu* is used here to denote someone who is deceased and *di* or even *vivo* (alive) to indicate someone is still alive. Also, the "o" (denoting male) or "a" (denoting female) after *fanciullo/a* and *nato/a* are the only indications, besides the name itself, of whether the child is male or female, so care should be taken in reading the act to make sure of the child's sex.

In this case the name of the village, Alpette, is stated. While the name of the town or city is often found in the baptismal act, sometimes, instead, the name of the parish is given. Often no location at all is mentioned, and rarely is the name of the diocese or province included.

Finally, the maiden name of the mother appears; separately, after her name, is the couple's family name. This is a fairly common format, and the mother's maiden name should not be confused with the child's family name. The surname, Ceretto Gianone, is a good example of the double surname—typical of this area not far from France, where the double surname is common. Both names make up the surname, as there are other variations of the Ceretto surname at Alpette that represent different lines. In modern civil records this surname would appear hyphenated as Ceretto-Gianone.

The remainder of the act follows:

. . . cui si amministro' il Battesimo dal *Vitonetti Giuseppe delegato* e si imposero i nomi *di Filippo* essendo padrino *Marchetti Pietro di Antonio* e madrina *Ceretto Gianone Catterina di Giacomo d'Alpette* rappresentati da

L'indicazione della nascita con richiesta del Battesimo
fu fatta dal *padre del neonato sottoscritto*
   Firma del richiedente
   Ceretto Giovanpietro
   Firma del Parroco
   Sacerdote Petrini Domenico

Translated:

. . . to whom the baptism was administered by
VITONETTI Giuseppe, the delegated priest, and to
whom was given the names *of Filippo*, the godfather
being MARCHETTI *Pietro, son of Antonio,* and the
godmother CERETTO GIANONE *Catterina, daughter of
Giacomo from Alpette,* represented by . . .
The indication of the birth, with the request for
baptism, was made by the *underwritten father of the
infant.*
   Signature of person who requested baptism
   Giovanpietro CERETTO
   Signature of the parish priest
   Priest Domenico PETRINI

Again, much interesting information is contained in this
section. In this case the baptism was not performed by the
parish priest. This was not a common practice, and it may
indicate that the family had a relative or friend who was a
priest in some other parish, or it may have been a way of
snubbing the parish priest. In any case, the office and
authority of the priest who performed the baptism is usually
indicated. In this act, it is stated *delegato,* or "delegated" by
the parish priest. Usually, though not here, it describes
where the other priest exercised his services.

The act indicates the name of the child and actually
states "names" in the plural. Usually only one or two given
names are given a child in Italy. The second given name
was often the name of a saint or some other religious name,
and it was not always listed in the civil records. Each day of
the year is dedicated to a different saint, and sometimes that
saint's name was given to a child born on that day. Each
town also has a patron saint, for whom the parish is often
named as well, and that saint's name often appears as a
child's name. For example, the patron saint of Naples is San
Gennaro. Gennaro is a popular name in the city but is
rarely found outside the region. Often, the use of several
middle names for a child indicates a wealthy or illustrious
family. This practice was a demonstration of a family's
distinction.

In all baptismal acts—even those of the 1500s, when not
even the maiden name of the mother was indicated—the
godfather and godmother were included. For all official acts
there were official witnesses to the act. For the christening,
these witnesses were the godparents; however, they had a
function that exceeded the legal aspect of witness: the
godparents were responsible for the child throughout his or

her life, and, if the child became an orphan, they often
became the guardians and providers for the child. Therefore, to be named the godparents of a child brought a
religious and moral responsibility. Usually, the godparents
were from the child's immediate family—often the aunts or
uncles—so this information is useful for genealogy. Who, for
example, was Catterina Ceretto Gianone? She has the same
surname but does not appear to be directly related; she may
be a cousin. Why was she chosen? Was she a good friend of
the mother? Members of noble or illustrious families in the
village were much sought after as godparents. The benefit,
or at least the hope, was that the child would have someone
important looking after him or her in life. Since there were
usually no more than one or two wealthy families in a town
or village, their members were often called on to be godparents, a role that the more generous rarely refused. Instead
of attending every baptism, however, which would have
become rather tedious, they often sent substitutes. The line
that has been crossed out and states *rappresentati da*
(represented by) would indicate the substitutes who
represented the godparents had they been necessary in this
case. It was the godparent, however, who bore the responsibility, not the substitute.

The document ends with the name and signature of the
father who reported the birth of the child and requested the
baptism, and the name of the parish priest. Even though, in
this case, another priest performed the baptism, the parish
priest was always responsible for filling out and signing the
act. Interesting is the fact that the father's signed name is
different from the name found within the act itself. The
father signed as Giovanpietro, but, in the act, his name is
given as Pietro. These seemingly small details can mean the
difference between a successful search and an unsuccessful
one. Which name will be on the father's marriage or
baptismal act—or will it be written Giovanni? Would you
recognize him as the direct ancestor if you were searching
only for Pietro? It is always preferable to read the entire act
and write down all of the information provided, including
the small details that later may make all the difference.

As stated, preprinted certificates on which the parish
priest simply fills in the appropriate information are typical
today, but they did not come into use until the late 1800s
in most dioceses. In some cases, as will be seen with the
marriage certificate, acts were written in Latin, which was
used in most areas of Italy for all parish records before the
unification of Italy in 1870. The exceptions are the former
Venetian Republic, the Trentino-Alto Adige region that was
under Austria, and Sardinia. In Sardinia, most records were
written in a dialect that was quite similar to Spanish, and in
Veneto a mixture of Italian and local dialect was used. In
the Bolzano province, formally under Austria (South
Tyrol), German was used in the records. Some examples
illustrating these language and regional differences follow.
They are from increasingly earlier periods, and they illustrate that less information was provided in earlier periods.

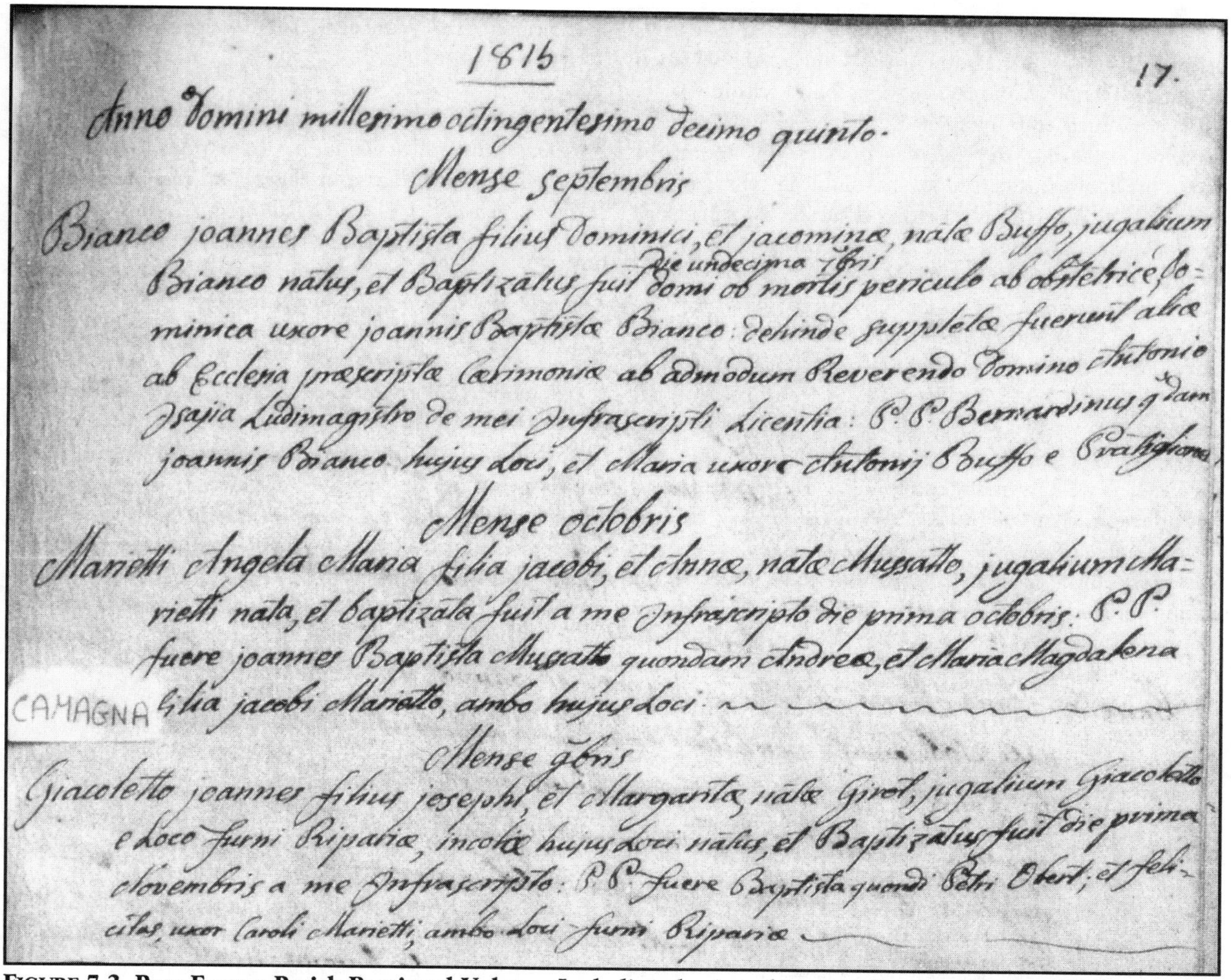
1815 17.
Anno Domini millesimo octingentesimo decimo quinto.
Mense septembris
Bianco joannes Baptista filius Dominici, et jacominæ, natæ Buffo, jugalium
die undecima 7bris
Bianco natus, et Baptizatus fuit domi ob mortis periculo ab obstetrice Do=
minica uxore joannis Baptistæ Bianco: dehinde suppletæ fuerunt aliæ
ab Ecclesia præscriptæ Cærimoniæ ab admodum Reverendo Domino Antonio
Isaija Ludimagistro de mei Infrascripti Licentia: P. P. Bernardinus q.dam
joannis Bianco hujus loci, et Maria uxore Antonij Buffo e Pratiglione,
Mense octobris
Marietti Angela Maria filia jacobi, et Annæ, natæ Mussatto, jugalium Ma=
rietti nata, et baptizata fuit a me Infrascripto die prima octobris: P. P.
fuere joannes Baptista Mussatto quondam Andreæ, et Maria Magdalena
CAMAGNA filia jacobi Mariotto, ambo hujus loci
Mense 9bris
Giacoletto joannes filius josephi, et Margaritæ, natæ Giret, jugalium Giacoletto
e loco furni Ripariæ, incolæ hujus loci natus, et Baptizatus fuit die prima
novembris a me Infrascripto: P. P. fuere Baptista quondam Petri Obert; et feli-
citas, uxor Caroli Marietti, ambo loci furni Ripariæ

FIGURE 7-2. Page From a Parish Baptismal Volume, Including the Act of Joannes Baptista Bianco, 1815, Camagna, Torino

Figure 7-2 contains acts from a baptismal volume from the town of Camagna, not far from Alpette, for 1815. Aiding research is the fact that the surname of each child is noted in the margin. The document is written in Latin; the first act is written:

Anno Domini millesimo octingentesimo decimo quinto
Mense Septembris
Bianco joannes Baptista filius Dominicis et jacomina nata Buffo jugalium Bianco natus, et Baptizatus fuit Die undecima 7bris domi ob mortis periculo ob obstetrice Dominica uxore joannis Baptista Bianco dehinde suppleta fuerunt alia ab Ecclesia prascripta Cerimonia ab admodum Reverendo Domino Antonio Isaiia Ludimagistro de mei Infrascripti Licentia: P.P. Bernardinus q.dum joannis Bianco huius loci, et Maria uxore Antonii Buffo e Pratiglione

Translated, this reads:

Year of the Lord one thousand eight hundred and fifteen
Month of September
BIANCO Joannes Baptista, son of Dominicus and of Jacomina born BUFFO and married to the BIANCO family, was born and baptized on the day eleven September, baptized in danger of death by the midwife Dominica, wife of Joannes Baptista BIANCO, in substitution according to the prescription of the Church, and the following ceremony administered by the Reverend Antonio ISAIIA LUDIMAGISTRO by authority of the here-written priest. Godparents Bernardinus, son of the deceased Joannes BIANCO of this place, and Maria, wife of Antonius BUFFO from Pratiglione.

Typically, the year was written at the top of the page and was not repeated in each act. Sometimes it was written only once, at the beginning of each year, and was not repeated again on any of the pages until the next year's acts began. Sometimes even the month was indicated only when it changed. Another interesting item found within the act (discussed further in chapter 12) is the use of *7bris* for September (seven, in Italian, is *sette*; the month is *Settembre*); obviously it does not indicate the seventh month of the year, i.e., July. Farther down on the same page is *9bris* for November—not for September (the ninth month).

In this example, and commonly in records of the late 1700s and 1800s, given names are in Latin, whereas the surnames are in Italian. Thus, Bianco, which is Italian, remains Bianco, but Giovanni Battista (John the Baptist) becomes Joannes Baptista; Domenico is written Dominicus; and so on. Often, in earlier records, the surname was Latinized as well, normally by placing a "De" before and an "is" after—so Bianco became De Bianchis and Buffo, the maiden name of the wife, De Buffis. In this parish, though not particularly common throughout Italy, most of the names were begun with lowercase letters—joannes instead of Joannes. There was no reason for this other than the preference of the parish priest.

This document, as does the next act, indicates that the baptism was performed by the midwife because the infant was in danger of dying. The midwife performed this sacrament by sprinkling the newborn with water and giving a name. If the infant survived, the ceremony was repeated by a priest with the godparents present. In this case, again, the second baptism was performed by a priest from outside the parish, but permission had to be given by the parish priest. Baptism in another parish was a rare event. It was not possible, for example, to take a child to a different parish to be baptized simply because the parish priest was disliked. It occurred only if the family moved for a time to another parish or if the mother was staying with relatives in another town at birth.

Once again, the godparents are mentioned, and more information is given about them than about the parents. However, the overall amount of information given is less than that in the first certificate examined (figure 7-1). In particular, no information is provided about the child's grandparents, nor is it specifically stated where either of the parents was born or where they lived. If nothing specific is stated, it can usually be inferred that both parents are from the same town and parish, but often the priest merely left out this very important information. In fact, while in the first example the town of Alpette was mentioned four times, here the name of the town is never stated.

The next two examples (figures 7-3 and 7-4) are from a small town called Vodo di Cadore situated in the midst of the Dolomite Mountains in the Venetian region. These examples were created approximately eighty years apart; they exemplify the use of dialectic forms in writing and the further decrease in the amount of information provided. In the first case (figure 7-3), each act is numbered and the year

is indicated. In act number 310, for Anastasia Zangrando, is written:

A di 31 d.o 1750
Anastasia fig.a di Zuane q. Zuane Zangrando e di Maria jugali fu batt.a in pericolo ad hac in vulva da Zuana v.a del q. Osvaldo Talamini, furono suplite le Cerimonie di chiesa santa e batt.a sub cond.e da me Cur. sud.o tenuta alle med.me et al sac.o fonte da Zuana moglie di Tomaso Zamichieli per nome di Zan Batta q Zu.e Zamichieli

Obvious even before the translation is that the parish priest, to save time, used a series of abbreviations: *fig.a* for *figlia*; *q.* for *quondam*; *batt.a* for *battezzata*; *v.a* for *vedova*; and so on. This practice renders the translation of the information that much more difficult, particularly for those who don't know the language well. Unfortunately, the use of abbreviations was very common throughout Italy. Another problem presented by this act is that the priest mixed Venetian dialect (e.g., the names) with Latin (*quondam*) and Italian. It is translated as:

On the day 31 of said month [August] 1750 Anastasia, daughter of Zuane, son of the deceased Zuane ZANGRANDO and of Maria, his wife, was baptized, in danger of her life, while in the womb, by Zuana, widow of the deceased Osvaldo TALAMINI, according to the ceremony of the Holy Church, and was baptized by me the Curate afterwards and held at the holy font by Zuana, wife of Tomaso ZAMICHIELI, representing Zuane Battista of the deceased Zuane ZAMICHIELI

This act demonstrates the standard form for most christening acts of the period. The exact date must be determined by carefully examining the whole page, and less information is provided than in later periods. There is no birth date. Even though the name of the paternal grandfather is provided with the name of the father, the mother's maiden name and place of birth are not indicated. Therefore, if a marriage record for this couple cannot be found at Vodo because Maria was from another village, the researcher will not know what her family name is or from what village she came.

Zuane, Zuana, and Zuane Batista are all dialectic forms of the Italian name Giovanni. Another dialectic variation is the use of only one consonant rather than the two that might be found in Italian—for example, Zuane instead of Zuanne, Batista instead of Battista, or Tomaso instead of Tommaso, or, as seen in the next example (figure 7-4), Batezato instead of Battezzato. Even the surname Zangrando, a dialectic form meaning Big John, in Italian would be Giovanni Grande.

Again, this act indicates that the midwife performed the baptism, this time when the infant was still in the womb

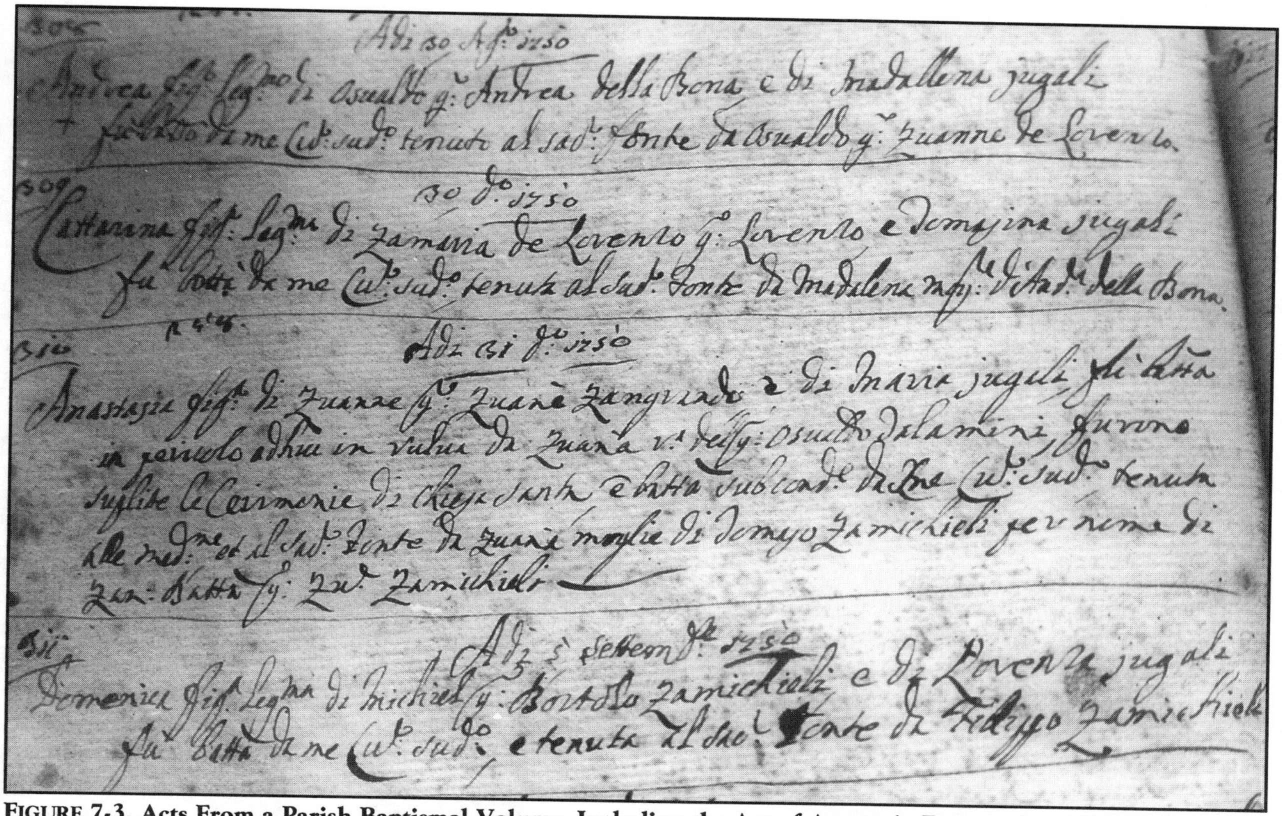

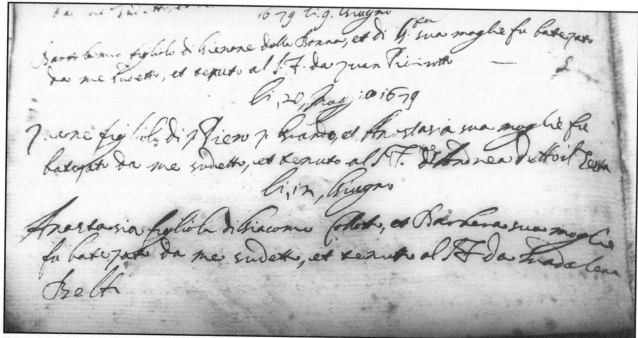

FIGURE 7-3. Acts From a Parish Baptismal Volume, Including the Act of Anastasia Zangrando, 1750, Vodo, Belluno

FIGURE 7-4. Acts From a Parish Baptismal Volume, Including the Act of Zuanne Zangrando, 1679, Vodo, Belluno (probably because it was a breech birth and the baby's survival was in doubt). This act also demonstrates one person's (Zuana Zamichieli) acting as a stand-in for the actual godparent (Zuane Battista). The responsible godparent was the person formally named, not necessarily the person who actually held the baby at the font.

The last baptismal act example (figure 7-4, middle act), for the same family but from seventy-one years earlier, clearly shows how the information included in the earlier records included only the essential minimum—especially as compared with the first example (of 1881). It reads:

li 20 Maii 1679
Zuane figliolo di Z.Piero Z.Grando, et Anastasia sua moglie fu batezato da me sudetto, et tenuto a S.F. da Andrea detto il Testa.

In this case, even the given names and surnames are abbreviated— for example, Z. for Zan—and *sacro fonte* (holy font) appears as *S.F.* The act is translated as:

20 May 1679
Zuane, son of Zanpiero ZANGRANDO *and Anastasia, his wife, was baptized by me, stated above, and held at the Sacred Font by Andrea, named the Brain* [a nickname].

While all civil records—both the Napoleonic and later Italian state records—have a general yearly index at the beginning or end of each volume of birth, marriage, and death records and usually have also a ten-year index for each decade, this is not true of parish records. Parish records are characterized by their extreme diversity, so, in some parishes (although rarely) there may be complete indexes in all volumes back to the 1500s; however, in most parishes indexes were begun in the late 1800s after the style of the civil records. An example (figure 7-5) from the parish records used as civil records in the Venetian region in the mid-1800s is a typical index, arranged alphabetically by surname. Only the name of the newborn infant and the page number are indicated; this limits the usefulness of the index because, for example, if you were searching for someone born in the Seren family, it would be necessary to examine all ten acts for 1869 to determine whether one of the children was from the family of interest. Sometimes the name of the child's father was also entered in the index, aiding research considerably.

For periods before the 1800s, indexes for individual parish record volumes are rare; therefore, each volume must be examined page by page, act by act. In some parishes, mostly in central Italy, each volume of records is divided alphabetically. Invariably, however, the records are arranged by the *given* name rather than by surname. Thus, under the letter "A" appear given names starting with A—Anna, Antonio, Achille, etc.—and under "B," Battista, Barbara, etc. For those given names beginning with common letters, such

as Maria, for which space sometimes ran out, subsequent entries were sometimes scattered throughout the volume in the empty space among other entries. The next example (figure 7-6) is from a baptismal volume of a small parish. The entries shown date from 1670 to 1745. Four children whose names begin with the letter "N," all Nicolaus, are shown. Entries for the letter "M" follow. (Note that the first act, from 1670, is almost illegible and did not reproduce well because of faded ink and the effects of humidity.)

This type of index is very useful if you wish to find a direct ancestor whose name is already known. For example, if Nicolaus, son of Antonius Martinelli, born in 1714, was the direct ancestor, it is a simple matter to search under the letter A in the same volume for an Antonius Martinelli born around 1690. Thus, the record facilitates the search for the known ancestor. Conversely, if you are searching entire family groups to find all the brothers and sisters of an ancestor, it is necessary to examine the entire volume, which spans more than a century, to find them all. In a normal volume that is arranged chronologically, all children in a family can usually be found within a relatively brief period of ten or fifteen years, and there is a certain order, with each child born every two years or so. In this case, instead, the siblings may be anywhere in the volume according to their given names, and it is difficult to perceive any order that makes research easier. Also, it may be that the Antonius above was known by his second name and that his full name at baptism was actually Matheus Antonius Martinelli. This, of course, would greatly complicate the research. This is true for each generation; a researcher may search one volume dozens of times to obtain the families of each generation. Therefore, records arranged in this manner are usually not favored by researchers because they render research more time consuming and less reliable.

In summary, do not expect to find indexes for periods before the 1800s. The normal procedure for research is to study each act and each page of the document. There are welcome exceptions—for example, at Chioggia, near Venice, there are indexes for each volume for all records back to 1595, when the parish was created. However, these indexes were created not many years ago by a priest who had a passion for genealogy; they were not part of the original records.

MARRIAGE RECORDS

As discussed in chapter 6, the civil record procedures for marriage instituted during Napoleon's rule were largely based on the ecclesiastical system used by the Catholic church. Thus, if a couple wanted to be married, they had to present themselves to the priest (usually with their parents or guardians), state their purpose, and obtain consent from the families. Then the banns were announced and, finally, the marriage was performed. Whereas each step of this procedure was documented in the civil records, the only documentation that remains, in most cases, in the parish

FIGURE 7-5. A Page From a Parish Baptismal Record Index, 1869–1870, Fonte Alto, Treviso

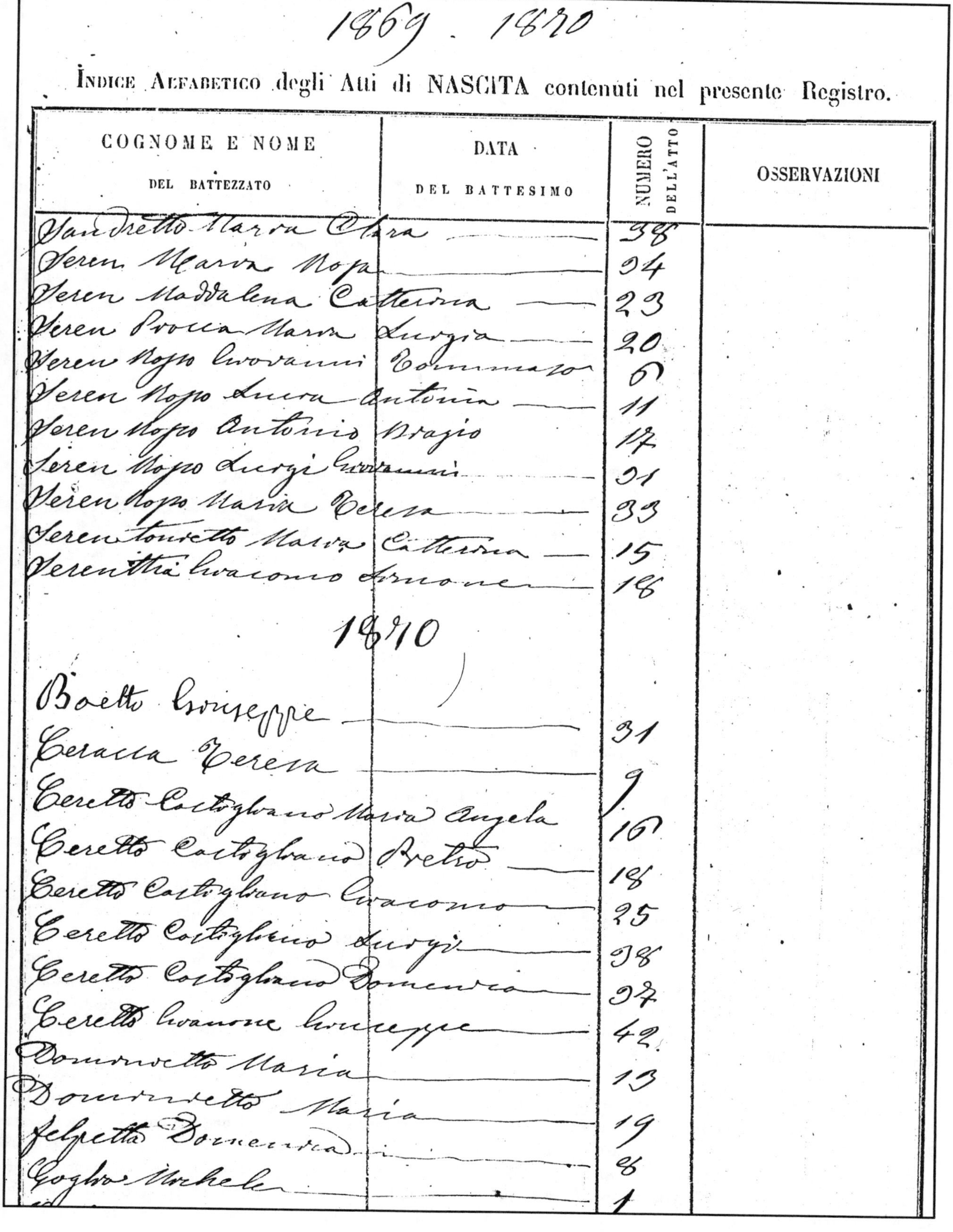

1869 . 1870

ÌNDICE ALFABETICO degli Atti di NASCITA contenuti nel presente Registro.

COGNOME E NOME DEL BATTEZZATO	DATA DEL BATTESIMO	NUMERO DELL'ATTO	OSSERVAZIONI
Sandretto Maria Chiara		38	
Seren Maria Rosa		24	
Seren Maddalena Catterina		23	
Seren Brocca Maria Luigia		20	
Seren Rosso Giovanni Tommaso		6	
Seren Rosso Anna Antonia		11	
Seren Rosso Antonio Biagio		14	
Seren Rosso Luigi Giovanni		34	
Seren Rosso Maria Teresa		33	
Seren touretto Maria Catterina		15	
Verenttia Giacomo Simone		18	

1870

Boetto Giuseppe		31	
Ceracca Teresa		9	
Ceretto Costigliano Maria Angela		16	
Ceretto Costigliano Pietro		18	
Ceretto Costigliano Giacomo		25	
Ceretto Costigliano Luigi		38	
Ceretto Costigliano Domenica		34	
Ceretto Giovanne Giuseppe		42	
Domenetto Maria		13	
Domenetto Maria		19	
Felpetta Domenica		8	
Goglio Michele		1	

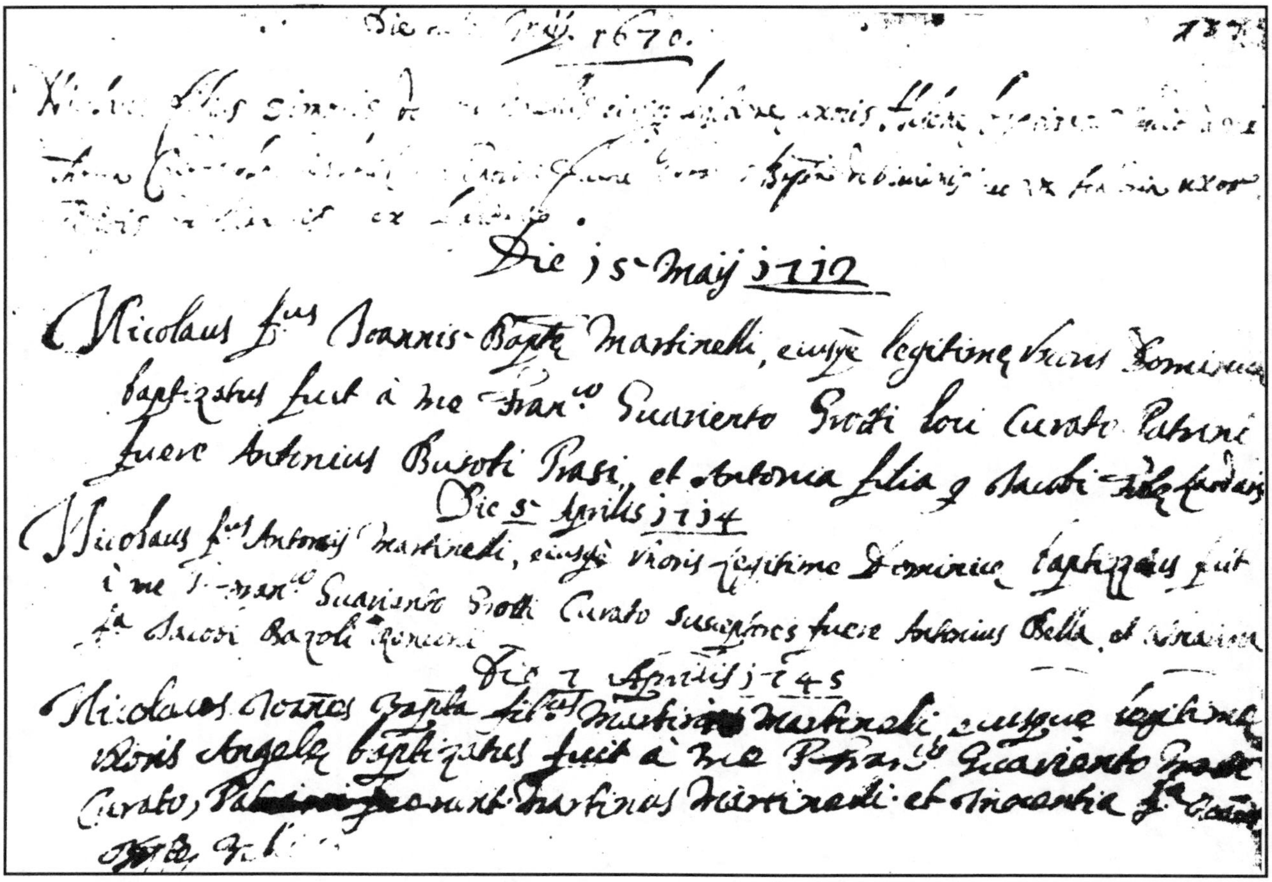

FIGURE 7-6. Parish Baptismal Acts Arranged in Alphabetical Order by the First Name of the Child, 1670–1745

records is that for the actual marriage act. There were also some differences in procedure from those used in the civil records. For the church, as established by the Council of Trent, three banns were declared rather than two. These usually were not written and posted for public viewing; rather, the marriage was formally announced during three consecutive Sunday Masses or at the Mass on a religious holiday. Occasionally only one announcement was made before the marriage—often due to premarital pregnancy and the obvious need to expedite the process. To eliminate one or two of the banns, however, was a decision made by special request and only by the presiding bishop of the *curia*, not by the parish priest. Documentation regarding requests to dispense with the banns is found in the *curia* archive in each diocese (see chapter 8).

Another prescription from the Council of Trent prohibited marriage between close relatives up to the fourth degree (second cousins) of consanguinity. In some unique instances marriage was permitted between first cousins, but to do so it was necessary to petition the pope himself, and the decision was made by the Holy See, not the parish priest. These prescriptions appear in the act itself and were a formal part of the act even back to the 1500s.

The first marriage act examined (figure 7-7) is from a relatively recent period. The preprinted form itself is in

Latin, as are all the names. This act originated in the Marche region in central Italy. The first part, which regards the banns, reads:

Pagina *1*
N. *1*
Philippus Semproni
Dominica Baldessari

Anno Domini Millesimo Octingentesimo *nonesimo* 1890 Die *sepima* Mensis *Junii* Denuntiationibus praemissis tribus contiuis diebus festivis, in hac Paroecia quarum prima die *decima octava* Mensis *Mai* secunda die *vigesima quinta* Mensis *Mai* tertia, die *prima* Mensis *Junii* inter Missae parochialis solemnia habita est nulloque legitimo detecto impedimento cum dispensatione Apostolica ex impedimento . . .

This act is for the first marriage of the year in this small village, so it is on page one and is number one in the volume. In the margin, also, are the names of the groom and bride in Latin. Many female names are the same in Latin as in Italian but, as discussed, male names can appear considerably different. In this act the groom's name, in Italian, would appear as Filippo. The above translates as:

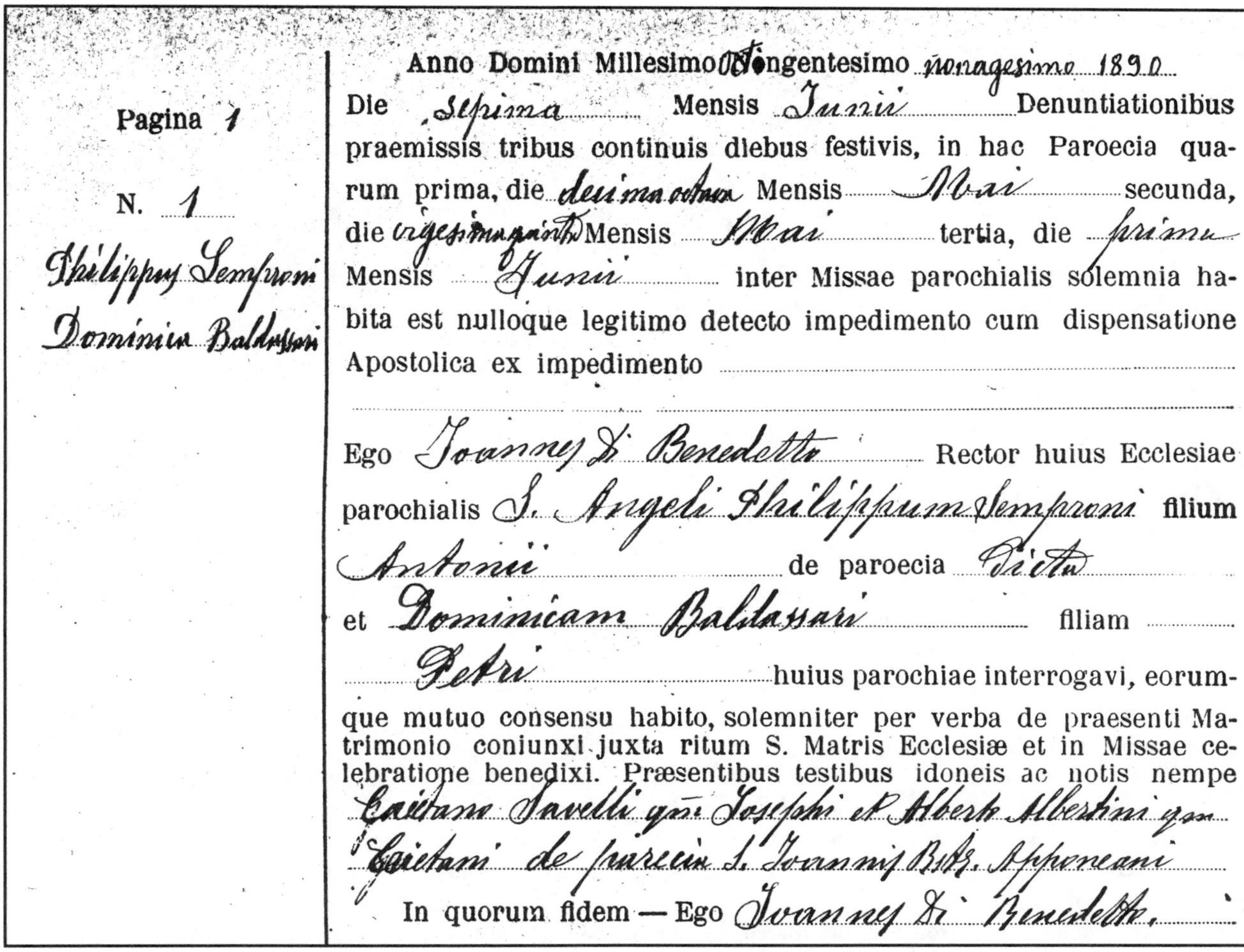

FIGURE 7-7. Parish Marriage Act of Phillipus Semproni and Domenica Baldessari, 1890, S. Angelo Parish, Acquasanta Terme, Ascoli Piceno

The year of the Lord One Thousand Eight Hundred and *ninety 1890*, on the *seventh* Day of the Month of *June*, having made the prescribed banns on three consecutive holidays in the Parish, the first on the day *eighteen* of the month of *May*, the second on the day *twenty-five* of the month of *May*, and the third on the *first day* of the month of *June* during the solemn Mass of this parish, and having detected no legitimate impediment or Apostolic impediment . . .

Here is indicated first the date of the marriage and then the days on which the three banns were announced. Note that the announcement was made during the Sunday Mass, when the whole community was gathered. If the groom or the bride had been from another parish, the banns would have been announced in that parish as well, and this information would have been noted in this part of the act. It was also necessary for the priest to note any legitimate objection to the marriage or any ecclesiastical objection—for marriage to a relative, for example.

The remainder of the act reads:

Ego *Joannes di Benedetto* Rector huius Ecclesiae parochialis S. Angeli *Philippum Semproni* filium *Antonii* de paroecia dictum Et *Dominicam Baldassari* filiam *Petri* huius parochiae interrogavi, eorum que mutuo consenso habito, solemniter per verba de praesenti Matrimonio conjunxi juxta ritum S. Matris Ecclesiae et in Missae celebratione benedixi. Praesentibus testibus idoneis ac notis nempe *Gaietano Savelli qm Josephi et Alberto Albertini qm Gaietani de parocia S. Joannis Bapt Apponeani.*

In quorum fidem—Ego *Joannes Di Benedetto*

Do not be confused by the change in spelling of the names according to the declension or the case of the noun in Latin. In this case, Philippus and Philippum refer to the same person, as do Dominica and Dominicam. The form of the name changes according to its position in the sentence. Names should be transcribed in the language used in the document, but in Latin they are usually expressed in the nominative case—Philippus or Antonius, for example (see the discussion in chapter 12). Thus, this part of the act appears in English as:

I, *Joannes* DI BENEDETTO, Rector of this parish church of *S. Angelo*, interrogated *Philippus* SEMPRONI, son of *Antonius* from said parish, and *Dominica* BALDASSARI, daughter of *Petrus from this parish*, and having their mutual consent, by the solemn word of those present, joined them in marriage according to the ritual of the Holy Mother Church, and during the celebration of the Mass gave them a blessing. Present were the appropriate witnesses, known as *Gaietano* SAVELLI, *son of deceased Josephus*, and *Alberto* ALBERTINI, *son of Gaietanus, parishioners from S. Joannes Baptista Apponeano.*

In faith I, *Joannes* DI BENEDETTO

Note that the bride's parish was assumed to be the parish where the marriage took place, while that of the groom was left blank, confirming the Italian tradition that the marriage take place in the bride's parish. In this case, both bride and groom were from the same parish. Another interesting fact is that the actual marriage bond was not pronounced by the priest but rather by the "solemn word of those present." The priest then performed the rites, celebrated the Mass, and gave his blessing, but the marriage was a social act of the community. As always, it was necessary to have two witnesses to confirm any act, and their names were always included as part of the record.

The next example (figure 7-8) originated in the Benevento province in the south of Italy during the 1800s. Although not preprinted and written in Italian rather than Latin, the important information provided remains the same. In the margin appear the names of the couple, Michele Lombardi and Celestina Patierne, and the number of the act, 432. The act begins with the date and the dates of the banns and follows almost the same pattern of information as does the previous act. It reads as follows:

A dì ventidue decembre milleottocento quarantanove Fatte le tre canoniche denuncie per tre domeniche sussecutive a dì 2, a dì 9, ed a dì 16 decembre premesse le solennita' dello stato civile, e non essendosi scoperto impedimento alcuno canonico, il sacerdote D. Antonio Manfredonio con licenza di me sottoscritto arcip.e ottenuto il consenso per verba de presenti dalli ziti Michele Lombardi di Plicolantonio, e Maria Teresa Marinaccio, e Celestina Patierne fu Giuseppe e Rosa Maria Marinaccio di questo Comune, previa la licenza della Ill.ma curia di Benevento, et S.S. gli ha solennemente congiunti in Matrimonio in faccia della chiesa alla presenza dei testimoni angelantonio d'Ardano fu Giovanni, e Giuseppe Ferritto fu Giovanni di questo comune, e gli ha celebrato la messa senza la nunziale benedizione atteso il Sagro avvento

ed in fede ecc.
Arcip. D'Amato

For the reader who is familiar with Italian, it is interesting to note that the Italian language was not fully developed in this period. Spelling and sentence structure here differ markedly from modern Italian. The disparity is often increased by the conciseness of the writing. Fortunately, in this example abbreviation is limited to S.S.—for the Latin *servatis servanda*, or "observing the rites." The full translation of this act is:

On the twenty-ninth of December, eighteen forty-nine, having announced the three canonical banns on three consecutive Sundays, on the second, on the ninth, and on the sixteenth of December, and having observed the prescriptions of the civil law [this area was part of the Kingdom of the Two Sicilies, and Napoleonic law, starting in 1809, continued there to the start of the Italian state in 1865], *and not having discovered any canonical impediment, the priest Don Antonio MANFREDONIO, with permission from me, the here undersigned Archpriest, having obtained their consensus, and by word of those present, joined in solemn marriage the couple Michele LOMBARDI, son of Plicolantonio and of Maria Teresa MARINACCIO, and Celestina PATIERNE, daughter of the deceased Giuseppe and of Rosa Maria MARINACCIO of this town, with permission of the Illustrious curia of Benevento, and observing the rites of the church, in the presence of the witnesses, Angelantonio D'ARDANO, son of the deceased Giovanni, and Giuseppe FERRITTO, son of the deceased Giovanni from this town, and he celebrated Mass without the wedding blessing due to the Sacred Advent.*

In faith, Archpriest D'AMATO

The format and the genealogical information provided are exactly the same as found in the previous example (figure 7-7). Some of the practices recorded were used throughout Italy from the beginning of the parish records; they were obviously prescribed by the Council of Trent. For example, all couples were married *per verba dei presenti*, or by "word of those present," and there were always two witnesses to the marriage. In this act there are also some local idiosyncrasies, such as the reference to permission from the *curia*, that are not commonly found in other records. An interesting item in this act is the absence of the wedding blessing due to the sacred Advent. Customarily, marriages did not occur during the period called Advent, which begins four Sundays before Christmas, or during Lent, the forty days before Easter that begin on Ash Wednesday. Marriage was not prohibited during these periods, as this act shows, but certain restrictions were observed. In this case the wedding blessing was not pronounced; during Lent, church

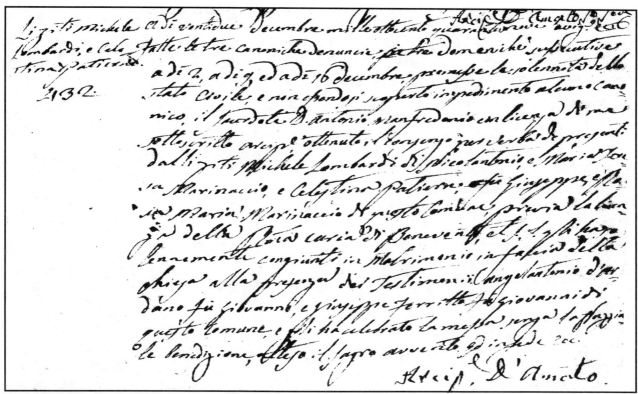

FIGURE 7-8. Parish Marriage Act of Michele Lombardi and Celestina Patierne, 1849, S. Angelo Parish, Acquasanta Terme, Ascoli Piceno

bells were not rung. These customs are still observed in Italy.

Two examples from the Vodo parish (figures 7-9 and 7-10), of the 1700s and 1600s, respectively, demonstrate how the form of the act can vary and that essential information about the parents of the couple does not appear. The first act, from 1703, is for the marriage of a widower and widow. It is an interesting variation of the normal act and reads as follows:

13 Gennaro 1703

Jacomo figlio di M.tro Titian Marchion Vedovo p. la morte d'Orsola della Bona, et Zuanna rel.a dal qm Bartholomio q.m Bastian di Lorenzo, dispensati da sua Beatitudine supra li quattro gradi di consanguita' e d'affinita', dispensati anche d'un unica pubblicazione furono sposati da me Curato sud.to alla presenza di Simon Marchion et di M.sto Antonio di Lorenzo.

This is translated as:

13 January 1703

Jacomo, son of Master Titian MARCHION, widower of the deceased Orsola DELLA BONA, and Zuanna, aggrieved widow of the deceased Bartolomio, son of the deceased Bastian DI LORENZO, with permission from His Beatitude [the pope] regarding the rule of the fourth

degree of consanguinity and affinity, and also dispensed for just one bann announced, they were married by me, the above stated Curate, in the presence of Simon MARCHION and Master Antonio DI LORENZO.

When one or the other of the couple (or, as in this case, both) was married for the second or even third time, his or her status as widow or widower was usually noted in the act. The abbreviations *ved.* or *v.*, for *vedovo/a* or, as in this case, *rel.a*, for *relicta* (bereaved), were commonly used to indicate this status. Occasionally, particularly for the male, *in seconda nozze* or *2.da nozze* would indicate a second wedding. The previous wife of a widower is not always mentioned; however, the name of a widow's first husband is usually included. Very often, as in this example, the given name and surname of the first husband are noted, but not the name of the widow's father or her maiden name. It is thus necessary to find the act for her first marriage, where her maiden name and father's name are included, to find the family name and continue the maternal line.

It is interesting that the first name Jacomo was modified from the Italian Giacomo and Latin Jacobus, while the name of the wife, Zuana, is dialect—again demonstrating how each priest was free to record information according to his ability or whim.

As discussed earlier, it was necessary to obtain permission from the pope through the *curia* to marry a relative of

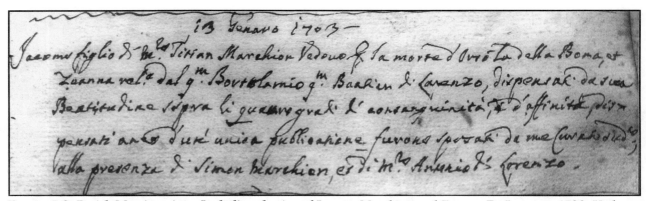

FIGURE 7-9. Parish Marriage Acts, Including the Act of Jacomo Marchion and Zuanna De Lorenzo, 1703, Vodo, Belluno

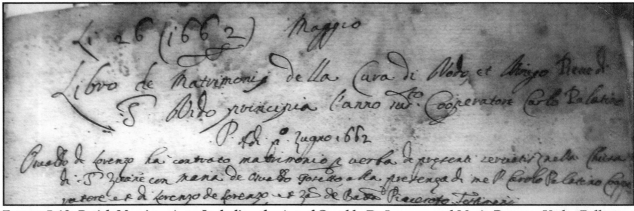

FIGURE 7-10. Parish Marriage Acts, Including the Act of Osvaldo De Lorenzo and Maria Rosetto, Vodo, Belluno

the third degree of consanguinity, such as a first cousin. Such permission is indicated in this act, together with the elimination of two obligatory banns. The reason, of course, is not stated in the marriage act but can be found in the petition to the pope found in the documents at the diocesan archive (see chapter 8).

The next act (figure 7-10, at bottom), from 1662, follows the normal format but, as is apparent, provides little information beyond the names and surnames of the couple. Even this information is important, however, because in the baptismal records of the same period the maiden name of the child's mother was not indicated; therefore, the marriage record provides the only clue to identify the family of the wife, allowing that line to be researched.

As may be seen, during this period there were many acts on each page of a record volume and no numbering or indexes, so research requires that each act be examined to find the one of interest. Normally, too, in documents from this early period the ink has faded and the handwriting is less regular, so research takes much longer.

Adì p.o Zugno 1662
Osvaldo de Lorenzo ha contratto matrimonio p. verba de presenti servatis S. nella chiesa di S. Zuanne con Maria de Osvaldo Rosetto alla presenza di me P. Carolo

Palatino Cooperatore et di Lorenzo de Lorenzo et Za de Batta Piveroto Testimonii

Or:

On the day One June 1662
Osvaldo DE LORENZO *was joined in marriage by word of those present, observing the prescribed rites, in the Church of S. John, with Maria, daughter of Osvaldo* ROSETTO, *in my presence, Father Carolo* PALATINO, *the Chaplain, and in the presence of Lorenzo* DE LORENZO *and Zuanne, son of Battista* PIVEROTO, *the witnesses*

That all early records were brief, providing little information, is contradicted by a record from Lonate Pozzolo, near Milan, from the year 1570 (figure 7-11). Though the ink is slightly faded, the act is as complete as those from later centuries examined previously:

M D L X X
A dì 5 Febraio
Fatte le tre denuntiationi nei tre giorni di festa infra. cio e' a dì 22 et 29 Genaio et a dì 2 Febraio ne havendosi inteso esser alcun impedimento tra Ambrogio fig.lo di Pietro buoni Bolazzi di lona' et Maddalena fig.la di

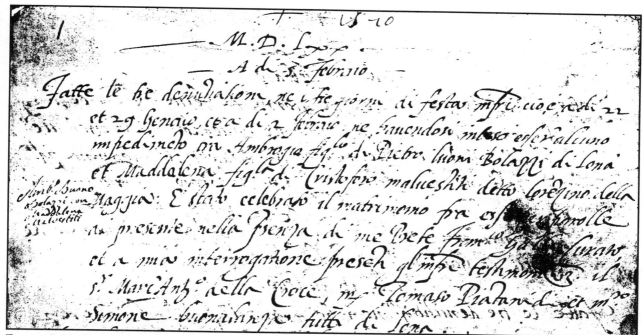

FIGURE 7-11. Parish Marriage Acts, Including the Act of Ambrogio Buoni Bolazzi and Maddalena Malvestiti Lorenzino, 1570, Lonate Pozzolo, Varese

Cristoforo malvestiti detto Lorenzino della Maggia. E stato celebrato il matrimonio fra esse per parolle di presente nella Presenza di me Prete Fran.co Galli Curato et a mia interrogatione presenti gli infra testimoni vz. il S.r Marc'Ant.o della Croce, ms Tomaso Piatani et m.o Simone buonalanza tutti di lona.

While there is a general tendency among the earlier records for the handwriting to be increasingly more difficult to read and the ink and pages to be more faded, such is not always the case. Very much depends on the individual parish priest. Some priests in the 1500s had excellent handwriting and included much information, while some in the 1800s had almost illegible handwriting and were careless in providing data. Written in Italian, this is similar to the second act examined. Translated, it reads:

1570

On 5 February

Having announced the three banns on three religious holidays, that is, on the 22nd and 29th of January and the 2nd of February, and not having found any impediment, the marriage was celebrated by word of those present, between Ambrogio, son of Pietro BUONI BOLAZZI *from Lonate, and Maddalena, daughter of Cristoforo* MALVESTITI, *called* LORENZINO DELLA MAGGIA, *both in my presence, Priest Francesco* GALLI, *the Curate, and at my interrogation of the couple were present the witnesses Sir Marc'Antonio* DELLA CROCE, *Master Tomaso* PIATANI, *and master Simone* BUONALANZA, *all from Lonate.*

Here, as was fairly common, names are abbreviated; thus, Antonio becomes Ant.o and Francesco becomes Fran.co (see the list of names and their abbreviations in chapter 12). As seen, the last letters in the abbreviation were usually written above the preceding letters. Often, too, one letter of a double consonant was omitted; a line above the first consonant indicated the missing consonant. This was commonly done, for example, with the Latin Joannes, which was written Joanes with a line above the "n" to indicate the second "n." There is a series of abbreviated titles in these acts, such as *M.s* for maestro and *Rev.* for reverendo.

DEATH AND BURIAL RECORDS

When going to Italy, many Americans mistakenly assume that they will find cemeteries in which their ancestors are buried; they hope to locate their ancestors' gravestones with genealogical information engraved. In the United States and most of North America, cemeteries contain graves and gravestones that sometimes date back hundreds of years and have genealogical information for the people buried there. Unfortunately, the same is not true in Italy. In most large towns and cities, a burial plot can be rented and a gravestone placed for ten, twenty, or thirty years. After this period of time the remains are exhumed and, if the family desires, placed in an urn and deposited more permanently in the wall of the cemetery. Otherwise, the remains are placed in a communal burial spot within the cemetery. In any case, the gravestone is removed and the burial plot is used for a new grave. Therefore, in most cities it is difficult to find a gravestone older than thirty years. This practice is due to the scarcity of land in Italy and the need to dedicate existing land to the living rather than to the dead.

In smaller villages there may be less demand for space and the grave may remain longer than thirty years, but rarely will you find graves that precede World War I, much less from periods when most people's ancestors were buried. A law states that any property rented for one hundred years or longer becomes the property of the renter. Since the cemeteries belong to the towns, a burial plot cannot be rented for longer than ninety-nine years, as after that time the town would have to relinquish property rights. This was true in earlier centuries as well because cemeteries were normally next to the parish church in the center of the village and were rarely very large. The exceptions are the noble families, whose members where often buried in family vaults in the floor or basement of the church, their names engraved in the marble flooring. Some families had private burial plots on their property. It is rarely possible to find the gravestone of an ancestor, and cemeteries are seldom helpful genealogical sources. However, parish death records usually date back as far as the other records and do provide vital information.

As will be seen, the death records are the least valuable and the most difficult and time-consuming records to consult in the parish, but no thorough genealogical research is complete without consulting them. A search of the death records not only rounds out research with additional information; it is also essential to consult death records for each direct ancestor to verify that he or she did not die in infancy. Otherwise, there is less assurance that the correct family line has been found. I researched a previously-completed genealogy project that was based on a family line starting from an ancestor in the 1800s. In actuality, however, this person was not the direct ancestor or even in the right line but, instead, had died in infancy. This fact would have become readily apparent if the previous researcher had taken time to consult the death records.

It is relatively easy to complete the births or baptisms for a family group and to find the marriage of a couple because the acts can be found within a limited and known period of time. However, it is usually much more difficult to find the death record of an ancestor because his or her death may be anywhere within a ninety-year period (unless an approximate death date is already known). Also, as will be seen, not always is enough information provided to identify with certainty the person of interest.

As with the previous records, the first act examined (figure 7-12) is from a fairly recent period. The first death act—atti di morte—again is from the town of Alpette in the Piedmont region and is for the year 1848. It reads:

ATTI DI MORTE (1848) Fol. *primo*
L'anno del Signore mille ottocento quarantotto ed alli *quattro del mese* di *Gennaio* nella Parrocchia de SS

Pietro e Paolo Comune di *Alpette* e' stata fatta la seguente dichiarazione di decesso
Il giorno *quattro* del mese di *Gennaio* alle ore *una pomeridiana* nel distretto *di questa parrochia,* casa *propria* munito de S Sacramenti Penitenza, Viatico, estrema unzione con ben. papale e' morto Giuseppe Dominietto d'eta' d'anni *settanta* di professione *magnano* nativo del Comune di *Alpette* domiciliato nel Comune di *Alpette* vedovo in prime nozze di *Maria Seren-Rosso* in seconde di ____ in terze di ____ maritato con ____ figlio del *fu* Domenico Dominietto di professione ____ domiciliato in ____ e della *fu* Maria Antonia Dominietto di professione ____ domiciliata in ____
Dichiaranti *Michaele Goglio* d'eta' d'anni *cinquanta-cinque* domiciliato in *Alpette* e *Goglio Pietro* d'eta' d'anni *quindici* domiciliato in *Alpette* ambi sottoscritti
    Firma del primo testimonio *Michele Goglio*
    Firma del secondo testimonio *Goglio Pietro*
Il cadavere e' stato sepolto il giorno *cinque* del mese di *Gennaio* nel cimitero di *Alpette*
    Firma del Parroco
    D. Demelchiore Iemo

This death act is fairly typical of more recent acts. It contains important genealogical information and imparts an understanding of the social and religious aspect of this event. The first part is translated as:

DEATH ACT (1848) Page *first*
In the year of the Lord eighteen forty-eight and on the *fourth of the* month of *January* in the Parish *of Saints Peter and Paul,* in the Commune of *Alpette,* the following declaration of death was made.
On the day *four* of the month of *January* at the hour *one in the afternoon* in the district of *the Parish,* and in his *own home,* provided with the *Holy Sacraments of Repentance, Eucharistia* and *Extreme Unction with the Papal Blessing* . . .

This first part of the certificate indicates the date and some of the religious sacraments involved with sickness and death. Important to note, once again, is the fact that the first date given is that of the declaration of death by the witnesses—the actual date of death is not indicated until the second paragraph. Usually these dates coincide. Often, however, if the person died in the evening or at night, the declaration would not be made until the following day.

Death was a natural part of the social and religious fabric of the epoch. More often than not it occurred in the home with family and loved ones nearby, and it was regarded as an important religious moment. Much of the

FIGURE 7-12. Parish Death Act of Giuseppe Dominietto, 1848, Alpette, Torino

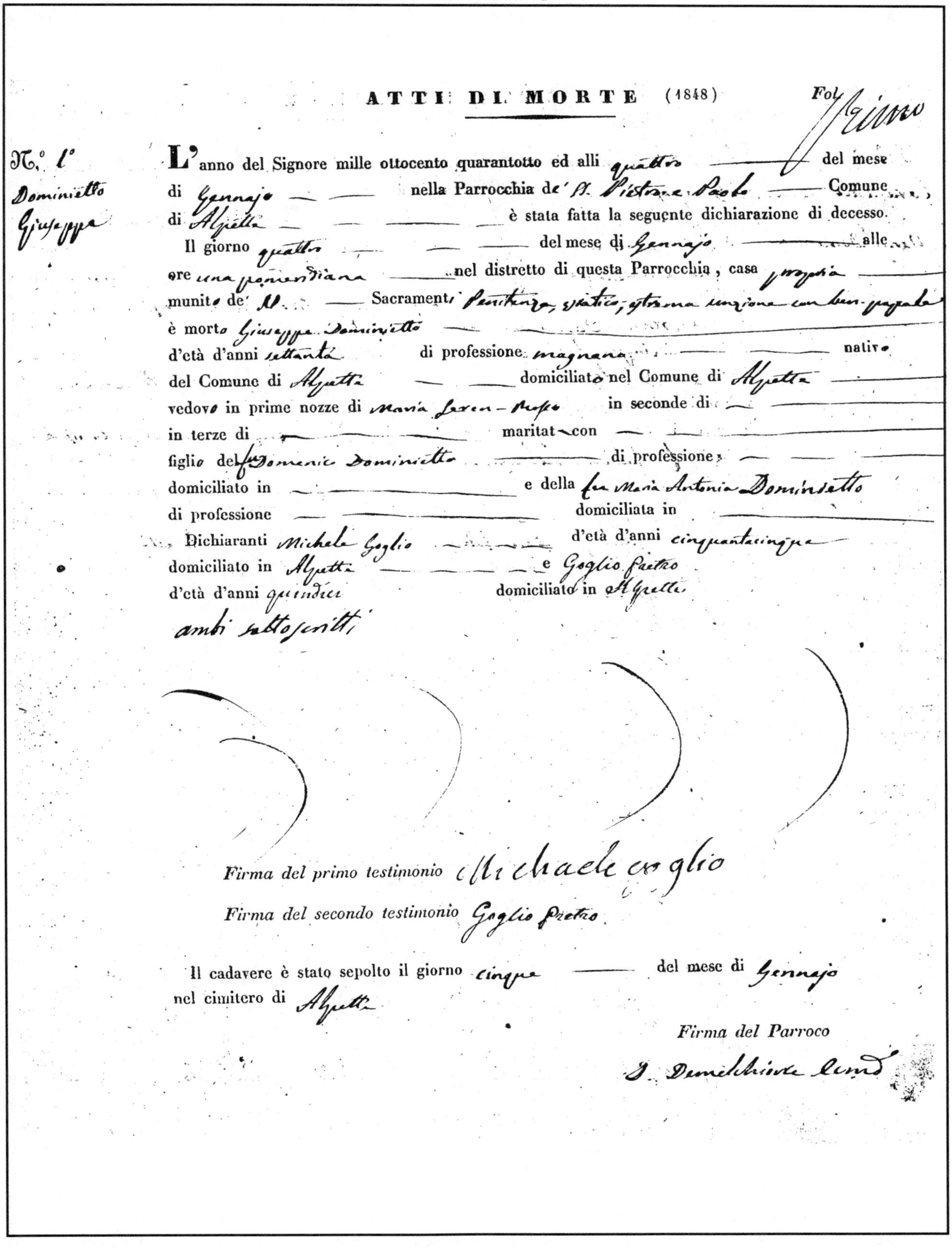

parish priest's time, as is true today, was dedicated to visiting the sick and comforting the dying. There was a series of church sacraments that were intended to comfort and assist the passage from this life; they are noted in almost all death acts. This was the moment in which the person could confess and repent of all his or her sins (*confessione* and *penitenza*) and receive forgiveness through the sacraments of Eucharistia and Extreme Unction. It was considered a great misfortune if sudden death did not allow time for these sacraments. For those who had long, drawn-out illnesses, the sacraments may have been given and repeated numerous times in case the person sinned and became impure from one administering to another. These sacraments were established and their inclusion in the parish death act decreed by the Council of Trent.

The act goes on to provide genealogical information about the deceased:

> . . . Giuseppe DOMINIETTO died at age *seventy*, by vocation a *landowner*, a native of the town of *Alpette* and living in the town of *Alpette*, widower of his first marriage to *Maria SEREN-ROSSO* in second marriage ___ in third marriage ___ married to ___ son of *the deceased Domenico DOMINIETTO*, by vocation a ___ living at ___ and of the *deceased Maria Antonia DOMINIETTO*, by vocation a ___ living at ___
> Those making the declaration, *Michele GOGLIO*, age *fifty-five*, living at *Alpette*, and *GOGLIO Pietro*, age *fifteen*, living at *Alpette*, are *both undersigned*
>   Signature of the first witness, *Michaele GOGLIO*
>   Signature of the second witness, *GOGLIO Pietro*
> The body was buried on the day *five* of the month of *January* in the cemetery of *Alpette*
>   Signature of the parish priest, *Don DEMELCHIORE Lemo*

Important genealogical information is provided here. The name, age, and profession of the deceased are given, and the name of the wife or husband for each of the deceased's marriages is also included. In this case, Giuseppe, the deceased, was a widower of one wife, but the form requests information about all possible marriages. The parents of the deceased are indicated, and space was provided for their vocations, although, in this case, the priest did not indicate what they did for a living.

As important as this information is, you should also be aware of some of the limitations. Some more recent death documents provide the exact date of birth or baptism, which is certainly more precise and helpful in identifying the subject as an ancestor and in continuing research. However, in many cases the stated age of the deceased is approximate. If the priest did not consult the deceased's baptism record, he probably estimated the person's age or accepted the word of relatives. I have documented cases in which the age listed in the records at the time of death was inaccurate by five, eight, or even ten years.

A fact that has been mentioned but that should be reemphasized is that, in Italy, even today, married females are known legally and socially by their maiden names (see chapter 5). In all documents, with few exceptions, the wife or mother is identified by her maiden name or, if it is not known, by no surname at all. In this case, the certificate indicates that the mother of Giuseppe is Maria Antonia Dominietto. However, this does not mean that she took the surname of her husband; rather, she too is from the Dominietto family, although from another branch.

A final note about the first death act (figure 7-12): once again, two legal witnesses (besides the priest) were required to ascertain and declare the death. It is interesting to note the use of a minor, Pietro Goglio, in this document. It may have been that the young man was studying with the priest and was readily available to sign his name, because he appears as a witness in almost all of the death records of Alpette in this period.

This document served also as a burial act and indicated the time and place of the burial. This information is commonly found in more recent records, but it was frequently omitted in earlier documents. In Italy, throughout the centuries, the corpse was buried within two days (at the most) from the time of death. This practice was established as law by Napoleon but was a fact of life even before then. Even today, with sophisticated means of preserving a corpse existing, the funeral must be held within two days from the death unless special permission is obtained from the civil authorities. Thus, the death date and burial date will be close, and the place of burial will always be the parish cemetery unless indicated otherwise.

An important omission in the example above (figure 7-12) is the cause of death. In most regions of Italy until the twentieth century, the cause of death was not included in either the parish or the civil death records (except for the parish civil records found in northeast Italy, as discussed in chapter 5)—probably because there were few doctors and understanding of illnesses was scarce, so often there was no way to determine the cause of death. Frequently, when a cause was mentioned, archaic terms such as *malore* (sudden sickness) and *deperimento* (wasted away) provide little medical data. This is unfortunate because families sometimes seek death certificates for their direct ancestors to confirm the existence or absence of certain congenital diseases, but this information is rarely available. Sometimes, when a death was caused by an unusual event, such as a person's being struck by a falling tree or drowning in a stream during a storm, the fact was noted in the records.

Parish civil records from the Venetian region include the causes of death because of an earlier order of the Serenissima Republic of Venice. In this republic, from 1576 on, it was necessary for the parish priest to indicate the cause of death in the records for each parishioner and to send copies of the records to the civil authorities. This practice was begun after the various plagues had ravished Europe from 1349 through the 1500s—in particular the last "plague" of cholera, which struck this area of Italy with particular intensity. The death record was then used by civil authorities to determine the beginning of any new plague or infectious disease epidemic. Many of these records can still be found in the state archives of Venezia, Padova, and Trieste, and they form a valuable source. The constant threat of epidemic is illustrated in a page from the death records of Cles in the Trento province (figure 7-13), which shows the deaths from cholera of thirty-five people from the village in an eighteen-day period. Similar pages follow. In a forty-day period just over one hundred years ago, more than 180 people from this village of around two thousand died of cholera.

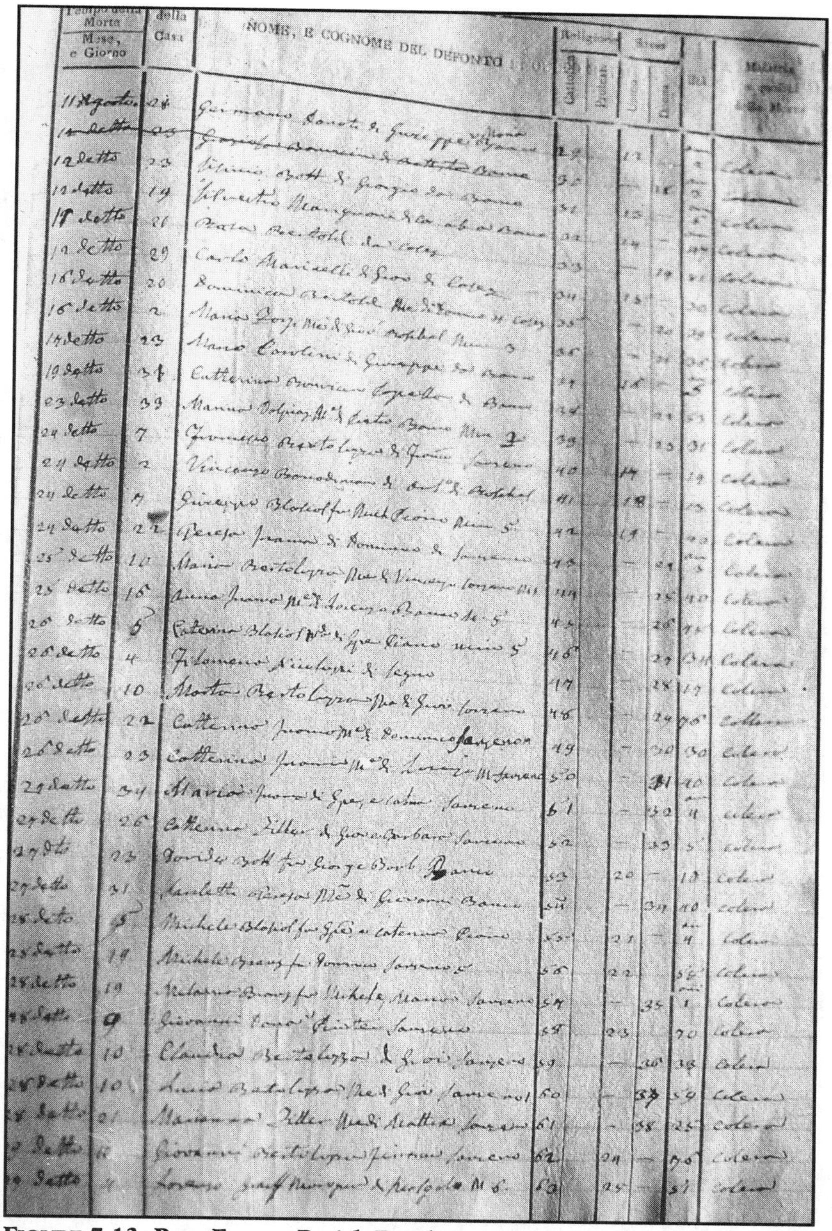

A further example of concern for the cause of death in the Serenissima Republic, from a parish in the Venetian region, is a death record (figure 7-14) in which much space is dedicated to the cause of death—*qualita' della morte*. This space is divided into three sections: *per malattia* (by sickness), *per violenza* (by violence), and *sorte o il male* (happenstance or illness). The first two of these are further divided. Sickness is described as common (*comune*), local, or epidemic, and violence is described as military (*servizio*), accident (*disgrazia*), or murder (*uccisione*). Each death is listed in one of these columns, and the last one describes the specific cause of death. In this example, one death resulted from a fall from a tree, and several infants died from convulsions (*convulsione*).

As stated previously, the use of preprinted forms for parish records was a practice that many dioceses imitated from the Napoleonic and Italian civil records, and they were used particularly in those dioceses where the *curia* kept a second copy of all parish records. Do not be under the impression, however, that all parish acts of the last century were written on preprinted, easy-to-read records. In many areas, particularly in the south of Italy, these records are still handwritten and no second copy is made at all. An example from just a few decades ago (figure 7-15) is in modern Italian:

FIGURE 7-13. Page From a Parish Death Record Volume Showing Deaths From Cholera, 11 to 26 August 1826, Cles, Trento

Li 7 Maggio 1952
9 Bonato Giovanni fu Gio Battista e fu Azzolin Maria coniugi. Nato a Crosara S. Bortolo li 21 Maggio 1863. Dimiciliato a Salcedo, marito della defunta Bonato Ellena. Mori' li 7 Maggio 1952 da paralisi progressiva alle ore 12, gli furono amministrati i sacramenti della Confessione, Comunione, ed Estrema Unzione. Gli fu impartita la Benedizione Papale con Indulgenza Plenaria. Non fu assistito fino alla fine per la morte repentina. Il di lui cadavere dopo le consuete esequie fu tumulato nel Cimitero Comunale di questa Parrocchia.
Vidale Don Bortolo Parroco

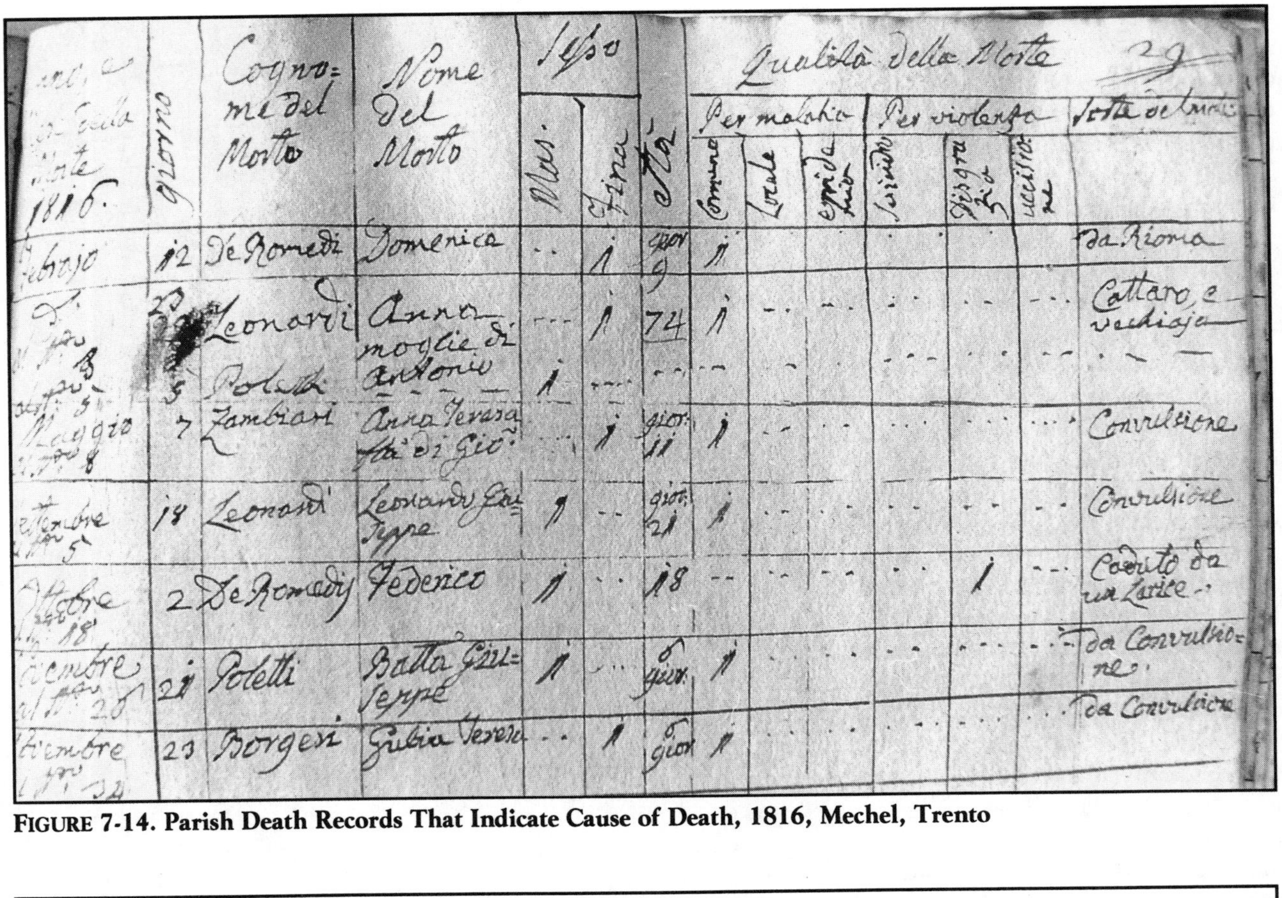

FIGURE 7-14. Parish Death Records That Indicate Cause of Death, 1816, Mechel, Trento

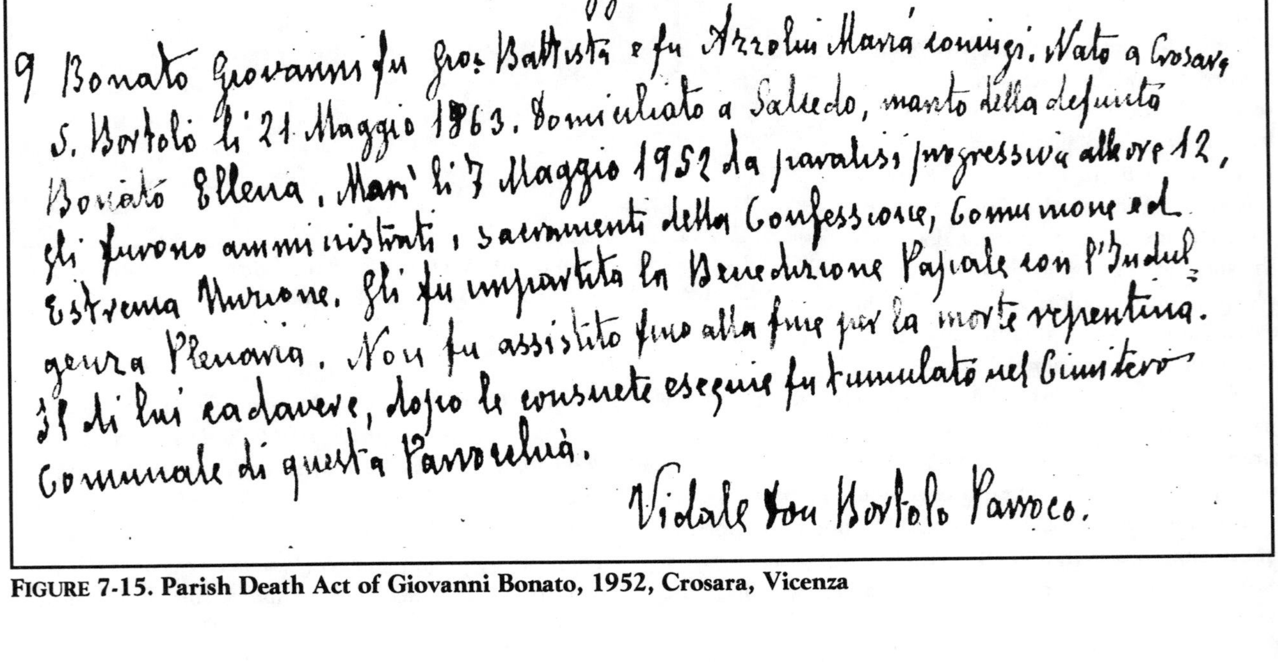

FIGURE 7-15. Parish Death Act of Giovanni Bonato, 1952, Crosara, Vicenza

This death act follows a format different from the initial example (figure 7-12) but provides much the same information. Translated, it reads:

On 7 May 1952
9 BONATO Giovanni, *son of the deceased Gio Battista and of the deceased AZZOLIN Maria, his wife. Born at Crosara S. Bortolo on 21 May 1863. Living at Salcedo and husband of the deceased BONATO Ellena, died on 7 May 1952 from progressive paralysis at the hour of 12. He was administered the sacraments of the Confession, Communion, and Extreme Unction, and he was given the Papal Blessing with full indulgence. He was not assisted to the very end because of the quickness of the death. His corpse after the normal administrations was buried in the Town Cemetery of this parish.*
VIDALE Don Bortolo, *Parish Priest*

Again, though the date at the top of the act and the death date are the same, do not assume that such is always the case. The first is the date when the priest wrote the act; only within the act itself is the death date indicated.

This act, compared with the previous one of approximately a century earlier, provides more precise data but omits some information. Both the exact birth date and place of birth are indicated. The cause of death is stated (though not in precise medical terms). On the other hand, the deceased's vocation is not stated at all, and the exact date of the burial is not indicated. Different terminology is used to indicate the sacraments that were administered, but they are the same as those indicated in the previous act. That a similar format for each of these acts was used in separate localities of Italy and spanning a century of time is strong testimony of the importance and influence of the decisions of the Council of Trent.

In most death acts, the most frequent form of death indicated was infant mortality. Before the 1900s, infant mortality or death at a young age was from twenty-five to fifty percent. In many large families of seven or eight children, only three or four lived to maturity and later married. Certainly this mortality rate was due to the limited medical facilities and knowledge of earlier periods, but it was also due to the harsh environment to which children were exposed. Rarely was there adequate heating, and food, even in the best of times, was scarce by modern standards. Childbirth was hazardous, and often both mother and child died during a difficult pregnancy.

Of six death acts shown in figure 7-16, four were of infants, one of whom died at age three, two at about one year, and the other at birth. The Latin act for Dominica Giacoletto (fifth from the top) reads:

Mense junii
Giacoletto Dominica filia Josephi et Margarita, nata Girot, jugalium Giacoletto e furno Riparia Infans unius

anni circiter abdormivit in Domino die quarta junii et die seguenti sepulta fuit in Cemeterio infantium Sancti Bartolomei.

This is translated as:

Month of June [1812]
GIACOLETTO Dominica, *daughter of Joseph and of Margarita born GIROT from Forno Rivara, an infant of about one year old, fell asleep in God on June fourth, and the following day was buried in the cemetery for infants of S. Bartolomio.*

For infants, none of the usual sacraments were given or required by the church if baptism had been performed. Thus, it was sufficient to identify the child and his or her parents and to indicate the date of death and burial. It is interesting to note that priests often used poetic phrases, such as "asleep in the Lord," to indicate death. Note also the use of the word *circiter* or, in Italian, *circa* (often abbreviated *c.a.*), which means "about" or "approximately." This word was used often in documents in regard to a person's age and indicates that the age was rounded off or was not known with assurance.

In the record above is another death act for a Bertoldo. In it, no name is indicated for the child; rather, the abbreviation N.N., for the Latin *nescio nomen*, or "of unknown name," is present. This phrase was commonly applied to stillborn children. The act states that the baptism was given in the womb because of the danger of death but that no name was given because she (the child was female—*filia*, which means "daughter," was used) was born dead. Very often such an infant was not included in the baptismal records; the only indication of the birth would be in the death records.

The final death acts (figures 7-17 and 7-18) again demonstrate the relative lack of information provided in earlier records. The first example is from death records of 1737. It shows that the basic format of the death act is the same as in more recent records, but less personal information is contained. The first act reads:

1737
Mille settecentotrentasette adì quatro Marzo Cattarina Milana moglie di Fran.co Specio Betiano d'anni trenta sette in circa munita de SS.mi Sagramenti Penitenza, ed estrema uncione passò da questa a miglior vita, fu sepolta in questa nostra pa.che di S. Ambrogio di Ionate pozzolo.

In English:

1737
Seventeen hundred and thirty-seven, on the fourth of March, Cattarina MILANA, wife of Francesco SPECIO

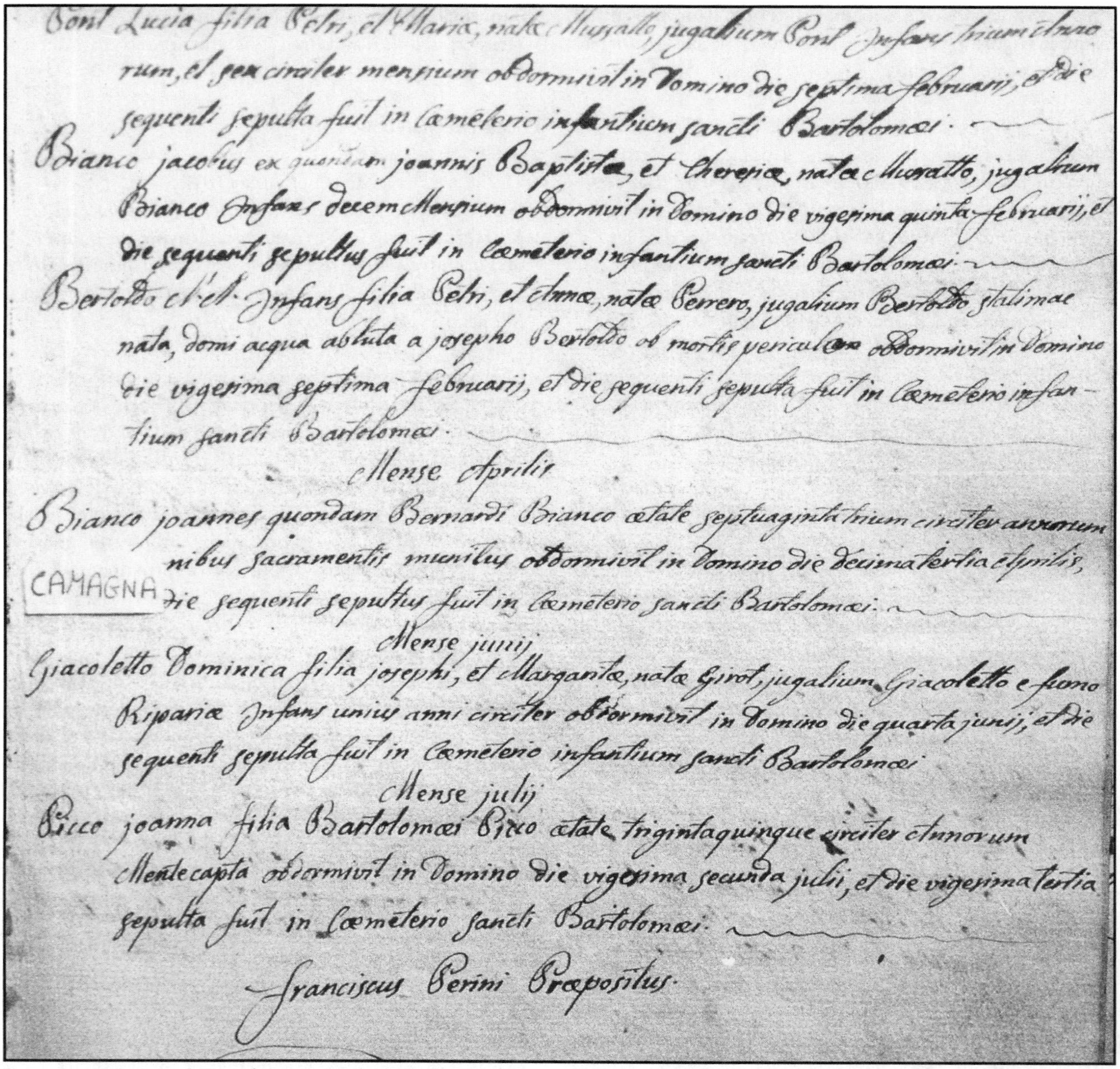

Pont Lucia filia Petri, et Mariae, natae Mussatto, jugalium Pont Infans trium circiter annorum, et sex circiter mensium obdormivit in Domino die septima februarii, et die sequenti sepulta fuit in Coemeterio infantium sancti Bartolomaei.

Bianco jacobus ex quondam joannis Baptistae, et Chericae, natae Muratto, jugalium Bianco Infans decem Mensium obdormivit in Domino die vigesima quinta februarii, et die sequenti sepultus fuit in Coemeterio infantium sancti Bartolomaei.

Bertoldo et ret. Infans filia Petri, et Annae, natae Perrero, jugalium Bertoldo statim nata, domi acqua abluta a josepho Bertoldo ob mortis periculum obdormivit in Domino die vigesima septima februarii, et die sequenti sepulta fuit in Coemeterio infantium sancti Bartolomaei.

Mense Aprilis

Bianco joannes quondam Bernardi Bianco aetate septuaginta trium circiter annorum omnibus sacramentis munitus obdormivit in Domino die decima tertia Aprilis, et die sequenti sepultus fuit in Coemeterio sancti Bartolomaei.

CAMAGNA

Mense junii

Giacoletto Dominica filia josephi, et Margaritae, natae Girot, jugalium Giacoletto e furno Ripariae Infans unius anni circiter obdormivit in Domino die quarta junii, et die sequenti sepulta fuit in Coemeterio infantium sancti Bartolomaei.

Mense julii

Picco joanna filia Bartolomaei Picco aetate triginta quinque circiter Annorum Mentecapta obdormivit in Domino die vigesima secunda julii, et die vigesima tertia sepulta fuit in Coemeterio sancti Bartolomaei.

Franciscus Perini Praepositus

FIGURE 7-16. Parish Death Acts, Including the Act of Domenica Giacoletto, 1812, Forno Canavese (Formerly Forno Rivara), Torino

BETIANO, age thirty-seven approximately, supplied with the Holy Sacraments of Repentance and Extreme Unction, passed from this to a better life and was buried in our parish of San Ambrogio of Lonate Pozzolo.

There is no reference to the parents of the deceased (though there likely would be if the deceased was a child) and information such as vocation, previous marriages, and the like is not provided. However, it was important to list the sacraments administered, and the place of burial is indicated.

In the last example, from 1656 (figure 7-18), poor handwriting makes reading the document difficult, and even less information is provided in each act. The first act reads:

1656 die p.a octobris
Caterina Tapella d'età di quaranta anni succeptis eccl.a sa.mis morta adì 30 setembre il p.o d'ottobre fu sepolta nella parochiale

All of the information found in acts from later periods has been reduced to the essential:

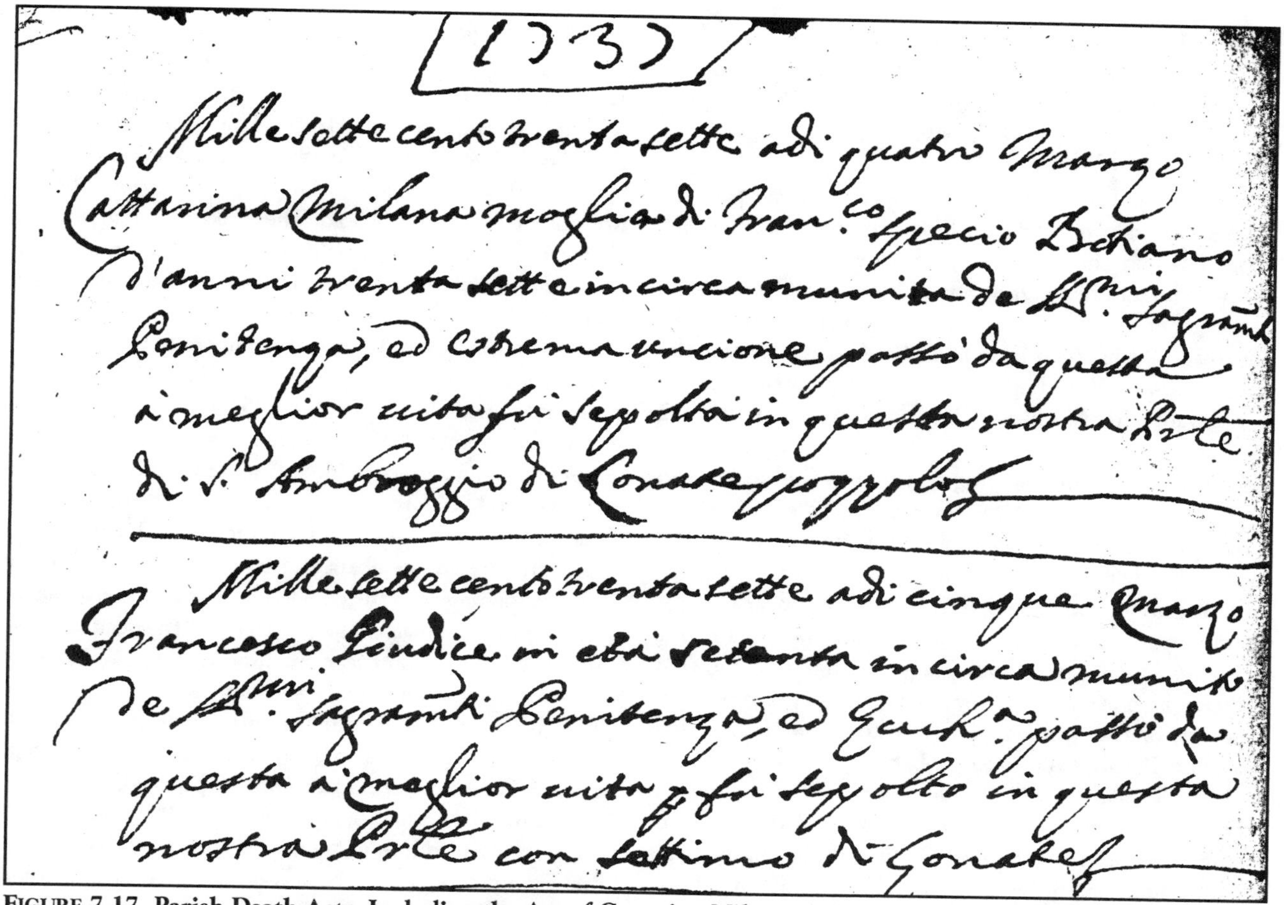

[7 3]

Millesettecento trentasette adi quattro Marzo Cattarina Milana moglie di Fran.co Speciо Bеharo d'anni trenta sette in circa munita de SS.mi Sagram.ti Penitenza, ed estrema uncione passò da questa a meglior vita fu sepolta in questa nostra P.rle di S. Ambroggio di Conate qui popolo

Millesettecento trentasette adi cinque Marzo Francesco Giudice in età settanta in circa munito de SS.mi Sagram.ti Penitenza, ed Euch.a passò da questa a meglior vita, fu sepolto in questa nostra P.rle con settimo di Conate

FIGURE 7-17. Parish Death Acts, Including the Act of Cattarina Milana, 1737, Lonate Pozzolo, Varese

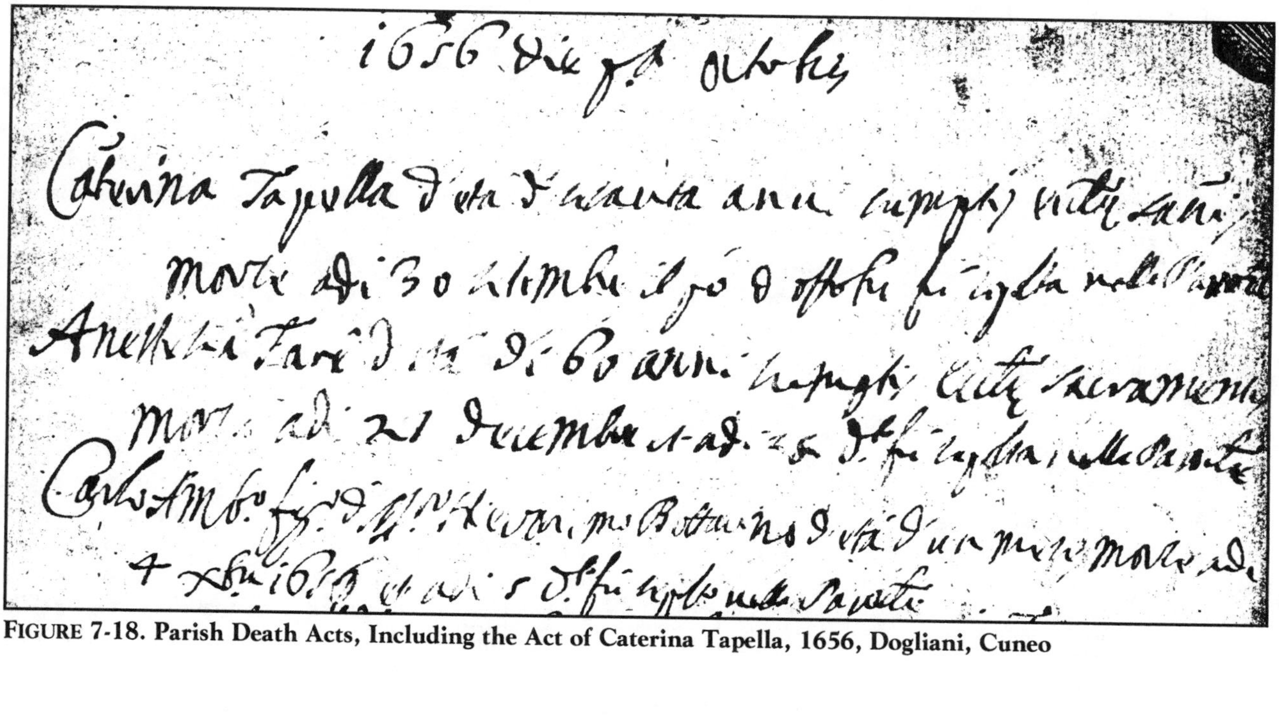

1656 die p.a ottobris

Caterina Tapella d'età d'ottanta anni compiti nelli anni, morte di 30 settembre il p.o d'ottobre fu sepolta nella Parochia

FIGURE 7-18. Parish Death Acts, Including the Act of Caterina Tapella, 1656, Dogliani, Cuneo

1656 First of October
Caterina TAPELLA, *age forty, supplied with the ecclesiastic sacraments, died on 30 september and on the first of October was buried in the parish cemetery*

It seems that Caterina was not married. (The acts for married women normally included the name of the husband. The opposite is true for men—rarely was the name of the wife mentioned. Only for children are the parents' names mentioned.) Besides the approximate age, no other personal information is included. There is a reference to the holy sacraments, but they are not listed separately. Still, the burial date and place are included; in the act from 1952 they were not.

It is quite common during research to find more than one child in a family with the same name. This is usually an indication that the first child of that name died before the second was born. Variations of the same name, however, were common and do not have the same meaning. For example, if there were two or more children named Petrus Antonius in the same family, it is probable that the first child died before the next infant of that name was born; if, however, one was called Petrus Antonius and the other Antonius Petrus, they were probably two separate, living individuals. A new child born later in the life of a couple or in a second marriage might have been named after a sibling who married and left the household and was still living.

Although parish priests should be commended for having left such precious and detailed records of their parishioners, mistakes and oversights were made and were not infrequent. A careful search of the records often leads to death records for children or adults for whom there are no baptismal records and vice versa. The names by which people were known and recorded in marriage and death records do not always correspond to their baptismal records. Sometimes acts were added at later dates when the priest realized that information was missing. Considering that priests often had jurisdiction over hamlets many miles away—perhaps atop a mountain—it is surprising how accurate they were, not that mistakes were made. This fact, however, reinforces the dictum that all available parish records should be examined to obtain the most complete information possible for each family.

STATUS ANIMARUM RECORDS

Though baptism, marriage, and death records are the standard documents found in all parishes of Italy, in the area that comprised the papal states in central Italy originated another interesting and useful record called the *status animarum* in Latin or *stato delle anime* in Italian. Both translate as "state of the souls." This record is basically a census that lists all the living members of each household, and it usually provides personal information, such as the age and relationship of each family member. These records were created by the papal states as a census of the population for tax purposes. Since, in the papal states, the ecclesiastical authorities were also the civil authorities, taxes were collected directly by the clergy. The census was taken periodically (usually every ten years, but the periods varied by diocese), and the taxes were based on the number of working males in a household. These records, similar to the civil certificates of *stato della famiglia* (see chapter 5), provide a comprehensive, easy-to-consult family group for every family in a parish.

The first example (figure 7-19) illustrates the wealth of information provided. It is a record from the province of Benevento, originally dating from 1852 but updated in 1882. It lists the members of household 904 of the town—the Tenisci family. The record identifies the head of the household, Angelo Maria Tenisci, his wife, Celeste Napolioni, and all of their children. It also provides the precise birth date for each of the family members and their relationships, and it indicates the names of the couple's fathers and the vocation of Angelo. The update to the record states the death date of Angelo and lists the marriage and families of two of his sons, who lived in the same household with their families. This information could take hours to find among the baptismal, marriage, and death records. In consulting the baptismal records it is possible to inadvertently skip a child, while here they are listed together.

At this point you might conclude that, where the *status animarum* records exist, there is no need to consult other records. However, a word of caution is necessary. First, earlier records, as will be seen, usually indicate only the age of the child, not the exact birth date, so this must be found in any case. Also, since the *status animarum* is a census record, only the children living in the household are indicated. Those who had married and left the household will be listed separately, and those who had died usually are not indicated at all. Finally, this record was compiled from other records, so the dates indicated, or the ages, may be inexact and should be compared with the original acts. Nevertheless, these are a precious source of information and can certainly expedite research. More importantly, they confirm family lines and family groups that might not be certain based on the original acts only.

The next example (figure 7-20) is from the town of Cautano and predates the previous example by a relatively short period (1814), but much less information is provided. The only exact birth date provided is for the head of the household, Filippo Massari; his wife and children are listed by age. Given the span between children, it is probable that other children were born and subsequently died but are not mentioned. In fact, the record notes that the youngest child of Filippo's family, Maria Giacinta, was the second of that name (*2da* [*seconda*] *di q.to* [*questo*] *nome*), but no other appears in the record. An interesting addition seen in the family of Giuseppe Massari (the last family shown) is a child named Giacomo Bucci. Giacomo is indicated to be a

FIGURE 7-19. Parish Stato delle Anime Record Showing the Tenisci Families, 1882, Cautano, Benevento

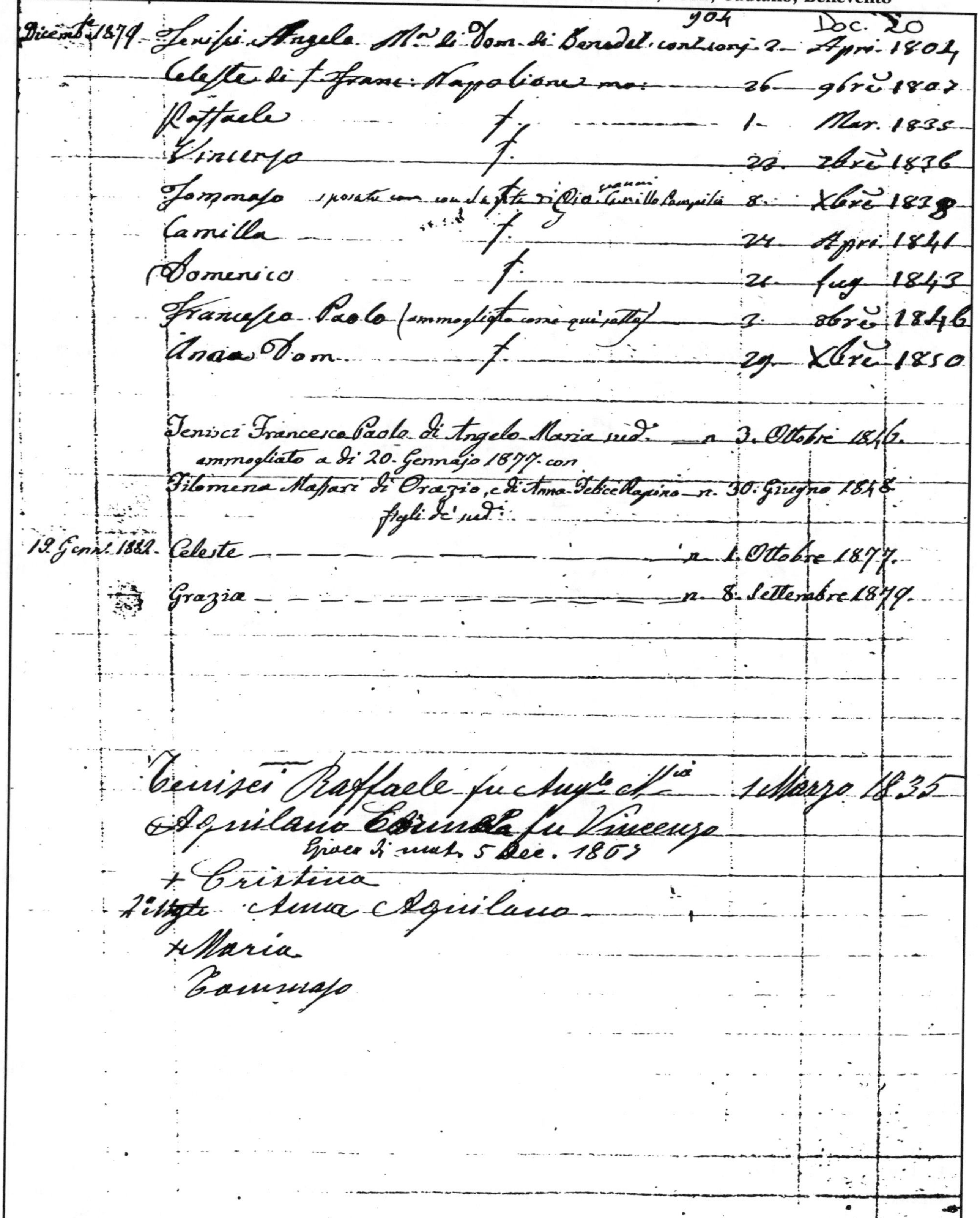

904 Doc. 20

Dicemb.re 1879 Tenisci Angelo M.a di Dom. di Benedet. contadino 2 Apri. 1804
Celeste di f. Franc. Napolione m.e 26 9bre 1807
Raffaele f. 1 Mar. 1835
Vincenzo f. 22 7bre 1836
Tommaso sposato con ... Gio. Camillo Pompilio 8 Xbre 1838
Camilla f. 24 Apri. 1841
Domenico f. 26 Lug. 1843
Francesco Paolo (ammogliato come qui sotto) 3 8bre 1846
Anna Dom. f. 29 Xbre 1850

Tenisci Francesco Paolo di Angelo Maria sud. n. 3. Ottobre 1846.
ammogliato a dì 20. Gennajo 1877. con
Filomena Massari di Orazio, e di Anna Felice Napino n. 30. Giugno 1848.
figli de' sud.
19. Genn. 1882 Celeste n. 1. Ottobre 1877.
Grazia n. 8. Settembre 1879.

Tenisci Raffaele fu Ang.o M.a 1 Marzo 1835
e Aquilano Carmela fu Vincenzo
Sposi di mat. 5 Dec. 1867
+ Cristina
figli Anna Aquilano
+ Maria
Tommaso

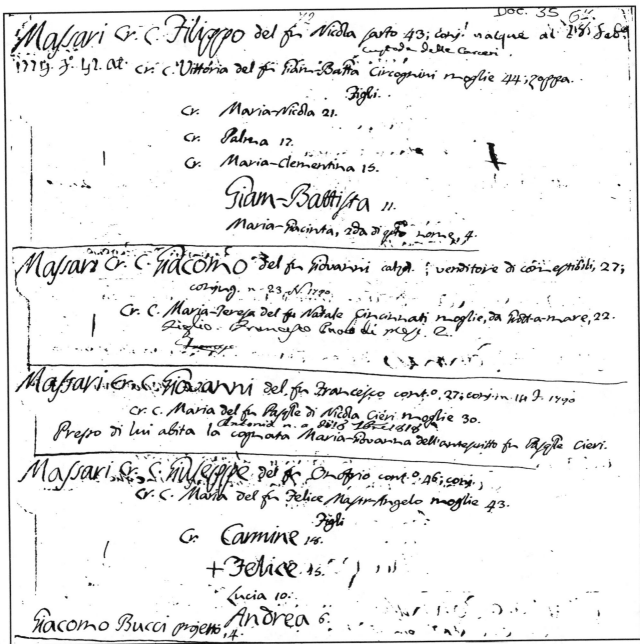

FIGURE 7-20. Parish Stato delle Anime Record Showing the Massari Families, 1812, Cautano, Benevento

proietto, or "foundling." As discussed in chapter 3, those foundlings or orphans who survived despite the high rate of infant mortality were usually taken in by families as servants or workers to earn their keep. Rarely, in normal parish records, is there any indication of who raised such children after baptism. Only in the *status animarum* record is found, as in this case, mention of foundlings and who raised them. Because this was a census record, these children were counted as part of the family that took them in, even though they were not legally adopted.

The next example (figure 7-21) is from a parish in the Abruzzo region; it was created during the 1700s. The clear and precise handwriting of the priest is noteworthy, and different information is provided. Across the top, different categories of information are listed: *nome* (name), *cognome* (surname), *professione* (vocation), *condizione naturale* (health), *num.o d' individui* (number of individuals), *num.o di casa* (house number), *stato* (marital status) and *eta'* (age). While most of these categories are normally found in the *status animarum* records, this is the only example I have found which records individuals as healthy (*sano/a*) or unhealthy (*ammalato/a*). Also, the number of people in a household was usually not listed separately. Noteworthy also is the fact that this is the only parish record that lists

FIGURE 7-21. Parish Stato delle Anime Record Showing the Mancini and Pantalone Families, 1756, S. Stefano, L'Aquila

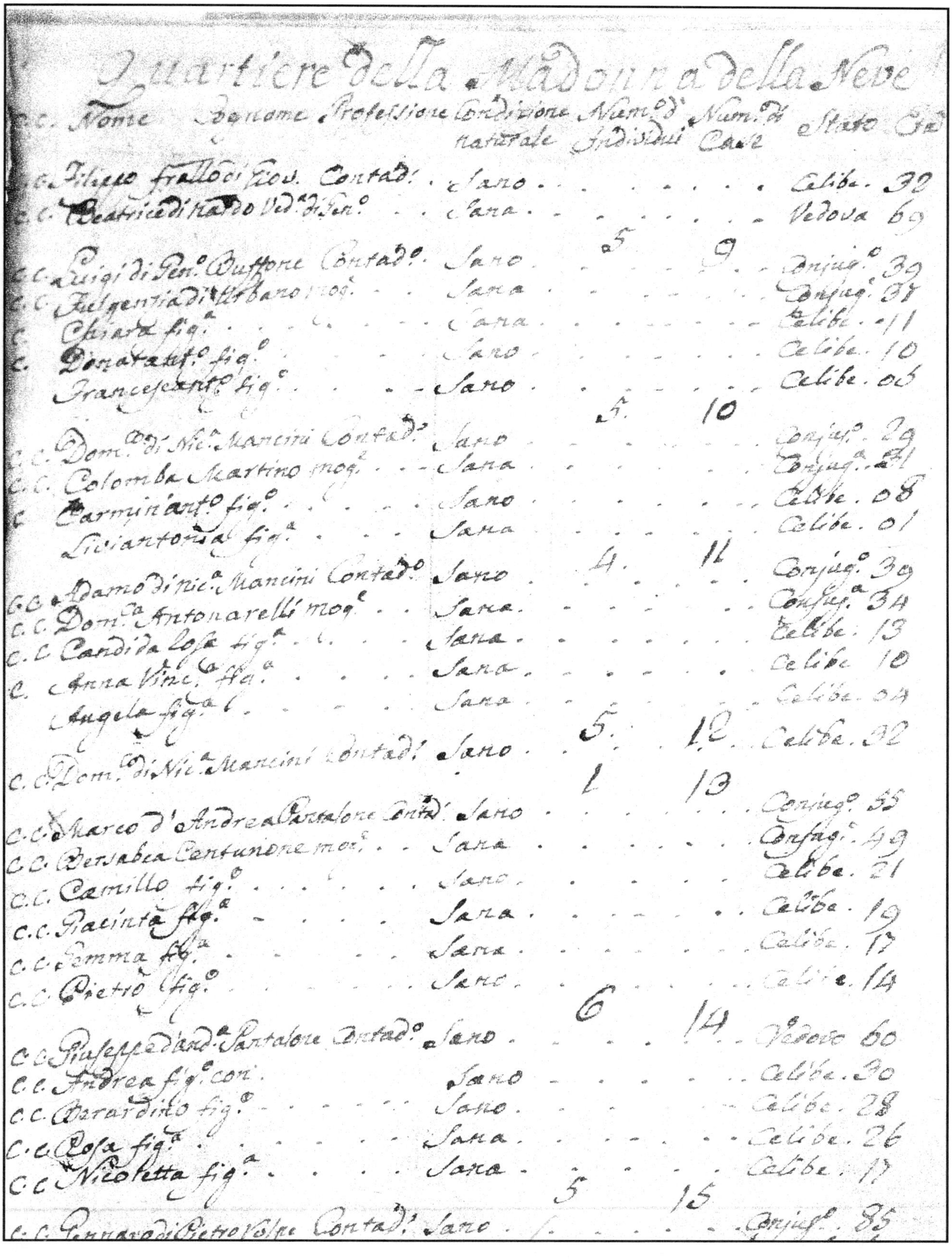

Quartiere della Madonna della Neve

C.C.	Nome Cognome	Professione	Condizione naturale	Num.o d'Individui	Num.o di Case	Stato	Età
c.c.	Filippo Frallocci fio.	Contad.	Sano			Celibe	32
c.c.	Beatrice di Nardo Ved.a di Fen.o		Sana			Vedova	69
				5	9		
c.c.	Luigi di Pen.o Buffone	Contad.o	Sano			Conjug.o	39
c.c.	Fulgentia di Urbano mog.		Sana			Conjug.	37
c.	Chiara fig.a		Sana			Celibe	11
c.	Donatant.o fig.o		Sano			Celibe	10
	Francescant.o fig.o		Sano			Celibe	05
				5	10		
c.c.	Dom.co di Nic.a Mancini	Contad.	Sano			Conjug.o	29
c.c.	Colomba Martino mog.		Sana			Conjug.a	21
c.	Carminant.o fig.o		Sano			Celibe	08
	Liviantonia fig.a		Sana			Celibe	01
				4	11		
c.c.	Adamo di Nic.a Mancini	Contad.o	Sano			Conjug.o	39
c.c.	Dom.ca Antonarelli mog.e		Sana			Conjug.a	34
c.c.	Candida Rosa fig.a		Sana			Celibe	13
c.	Anna Vinc.a fig.a		Sana			Celibe	10
	Angela fig.a		Sana			Celibe	04
				5	12		
c.c.	Dom.co di Nic.a Mancini	Contad.	Sano			Celibe	32
				1	13		
c.c.	Marco d'Andrea Pantalone	Contad.	Sano			Conjug.o	55
c.c.	Bersabea Centunone mog.		Sana			Conjug.	49
c.c.	Camillo fig.o		Sano			Celibe	21
c.c.	Giacinta fig.a		Sana			Celibe	19
c.c.	Somma fig.a		Sana			Celibe	17
c.c.	Pietro fig.o		Sano			Celibe	14
				6	14		
c.c.	Giuseppe d'And.a Pantalone	Contad.o	Sano			Vedovo	60
c.c.	Andrea fig.o con.		Sano			Celibe	30
c.c.	Berardino fig.o		Sano			Celibe	28
c.c.	Rosa fig.a		Sana			Celibe	26
c.c.	Nicoletta fig.a		Sana			Celibe	17
				5	15		
c.c.	Gennaro di Pietro Volpe	Contad.	Sano			Conjug.o	85

the vocations of the family members. Vocation was commonly noted in the civil records but is rarely found in parish records. In this case, of course, it was an important element in determining the taxes due.

The last two examples (figures 7-22 and 7-23) are from the town of Agnone in the province of Isernia. At one time an important agricultural and commercial center, Agnone was the most important town of the region and the seat of the diocese. It is an isolated town of seven thousand inhabitants today. It has seven parishes, each of which has *status animarum*, marriage, and death records dating back to 1595. Only one parish had a baptismal font, so the baptismal records for the whole town were kept in that parish. At Agnone, the parishes took a census every two or three years. By comparing these records, complete family groups can be created. The two examples are from the late 1600s. Each house is numbered, and all members of the household are listed by name, family relationship, and age. Both parents' names are listed for the mother and father, but there is no information about marriage or death among the family members. It is noteworthy that, at the end of each record (as seen in figure 7-23), a total of the population was made. There were 339 men and 350 women; 8 boys and 6 girls were born; and there were 10 priests with an altar boy and deacon for a total of 713 for the parish. There were no deaths.

Though these records are unique to the papal states, similar records begun after the creation of the Italian state can be found in many parishes. These are called *anagrafe* records, and they are census records, as are the *status animarum*. Usually, however, they were made out every twenty years, and they were discontinued by 1900. For research regarding people who lived in the nineteenth century, in any case, they may prove very useful.

Because parish records are the principal source of data for periods before the advent of Napoleonic records and, in some regions of Italy, before the Italian civil records, they are very valuable. Seldom is there a source of records, kept with such care, that provides all important genealogical data for more than ninety-eight percent of a population dating back to the 1500s. Italian descendants and genealogists should be very grateful for the care of the priests and the decisions of the Catholic church at the Council of Trent, which have created such a rich source of family information.

FIGURE 7-22. Parish Stato delle Anime Record Showing Households , 1695, Agnone, Isernia

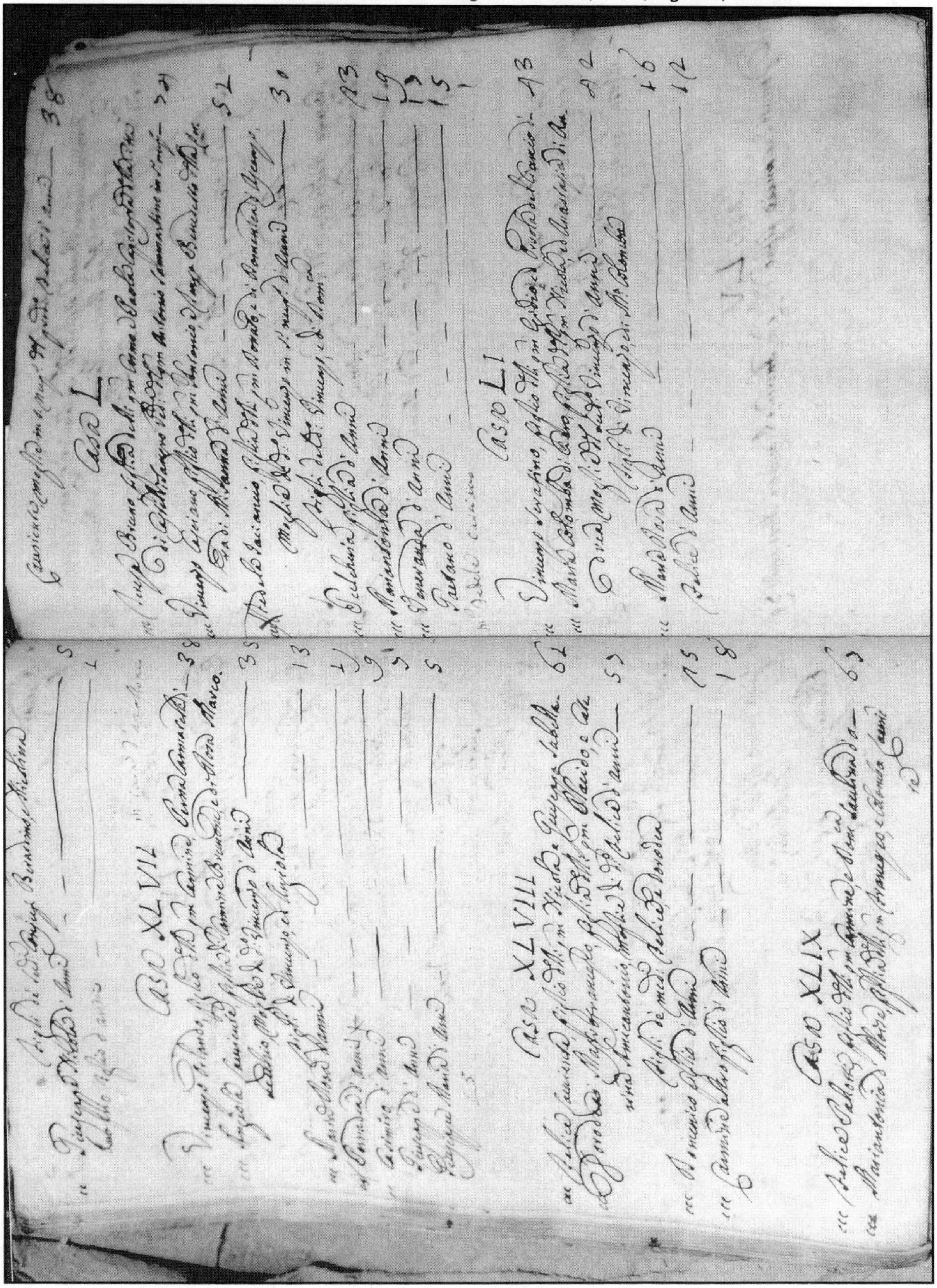

FIGURE 7-23. Parish Stato delle Anime Record Showing Total Number of Parish Inhabitants, 1695, Agnone, Isernia

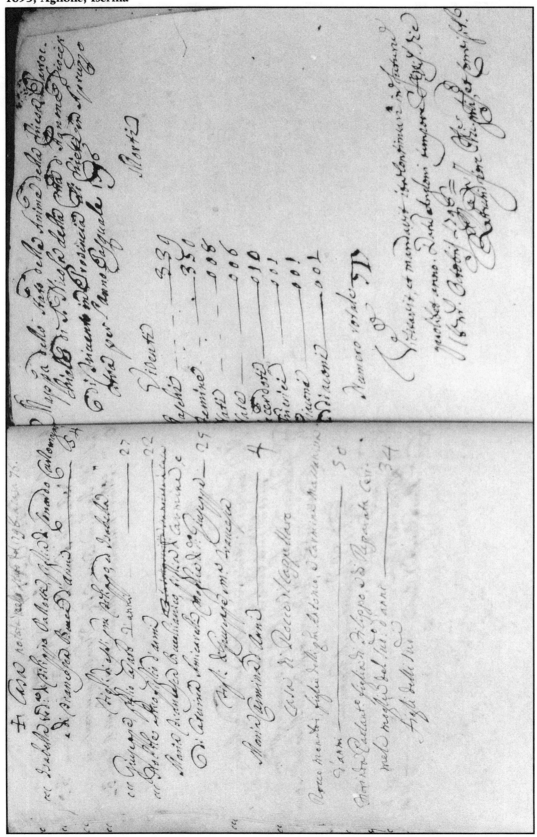

Chapter 8

ALTERNATIVE ECCLESIASTICAL RECORDS

WHILE THE PARISH RECORDS OF THE ROMAN CATHOLIC church are the major source of ecclesiastical records in Italy, another source of Catholic records is the *curia vescovile* (bishop's office or diocese seat). Some records also exist for other religious groups, such as the Waldensian sect, the Greek Orthodox church, and Italian Jews. This chapter discusses the records that are available for all of these groups, beginning with the records held by the *curie vescovili*.

DIOCESAN RECORDS

As discussed in chapter 7, the major sources of ecclesiastical records in Italy are the Catholic parishes. A parish serves one town, a group of small villages, or one neighborhood in a large city. In some areas, particularly in the alpine (northern) regions that were once under Austrian control, a group of parishes was combined into a *pieve*. The archpriest of the *pieve* kept the records for several parishes.

The diocese has jurisdiction over all the parishes and *pievi* within a geographical area. Each diocese is headed by a bishop (*vescovo*), who regulates the religious affairs of the diocese. As described in chapter 2, several centuries ago the bishops had both religious and political power in the areas of their jurisdiction. As bishops lost or gained power, the boundaries of their dioceses changed accordingly. When the ecclesiastical leaders lost political power and the current political divisions of provinces and communes were established, the boundaries of the provinces were often formed from the existing dioceses.

The seat of each diocese—the *curia vescovile*—is usually in the largest city of the province, and the boundaries of the diocese are usually similar to those of the province. Some diocese boundaries have changed because of the considerable shift in the population toward the coastal areas and the industrial north. Some dioceses have been combined, such as Belluno and Feltre or Bressanone and Bolzano; the combined dioceses have their seat in the province's capital. Even some of the new provinces that have been established, such as Crotone and Vibo Valentia, were formed around existing dioceses. The exception is in the former papal states of central Italy, where there are many more dioceses than provinces. (Appendix B contains the addresses of the *curie vescovili* of current dioceses in Italy.)

Most often, therefore, if an ancestor's parish of origin is in the province of Padova, for example, it is likely that the parish will be in the diocese of Padova, and the *curia vescovile* will be in the city of Padova (Padua). The *curia* is always near the city's *duomo*, or cathedral. The *duomo* is, in fact, the bishop's church, where he officiates. Even small cities that have a *duomo* are the site of (or were in the past) the *curia vescovile* and were the center of a diocese. The *curia* is usually a large building attached to the *duomo* or situated nearby and is adorned by the bishop's coat of arms over the doorway. It houses offices that deal with church records and other affairs of the church, and it also contains the diocesan library and archive.

Although a less rich source of information than the records held by the parishes, the *curia* archives are an important alternative source of records. When there are gaps in the parish records or the records are missing entirely, a *curia* may be able to provide additional information. The majority of records concern the bishops and their affairs, and usually there are biographies of the various bishops who served in the diocese—especially those bishops who were powerful political and historical figures during the Middle Ages. There are ordination records containing biographical data about priests and nuns and records of the religious orders. There are also records concerning members of religious confraternities, charities, and pious institutes.

Many confraternities developed in the Middle Ages after the plagues. They were the first organizations of mutual assistance for the sick and needy. The first hospitals in Italy were often built with funds and assistance from these groups. Although religious in nature, they were not made up of ecclesiastical officers or priests; rather, their members were prominent citizens of the community. Many still exist today, and they continue the customs and rituals of centuries past. (One of the most famous is the Arciconfraternita della Misericordia of Florence, also called *i capucciati*—"the hoods"—because its members appear only with hoods over their heads. Cloaks and hoods conceal their identities as they accompany funeral marches, drive ambulances, and perform other acts of charity. The giving of time, money, and assistance is done with humility and is not demonstrated to the community.) These organizations were quite secretive, and the only records with the names of the members and the minutes of their meetings were kept by the bishop at the *curia*. Although they contain little genealogical information other than the names of the group members, they are fascinating to examine; you might even find an ancestor as a member.

Church property records are also held by the *curia vescovile*. They list the properties of each parish and of the diocese, including houses, fields, and churches. Many *curie* retained possession of vast quantities of land for centuries and were the landlords for many of the *mezzadri* (tenant farmers) who cultivated the land. Generally, these records are of little interest to the genealogy researcher, but they may contain the names of people who willed property to the church, and even a will itself may appear.

Other interesting records are those that deal with people who were excommunicated and Protestants who were converted. Often the former, besides stating the reason for excommunication, also state the name and age of the person and often the names of the father, spouse, and other family relations. The most frequent reason for excommunication was heresy. The excommunicated person would be listed as a "Protestant," although he or she may never have belonged to another church. In some of the older records, the person may be listed as a witch or as possessed by the devil. These records do not contain the minutes of the ecclesiastical courts of the inquisition; these courts were formed and governed by priests who were chosen by the pope, and they were responsible only to the Holy See. The records of Protestants who became Catholics (very often the same who had been excommunicated or their children) list the name, age, and family relationships. Often, too, the date of baptism or the baptismal annotation is included. These records are not voluminous; apparently there were few cases of heresy over the centuries outside of the Inquisition.

The worth of some of these ecclesiastical records, of seemingly little genealogical value, became obvious to me in a research project. A family was trying to locate the birthplace of a great-grandmother who supposedly had been born somewhere in the Ticino region of Switzerland around 1820. First, telephone books of towns that had a high concentration of the surname Franzioli were searched. However, since there were several towns with many occurrences of that surname, and since none of those with the greatest concentration proved to be the birthplace of the ancestor, Josephine, another tactic was needed. The family knew that Josephine's brother, Joseph, had been ordained a priest at Milan and later served as a parish priest in Switzerland, so the ordination records of the *curia* at Milan were

examined. These records contain the registrations of ordination to each office in the priesthood for those seeking to become priests. The records at Milan date back to the 1600s, and back to the mid-1700s they are very complete. Careful scrutiny of the records after 1830 revealed several for Joseph. He was first confirmed as a *chierico* (altar boy), then as an assistant deacon, then a *diacono* (deacon), and finally as a priest in 1840 (figure 8-1). In his ordination as a deacon, even his birth certificate was enclosed with other documents, establishing his birthplace as the town of Dalpe in Switzerland. Further research confirmed this as the birthplace of Josephine and as the family's town of origin. This case demonstrates the usefulness of alternative sources and why no stone should be left unturned.

Records that are normally of more assistance to the researcher interested in family history are the confirmation records and the records of marriage among relatives. Probably the largest section of each diocesan archive is dedicated to what are called *visite pastorali* (pastoral visits). These are visits that the bishop makes, presently once a year but in earlier times less regularly, to each parish in the diocese. The major purpose of this visit is for the *cresima* (confirmation) of each child in the Catholic church. These records, besides providing information about the bishop and the dates of his visits, list by parish all of the children in each village who participated in the *cresima*. In many cases only the names of the children are listed. Exact birth dates are not provided, but the age of a child can be presumed because confirmation usually took place between age eight and about twelve. Presently, the *cresima* is celebrated every year for children aged thirteen and fourteen. Because in earlier times the bishop's visit was made only once every few years, sometimes more than one sibling in a family participated in the *cresima*. Occasionally, the age of the child or the name of the father was listed, making these records more valuable. When there is a gap in the parish baptismal records or when earlier records are missing, the confirmation records can be used to verify the existence of children. When death records are missing or are incomplete, the confirmation can also establish that a child survived infancy and was still alive at the time of confirmation.

Other records are even more interesting. As discussed in chapter 7, marriage to someone of the third degree of consanguinity (a second cousin) had to be approved by the bishop and, for second-degree relatives, by the pope himself. Also, any couple that wanted to forgo the banns on three successive Sundays to marry sooner needed the bishop's approval. (The most frequent reason for either of these requests was an unexpected pregnancy.) In the *curie* are records, for all of the parishes, of such marriages that were approved by the bishop. Besides the names of the couple, these records also provide the names of their parents, their place of residence, and the petition of the couple stating the reason for the marriage. (A petition may even have a small pedigree chart showing the relationship between the

FIGURE 8-1. Record of Giuseppe Franzioli's Ordination to Priest, 1840, Milan; From the Curia Vescovile at Milan

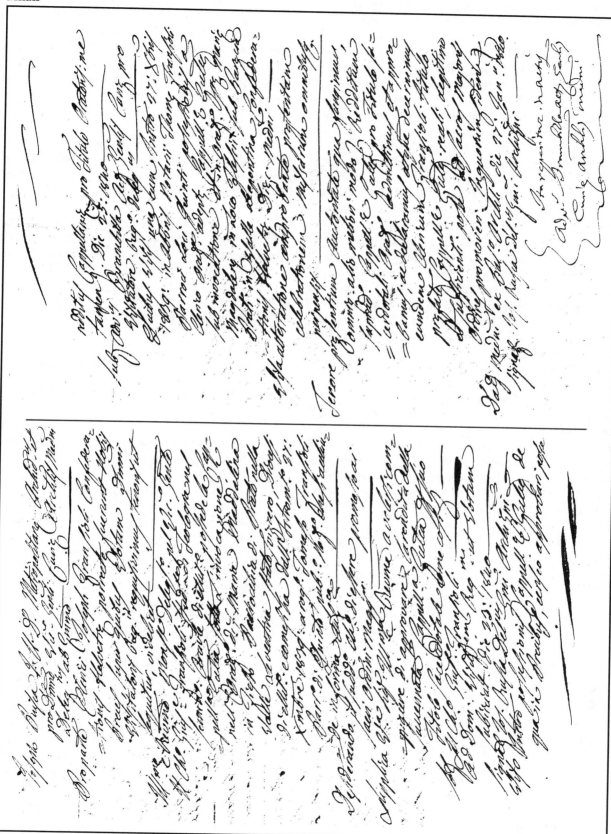

couple.) When parish marriage records are missing or if you want more information about a marriage that took place under these circumstances, these records become an interesting alternative source. Obviously, the percentage of marriages approved by the bishop was very small, but these records may be vital in continuing one or more lines.

Finally, the most useful records held by the dioceses are the copies of parish records. As discussed in chapter 6, preprinted civil record forms and duplicate copies were introduced by Napoleon. The idea took hold and was imitated later by the Italian state for civil records and by the Catholic church for ecclesiastical records. Thus, starting in the early 1800s, many dioceses began keeping second copies of the parish records at the *curia vescovile*. Most dioceses, particularly in the central-north regions, have these records; throughout most of southern Italy, duplicate records were not created until the late 1800s or the early 1900s. If the parish copies have been lost or if it is impossible to consult them due to an uncooperative parish priest, these copies become an invaluable source. For example, in the mountainous area of the Vicenza province around Asiago, almost all of the parish records were destroyed in World War I during heavy fighting with the Austrians; however, copies of these records, dating back to 1812, exist for the towns in that diocese in the diocesan archive at Padua. Parish records of nearby towns in the Trento diocese, however, have been irrecoverably lost because no copies were made.

The actual acts held by the *curia* are identical to those of the parish, as can be seen in the following example (figure 8-2). These acts, from the parish of Airali in the commune of Chieri in Torino province, show the typical format for these copies. They were preprinted and have a standardized format. The baptismal record begins with the heading, the date, and the place, as follows:

ATTI DI BATTESIMO
N.o 1
L'anno del Signore mille ottocento *quaranta* ed alli *tredici* del mese di *febbraio* alle ore *undici di mattina* nella Parrocchia d'*Airali* Comune di *chieri*

Or:

BAPTISMAL ACT
Number 1
Year of our Lord eighteen hundred and *forty* and on the *thirteenth* of the month of *February* at the hour *eleven in the morning* in the Parish of *Airali* in the Town of *Chieri.*

Each act is on a separate page and is numbered. This act goes on to state the child's birth date, the names of the parents and their professions, and finally the name of the child:

È stato presentato alla Chiesa un fanciullo di sesso *feminina* nato li *tredici* del mese di *febbraio* alle ore *due di mattino* nel distretto di questa parrocchia, figlio di *Michele Quaglino* di professione *contadino* domiciliato in *Airali* e di *Giuseppa Mensio* di professione *contadina* domiciliata in *Airali* conjugi *Quaglino* cui fu amministrato il Battesimo da me sottoscritto e sono stati imposti li nomi di *Virginia.*

This part is translated as:

A child of *female* sex was presented to the Church, born on the *thirteenth* of the month of *february* at *two o'clock in the morning* in this parish, *daughter of Michele* QUAGLINO, by profession a *farmer* living at *Airali,* and of *Giuseppa* MENSIO, also by profession *a farmer,* living at *Airali* and married to QUAGLINO. The baptism was administered by me, the underwritten, and the name of *Virginia* was given to the child.

The last section states the names of the godfather and godmother and their professions:

essendo stati padrino *Mensio Luigi*
di professione *contadino* domiciliato in *Airali*
e madrina *Margarita Mensio nata Bechi*
di professione *contadina* domiciliata in *Airali*
rappresentati da . . .
e da . . .
L'indicazione della nascita con richiesta del Battesimo fu fatta dal *padre neonato*

Translated:

The godfather, being MENSIO *Luigi,* by profession a *farmer* and living at *Airali*
and the godmother, MENSIO *Margarita, born* BECHI, also by profession a *farmer,* living at *Airali* represented by . . .
and by . . .
The indication of the birth, with the request for baptism, was presented by the *father of the newborn*

The format follows that of the more recent parish records. Each diocese supplied preprinted forms for both the parishes and the diocese. It is noteworthy that at this time (1840) there was already collaboration between the civil authorities and the parishes in this area, as indicated by the last line of the document. In fact, the House of Savoy, which ruled in Piedmont from Napoleon's time, began keeping civil records there in 1839. Since these are authorized parish records, the *curia* can release baptism or marriage certificates after research has been completed. It may even be possible to obtain these certificates by mail (see chapter 11). Figure 8-3 is a baptismal certificate released by

FIGURE 8-2. Baptismal Act of Virginia Quaglino, 1840, Airali, Chievi, Torino; From the Curia Vescovile at Turin

ATTI DI BATTESIMO.

N.° 1

uglino

ginia

L'anno del Signore mille ottocento *quaranta* ed alli *tredici* del mese di *febbrajo* alle ore *undici di mattina* nella Parrocchia d'*Airali* Comune di *chieri*

È stato presentato alla Chiesa un fanciullo di sesso *feminino* nato li *tredici* del mese di *febbrajo* alle ore *due di mattino* nel distretto di questa Parrocchia, figlio d'*Michele Quaglino* di professione *contadino* domiciliato in *Airali* e di *Giuseppa Mensio* di professione *contadina* domiciliata in *Airali* conjugi *quaglino* . cui fu amministrato il Battesimo *da me sottoscritto* e sono stati imposti li nomi di *virginia*

essendo stati

padrino *Mensio Luigi* di professione *contadino* domiciliato in *Airali* e madrina *Margarita Mensio nata Bedus* di professione *contadina* domiciliata in *Airali* ~~rappresentati da~~ ~~e da~~

L'indicazione della nascita con richiesta del Battesimo fu fatta *dal padre neonato*

Firma del Richiedente + *Michele quaglino*   Firma del Parroco *V. Pattan*

FIGURE 8-3. Certificate of the Birth and Baptismal Acts of Bernardus Petranegra, 1767, Quinto al Mare, Genova; From the Archdiocesan at Genoa

ARCHIDIOCESI DI GENOVA

PARROCCHIA di

Atto integrale di Nascita e Battesimo

L'anno del Signore mille ~~novecento~~ settecentosessantasette

lì 26 del mese di APRILE alle ore

la Parrocchia di "S. PIETRO" QUINTO AL MARE

mune di QUINTO AL MARE

E' stato presentato alla Chiesa un fanciullo di sesso MASCOLINO

to il 23 del mese di APRILE alle ore

Laurentius PETRANEGRA figlio d

vivo di di condizione

la Angela Maria · figlia d

iva di di condizione

iugi, abitanti in questa parrocchia, via n.

fu amministrato il S. Battesimo da Rev Joannes Baptista

GHIO e si impose il nome di Bernardus

Fu padrino Bernardus CORTESE figlio di

Laurentius, domiciliato in ;

drina Antonia SCIACALUGA figlia di

niciliata in rispettivamente

presentati da

L'indicazione della nascita con richiesta del Battesimo fu fatta da

IL RICHIEDENTE   IL PARROCO

Foglio N.

N.

Cognome e Nome

Bernardus

PETRANEGRA

Spazio
riservato alle correzioni

a) Il battezzato sopra descritto ricevette la S. Cresima in

di mese di anno adr.

Mgr.

b) Contrasse matrimonio ecclesiastico con figli di

la parrocchia di Diocesi di

lì mese di anno

Rilasciato in carta libera per uso

In fede: dalla Parrocchia di

lì 19

(bollo parrocchiale)

Parroco

V. Per l'autenticità della firma dicente

Genova, dalla Curia Arciv.,

Il Cancelliere Arciv.

the diocese of Genova.

Although the format of the various acts in the *curia* is the same as that for the parishes, the organization of the volumes is often quite different. At the *curia* of Torino province in the Piedmont region, for example, there are thick volumes of records labeled alphabetically for each year. In volume "A" for 1840 are all of the baptismal records for all of the parishes in the diocese that begin with "A," such as Airali, for that year. Separate volumes using the same system exist for marriage and burial records. A baptismal record for the nearby parish of Chieri would be in volume "C" alphabetically under "Chieri" among the other parishes. These records contain no indexes. At other *curie* there are separate records for each parish in one-year or ten-year volumes, much like the civil vital records, and indexes for them may exist.

These duplicate records are vital when parish records have been destroyed or are not available for consultation, but there are other occasions as well when they can be very helpful for research. If, when researching in a large city, you don't know from which parish a family originated and can't find this information in the civil records, it is much easier to consult the records of all the parishes in the city in the diocesan archives rather than to consult the records at each individual parish. The latter course might require weeks to find all of the parish priests at home and to gain access to their records, whereas researching in the *curia* might require only hours. The duplicate records can also be useful when a maternal line leaves the parish, cannot be found in earlier records, and there is no mention of the place of origin. In the *curia* the parish marriage or baptismal records of all the surrounding villages can be searched to find the line without the need to travel to each village. A major disadvantage is that copies of parish records do not exist for records made before the early 1800s.

Curia archives are very often also a major source of information about parishes that existed in earlier years and have since been closed. Often, the records of these closed parishes are stored in the *curia* and can be consulted there. In some dioceses it is necessary to first obtain permission from the *curia* before consulting the records of the parishes in that diocese. In Lucca province in the Tuscany region, for example, parish priests cannot allow research without the bishop's permission.

Some dioceses have begun collecting or microfilming baptismal, marriage, and burial records from the parishes in the diocese. At Arezzo diocese in Tuscany, all of the parish records from before 1860 are stored in the *curia* and can be consulted there, allowing better preservation, restoration, and supervision of the records. The diocese of Pordenone province in Friuli-Venzia Giulia is following this example, and in the future other *curie* may follow suit. All of the parish records in the dioceses of Trento, Bolzano, Ivrea, and Vercelli have been microfilmed, and they are available for consultation in each of these *curie*.

WALDENSIAN RECORDS

Although the vast majority of Italians are Roman Catholics, there are some important exceptions to be considered. The first is a major Protestant movement that began centuries ago in France. Its followers were called the Waldensians.

This religious movement was begun in 1170 in Lyons, France, by a wealthy merchant named Valdesius (in Latin—probably Valdes in French). It was not originally intended as a Protestant movement; Valdesius lived more than three hundred years before Martin Luther, and the time was not ripe for such a movement. Valdesius' objective, rather, was a return to simplicity within the church. At some point in his life Valdesius had a religious experience and decided to dedicate the rest of his life to Christ. He first had parts of the Bible translated and written in the "vulgar," or language of the people. Then, he gave up all of his riches and, living from alms, began preaching the gospel of Christ, declaring that the Catholic church and the people should give up their riches and return to Christ as well. He created a considerable following, particularly among the merchants and working class of Lyons. They became known as the "poor in spirit of Lyons" or just the "poor of Lyons." Valdesius was not trying to create a separate religion but to teach repentance to the church; to confirm this he signed a declaration of loyalty to the bishop of Lyons.

Catholic church leaders, though they considered Valdesius and his followers ignorant, felt threatened by his preaching and finally prohibited Valdesius and his followers from continuing any form of preaching. Valdesius, of course, felt that he was following his calling and would not give in. He and his followers were excommunicated, and centuries of persecution began. The movement gained force in the early 1200s from dissident religious groups in the Lombardy region of Italy. As a result, the center of the movement moved from Lyons, where the Waldensians were unwelcome and discriminated against, to Bergamo and the Lombardy region. They became known then as the "poor of Lombardy."

During the Council of Laterano in 1215, Catholic leaders decided that the only way to deal with heresy and dissidence was by force. The Waldensian movement was one of those labeled as heretic, and active persecution was enacted to stamp out this movement. Seemingly, however, the more the church tried to eliminate the followers of Valdesius, the more rapidly the movement grew. Soon there were followers as far away as Austria, Switzerland, and Bohemia in the north and in the Puglia and Calabria regions in the south of Italy. The first documentation of Waldensian heretics being burned at the stake by the Inquisition begins as early as 1312 at Pinerolo, near Turin. The practice continued for centuries.

Between 1476 and 1489 the Waldensians become the object of several crusades to destroy them, and they were run out of their strongholds in Val Luserna and Pinerolo.

As the Protestant movement gained strength with Huldrych Zwingli, a Swiss Reformation leader, and Martin Luther, the Waldensians united themselves with this reform movement but never received the political backing and popular support that was available to the Lutheran church in the Germanic regions. However, the Waldensians translated the entire Bible into French for the first time and were instrumental in preaching the words of Christ. As a result, the Catholic church became even more severe in its persecution, and the Waldensians migrated continually between France, Switzerland, and the Piedmont area of Italy. In 1545 there was a massacre of Waldensians in the Provence region of France at Luberon, and in 1561 a group in Calabria was exterminated. There is a record of continual persecution over the next century and a half; many Waldensian religious leaders were imprisoned and executed. In 1686 another massacre occurred in Italy and many Waldensians were imprisoned. The remainder were exiled to Switzerland. Finally, in 1688, Waldensians returned to the valleys of Piedmont, near Pinerolo, and in 1690 they were granted acceptance by the Duke of Savoy. From this time on, while not free from religious discrimination, they were no longer actively persecuted. In 1805 Napoleon gave the Waldensians official recognition as part of the Reformed Church of France, and over the last two centuries they have prospered and grown, with groups and temples throughout Italy from Venice to Palermo. A group as far away as Uruguay was founded in 1859.

The Waldensians are significant not only because they represent the largest Protestant group in Italy. In 1849, Lorenzo Snow, an apostle of the LDS church, began a missionary effort in Italy that ended with the conversion of more than six hundred Waldensians, who soon after emigrated to America and the Salt Lake Valley in Utah. Today thousands of their descendents in that area are interested in their genealogy and family history. As a result, the LDS church has microfilmed the records of the sixteen Waldensian parishes in the Pinerolo district in northwest Italy and the notary records concerning the Waldensians at the state archives of Torino province (see chapter 10). Some of the parish records date back to 1686, while most date to 1692; the rest were begun during the 1700s. All earlier records were destroyed in the massacre of 1686.

The Waldensian acts are similar in most aspects to Catholic parish records. They consist of baptismal, marriage, and burial records. Unlike some Protestant churches, the Waldensians performed baptism at birth, as did the Catholics. Even the format of the records themselves follows that used by the Catholic church, although there are some differences. As is true of most of the Piedmont region, the baptismal records state the exact birth date, but the date of baptism is not always included. Thus, preference is given to the birth date and not the baptismal date. The other major difference is that the early records in these sixteen parishes were written entirely in French, including the names and surnames. There was a gradual shift in this tendency over the years so that, by the end of the eighteenth century, the acts were written in Italian, but many names remained in French. Thus, surnames like Revel, Pons, Coombs, Vinay, and Tourns, which have French origins, are common in these records.

In examining the following examples of baptismal, marriage, and death acts from the parish of Luserna S. Giovanni, note the extreme scarcity of information provided. The first marriage act of 1709 (figure 8-4) is written simply in French:

Ce 9 Janvier 1709 J'ai beni le marriage de Jean Pierre Gofs avec Lucie Bellonal tous deux de S. Jean.
    Cyprien Appia Pasteur

This is translated as:

On 9 January 1709, I blessed the marriage of Jean Pierre GOFS with Lucie BELLONAL, both from S. Giovanni.
    The Priest Cyprien Appia

The names of the couple's parents are not given, nor is any of the other information normally found in the Catholic parish records, such as the names of the witnesses, information about the banns, and so on. Later records provide information about the parents of the bride and groom, but they as well are striking in their brevity.

In the baptismal and death records only the names of the parents were mentioned, so it is difficult to research earlier generations. In figure 8-5, for example, only the given name of the child's mother is mentioned; her surname is not. However, the names of godparents appear regularly, just as they do in Catholic records. The death records are briefer still, giving only the burial date and name of the deceased or, for a child, also the name of the father. The first act in the next example (figure 8-6) reads: Le 8 Decembre a Enterre' David Malan, or simply, "On 8 December [1749], David Malan was buried." The last act on the page includes a bit more information; it reads: Le 10e Mars on Enterre' Susane fille de David Gonin des Nazerot. Again the burial date, 10 March, and the name of the deceased, Suzanne, are mentioned, but the names of the father and paternal grandfather are given as well: David Gonin, son of Nazerot. Suzanne was probably a child, but there is no mention of her age, and there is little else to determine the person's exact identity.

This scarcity of information is characteristic of some Catholic parish records as well, but normally only those of a much earlier date. Obviously this scarcity renders research more difficult, as less information is available to establish family lines. However, in view of the centuries of persecution endured by the Waldensians, it is a wonder that any trace of these families has remained at all. Other persecuted religious groups have left even fewer recorded traces.

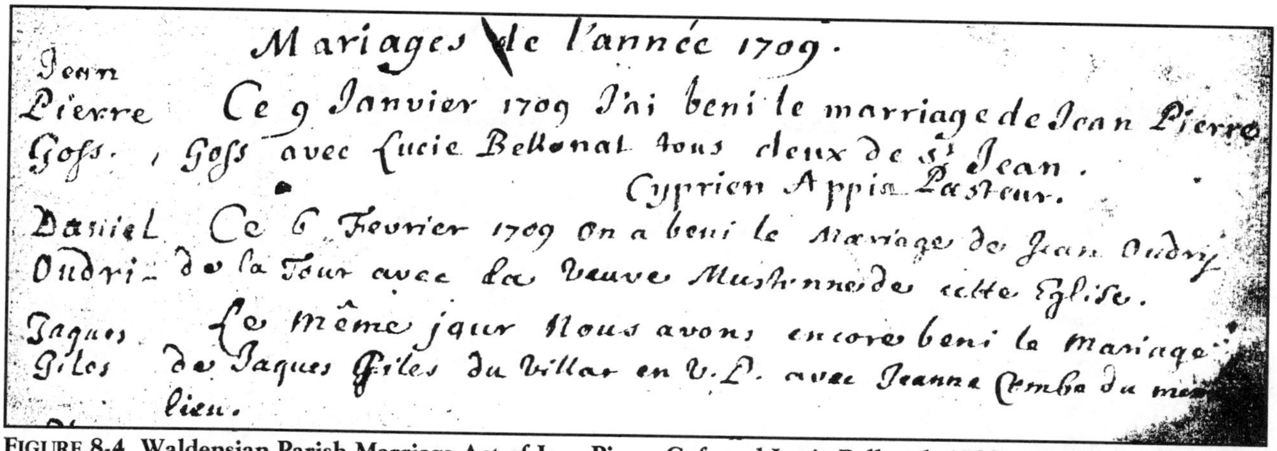
Mariages de l'année 1709.

Jean Pierre Gofs. — Ce 9 Janvier 1709 J'ai beni le marriage de Jean Pierre Goss avec Lucie Bellonat tous deux de St Jean. Cyprien Appia Pasteur.

Daniel Oudri — Ce 6 Fevrier 1709 On a beni le Mariage de Jean Oudry de la Tour avec la veuve Mustonne de cette Eglise.

Jaques Giles — Le même jour Nous avons encore beni le Mariage de Jaques Giles du Villar en V. L. avec Jeanne Combe du meme lieu.

FIGURE 8-4. Waldensian Parish Marriage Act of Jean Pierre Gofs and Lucia Bellonal, 1709, Luserna S. Giovanni, Torino

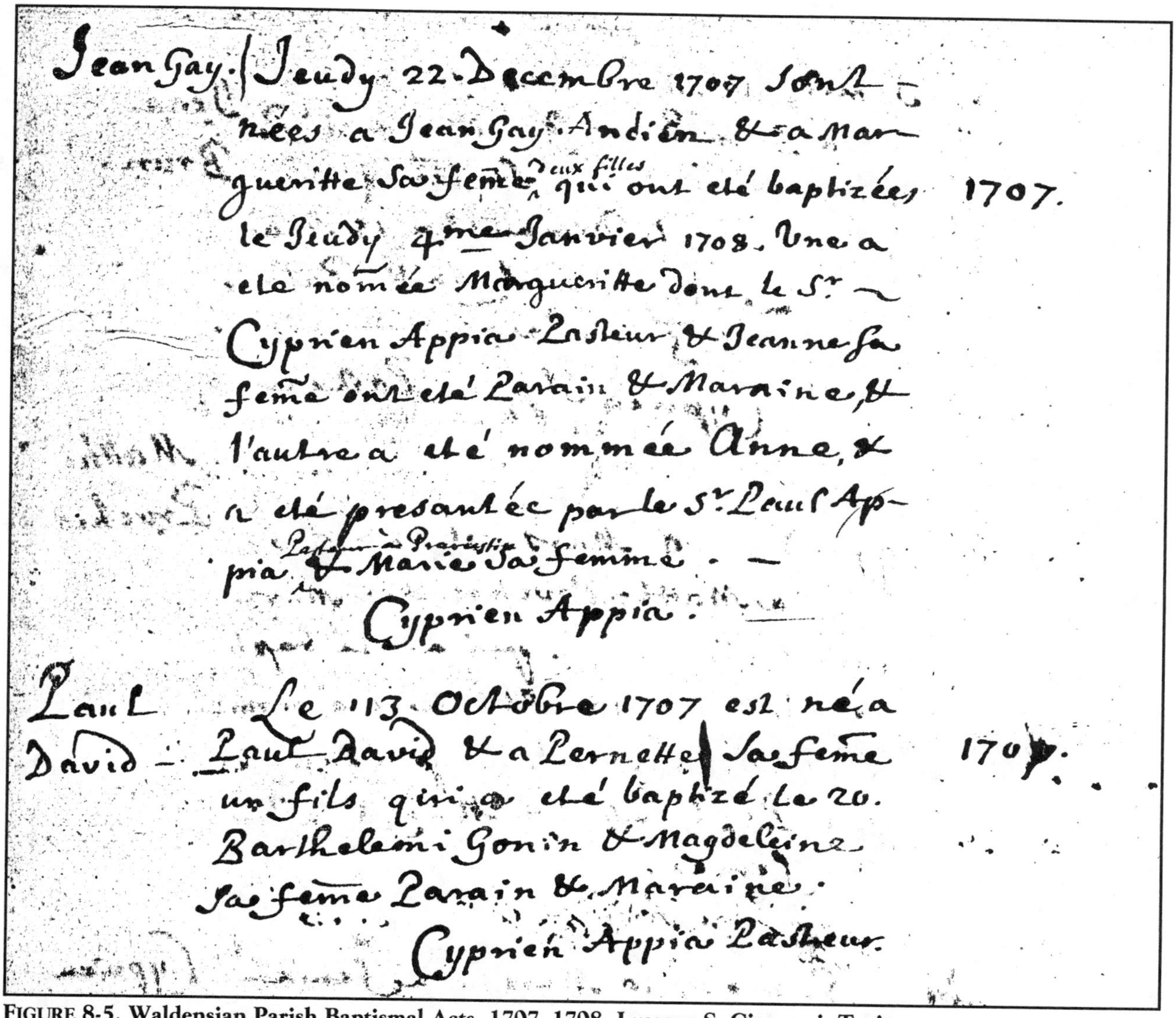
Jean Gay. — Jeudy 22 Decembre 1707 sont nées a Jean Gay Andien & a Marguerite sa feme deux filles qui ont eté baptizées le Jeudy 4me Janvier 1708. Une a eté nommée Marguerite dont le Sr Cyprien Appia Pasteur & Jeanne sa feme ont eté Parain & Maraine, & l'autre a eté nommée Anne, & a eté presantée par le Sr Paul Appia Pasteur a [illegible] & Marie sa femme. — Cyprien Appia. 1707.

Paul David — Le 13 Octobre 1707 est né a Paul David & a Pernette sa feme un fils qui a eté baptizé le 20. Barthelemi Gonin & Magdeleine sa feme Parain & Maraine. Cyprien Appia Pasteur. 1707.

FIGURE 8-5. Waldensian Parish Baptismal Acts, 1707–1708, Luserna S. Giovanni, Torino

FIGURE 8-6. Waldensian Parish Burial Acts, Including the Act of David Malan, 1749, Luserna S. Giovanni, Torino

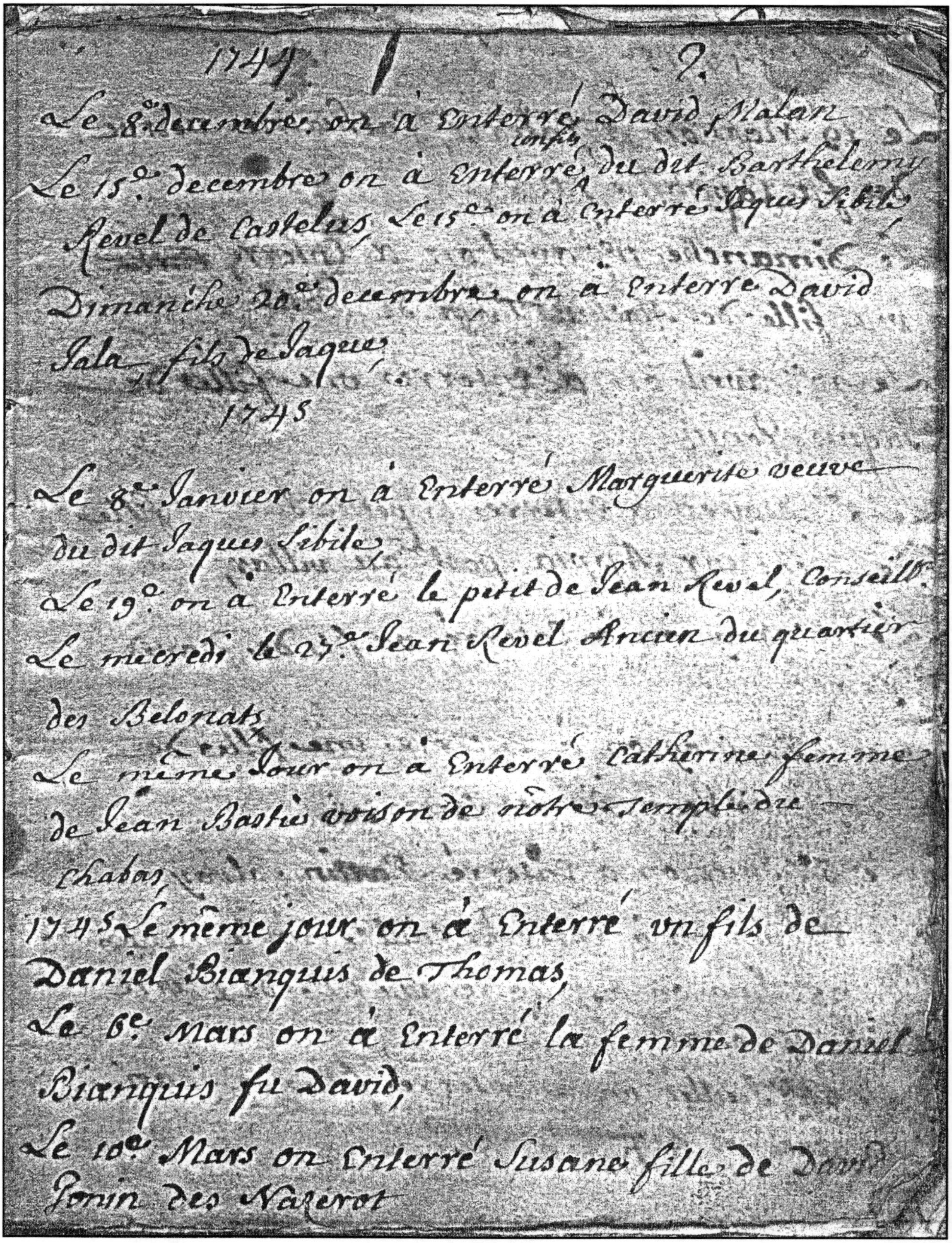

1744 9.

Le 8e decembre on a enterré David Malan

Le 15e decembre on a enterré confis du dit Barthelemy
Revel de Castelus, Le 15e on a enterré Jaques Sibile

Dimanche 20e decembre on a enterré David
Sala fils de Jaques

1745

Le 8e Janvier on a enterré Marguerite veuve
du dit Jaques Sibile

Le 19e on a enterré le petit de Jean Revel, Conseill.

Le mecredi le 27e Jean Revel Ancien du quartier
des Belonats

Le même Jour on a enterré Catherine femme
de Jean Bastie voison de notre semplidre
Chabas,

1745 Le même jour on a enterré un fils de
Daniel Bianquis de Thomas,

Le 6e Mars on a enterré la femme de Daniel
Bianquis fu David,

Le 10e Mars on enterré Susane fille de David
Ponin des Nazerot

JEWISH RECORDS

The Jewish people were persecuted throughout Europe and elsewhere for centuries. The first Jews arrived in Italy during the period of the Roman empire around the time of Christ. More were brought in, most as slaves, soon after the destruction of Jerusalem and the dispersion of the Hebrews as a nation. Thus, small concentrations of Jews existed in Rome and some other major cities of Italy from that period on, and theirs is the only religious and ethnic group that has maintained a separate identity within Italy from this early period.

There was little change in the population of Jews in Italy until 1492. From this time and culminating in 1692, the Jews were driven out of Spain and Portugal, many of them immigrating to Italy. Even so, Jews were never numerous in Italy; at the beginning of World War II they numbered only 35,000. In Italy, Jews were never persecuted as severely as in many other European countries, and there were none of the pogroms of Russia and Poland, nor the torture and persecution of the Spanish Inquisition. However, there was discrimination, and Italian Jews were not free to live as they wanted. From the beginning of the Holy Roman Empire and probably even before, Jews were not allowed to own land or to practice agriculture; they were required to live in segregated areas of the cities called "ghettos."

Even in the cities, Jews could not own property outside the ghettos; this led to curious architectural styles. Houses were built ever higher because they could not be expanded to surrounding terrain. Thus, the wealthier families added new floors to their homes, and some of the houses in the ghettos became the tallest in the cities, as seen today in Venice. Because Jews were not allowed to own land at a time when more than ninety-eight percent of the population lived from agriculture, they became merchants and bankers in the cities, laying the foundation for the middle class that was to become so important in the economic development and wealth of Italy during the Renaissance. Thus, the Jews of Italy, on the whole, were a wealthy class of people who nevertheless were objects of discrimination. At the height of the Spanish Inquisition in Spain and Portugal in the fifteenth century, there was a consistent effort throughout Europe to convert Jews to Christianity and to persecute or exile those who refused. This occurred in Italy as well, and many Jews converted (at least publicly), changing their names to escape persecution. As discussed in chapter 3, very often they took the names of cities, so surnames such as Trieste, Genova, and Torino today are known as typically Jewish names.

During World War II, though Italy was allied with Germany, most Italians did not approve of or participate in the persecution or extermination of the Italian Jews, and some Italians went to great personal risk to help them. Giorgio Perlasca was an Italian who imported meat from Italy into Budapest, Hungary, during the war. Witnessing the fate of the Jews there, he passed himself off as the consul of neutral Spain. At great personal risk and with typical Italian creativity, he set up office in the Spanish consulate and issued false passports and Spanish visas to thousands of Hungarian Jews, saving them from deportation and death.

In the last years of the war, however, the Germans effectively took control of the politics and war machine in Italy, and the same treatment that had occurred in Germany and in Poland and other occupied countries was in store for the Italian Jews. More than 8,000 Italian Jews were sent north to the extermination camps in Germany and Poland, and only a few hundred returned. An extermination camp was set up in a rice factory at San Sabba, near Trieste, where, in the last eighteen months of the war, approximately 15,000 to 20,000 Jews and "undesirables" from Italy and Yugoslavia were killed. Some Jews managed to escape, and many were hidden and survived the war. Only a few thousand remained in Italy after the war, the largest concentrations in Rome, Turin, and Venice. Their numbers were increased when many Jews from northern and eastern Europe, who often used Italy as a way station while emigrating to Israel or the United States, decided to remain. Several thousand Jews now live in Italy, but few are related to the Jewish families of the Middle Ages.

Genealogical record sources for the Jewish community are not very complete or readily available for consultation. While the parish priests of the Catholic church kept written records for each of the important sacraments, such as baptism, marriage, confirmation, and death ordinances, genealogy for those of the Hebrew faith is and has been a family affair. The Bible indicates that genealogy was very important in the Hebrew nation; however, it was not recorded by the clergy but by the family patriarchs. In Italy, no member of the Jewish community is obligated to register the birth of a child with the Jewish clergy; registration is a civil matter, as with any other Italian citizen. The rabbi of each synagogue keeps a record of those who voluntarily register the births of children, but these records (at Venice and Turin, for example) date back only to approximately 1900.

Earlier records, which date back to the 1700s, are those of *il libro della circoncisione*—"the book of circumcision"—and the marriage records. The former records the circumcisions of the males of each community, containing the infant's name, the parents' names, the date of birth, and the date of circumcision. (Circumcision usually took place within eight days of birth.) These are held in the synagogues but can be consulted only by members of the community or by people known to them. They are not open to public consultation, and photocopies or photographs of the documents are prohibited.

There are two types of marriage records. One is the marriage contract, usually written by hand in Armenian, between the bride and groom and their families. These are private contracts that are held by the families themselves. The other marriage record is the registration of the marriage in books held by the community. These state the names of the bride and groom, their ages, the names of their parents, and the date of marriage. It is an excellent source of genealogical information and is almost the only source for Jewish females. However, it is not open for public consultation. In theory, these records date back as long as the community has existed. For the ghettos of Venice and Rome, this would amount to centuries. During World War II, however, most documents were burned or otherwise destroyed by the Nazis, so most Jewish records have been lost.

The government of Israel has attempted to record and preserve both the communal marriage records and the books of circumcision from Jewish communities throughout the world. Many of the documents from Italy are available in Israel with computerized indexes. Therefore, it may be much easier and more fruitful to research these documents by consulting the records held in Israel rather than pursuing research in Italy. Contact an Israeli consulate for information on consulting these records.

FIGURE 8-7. Tombstone in the Jewish Cemetery at Turin

Tombstone inscriptions represent the one source of information on Jewish ancestry that is readily available in Italy. Christians believed that burial of a Jew in a Catholic cemetery was an act of desecration, so from early times Jewish dead were confined to their own cemeteries. Unlike Italian Catholics, however, who reuse the same plots over and over, Jews traditionally leave burial plots untouched. As a result, there are tombstones and family plots that date back several centuries. Usually the deceased's name and the years of birth and death are engraved on the tombstone, so, besides being fascinating relics of history, tombstones also contain important genealogical information. As can be seen on tombstones from the Jewish cemetery at Turin (figure 8-7), the inscriptions are typically in Hebrew. Unfortunately, many of the older stones have been worn by time and weather and are illegible, but much information can be obtained from the more recent ones.

It is not always easy to locate and visit a Jewish cemetery. In Padua the oldest cemetery, no longer in use, is inaccessibly located in a courtyard behind some abandoned buildings in the city's old ghetto. In Rome, however, which has the largest and oldest Jewish community in Italy, there is a large cemetery in the center of the city. Unfortunately, because it is open to the public, it has recently been the object of anti-Semitic desecration.

If you are of Italian-Jewish descent and wish to obtain more information about Italian ancestors, you should visit or write directly to the rabbi at the synagogue in the city of interest; you can also write to an Israeli consulate in the United States to learn what information is available in Israel. Non-Jewish researchers, even professional genealogists, do not have access to these records. At best, they can visit a cemetery to search for names and dates.

GREEK ORTHODOX RECORDS

Given Italy's proximity to Greece and Albania, where the Greek Orthodox church is prevalent, it is logical to assume that there was considerable migration from these countries to southern Italy, particularly along the coastline of the Puglia and Molise regions. Surnames like Greco (Greek), Del Greco, Dei Greci, and De Albanesi, which are common in Puglia, are evidence that many people from those areas have come to Italy and settled there. Surprising, however, is the fact that along the coastline there have been no Greek settlements that maintained their original tongue, customs, or religion. Those Greeks and Albanians who did migrate to Italy were, for the most part, absorbed by the existing culture. The exception is in Sicily.

During the fifteenth century, the Ottoman Empire of Turkey invaded the Macedonian Empire—what is today Albania, Macedonia, and

Bosnia—leading to cultural and religious conflicts that still exist. In 1431, Giovanni Castriotta, king of Albania, was forced to cede his crown to the Turks, beginning a long period of persecution. Under the repression of the Muslim Turks there was a massive migration of Albanian Christians to Italy. Many of them settled along the coastline and in the sparsely inhabited internal regions of Basilicata and Molise. Few of these settlements survived. The people went to work for the feudal lords of the region or were driven out. In Sicily, however, the immigration was so massive that entire cities were built or settled by the Albanians, and several remain today. The most famous of these is Piana degli Albanesi, near Palermo, but there are others, such as Contessa Entellina, Mezzojuso, Biancavilla, Santa Cristina Gela, Sant'Angelo Muxaro, and S. Michele di Ganzaria, that still have large populations of Albanian and Macedonian descent. Here, as elsewhere, there has been considerable mixing of the Italian Catholic and Albanian cultures, and many customs and traditions have been lost over the centuries. However, in some towns, such as Piana degli Albanesi and Contessa Entellina, many people still speak the Abresche dialect, practice the Greek Orthodox religion, and maintain their culture as much as possible. There is presently a revival in these towns of old customs, food, and clothing from the homeland.

In many of these towns, the major religion was Greek Orthodox. In earlier centuries the archbishop of the Monreale Archdiocesan gave permission to the Greek Orthodox to establish churches and perform their rites. For the Italian Catholics living in these towns, which were usually governed by Greek authorities, it often was convenient to be baptized and to baptize their children in the Greek parishes. When the Catholic priests saw that they were losing their flocks, the Roman Catholic church began an effort to expand its own parishes and to convert Greek Orthodox parishioners. Therefore, through the centuries there was considerable rivalry between the two churches, but there was little persecution or active discrimination. During the tumult of the nineteenth century and the unification of Italy in 1865, the land and political conflicts that ensued caused many of these Italians of Albanian origin to emigrate to the United States. From Contessa Entellina, more than one hundred emigrants arrived together at New Orleans and settled in the area. They created a Contessa Entellina Society that still exists as one of the least-known ethnic groups in the city.

The Greek Orthodox church at Contessa Entellina is pictured in figure 8-8. In Contessa Entellina, of the present population of approximately five thousand inhabitants, three thousand, including the town mayor, are of Greek or Albanian descent. There is still considerable rivalry between the two groups and the two parishes, each claiming slights by the other group, but the same families have been living together for centuries. The records of the Roman Catholic parish date back to 1640, although apparently there were earlier records that have been lost. The records of the Greek Orthodox parish are well preserved, however, and they date back, with some minor gaps, to 1541.

These records are written in archaic Italian rather than Greek or Latin and are similar in all respects to the Roman Catholic parish records discussed in chapter 7. There are birth records, marriage records, and burial records, much the same as in the nearby Catholic parish. (I do not know whether this practice conforms to the normal practice of the Greek Orthodox church or whether it resulted from the agreement made with the bishop at Monreale in the sixteenth century to coexist in Italy.)

When pursuing genealogy in these towns, be aware that some families alternated between Greek Orthodox and Roman Catholic parishes. Although most families remained within their own ethnic and religious group and most people married within their own groups, some families, for convenience or because of mixed marriages, attended both churches. In some cases, even within one generation, some siblings were baptized in one church and some in the other, or at times they were registered in both parishes.

Though Catholic parish records are the most common records of religious sacraments, alternative ecclesiastical record sources certainly exist in Italy. With the exception of the Jewish records, these sources give valid genealogical information for these religious groups. When sufficient information cannot be found in any ecclesiastical record, or when you wish to supplement these records or need earlier records, further alternative record sources, discussed in chapter 9, may be helpful.

FIGURE 8-8. Interior and Exterior of the Greek Orthodox Church at Contessa Entellina, Palermo

ALTERNATIVE RECORD SOURCES

MOST GENEALOGICAL RESEARCH CAN BE ACCOMPLISHED using the civil and ecclesiastical records discussed in preceding chapters. These are the principal Italian record sources, and they contain the greatest amount of genealogical information. As discussed in chapter 7, however, many parish records and even civil records have been lost or destroyed. Others have simply faded or been rendered illegible by humidity and time. As a result, when research cannot be pursued with these sources, alternative sources are necessary. Also, while the civil and parish records provide complete genealogical data, they contain little personal information about the ancestor or the family.

For those who are interested in expanding their family histories with facts and information that are not found in these principal sources, again, alternative sources are needed. For example, military records provide not only vital information but a physical description of the ancestor as well, and notary records may provide an idea of a family's property holdings and wealth. This chapter examines the most readily available alternative sources of genealogical and historical information, including conscription and military records, notary records, census and tax assessments, university records, and miscellaneous sources.

Most of these records are found in the *archivio di stato* (state archive) of each province, which is usually in the province's major city. (Appendix A contains the addresses of all the provincial state archives.) Each province is responsible for records under its geographical jurisdiction. Many of the newly organized provinces have no state archives as yet; the relevant records are still located in the archives of the larger, original provinces. Several provinces have branch offices of their state archives in other major cities of the province; these contain the records for those districts. For example, at Vicenza, in the Venetian region, the state archive is in the city of Vicenza, but a branch archive at Bassano del Grappa has the military, notary, and census records of Bassano and all the towns in the northern part of the province.

CONSCRIPTION AND MILITARY RECORDS

In 1865, one of the first acts of the newly formed Italian state was the imposition of the draft—conscription of all able males at the age of eighteen. This measure was extremely unpopular, particularly in the agricultural south, where it meant the loss of seasoned farmhands to the state for three years and was perceived as an imposition by the northern government. The practice was continued despite the protests and still exists today, although service has been reduced to one year from the original three.

Every Italian male, at the age of eighteen, must report to the draft board and undergo a physical examination that determines his eligibility. Even men who are obviously disabled or ineligible for reasons such as being the only son of a widow or the son of a father who died in war must still report to the board, undergo the physical examination, and be declared ineligible for physical or other reasons. As a result, conscription records document every Italian-born male born from approximately 1855 to the present who did not emigrate at a young age. The year in which the records were begun varies from one area to another with the year in which the area became part of unified Italy, but in most of Italy they are present from around 1873, starting with men who were then eighteen years old and thus born in 1855.

The conscription records, called the *registro di leva*, list all males, by year of birth, for each military district. Usually these records are indexed and are very easy to consult. There are two copies of them; one is held in the military archive of each military district, and the other copy is initially held by the *procura della repubblica*, usually at the court (*tribunale*) archive. After seventy-five years, the latter copy is usually turned over to the state archive and made available for consultation. The state archive contains the records of each military district within the boundaries of the province. Usually the military districts are within the geographical area of a province, with one to three districts per province, but one military district may span two provinces, particularly where new provinces have been created. In such a case it may be necessary to consult the archives of both provinces.

Figure 9-1 is an example of the *registro di leva*. It provides much essential genealogical information, including information that will not be found in any other source. This example, which originated in the province of Sondrio in Lombardy, begins with the number of the document (296) and the prospective draftee's name: Nazzareno Paindelli. The next column provides the names of the parents: Battista and Gioconda Isabella Paindelli. The commune of residence, Albosaggia, follows. The next columns provide the date of birth (30 November 1888) and the commune and province of birth: Albosaggia, Sondrio. This document, as is typical, spans two pages and has several entries per page. The last column on the left-hand page gives Nazzareno's vocation as *contadino* (farmer) and then indicates whether he was capable of reading and writing (*leggere, scrivere*). In this case, *si* (yes) is indicated for both.

On the right-hand page is a column for a physical description of the person. In this example it was not filled in because Nazzareno had already emigrated to the United States and was not present for his physical examination. Usually in this space is noted the height in meters (*statura metri 1*), chest measurement (*torace m. 0*), color and form of the hair (*capelli–colore, forma*), eye color (*occhi*), skin color (*colorito*), condition of the teeth (*dentatura*), and any scars or birthmarks (*segni particolari*).

The last column concerns the draft board's decision regarding fitness for military service. Normally the decision was indicated as *abile* (able), followed by the branch of service for which the draftee was destined and when service

was to begin and end. *Inabile* (not able) indicates that there was some physical disability that precluded regular military service. In this case, however, *renitente* (delinquent) followed by *America 28 Luglio 1908* and *abile* indicate that Nazzareno had left the country for the United States without reporting to the board and was declared eligible to serve as of July 1908. In this period, males sixteen years of age or older were not allowed to emigrate or leave the country even temporarily without permission from the draft board. The notation below indicates that Nazzareno was enrolled in the service in a deferred status because his father was already older than sixty-five and that he was the first male child and was responsible for the family: *arruolato in 3.a categ. quale primogenito di padre entrato nel 65 anno di eta'*—as shown by documents presented by the family. His address is given as the Italian consulate at San Francisco. (The same column of the entry above this one indicated that the person was exempted from serving in the military because he emigrated before the age of sixteen.)

The conscription records are very important for beginning research on an ancestor when only the province or region of origin is known. Because there are no central or regional archives of parish or civil records, research must normally begin in the commune or parish of origin. Thus, it is important to know an ancestor's town of origin to begin the search. Sometimes, however, this information is difficult to obtain from record sources outside Italy. Therefore, if you know only that a male ancestor born after approximately 1855 came from, for example, northern Italy or from the province of Venice, research can begin with the conscription records of those provinces that are most likely to be the place of origin. If only the region is known, all of the military districts in that region must be searched, but results can be obtained that way. Sometimes research can be performed by mail at less expense.

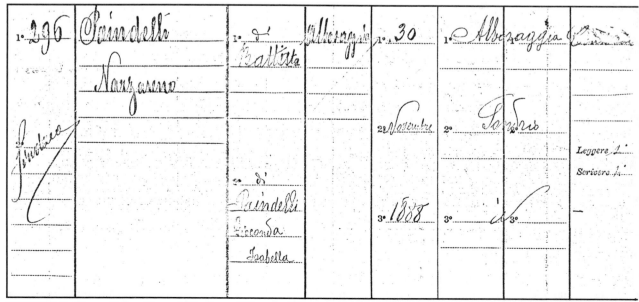

FIGURE 9-1. Conscription Record (Registro di Leva) of Nazzareno Paindelli, 1906; From the State Archive, Sondrio

In a research project with which I am familiar, it was known only that the ancestor, Antonio Dal Ponte, was from the province of Vicenza. His exact birth date was unknown but was supposed to have been between 1864 and 1874. His father's name was Bortolo. Beginning with the index for 1864 and continuing with the indexes for the next ten years, I found seventeen Dal Pontes from thirteen different towns, including Vicenza, who were born in this period. Four of them were named Antonio, and further investigation of the records revealed that only one of them was the son of Bortolo; he had been born at Lusiana. Subsequent research at Lusiana confirmed that he was indeed the correct ancestor.

A separate record called the *registro dei fogli matricolari* (record of draftee curriculum) documents the individual's military service, indicating promotions and other changes in status. As discussed in chapter 1, the period from 1890 to 1914 saw mass emigration of Italians to the United States, mainly due to open immigration laws in the United States and consistent poverty in parts of Italy. This period of emigration ended with the beginning of World War I; Italy ceased allowing males to leave the country so that they would be available for service in the war. Even those who had already served for two years but were under age forty were called again to arms in 1915—whether they had emigrated or not. As a result, many Italians returned from the United States in this period to serve in the army. Many more who stayed in the United States were labeled deserters by the draft board, and such was indicated on their military records. Desertion was punishable by imprisonment and even by death during wartime, so those who were listed as deserters were afraid to return to Italy permanently, or even to visit, for decades after.

Figure 9-2 is the *foglio matricolare* of Nazzareno Paindelli, who was not present for the draft in 1888 because he had emigrated to the United States. His military record first repeats the vital information and includes space for a description of his physical appearance. It further provides all of the decisions made by the military board concerning his case until his final dismissal in 1945. It is interesting to note that he was given *congedo illimitato* (unlimited discharge) when his case was examined in 1908. However, on 31 December 1915, after he failed to report for the general call to arms, he was listed as a deserter. After the war, in 1920, he was discharged again, but the charge of deserter was maintained until 1927, when a law was passed to allow the reentry of all those who had been labeled deserters. He was finally given an absolute discharge in 1945. All of these decisions were made without the knowledge of Nazzareno!

With the *foglio matricolare*, or in a separate record called the *registro di ruolo* (military record), other documents may be found. The *foglio di congedo illimitato* (discharge record—figure 9-3) documents discharge from military service. It repeats the vital information and names the parents under the heading *stato civile*, gives physical appearance under *contrassegni personali*, and includes vocation and educational information in the next section. It is fascinating to note that in the description of personal appearance even the color of the eyebrows and the shape of the face and chin are indicated. In the example shown, Bernardo Bonato is indicated to have been 1.68 meters tall (*statura metri 1.68*); have hair (*capelli*) of brown; eyes (*occhi*) of gray (*grigi*); dark (*bruno*) skin color (*colorito*); healthy (*sano*) teeth (*dentatura*); no scars (*segni particolari*); and brown eyebrows (*sopracciglia*); and his forehead (*fronte*), nose (*naso*), mouth (*bocca*), chin (*mento*), and face (*viso*) were all normal (*regolare*).

The next section, *arruolamento e prima venuta alle armi*, indicates when the person was drafted and the length of his service. Bernardo was drafted in September 1913, but World War I broke out while he was under arms and he continued to serve until 1919, when he was given an unlimited discharge. The next section indicates change of service or transfer from one unit to another, and another section indicates war campaigns, medals, and wounds. One copy of this discharge record was given to the soldier when he left the armed forces, and one copy was held in his file. Even documents regarding medals or other special military honors may be found in this record, as shown in the next document (figure 9-4) regarding the World War I campaign medal awarded to Bernardo Bonato.

Whereas conscription records began only after 1865, military records sometimes date from before the beginning of the Italian state. In some regions, such as the Granducato of Tuscany and Savoy, there were career military officers and soldiers whose records of military service can be

FIGURE 9-2. Military Service Record (Foglio Matricolare) of Nazzareno Paindelli; From the State Archive, Sondrio

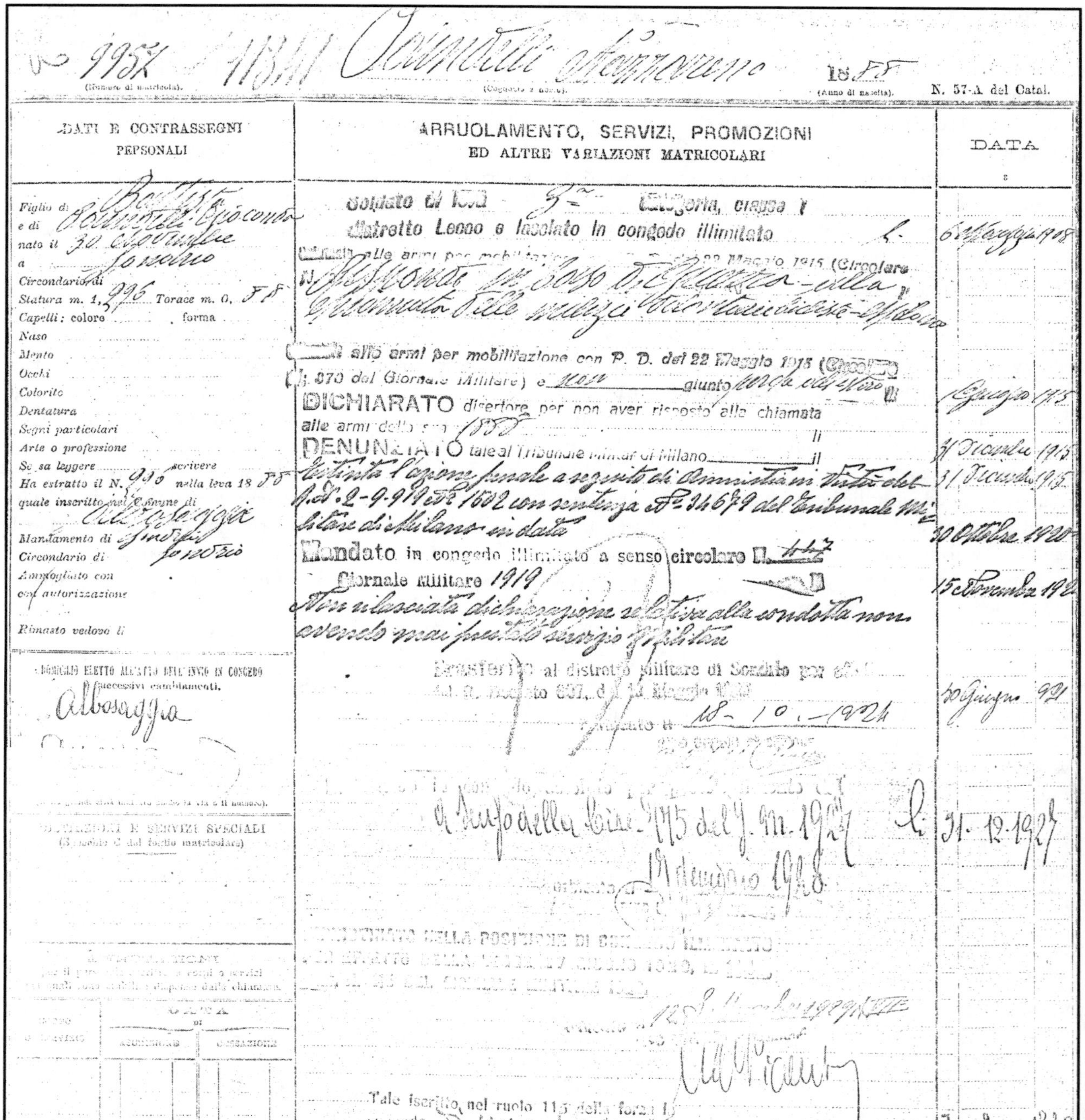

N. 9957 (Numero di matricola) Paindelli Nazzareno (Cognome e nome) 1885 (Anno di nascita) N. 57-A del Catal.

DATI E CONTRASSEGNI PERSONALI	ARRUOLAMENTO, SERVIZI, PROMOZIONI ED ALTRE VARIAZIONI MATRICOLARI	DATA
Figlio di Battista e di Paindelli Gioconda; nato il 30 Novembre a Sondrio; Circondario di; Statura m. 1,[illegible]; Torace m. 0,[illegible]; Capelli: colore, forma; Naso; Mento; Occhi; Colorito; Dentatura; Segni particolari; Arte o professione; Se sa leggere, scrivere; Ha estratto il N. [illegible] nella leva 1885; quale inscritto nel Comune di Albosaggia; Mandamento di Sondrio; Circondario di Sondrio; Ammogliato con; con autorizzazione; Rimasto vedovo il	Soldato di leva 3ª categoria, classe 1885 Distretto Lecco e lasciato in congedo illimitato	6 Maggio 1908
	Chiamato alle armi per mobilitazione con R. D. del 22 Maggio 1915 (Circolare N. 370 del Giornale Militare) e non giunto	
	DICHIARATO disertore per non aver risposto alla chiamata alle armi	1 Giugno 1915
	DENUNZIATO tale al Tribunale Militare di Milano	31 Dicembre 1915
	Estinta l'azione penale a seguito di amnistia ... con sentenza ... del Tribunale Militare di Milano in data	30 Ottobre 1920
	Mandato in congedo illimitato a senso circolare N. ... Giornale Militare 1919	15 Novembre 1920
	Non rilasciata dichiarazione relativa alla condotta non avendo mai prestato servizio militare	
Domicilio eletto all'atto dell'invio in congedo e successivi cambiamenti: Albosaggia	Trasferito al distretto militare di Sondrio ...	30 Giugno 1921
Decorazioni e servizi speciali	...	31-12-1927
	Tale iscritto nel ruolo ... della forza in congedo del Distretto Militare di Sondrio	9 2 1930
	MANDATO IN CONGEDO ASSOLUTO per proscioglimento dal servizio a senso dell'art. 165 del T. U. delle disposizioni legislative sul reclutamento del R. Esercito e della circ. N. ... data 25-11-1915 ...	
	IL CAPO UFFICIO	

FIGURE 9-3. Discharge Papers (Foglio di Congedo Illimitato) Among the Military Records (Registro di Ruolo) of Bernardo Bonato; From the State Archive, Vicenza

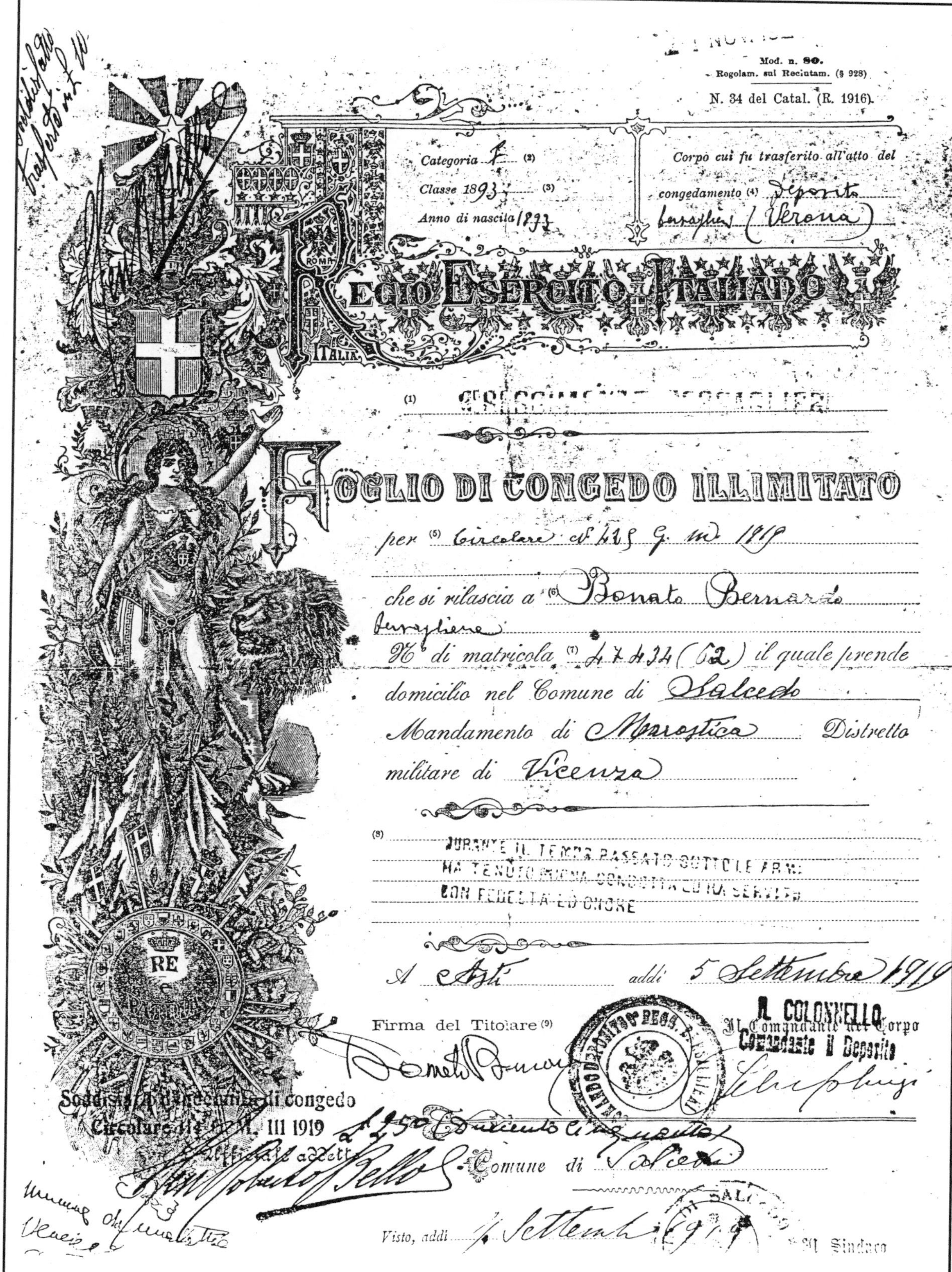

Mod. n. 80.
Regolam. sul Reclutam. (§ 928)
N. 34 del Catal. (R. 1916).

Categoria 1 (2)
Classe 1893 (3)
Anno di nascita 1893

Corpo cui fu trasferito all'atto del congedamento (4) Deposito bersaglieri (Verona)

REGIO ESERCITO ITALIANO

(1) .... REGGIMENTO BERSAGLIERI

FOGLIO DI CONGEDO ILLIMITATO

per (5) Circolare N° 425 G. M. 1919

che si rilascia a (6) Bonato Bernardo bersagliere

N° di matricola (7) 47434 (62) il quale prende domicilio nel Comune di Salcedo

Mandamento di Marostica Distretto militare di Vicenza

(8) DURANTE IL TEMPO PASSATO SOTTO LE ARMI HA TENUTO BUONA CONDOTTA ED HA SERVITO CON FEDELTÀ ED ONORE

A Asti addì 5 Settembre 1919

Firma del Titolare (9) Bonato Bernardo

IL COLONNELLO
Il Comandante del Corpo
Comandante il Deposito

Soddisfatta l'indennità di congedo
Circolare 414 G. M. 111 1919
L. 250 Duecento cinquanta

Comune di Salcedo

Visto, addì 14 Settembre 1919

Il Sindaco

FIGURE 9-3. Discharge Papers of Bernardo Bonato (continued); Left-Hand (below) and Right-Hand (right) Facing Pages

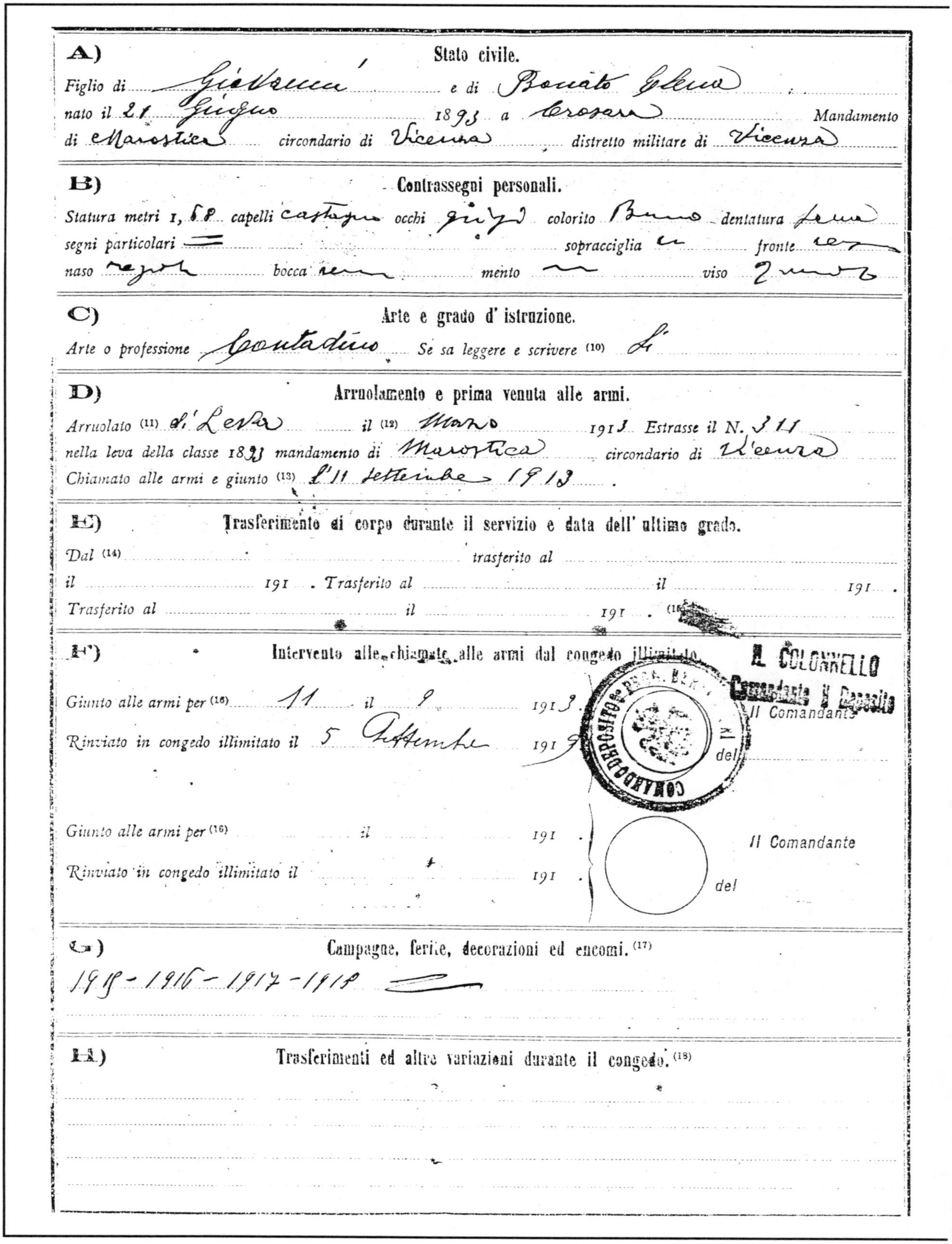

A)　　　　　　　　　　　　Stato civile.

Figlio di *Giovanni* e di *Bonato Elena*

nato il *21 Giugno* 189*3* a *Crosara* Mandamento

di *Marostica* circondario di *Vicenza* distretto militare di *Vicenza*

B)　　　　　　　　　　　Contrassegni personali.

Statura metri 1, *68* capelli *castagni* occhi *grigi* colorito *Bruno* dentatura *sana*

segni particolari — sopracciglia *ca* fronte *reg*

naso *regol* bocca *reg* mento *reg* viso *ovale*

C)　　　　　　　　　　Arte e grado d'istruzione.

Arte o professione *Contadino* Se sa leggere e scrivere [10] *Sì*

D)　　　　　　Arruolamento e prima venuta alle armi.

Arruolato [11] *di Leva* il [12] *Marzo* 191*3* Estrasse il N. *311*

nella leva della classe 189*3* mandamento di *Marostica* circondario di *Vicenza*

Chiamato alle armi e giunto [13] *l'11 settembre 1913*.

E)　　　Trasferimento di corpo durante il servizio e data dell'ultimo grado.

Dal [14] .... trasferito al ....

il .... 191 . Trasferito al .... il .... 191 .

Trasferito al .... il .... 191 . [15]

F')　　　　Intervento alle chiamate alle armi dal congedo illimitato.

Giunto alle armi per [16] *11* il *9* 191*3*.

Rinviato in congedo illimitato il *5 Settembre* 191*9*

Giunto alle armi per [16] .... il .... 191 .

Rinviato in congedo illimitato il .... 191 .

IL COLONNELLO
Comandante il Deposito
Il Comandante
del

Il Comandante
del

G)　　　　　Campagne, ferite, decorazioni ed encomi. [17]

1915 – 1916 – 1917 – 1918

H)　　Trasferimenti ed altre variazioni durante il congedo. [18]

INDENNITÀ DI VIAGGIO PAGATE.

a) — PER L'INVIO IN CONGEDO

Il titolare del presente parte da _Arti_ per recarsi in congedo a _Salecda_

soddisfatto di soldo a tutto il .... e di indennità di trasferta per N. .... giornate,

come pure di indennità di trasporto:

per ferrovia { da .... a .... in L. ....
{ da .... a .... in L. ....

per mare — da .... a .... in L. ....

A _Arti_ addì _Settembre_ ~~191~~   L'Aiutante maggiore

b) — PEL RINVIO IN CONGEDO DOPO IL PRIMO RICHIAMO

Il titolare del presente parte da .... per recarsi in congedo a ....

soddisfatto di soldo a tutto il .... e di indennità di trasferta per N. .... giornate.

come pure di indennità di trasporto:

per ferrovia { da .... a .... in L. ....
{ da .... a .... in L. ....

per mare — da .... a .... in L. ....

A .... addì .... 191 ....   L'Aiutante maggiore

c) — PEL RINVIO IN CONGEDO DOPO IL SECONDO RICHIAMO

Il titolare del presente parte da .... per recarsi in congedo a ....

soddisfatto di soldo a tutto il .... e di indennità di trasferta per N. .... giornate,

come pure di indennità di trasporto:

per ferrovia { da .... a .... in L. ....
{ da .... a .... in L. ....

per mare — da .... a .... in L. ....

A .... addì .... 191 ....   L'Aiutante maggiore

ANNOTAZIONI.

(1) Corpo che rilasciá il congedo.

(2) Per coloro che vanno in congedo per trasferimento alla 2ª e alla 3ª categoria. si indicherà la categoria alla quale vanno ad essere ascritti all'atto del congedo.

(3) Alla quale. o per arruolamento o per trasferimento, risulta ascritto al momento che va in congedo.

(4) Per coloro che nel momento del licenziamento, anziché essere trasferiti ad altro corpo, debbono essere ascritti alla milizia mobile o alla milizia territoriale, s'indicherà. inoltre che sono ascritti alla milizia mobile o territoriale del ... reggimento .... o del distretto di ....

Pei trasferimenti successivi vedasi la casella H nella 2ª pag.

(5) Indicare la causa per la quale si rilascia il congedo, e cioè per:

a) fine di ferma;

b) anticipazione;

c) trasferimento alla 2ª o alla 3ª categoria per modificazioni sopraggiunte nello stato di famiglia;

d, effettuata surrogazione di fratello per iscambio di categoria;

e) compiuta istruzione (se di 2ª o 3ª categoria);

f) compiuta raferma;

g) collocamento a riposo prima dell'invio in congedo assoluto della classe cui appartiene.

Se il militare viene inviato in congedo illimitato per una causa qui non prevista, occorre sempre che sia indicata.

(6) Cognome e nome, grado ed impiego speciale e, se il corpo è suddiviso in specialità, indicare tra parentesi la specialità nella quale ha prestato servizio. Aggiungere inoltre le indicazioni che occorra aver presenti in caso di richiamo alle armi e che, a tale scopo, siano state apposte sul quadro C del modello 59.

(7) Indicare il numero di matricola avute nell'atto dell'inscrizione sul ruolo numero 57 del distretto.

(8) Spazio per il giudizio sintetico sulla condotta (§§ 942 e segg. Regolam. sul Reclutam.).

(9) Da apporsi quando nella casella « arte e grado d'istruzione » è dichiarato che sa leggere e scrivere.

(10) Apporre secondo i casi in tutte lettere l'annotazione: « sa leggere e scrivere » — « sa leggere ma non sa scrivere » — « non sa nè leggere, nè scrivere ».

(11) Di leva in ... categoria o volontario o surrogato di fratello.

(12) Se di leva o surrogato avanti il consiglio di leva, data dell'arruolamento al consiglio di leva. Se volontario o surrogato al corpo, data dell'arruolamento alle armi.

(13) Data, per gli arruolati di leva, nella presentazione al distretto.

Non occorrono, oltre la data, altre indicazioni, come ad esempio i motivi della ritardata presentazione, ecc.

(14) Corpo cui fu assegnato dal distretto di leva nella prima venuta sotto le armi.

(15) Grado rivestito al momento del congedo.

(16) Istruzione (o per rassegna, per mobilitazione od altra indicazione che fosse stabilita dal Ministero). Per ogni chiamata occorre sia apposta la firma del Comandante del distretto o del deposito, ecc., secondo i casi e il bollo d'ufficio.

(17) Tanto prima del rilascio del presente congedo quanto in occasione di richiami alle armi.

(18) Quando il trasferimento è accompagnato da passaggio alla milizia territoriale dovrà farsene cenno. In questa casella si dovranno registrare anche le più importanti modificazioni che potranno avvenire nella posizione del militare in congedo, cioè: retrocessioni, rimozione dal grado, ecc.

N-B. — Occorrendo di rilasciare un duplicato, il foglio porterà la data del rilascio del duplicato stesso; ma al di sopra della firma del Comandante del corpo si scriverà :

« Per duplicato dell'altro smarrito che fu rilasciato in data .... 191... ».

FIGURE 9-4. World War I Military Campaign Medal Awarded to Bernardo Bonato, 1921; From the State Archive, Vicenza

a notary. In the early Middle Ages this title was given to the secretary of the emperor of the Holy Roman Empire. Later, as the noble class formed and property rights became important in preserving family patrimony, public officials were chosen directly by the emperor to regulate and record all property transactions. Later still, the same officials were charged with tax collection, and the property transactions were taxed. Debts and loans were also regulated by the notaries to avoid contention or misunderstanding between the parties involved. Since the notaries directly represented the emperor or the local rulers and had to be able to read, write, and calculate, the position was open only to those who were educated—usually with a law degree—and were in favor with the authorities. In the Middle Ages, only those from wealthy and noble families could study and receive a degree. Therefore, the office of notary public was a mark of power and prestige. And since the notaries were well compensated for their services, the position enabled the wealthy to get wealthier. In many families the position was passed from father to son for generations.

Today, in Italy, the notary public has the same function and responsibilities. He or she must have a law degree, and only when an existing position becomes vacant, usually through the death of a notary, and by selection by a special board of notaries and with government approval can an individual aspire to become a notary. Every property transaction in Italy, from the purchase or sale of a car, house, or land, must be registered by a notary and taxed. Also, the establishment of a new company, change of company name, or closure of any business is registered by a notary, as is any kind of loan. The notary is responsible for collecting the state tax on these transactions and collects a fee for the service. The notary is also responsible for ensuring that there are no liens or other ownership complications that could affect the transaction. Thus, as they have been for centuries, notaries are important figures in Italy's economic and commercial organization today.

found as far back as 1792. In these cases the documents actually precede civil records and can be important genealogical sources. Military records also can be found in the state archives. The LDS church has begun microfilming conscription and military records in archives throughout Italy, and some are now available for consultation (see chapter 10).

NOTARY RECORDS

In each important household of ancient Rome, a servant, usually a literate slave, was chosen to make notes and to keep correspondence for his owner. This servant was called

Notary records are found in each state archive throughout Italy; they primarily document property transactions. Although some records date back to the year 1000, most of the records date to the fifteenth and sixteenth centuries. There was no established format for these records; each notary created the record according to his style and the desires of the parties involved. Some documents consist of only one page, while many consist of several pages, particularly when much property was involved. Until around 1865, the official language used by notaries was Latin, and they used abbreviations and codes to make documents as obscure as possible so that only notaries could read them.

A notary would create two copies of each document, read the contents to each party, have each sign it, and authenticate the signature, which sometimes was only a mark (X). The notary kept one copy on file, and the other copy was registered in the master file of the notary district. Therefore, two sets of notary records can usually be found in the state archive: those of each notary, which contain all of the documents created by the notary (listed in chronological order under the name of the notary); and those of the master file. Notaries rarely made indexes, so it is necessary to read each of the documents to discover to whom it refers. Given the illegibility of the older documents, the special abbreviations and codes used by the notaries, the classic Latin, and the length of each document, it can take hours or days to examine one volume of records.

In larger towns and cities there were many notaries, and there is no way of knowing which of them may have been consulted by an ancestor. Traditionally, the person who purchased the property could choose the notary of his or her preference. This could be a notary from the same town or someone from another town who had a better reputation. As a result, records of all of the notaries in a district may have to be consulted to find documents concerning an ancestor.

The other notary copy is found in either the state archive or in the notary district. These records comprise copies of all documents created by all of the notaries in a district. They are usually divided into volumes of five or fewer years (depending upon the quantity of documents). These documents are arranged in the order in which the notaries in the district registered them in the master file. The order of registration of the documents does not always represent the order of the dates on the acts; often the notaries registered documents months or even years after they were created. These records sometimes have indexes known as *lista delle parti* (list of the contractors) that give the names of the contracting parties. More commonly, however, there are no indexes, and these volumes are cumbersome and time consuming to search because there can be many documents in a five-year period. The master file is a more effective source, however, if you are searching for a specific act and know approximately when the act took place but do not know who the notary was. For example, if you were looking for a notary act concerning a will or inheritance and knew when the ancestor died (and thus an approximate date for the act) but not the name of the notary, the master file would be the easier source to consult.

In spite of their limitations, notary records are a very important source for several reasons. Anyone who wishes to pursue research beyond the beginning of the parish records will probably have to use these records; they (and heraldry records—see chapter 4) are the only existing documents predating 1560 that contain genealogical information. Also, anyone who desires information about a family's property or financial status will want to use these records. When the parish records have been lost or destroyed, the notary records are often the only, or certainly the most complete, source of genealogical information.

There were several major purposes for which people used a notary's services: for the creation of wills and dowries, for the purchase and sale of property, and for registering debts. The first two are of major interest to genealogists.

At the death of the head of a household, the family's property was passed on to certain members of the family. If the death occurred suddenly and there was no will, precise laws regulated the division of the property. For many centuries, all property passed to the firstborn male. This practice kept the land intact so that it would always be sufficient to maintain the family. (If land had been divided and re-divided, in only a few generations the plots would have been too small to support anyone.) If the head of a household wanted to cut off a son from his inheritance and give it to another or in any way modify his estate, it was necessary to make out a will with a notary.

Figure 9-5 is an example of such a will. It includes the name of the family head, here Sante Maffei, and the name of at least one of his children. (Sometimes all of the children and the wife were mentioned.) Usually the name of the town of residence was also mentioned; in this case it was Apella, a *frazione* in the commune of Varano. No vital statistics are provided, but family members can be identified. Sometimes, if the property was divided after the death of the head of the household, his date of death may appear.

The term "head of the household," instead of "father" or "head of the family," is proper because normally, in the agricultural society that prevailed for centuries in Italy until World War II, extended families lived together in the same house, sometimes with three or four generations—sons and their families, grandchildren, and their wives and children—present. The property belonged to the head of the household until he died. Only then did his first son become the property owner.

Within this family system, daughters were considered liabilities because they did not work the land. If they did not get married, the family had to continue to maintain them. The daughter's right to marriage lay in her dowry. Very

FIGURE 9-5. Will of Sante Maffei, 1579, Apella, Varano, Massa Carrara; From Notary District of Aulla, Lucca

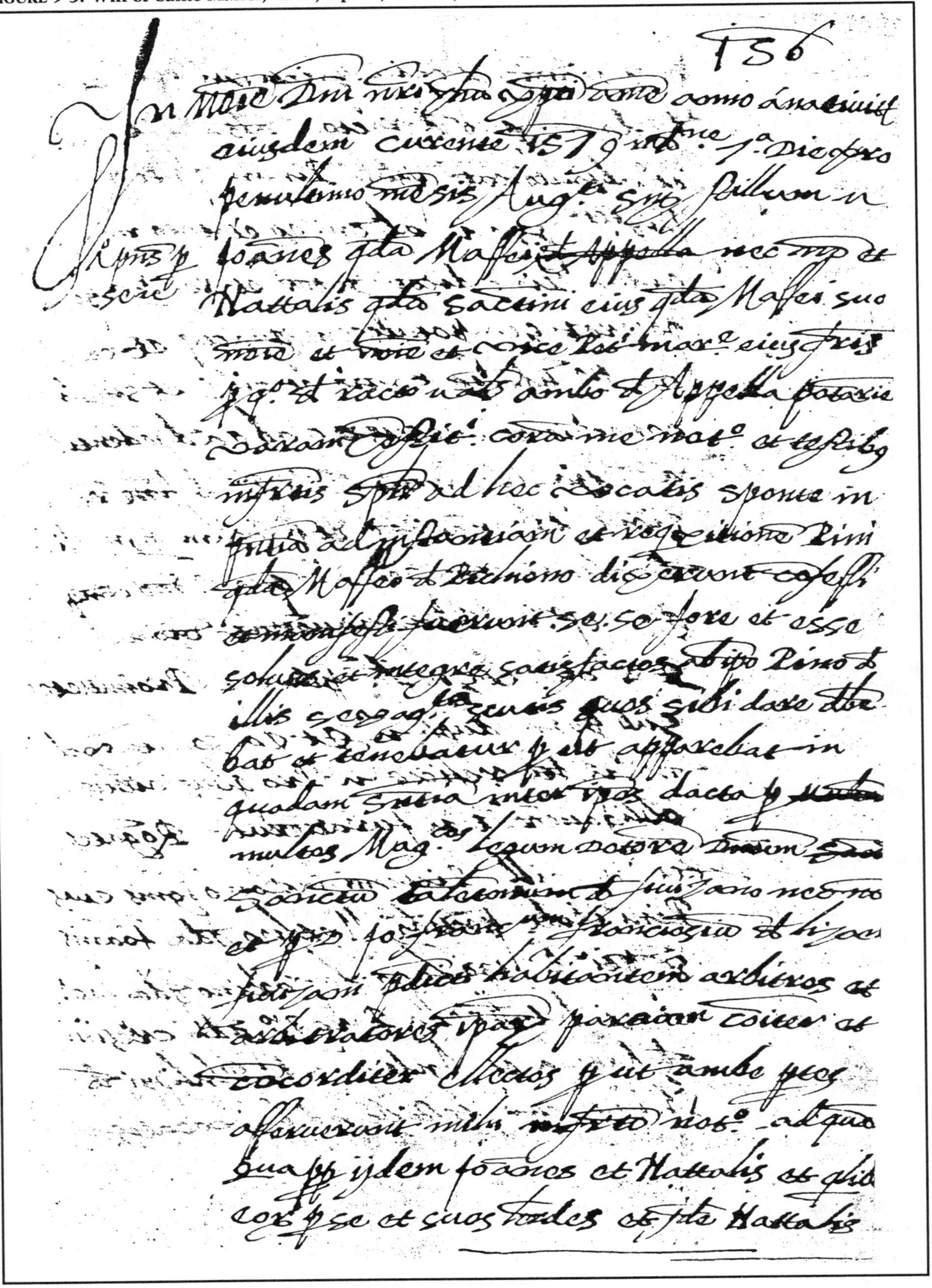

often, even well-to-do families had very little cash available, so the dowry came from the family property. This property transaction would be registered with a notary and would be found among these records.

The second example of a notary record (figure 9-6) is the first page of a long and fascinating document concerning Catterina Maffei. She was left without a dowry in her father's will and therefore was unable to marry until she persuaded her brother, Sante Maffei, who was the universal inheritor, to provide a dowry. This document names Catterina and her brother; their father, Giovanni, from Apella; and Catterina's husband-to-be, Francesco Boschetti. The date of the act, 18 December 1786, is given but the date of the marriage is not. The money and property given as a dowry are listed, giving an indication of the family's wealth. The genealogical information is fairly scarce, but the insight into family relationships and the cultural and social aspects of life two centuries ago is fascinating.

Some notary acts, particularly in Sicily and elsewhere in the south, dealt with the marriage contract (or betrothal). These acts include the names of the bride and groom and their parents, the marriage or betrothal date, and information about the money and property involved in the dowry. These records thus include important genealogical information similar to a civil or parish marriage act.

Other notary records dealt with the purchase or sale of property. Figure 9-7 concerns Paolo Maffei's sale of land to Francesco Michelini. Besides the date and the names of the seller and purchaser, an exact description of the land is given with precise descriptions of the borders. The price and payment are stated, indicating whether payment was in cash or on credit. A will required the testimony of one or two other witnesses, but most of these documents were signed only by the notary and by the participants (if they could write)—evidence of the authority and trust invested in notaries.

A final form of notary record is that regarding debts. Merchants often registered debts incurred by farmers and others with a notary. In these cases, the merchandise taken, the purchase price of the goods, and the penalty or property put up as a guarantee on the "loan" were all listed. When a debt was repaid, another notary act extinguishing the debt was created. In both instances the buyer had to pay for the services of the notary.

Notary recoards provide names of family members and certainly much interesting information about the customs, economic interactions, and property of one's ancestors. However, compared with the civil and parish records, and taking into account the time and effort necessary to extract the genealogical data, they are not efficient sources of information. There are other drawbacks and limitations to them that should be considered as well.

These are records of property transactions, which implies that, if an ancestor had no property, he or she will not appear among these records. Throughout most of Italy,

particularly in mountainous regions, it was very common for even the poor to have property of some sort, even if only a house and a small plot of land. However, there were huge land areas in the plains of Sicily, Puglia, Calabria, Basilicata, Lazio, and the Val Padana in the north that were owned by a only a few landowners. The rest of the population worked for the owners or for the church and were given a portion of the crops, but they owned no property of their own. My wife's Segato family were *mezzadri*—farm workers who for generations worked the land of the Trieste family in Veneto. The Triestes had farmland in diverse parts of the region, so Segato family members moved from one province to another as the owners directed, a practice that has made it very difficult to trace the family's genealogy. Not until after World War II did a major land reform (*patti agrari*), bitterly attacked by the powerful landowners, break up these large plots of land and allocate the land to the *mezzadri* who had farmed it for centuries. This reform, although opposed by many, laid the foundation for much of the prosperity and the middle class that has developed since the war.

Another limitation of the records is that often the family head made no will. The property simply passed on to the firstborn son; if there were no contestants, no notary act was needed. So even if your ancestors did own property, they may never have sold or acquired new land nor made wills or debts; thus, they will not be found among the notary acts. More likely, a few isolated acts were created—but not enough to create a continuous family tree. Daughters were often left out, and even second and third sons were often ignored. Children who died in youth were not mentioned, and wives rarely were unless they were associated with a will. For most families, notary records are not a promising source, but they may help to fill in some blanks.

However, these records can be very useful in regard to noble or wealthy families. These families, obviously, had money and property, often purchased other property, provided generous dowries for their daughters, and often willed land or money to sons who were not first-born. They owned the stores that lent merchandise and often were the only ones that could afford to make debts to buy from these stores. Perhaps eighty percent of the notary records are concerned with the wealthy families that made up two or three percent of the population. Many documents tend to exist for these families, so much more complete genealogical and historical information can be gathered from them.

This discussion is not intended to discourage anyone from using this source, but you should be aware of the difficulties inherent in this type of research. Generally, it is very time consuming to consult these records, and the amount of genealogical information in them is limited. If you desire historical information about a family, however, they are an excellent source that can provide deep insights into how the family functioned and what it owned.

FIGURE 9-6. Notary Record Concerning the Dowry of Catterina Maffei, 1777; From Notary District of Aulla, Lucca

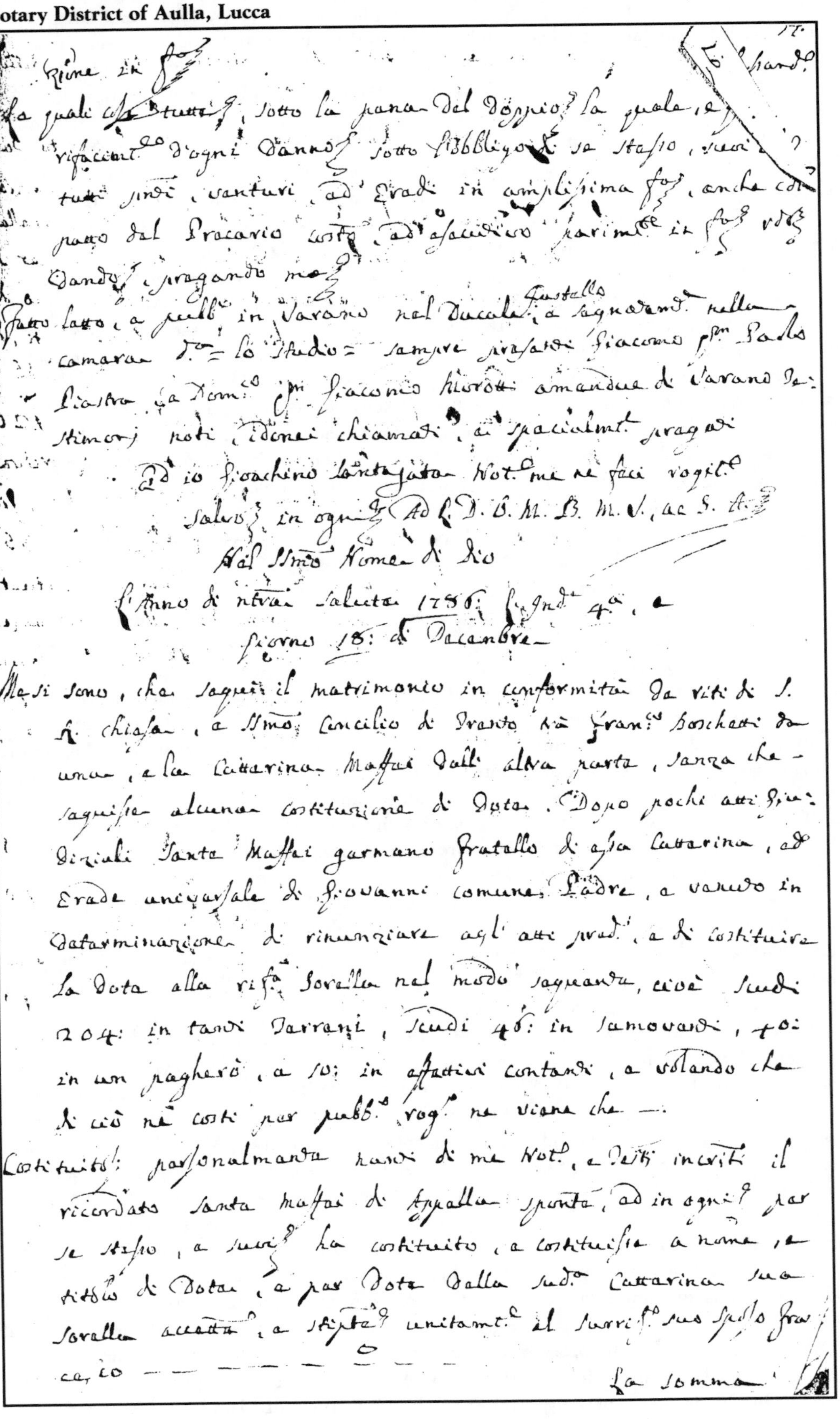
la quale ... tutti, sotto la pena del doppio, la quale, e ...
rifacimento d'ogni danno, sotto l'obbligo di se stesso, suoi
tutti, juri, venturi, ed eredi in amplissima forma, anche col
patto del Precario costituto, ed assicurato parimente in forma
Dando, pregando me
Fatto letto, e pubblicato in Varano nel Ducale di Guastalla, e segnatamente nella
camera detta lo Studio = sempre prefatto Giacomo fu Paolo
Piastra, e Domenico fu Giacomo Morotti amendue di Varano te-
stimoni noti, idonei, chiamati, ed specialmente pregati
Ed io Gioachino Cantagalli Not. me ne feci rogito
Salvo in ogni ... Ad L. D. O. M. B. M. V. ac S. A.
Nel Santissimo Nome di Dio
L'Anno di nostra Salute 1786 Ind. 4a, e
Giorno 18: di Decembre
Mesi sono, che seguì il matrimonio in conformità de riti di S.
Chiesa, e Santissimo Concilio di Trento tra Francesco Boschetti da
una, e la Cattarina Maffei dall'altra parte, senza che
seguisse alcuna costituzione di Dote. Dopo poche atti giu-
diziali Santo Maffei germano fratello di essa Cattarina, ed
Erede universale di Giovanni comune Padre, e venuto in
determinazione di rinunziare agl'atti pred., e di costituire
la Dote alla rifa. Sorella nel modo seguente, cioè Scudi
204: in tanti Terreni, Scudi 46: in Semoventi, 40:
in un pagherò, e 10: in effettivi contanti, e volendo che
di ciò ne costi per pubbl. rog. ne viene che —
Costituito personalmente avanti di me Not., e detti incritti il
ricordato Santo Maffei di Appella sponte, ed in ogni par
se stesso, e suoi ha costituito, e costituisce a nome, e
titolo di Dote, e per Dote della sud. Cattarina sua
Sorella accetta, e stip. unitamente al sudd. suo Sposo Francesco — — — — — — —
La somma

FIGURE 9-7. Notary Record Concerning a Property Transaction Between Paolo Maffei and Francesco Michelini, November 1777; From Notary District of Aulla, Lucca

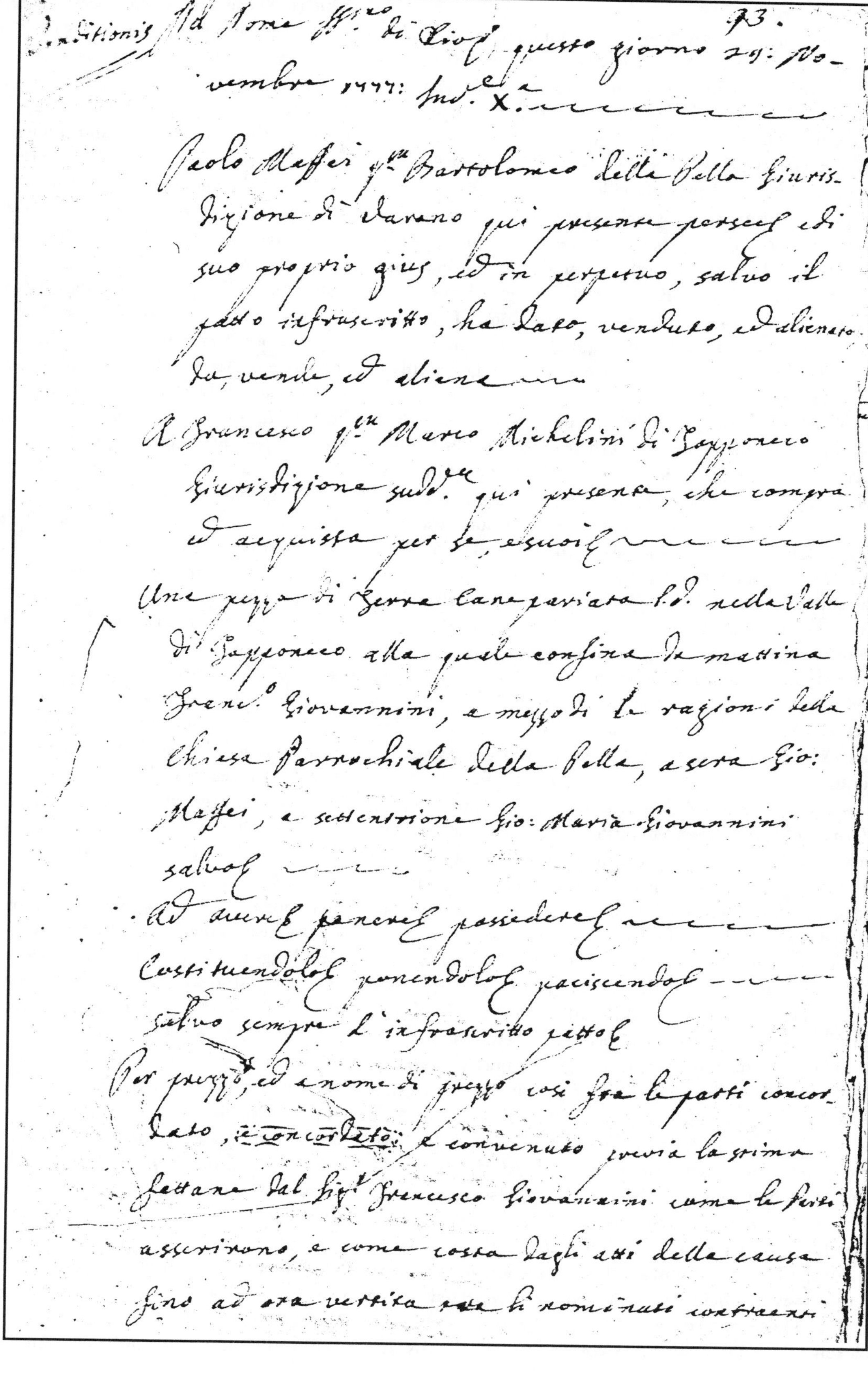

Conditionis Ad Nome SS.mo di Dio questo giorno 29: Novembre 1777: Ind.e X.a
Paolo Maffei q.m Bartolomeo della Bella Giurisdizione di Varano qui presente per se, e di
suo proprio gius, ed in perpetuo, salvo il
patto infrascritto, ha dato, venduto, ed alienato
da, vende, ed aliena
A Francesco q.m Marco Michelini di Zapponeco
Giurisdizione sud.a qui presente, che compra
ed acquista per se, e suoi &c
Una pezza di Terra Campiva, l.d. nella Valle
di Zapponeco alla quale confina da mattina
Franc.o Giovannini, a mezzodì le ragioni della
Chiesa Parrochiale della Bella, a sera Gio:
Maffei, a settentrione Gio: Maria Giovannini
salvo &c
Ad avere &c tenere &c possedere &c
Costituendolo &c ponendolo &c paciscendolo &c
salvo sempre l'infrascritto patto &c
Per prezzo, ed a nome di prezzo così fra le parti concordato, e concordato, e convenuto previa la stima
fattane dal Sig.r Francesco Giovannini come le parti
asserirono, e come costa dagli atti della causa
fino ad ora vertita tra li nominati contraenti

TAX ASSESSMENT AND CENSUS RECORDS

Normally called *catasti* or *estimi catastali*, records of census and tax assessment differ widely from one area of Italy to another according to historical context and political divisions. The oldest such records were created in the papal states and date back to the late fourteenth century. This was the time of the first such census of the population; its purpose was to identify families' property for taxation purposes. This first census covered the present provinces of Ancona, Ascoli-Piceno, Macerata, Pesaro, Perugia, Terni, Frosinone e Latina (formerly Littoria), Rieti, Roma, and Viterbo. These records are held in the secret archives of the Vatican (*archivio segreto del vaticano*) at Rome. The papal states were also the first to begin the *status animarum* records, which were ecclesiastical censuses used to calculate taxes (see chapter 8).

The Serenissima Republic of Venice, too, began a tax assessment of the populace and their property. The earliest recorded *catasto* of Venice is from 1379, but beginning in 1453 regular property censuses were taken in all the territory of the republic to create a more equal tax base. The heavy debts incurred in a war with the Turks could no longer be sustained only by the wealthy property owners; the support of the entire population was needed, including the merchants and craftsmen.

From 1446 the ruling body imposed a tithe of ten percent on commercial earnings and agricultural production, and a census was begun soon after to ascertain the commercial worth of each merchant and property owner. These censuses were taken every few years and continued for centuries. A *catasto* of 1661 (figure 9-8) for two families—Zellarin and Zello—indicates how much wheat (*formento*) and wine (*vin di pasto*) each section of property produced, how many hogs (*carne porcina*) they owned, and the rent (*affitto*) they received from their tenants. It was not a property tax, then, but rather an income tax that had to be recalculated every few years. The genealogical information to be gleaned from these records is quite sparse, as only the property owners or the tenants were mentioned, not family members. Even for the head of the household, age, family relations, and other information were omitted.

These *catasti* were continued regularly until the republic fell to Napoleon in 1797. A major population census that included not only the property owners but family members as well was enacted by Maria Teresa of Austria in 1840 for the entire Austro-Hungarian Empire. At the time, the empire included most of the former Serenissima Republic and the Lombardy region in northeastern Italy. These *catasti* and *censi* can be found in the state archive at Venice.

In the Tuscany region, another population and property census was taken in the 1600s and was repeated in the 1800s. These records are now in the state archive at Florence. The tax assessment covered the whole Tuscany region except for parts of Massa Carrara province (formerly named Apuania) that were in the Duchy of Modena and Liguria. These first census records listed only the head of the household or taxpayer, the place of residence, and the property to be taxed, or just the amount of taxes assessed.

From 1747 to 1755, a census was taken in the city of Naples. It differed from previous tax records in that the names of the husband, wife, and children and their approximate ages were all included, as were the occupations of the adults and the places of origin of non-residents. Also, a list of property was made and the tax established. This type of census was carried out in the Kingdom of the Two Sicilies at various intervals during the eighteenth and nineteenth centuries but did not include the city of Naples.

Figure 9-9 is an example of such a census taken in the province of L'Aquila and now held in the state archive in the commune of Aquila. The census was first taken in 1791 and was updated in 1802 and 1808. The name of the head of the household, Adamo Battistone, heads the document. His vocation, *pastore* (shepherd), and his age, thirty-two, are given. His wife and children follow: Anna Maria Teresa, *moglie* (wife), age twenty-two; Pietro Paolo, *figlio* (son), age three; and Lonard'Antonio, *figlio*, age one. *Testa* (heads) and *due* (two) mean two adults. Next, *industria* (industry) is indicated by a number expressed in *ducati* (or another monetary denomination according to the geographical area); this is the total tax assessed the household for its production, which is broken down in the following pages by the different crops produced. Then is written *Abita in casa propria e possiede i seguenti beni*: "He lives in his own house and owns the following goods:" The property and goods of the family are then listed. In this case the original document was four pages long, the three not shown continuing the property list. Obviously this record provides much vital genealogical data and information about the property of each household. It is a source that should not be overlooked.

Another major use for this type of tax record was also mentioned in discussing the parish census records (chapter 7). Because formal, legal adoptions were rare, orphans and foundlings raised by families were seldom mentioned in the civil or parish records. However, you may want information about a family that raised such a person, perhaps even to continue that line. The census or tax assessment records become a valuable source because from the late 1700s they listed all members of the household, including servants or anyone else living in the same house. The problem, of course, is in not knowing which family might be the correct one; then, all of the households must be examined. This method would be impractical for a large city, but for many towns and small villages it would not be prohibitively time consuming.

The major drawbacks of these records are their relative scarcity and the lack of indexes. In central Italy, where the papal states were located, the tax assessment records were replaced by the *status animarum* records (see chapter 5).

FIGURE 9-8. Tax Assessment (Catasto) of Two Venetian Families, Zellarin and Zello, From the Catasto of 1661 in the Serenissima Republic; From the State Archive, Venice

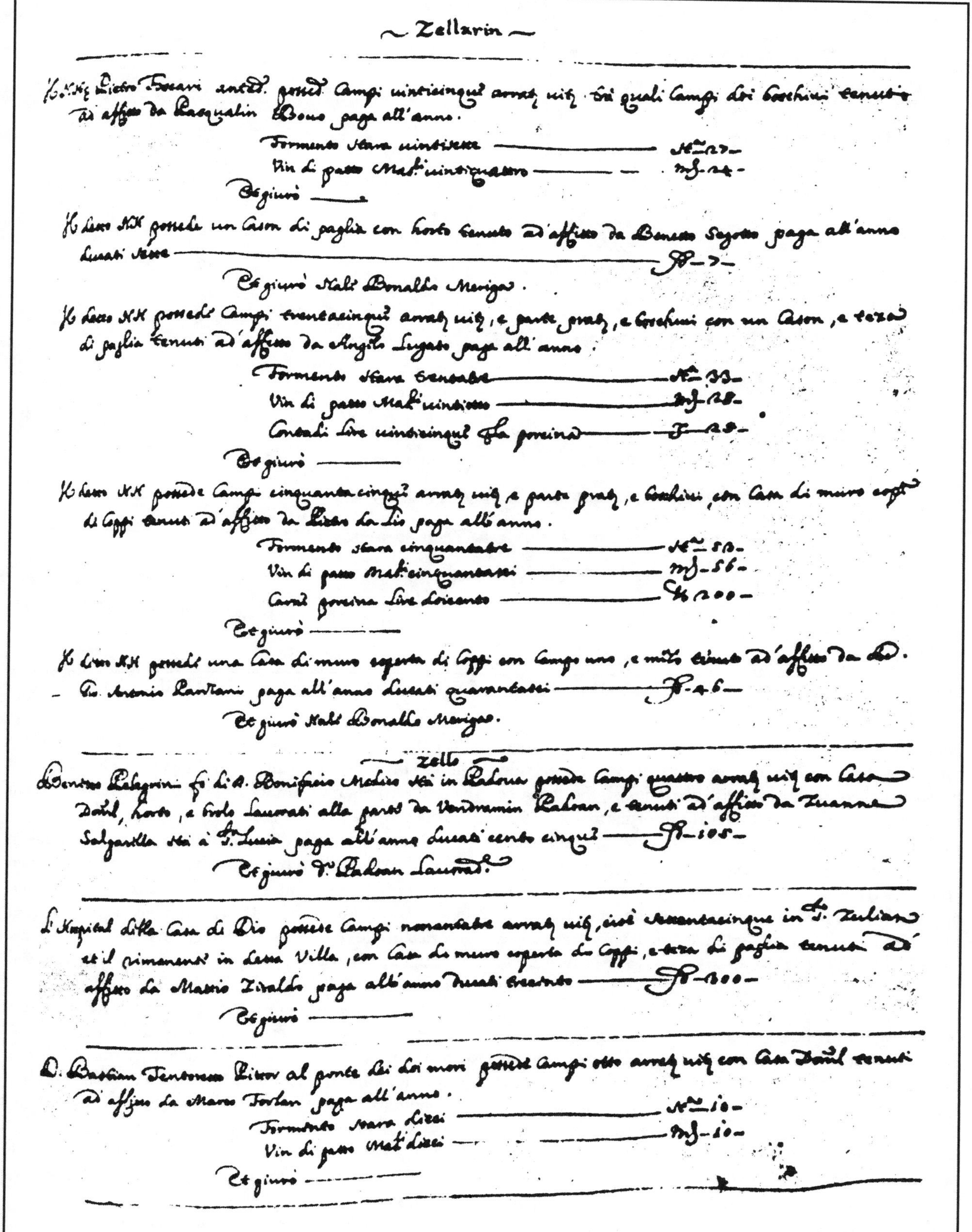

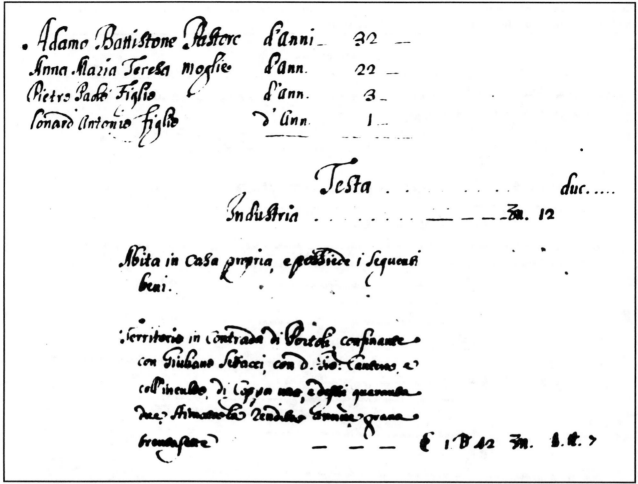

FIGURE 9-9. Tax Assessment/Census Record of the Battistone Family, 1791, S. Stefano, L'Aquila

For some cities, *estimi catastali* listing property and owners exist, but they are rare for residents of the countryside. Because none of the early *catasti* are indexed, they must be examined in detail to find relevant information.

The Italian state government began a general census in 1861, continuing it at ten-year intervals thereafter—1871, 1881, 1891, 1901, and so on. These earliest census records, up to the census of 1911, are held in the state archive of each province. Although intended to be general census records, they differ little from earlier tax assessment records. These records are of limited use. They are not uniform in the information included, and for most regions only the head of each household was named, including a description of the household head's occupation and indicating whether he or she was a property owner. They also indicated the head's civil status—whether single, married, or widower. Women were usually not named; other than the head of household, only men who worked were named. The total number of people in a household was indicated as well.

Not until the census of 1911 were all Italians named along with age, birthplace, and civil and occupational status. Censuses were also taken in 1921, 1931, 1936, 1951, 1961,

1971, 1981, and 1991, but none of these records (including the 1911 census) are available to the public. They are used by each commune's *anagrafe* office to update current records.

In the south, only two or three censuses were taken before the twentieth century; rarely is anything found from before 1740. For example, in Sardinia, a census was taken in 1848 and another in 1857, but there are no earlier records. In the records for the Kingdom of the Two Sicilies, which are the most complete, children who died or moved away were not listed with the family, and only approximate ages were included. However, when other record sources are lacking, tax and census records should certainly be consulted. Because there is so much variation from one province to another and even from one town to another, you should always attempt to consult these records through the state archive—sometimes you can find a gold mine!

The state archives contain many other sources of records that you could spend a lifetime examining. Usually there are old maps of towns and cities showing the location of each house. There are records of town council minutes and political decisions made in each commune. There are legal records and court records with statements of arrests and condemnations, and usually there is a small library of local history, history of local noble families, etc. With the exception of these last (discussed in chapter 4), most of these documents are of little interest to the genealogist. They contain important and stimulating historical information, and they certainly allow a glimpse into legal and political events, but they contain little personal data and are not indexed in a way that would enable a researcher to quickly find information about an ancestor.

Exceptions are court records, which can date to the fifteenth century and some of which are indexed by the names of those arrested. Only the most extreme cases of crimes ever arrived at the courts; most decisions were made at the local level without arrests or at ecclesiastical courts of the Inquisition (chapter 8). In any case, as a supplement to other records (and at the risk of finding an ancestor to be a criminal), you can consult these records.

From the beginning of the Italian state, police records have been maintained on all Italian citizens. When applying for certain jobs or for public office, it is necessary to present a court record known as the *certificato penale* (felony certificate) which declares that the person's record is clear. These records are held by the court (*tribunale*) of each province and can be obtained from the office of the *casellario giudiziale*. An example (figure 9-10) is the *certificato penale* of Giuseppe Antonio Ferrante from the *casellario giudiziale* of the court of Campobasso province. The record states his name and those of his parents (Francesco Paolo and Maria Carlotta), his birth date (22 June 1889), and place of birth (Campobasso). It also indicates who requested the document: *sulla richiesta di stesso interessato* (requested by [Giuseppe] himself) *per uso di legge* (for the use allowed by the law); *si attesta che in questo Casellario giudiziale risulta* (attest that in this court office results as) *incensurato* (with a clean record). *Censurato* would indicate that the court records could be searched for a felony record.

PASSPORT AND EMIGRATION RECORDS AND PASSENGER RECORDS

Because, almost invariably, Italian-Americans are descended from ancestors who emigrated from Italy to America or elsewhere in the world, passport records would seem to be among the first sources to search for more information. Because the passport record indicates the town of birth, these would be especially helpful if you had no idea where an ancestor originated. However, passport records are one of the most difficult sources to research. The concept of a document necessary to emigrate from a town or region did not appear in Italy until Napoleon introduced it with his many administrative reforms. These documents began as traveling papers that allowed free movement of people from one duchy or province to another. Later they became forms

of permission from the ruling powers for a person to relocate to another area.

Italy, and most of Europe, had a closed society. Land was scarce and ownership of it was already established. Even uninhabited countryside in the mountains was the common property of the townships and their citizens and was necessary for their survival, so new families moving in were often not welcome or even allowed. Therefore, resettlement meant finding open lands free to settle on. The obvious such place was America.

After Napoleon's defeat in 1815, the use and need for passports ceased in most areas of Italy. Sometimes permits for travel or relocation were released by local authorities, such as the king of Naples or the duke of Tuscany, but these were few. These early permits can be found in the state archives. Not until 1869, after the unification of Italy, did passports became required. They were not required at that time by the United States or by many foreign states, as there was a policy of open immigration; many Italians simply boarded ships and traveled to the United States or South America without an official passport.

In Italy, passports allowed further control of Italian citizens by the state. In fact, one of the first reasons for regulating emigration was to ensure that young Italian males did not go abroad to avoid the draft. As a result, passports became the responsibility of the police and are issued even today by the *questura* in each province, which is the headquarters of the internal police. These records are kept in the archive of the *questura* and are not open for public consultation. You can make a written request to the *prefettura* (district attorney's office—see chapter 5) of the province of origin (on "legal" paper—with an official stamp presently costing L15,000) for a photocopy of the passport documentation. To date, however, I have had no success in obtaining passport records that predate the beginning of the twentieth century from this source. Some of the older passport records have been placed in state archives and are listed under *polizia* (police) or *questura*.

Another source is the *registri delle vidimazioni dei passaporti* (passport records). Every request for a passport had to be approved by the *ministero degli interni* (minister of internal affairs) at Rome. (You can imagine the months it took to obtain a passport!) A list of passport requests and approvals is kept by the *ministero* at Rome and can be requested from it. These are indexed by town or province for each year, so it is necessary to know the ancestor's commune of origin and the year the passport was released. The record gives the name of the ancestor, birth date, town of residence, and date of application. In some cases the port of emigration departure and the destination are also indicated.

These records are difficult to access and contain little information of real worth. They do not even specify the exact date of departure, as the passport may have been requested months or years before the actual emigration. However, as noted in the discussion of civil vital records

FIGURE 9-10. Court Felony Record (Certificato Penale) of Giuseppe Antonio Ferrante; From the Casellario Giudiziale of the Tribunale at Campobasso

AUMENTO DEL DUE PER CENTO

ANNULLATO

L. 2,40 tassa di bollo compreso l'aumento di 2/10

L. 0,60 tassa di casellario

L. 3. AUMENTO DI 2/10

CASELLARIO GIUDIZIALE

Certificato[a] Penale

Tribunale di CAMPOBASSO

Al nome di [b] Ferrante Giuseppe Antonio

(di ~~o fu~~) [c] Francescopaolo (di ~~o fu~~) [d] Maria Carlotta Sedenini

nato il 22 giugno 1889 in Campobasso

Provincia (o Stato [e]) di

sulla richiesta di [f] se stesso interessato

per [g] uso di legge

si attesta che in questo Casellario giudiziale risulta:

[h] NULLATO 2/4/1913 POSTO DI CANCELLERIA

(a) Generale, penale o di capacità civile.

(b) Cognome e nome della persona, che forma oggetto del certificato.

(c) Nome del padre. (d) Cognome e nome della madre.

(e) Nel caso che sia nato all'estero.

(f) Cognome e nome del richiedente.

(g) Motivo della richiesta.

(h) Segnare le decisioni in ordine cronologico; indicando per ciascuna: 1° la *data*; — 2° il *magistrato* che la pronunziò e la sua sede; — 3° il *dispositivo*; — 4° (per le decisioni penali) il *titolo* del reato, con le *aggravanti* e *diminuenti*, indicando se *tentato* o *mancato* e se *continuato*; — 5° gli *articoli* di legge applicati — ovvero: Nulla.

Seguono la data, la firma del Cancelliere, il bollo d'ufficio e il *Visto* del Procuratore del Re.

(chapter 5), a record of any change in residency, including emigration, with the date and destination, is kept by each *anagrafe* office. Consult this source, rather than the passport record, for an ancestor who emigrated in the twentieth century. Often, however, for persons who traveled between America and Italy more than once ("birds of passage") before permanently settling in America, only the final move will be indicated.

Locating the actual passport of an ancestor can be a very rewarding experience, but they are typically found among personal documents in the land of destination. As seen in figure 9-11, the passport provides the names of the person and his or her parents, birth date, place of residence, and vocation–in this case *bracciante*, or "farm worker." Inside there is a physical description, including height, age, forehead, eye color, nose, mouth, hair, whether a beard (*barba*) or mustache (*baffi*), coloring, and particular marks. It also indicates the destination, usually just stating America (if the United States) but in this case Washington also, and the date the passport was released. Later passports also contain a photograph of the holder.

Other sources that are frequently requested by Americans beginning their Italian genealogy are the passenger lists or emigration records at the port of emigration. This is because the port of emigration is one of the few items of information found in U.S. customs or immigration records.

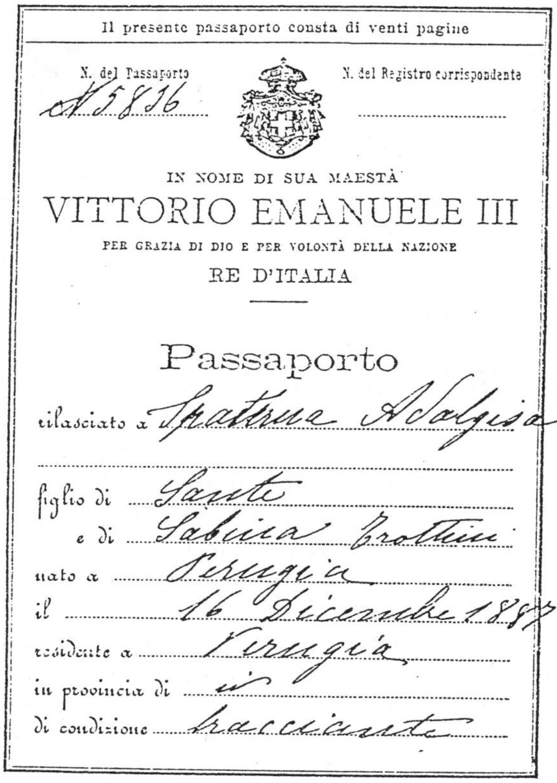

Il presente passaporto consta di venti pagine

N. del Passaporto N. 5816

N. del Registro corrispondente ....

IN NOME DI SUA MAESTÀ
VITTORIO EMANUELE III
PER GRAZIA DI DIO E PER VOLONTÀ DELLA NAZIONE
RE D'ITALIA

Passaporto

rilasciato a Spaterna Adalgisa

figlio di Sante
e di Sabina Trottini
nato a Perugia
il 16 Dicembre 1887
residente a Perugia
in provincia di id
di condizione bracciante

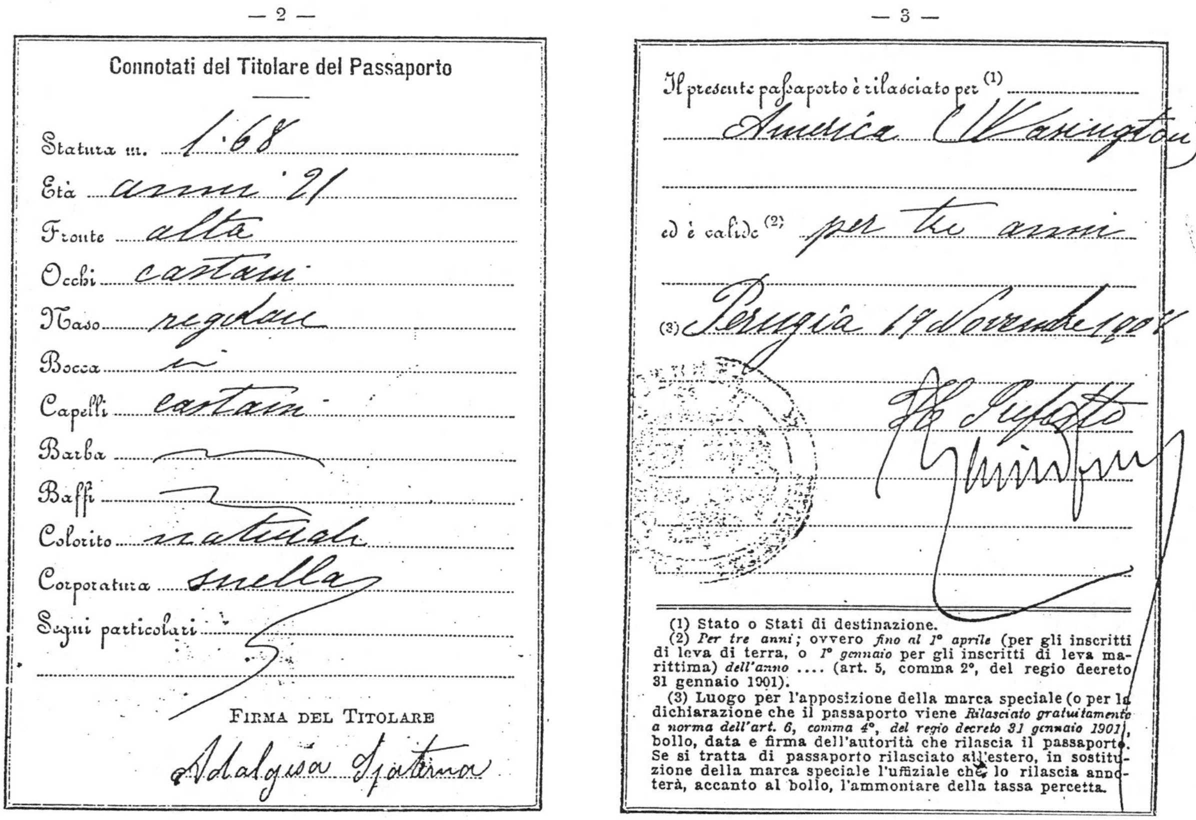

— 2 —

Connotati del Titolare del Passaporto

Statura m. 1.68
Età anni 21
Fronte alta
Occhi castani
Naso regolare
Bocca id
Capelli castani
Barba —
Baffi —
Colorito naturale
Corporatura snella
Segni particolari —

FIRMA DEL TITOLARE
Adalgisa Spaterna

— 3 —

Il presente passaporto è rilasciato per (1) America (Washington)

ed è valido (2) per tre anni

(3) Perugia 19 Novembre 1904

Il Prefetto

(1) Stato o Stati di destinazione.
(2) *Per tre anni*; ovvero *fino al 1° aprile* (per gli inscritti di leva di terra, o *1° gennaio* per gli inscritti di leva marittima) *dell'anno* .... (art. 5, comma 2°, del regio decreto 31 gennaio 1901).
(3) Luogo per l'apposizione della marca speciale (o per la dichiarazione che il passaporto viene *Rilasciato gratuitamente a norma dell'art. 6, comma 4°, del regio decreto 31 gennaio 1901*), bollo, data e firma dell'autorità che rilascia il passaporto. Se si tratta di passaporto rilasciato all'estero, in sostituzione della marca speciale l'ufficiale che lo rilascia annoterà, accanto al bollo, l'ammontare della tassa percetta.

FIGURE 9-11. Passport of Adalgisa Spaterna, 1904; Released by the Prefetto of Perugia for Emigration to America

Thus, the port of departure from Italy is often the only reference point an American researcher has. The major ports of departure during the 1800s were Marseilles and Nice in France and Genoa, Naples, and Palermo in Italy; Venice and the Adriatic ports were seldom used for departure to America. Although the port authorities in these cities do have some lists of ships and departures into the 1800s, they have no passenger lists. The passenger lists were kept by each individual shipping company, and most seem to have been lost or ruined with time. As a result, except for more recent travel, this is not a very likely source.

UNIVERSITY RECORDS

The university is a legacy of the Middle Ages that emerged during the twelfth and thirteenth centuries. A medieval university was known as a *studium generale* and was staffed by professors of the seven arts and at least one of the higher disciplines of theology, medicine, physics, and law. Initially the term "university" referred not to the school itself but rather to the individual student guilds or unions. There were no salaried professorships; each teacher depended on the tuition of the students he was able to draw. As a result, teachers were also forced to comply with the students' rules. For example, a teacher could not leave town without their permission, could not go faster or slower than the course syllabus prescribed, and had to attract at least five students. If his lectures went overtime, the students were obliged to walk out on him!

Around 1215, the first *studium generale* in Europe was organized in Italy at Bologna, where masters of ecclesiastical law and the arts joined masters of Roman (civil) law. It was secular in constitution, and two universities were formed: one for Italian-speaking students and one for Germans. A few years later, in 1222, some masters of law left the *studium* at Bologna, where they felt there was too much ecclesiastical control, and founded the university at Padua. It later became famous for the study of medicine, with such illustrious researchers as Morgagni and Falloppio, and became foremost in the study of physics—Kepler studied there and Galileo was a professor and researcher there. These universities were followed by others in Italy and elsewhere in Europe, such as the Sorbonne in Paris and Oxford in England.

In Italy there are records of student enrollment and academic records dating back almost to the beginning of the universities, making these among the earliest sources of records available. They are found either at the historical archive of the university—for example, at the universities at Padua, Rome, and Bologna—or at the state archive for many others, such as those in Pavia, Naples, and Salerno.

The enrollment record (*registro matricolati*) lists all first-year students for each year, in alphabetical order, but they are divided according to the degree program to which the student applied. Therefore, there are separate enrollments for the schools of law, medicine, physics, etc. At some schools, such as at Bologna and Padua, there were also separate enrollment records for the two universities: Italian and German. The enrollment records for Padua date back to the early 1400s, and they are even older at Bologna. The records contain the name of the student, usually the name of his or her father, often the birth date, and the town of residence.

The most interesting information, however, is contained in the academic file maintained for each student. This file documents the student's entire academic career, from examinations (figure 9-12) to report cards (figure 9-13) and the final degree conferred (figure 9-14). In this student's file even the thesis written for his degree was present and was photocopied for his descendants. This material represents a wealth of information for anyone's family history.

To understand the genealogical value of these records, it is interesting to follow the process by which the person in this example was found. Alessandro Volpi's son had been born in Venice, and some information about the son had been gathered. Unfortunately, however, no records concerning Alessandro were found in Venice, and there were no clues there as to where he originated. In the son's baptismal record, however, the father was mentioned with the title *dottore* (doctor), indicating that he had a degree. Another clue was found in a volume listing Italian publications from the 1800s (figure 9-15); it listed an article published by an Alessandro Volpi in 1853 at Padua. Research in the historical archive at the University of Padua revealed Alessandro's records. In the records his place of birth was given as Trento in Tyrol, and research continued there. His birth record and that of his mother were found at Trento, but there was no further trace of his father or the Volpi family. However, Alessandro's thesis, located with his university records, was dedicated to his uncle, Antonio Volpi, *rettore* (president) of the University of Pavia (figure 9-16). Further research continued at Pavia, where it was found that his uncle and father had both studied. That was the city of origin of the Volpi family.

Clearly, these records represent another source of valuable information and potentially another valuable genealogical tool. The major drawback, of course, is that they are limited to the few people who were able to attend universities; they were usually of noble and wealthy families. The University of Padua has a large room decorated with the coats of arms of students from the noble families of Italy, Germany, and elsewhere in Europe who attended the school. For those who descend from one of these illustrious families, however, the university records are just one of many valuable historical sources that are availabe (see chapter 4).

FIGURE 9-12. Page From a University Document Containing Alessendro Volpi's Final Examinations in the Subjects of Optometry, Legal Medicine, Clinical Medicine, and Chemistry, 1852; From the University of Padua Historical Archive, Padua

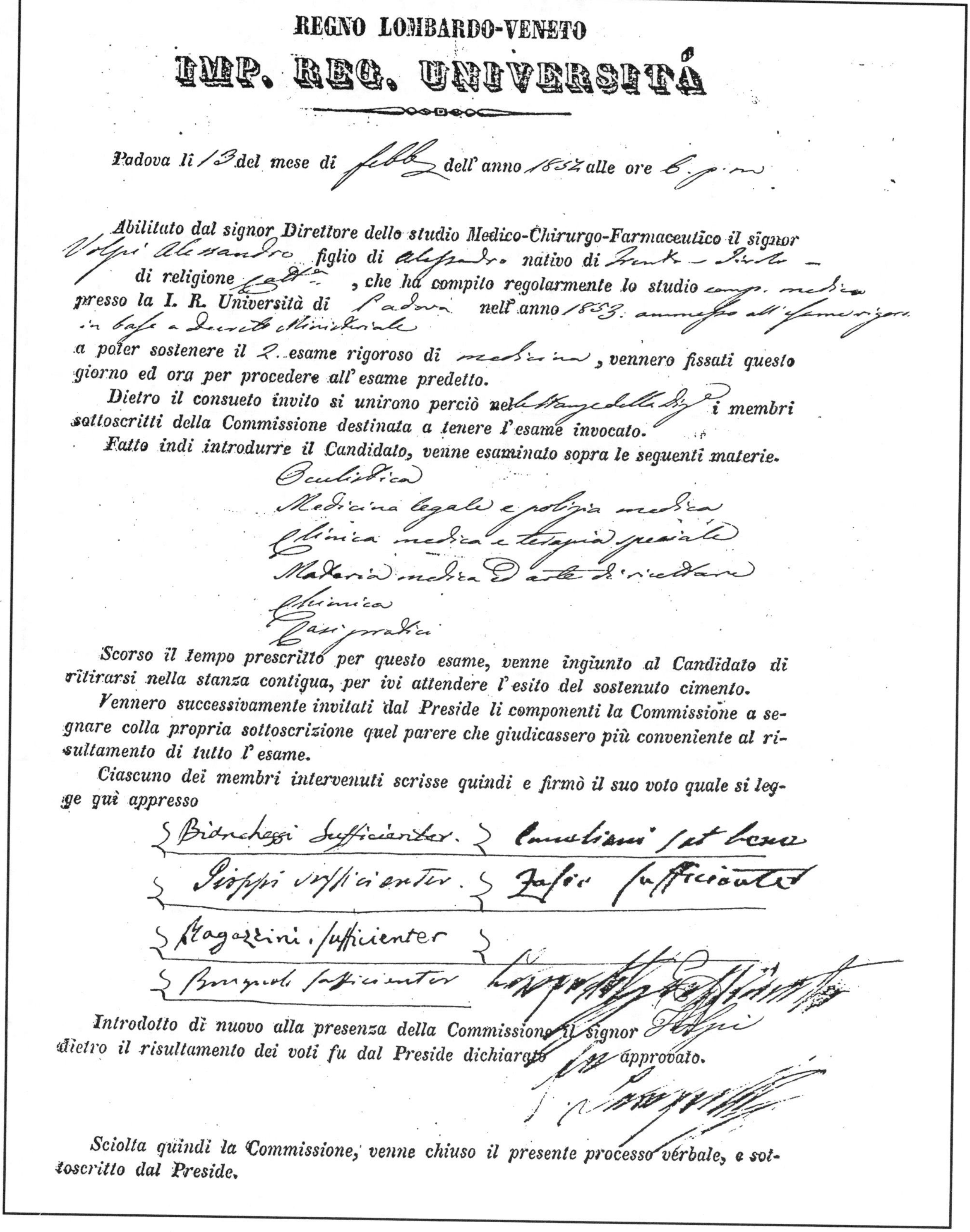

FIGURE 9-13. University Report Card of Alessandro Volpi, 1852; From the University of Padua Historical Archive, Padua

NOME DELLO STUDENTE *Volpi Alessa*

Medicina e Chirurgia di Laurea

1851/52

	Costumi	Applicazione	Progresso
Anatomia	—	—	—
Storia Naturale	dist	mod	I
Botanica	»	»	I
Fisiologia	conf	dil	I
Chimica	dist	»	I
Patologia	—	—	—
Ostetricia	—	—	—
Farmacologia	—	—	—
Veterinaria	—	—	—
Clinica medica	—	—	—
— chirurgica	—	—	—
Clinica medica	dist	dil	I Em
— chirurgica	—	—	—
— oculistica	dist	dil	I Em
Medicina legale e Polizia medica	»	mod	I Em

Magistero di Chirurgia e Chirurgia minore

	Costumi		Applicazione		Progresso	
Fisica						
Botanica						
Chimica						
Anatomia						
Patologia						
Farmacologia						
Ostetricia						
Veterinaria						
Clinica medica						
— chirurgica						
— oculistica						
Medicina legale						

FIGURE 9-14. Certificate of a Degree in Medicine Awarded to Alessandro Volpi By the University of Padua; From the University of Padua Historical Archive, Padua

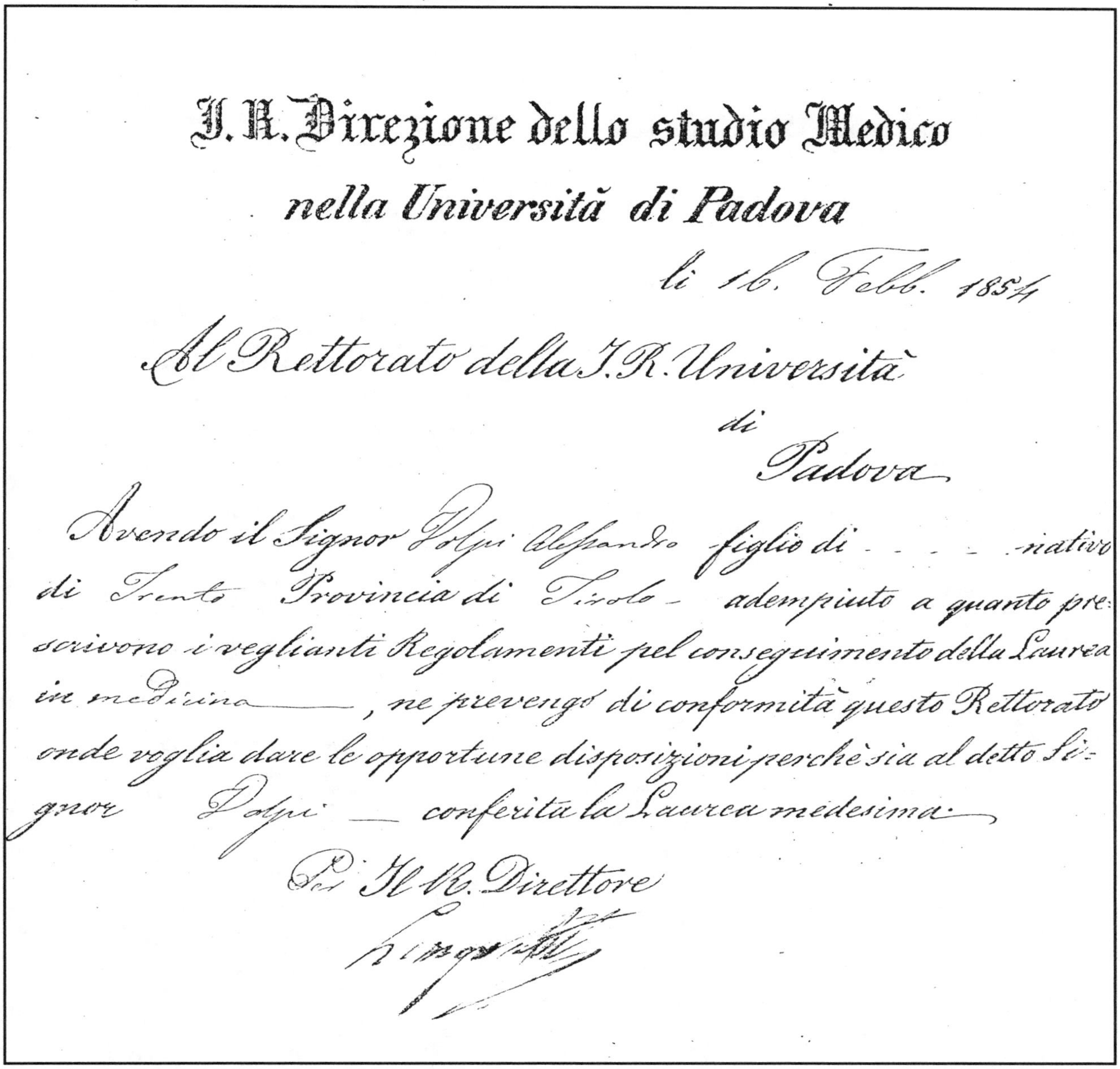

FIGURE 9-15. A List of Italian Scientific and Literary Publications of the Nineteenth Century, Including Articles Written by Alessandro Volpi

808	VOLPE	VOLPICELLA

VOLPE

Volpe Ricc. La vallata di Zoldo: escursione alpina. Belluno, De liberali, '84. 8°.   L. — —

—— Panfilo Castaldi in una seduta del consiglio dei nobili della città di Belluno ai 12 luglio 1464. Belluno, Deliberali, '88, 8°, p. 12.

—— Sui boschi e sul commercio del legname nella provincia di Belluno. Belluno, De liberali, '73, 8°.

—— Terra e agricoltori nella provincia di Belluno. Belluno, Deliberali, '80, 8°, p. 351.   » 5 —

—— *Vedi*: Pellegrini Fr. Fatti dell'anno 1809.

Volpe Landi G. B. L'emigrazione: sue cause, suoi bisogni, provvedimenti. Piacenza, Marchesotti e Porta, '92. 8°, p. 19. » — —

—— Le missioni nei rapporti coll'espansione coloniale. Genova, t. Sordomuti, '92, 8°, p. 8.

Volpe-Rinonapoli Ern. Francesco II di Borbone, ex re delle Due Sicilie. Napoli, Ruggiano, '95. 16°, p. 64.

Volpe-Rinonapoli Luigi. Ai mani di Fel. Cavallotti: conferenza. Penne, Papa, '98, 8°, p. 30.

—— Canti ribelli. Napoli, Carluccio, '79, 16°, p. 88.   » 1 —

—— Chiavi dicotomiche per la fauna italiana. Parte 1ª. Trani, t. Fôro tranese, '94, 16°, p. 48.   » 1 —

—— Di Dante da Majano e di una recente monografia del prof. Borgognoni. Napoli, Pierro, '83. 8°. p. 31.

—— Evanescenze: versi. Napoli, Carluccio, '82, 16°, p. 199. » 2 50

—— Il mito di Lilith: studi di mitologia ebraica. Penne, Valeri, '99, ?°, p. 26.   » — —

—— Inno ai forti. Napoli, De Lella, '78, 16°.   » — —

—— L'ipercritica della scienza e la filosofia. Napoli, De Lella, '78, 16°, p. 32.   » — —

—— Nemêli: fantasia allegorica. Napoli, t. del Vaglio, '78, 16°, p. 16.   » — 70

—— Pel natale di Roma: ode. Benevento, t. Forche caudine, '98, 16°, p. 12.   » — —

—— Quattro anni: bozzetto drammatico. Trani, Paganelli, '95, 16°, p. 45.   » 1 —

—— Reminiscenze e parafrasi: versi. Licata, Sciacca, '97, 24°, p. 22.   » — —

—— *Vedi*: Murger Enr. Le notti d'inverno. — Perrone G. M. e Volpe-Rinonapoli Luigi. Niobe.

Volpes Ces. Studio sulla questione sociale. Palermo, Puglisi, '84, 16°, p. 67.   » — 80

Volpi Aless. Consideraz. sul sangue nello stato sano e morboso in rapporto alla medicaz. deplctiva. Padova, t. del Seminario, '53, 8°. » 1 25

—— Manuale popolare di veterinaria. Padova, t. del Seminario, '53, 16°.   » 4 50

—— Nuovo ricettario scientifico di veterinaria. 2ª ediz. Milano, Gnocchi, '91, 16°, p. 208.

—— Ricettario ragionato magistrale ed officiale di veterinaria. Milano, Gnocchi, '59, 16°.   » 1 50

—— Sunto delle principali disposizioni di polizia veterinaria. Padova, '54, 8°.   » 2 —

—— Trattato delle malattie epizootiche e contagiose degli animali domestici. Milano, '56, 8°.   » — —

—— Enrico e Giulietta: racconto storico del secolo XV. Padova, Sicca, '53, 8°.   » — —

—— L'attentato del 18 febbraio 1843 contro la preziosa vita di S. M. Francesco Giuseppe I, imperatore d'Austria: ricordo storico. Padova, t. del Seminario, '53, 8°.

—— *Vedi*: Andreis Gir. Andrea Hoffer e la sollevazione del Tirolo del 1809. — Hitzinger Giorgio. Precetti elementari di ferratura teorico-pratica.

Volpi Ant. Proposta sulla utilizzazione del sangue di bue per combattere la pellagra. Bergamo, Gatti, '99, 8°, p. 28.   » — —

Volpi Ern. Commemorazione di Gius. Garibaldi. Venezia, Visentini, '83, 8°, p. 22.   » — 50

—— Distretto e podesteria di Noale: note e ricordi. Venezia, Visentini, '93, 4°, p. 16.

—— Guida commerciale amministrativa della città e provincia di Venezia. Venezia, Visentini, '88, 8°, p. XVI-186.

—— Il leone di s. Marco sulla colonna in piazzetta: polemica e note del giorno. Venezia, Visentini, '91, 8° f., p. 31.   » 2 —

—— Lapidi murate in Venezia nel secolo XIX: note e ricordi illustrativi. Venezia, Visentini, '90, 8°, p. 108.   » 3 —

—— Manuale teorico-pratico sulla nuova legge del macinato. 2ª ediz. Venezia, Grimaldo, '74, 8°, p. 254.

—— Profili biografici di Giov. Ant. e Fr. Dorigo: note e ricordi. Venezia, Visentini, '93, 4°, p. 24.

—— Storie intime di Venezia repubblica, con prefazione di G. Occioni Bonaffons. Venezia, Visentini, '93, 16°, p. 330, c. t. » 10 —

—— Zig-zag per Venezia: abbreviata nuova guida pel forastiero. Venezia, Visentini, '87, 16°, p. 133.   » — 75

—— Fede nuova ossia la legge di perfezionamento e lo spiritismo. Mantova, Botta, '77, 16°, p. 156.   » 2 25

VOLPICELLA

Volpi Ern. Religione e sacerdozio traverso la storia e davanti la scienza. Milano, Battezzati, '83, 8°, p. 199.   L. 3 —

Volpi Fr. Il manicomio: lettera. Mantova, Segna, '74, 8°, p. 10.

Volpi G. *Vedi*: Gregorio d'Arezzo. Canzone a Sennuccio del Bene. — Montecatini Nic. Carlo V a Lucca nel 1536.

Volpi Giov. Guida medica popolare per l'uso delle acque ferruginose di Zogno. Bergamo, Cattaneo, '73, 16°, p. 50.

—— La Madonna rifugio de' peccatori, detta di Ponte Rosso, chiesa di s. Michele. Lucca, t. s. Paolino, '95, 16°, p. 43.

—— Matteo Civitali, artista del rinascimento cristiano: discorso. Lucca, Baroni, '93, 16°, p. 58.

—— *Vedi*: Ossequî e preghiere in onore dello Spirito santo. — Ruiz De Medina Giov. La rosa di Granata.

Volpi Gius. Rocco. Il giglio fra le spine ossia breve compendio della vita di s. Luigi Gonzaga. Siracusa, Miuccio, '75, 16°, p. 16.

Volpi Gugl. Affetti di famiglia nel quattrocento: spigolamenti. Firenze, t. Cooperativa, '91, 8°, p. 11.

—— Dante nella poesia italiana del secolo XIII e XIV. Firenze, t. Cooperativa, '90, 8°.

—— Del tempo in cui fu scritto il *Morgante*. Modena, t. Modenese, '90, 8°.

—— Il bel giovine nella letteratura volgare del secolo XV. Verona, Tedeschi, '91, 16°, p. 16.

—— La carità nei *Promessi sposi*. Firenze, Paggi, '95, 16°, p. 32.

—— *Vedi*: Poesie popolari italiane del secolo XV.

Volpi Luigi. Paralleli storici fra Corradino e Massimiliano. Napoli, '75, 8°.

Volpi Paolo. La evoluzione della beneficenza. Lucca, Amedei, '95, 8°, p. 63.

—— Siate felici!: racconto. Firenze, t. Gazzetta d'Italia, '77, 16°, p. 74.

Volpi Pietro. La questione dell'ospedale: lettera. Milano, Civelli, '82, 8°, p. 12.

—— Sui provvedimenti alla pellagra. Milano, t. Perseveranza, '90, 8°, p. 35.

—— Sull'opuscolo del sig. Enr. Cornuschi: osservazioni. Milano, Dumolard, '61, 8°.

Volpi Raimondo. Lectiones philosophiae moralis. Vol. 1ᵐ. Roma, t. di Propaganda, '99, 8°, p. 202.   » 3 —

Volpi Rob. Introduzione allo studio dell'algebra. Modena, '900, 8°, p. 50.

—— e Zoccoli E. G. Di un'applicaz. della teoria dei gruppi del Cantor al problema gnoseologico. Modena, Moneti, '95, 8° f., p. 15.

Volpi Romualdo. Allocuzione a tutti i sacerdoti italiani nella guerra dell'indipendenza ital. Lucca, Giusti, '59, 8°, p. 50.

—— Appello agli abitanti dell'Italia centrale per l'anima ed alla Sardegna. Lucca, Balatresi, '60, 16°, p. 16.

—— Il potere temporale del papa deve cessare o perchè: parola di un cattolico italiano. Lucca, Giusti, '60, 8°.

—— La Toscana abbandonata da Leopoldo II ha trovato un padrone migliore: ragionamento. Lucca, Giusti, '59, 8°, p. 60.

—— Lettera a S. S. Pio IX sulla rinunzia del governo temporale e il riscatto della Venezia. Lucca, Balatresi, '60, 8°, p. 20.

—— L'unità d'Italia è necessaria alla futura sicurezza delle potenze occidentali rispetto all'Oriente. Lucca, Balatresi, '60, 8°, p. 51.

Volpicella Fil. Della pena di morte e dell'imprigionamento dei debitori. Salerno, Migliaccio, '49, 16°, p. 133.

Volpicella Luigi. Bibliografia storica della provincia di Terra di Bari, pubblicata da Gaet. Anfora, con prefazione di R. Capasso. Napoli, t. dell'Accad. delle scienze, '84-87, 8°, p. XVI-533.

—— —— S. l., '71, 8°, p. 52.

—— Degli antichi ordinamenti marittimi di Trani: discorso. Potenza, '52, 8°.

—— Degli scrittori della storia di Giovinazzo: discorso. Napoli, '84, 8°.

—— Del diritto di albinaggio. 8ª ediz. Napoli, t. del Fibreno, '81, 8°, p. 112.

—— Della vita e delle opere di Andrea Bonello da Barletta, giureconsulto del XIII sec. Napoli, t. del Fibreno, '72, 8°, p. 62.

—— Dello studio delle consuetudini e degli statuti della città di Bari: discorso. Napoli, Nobile, '56, 8°, p. 41.

—— Di uno statuto aquilano del 1333: breve discorso. Napoli, Nobile, '61, 16°, p. 10.

—— Fra Francesco da Guevara ovvero un duello nel XVI secolo. Napoli, t. del Fibreno, '75, 16°, p. 24.

—— Gli statuti per il governo municipale della città di Giovinazzo. Napoli, Giannini, '81, 8°.

—— Intorno alle consuetudini di Trani: lettera a Nic. Alianelli. Napoli, '68, 8°.

—— Notamento delle opere relative alla storia ed alla topografia della provincia di Basilicata. Napoli, '52, 8°.

FIGURE 9-16. Title (bottom) and Dedication Pages of Alessandro Volpi's Doctoral Dissertation for His Degree in Medicine, 1854; From the University of Padua Historical Archive, Padua

ALL'ILLUSTRE SIGNORE

ANTONIO VOLPI

CAVALIERE DELL'ORDINE FRANCESCO GIUSEPPE

DOTTORE IN AMBO LE LEGGI

PROFESSORE DI DIRITTO

E

RETTORE MAGNIFICO

DELL'IMP. REGIA UNIVERSITÀ

DI PAVIA

L'UMILE NIPOTE

IN SEGNO DI RISPETTO E DI RICONOSCENZA

D. D. D.

DALLA

MEDICINA VETERINARIA

DEVESI PURE PROSTITUIRE L'EMPIRISMO

DISSERTAZIONE INAUGURALE

PER OTTENERE

LA LAUREA IN MEDICINA

DI

ALESSANDRO VOLPI

PADOVA

COI TIPI DI A. BIANCHI

—

1854

Part III

Research

Chapter 10

RESEARCH PROCEDURES

PERFORMING RESEARCH, WHETHER USING ORIGINAL RECORDS or microfilmed copies, requires a basic knowledge of genealogical research procedures. Because much of this information can be found in books that discuss how to begin a family history and how to pursue your own genealogy, it is not discussed in depth here. However, some aspects of genealogical research specific to Italian research need to be examined.

As explained in chapter 1, the first goal of research should be to discover the Italian commune of your ancestor's origin. The best source is your own family. Talk to older relatives about your family's history and ask to view old letters, documents, and photographs. Usually this step will be the most fascinating and rewarding part of a family history, and it should never be ignored.

As a complement to family sources or as an alternative (if relatives are not a viable source), there are other sources of information in the United States, such as customs records, passenger lists, and census and naturalization records, that may provide information about an ancestor's place of origin. It is normally more efficient and less expensive to consult U.S. or Canadian sources than to start with Italian sources, so do not neglect them.

If you have explored all family sources and available U.S. sources and still have found no mention of an ancestor's place of origin, it may be possible to locate the family in Italy through a search for the surname variation (see chapter 3) or through the military and draft records in each military district (see chapter 9). Such a search can be expensive and time consuming, but often the family can be located in this way and research in the parish or civil records can begin.

After you have discovered an ancestor's town of origin, there are several possibilities for continuing research; much depends on various considerations, such as how much and what type of information you desire and how much money you can spend. There are three research options: 1) Do as much research as possible by mail (see chapter 11) and by using sources available on microfilm; 2) travel to Italy to consult records at the town or parish; or 3) entrust someone else—a professional researcher or perhaps a relative—to perform the research. Even if you choose to go to Italy or to entrust the research to someone else, you may first want to do as much as possible by mail and by using immediately available records to become personally involved in the research and to reduce the cost.

MICROFILM RECORDS

The Family History Library of The Church of Jesus Christ of Latter-day Saints (LDS church) has been microfilming records of genealogical significance from all over the world for decades. Copies of these records are deposited in a vault beneath the mountains near Salt Lake City, Utah, to be preserved in the event of catastrophe. Other copies are provided to the repository where the records originated. Finally, master copies are used by the Family History Library in Salt Lake City to make additional copies for consultation. The Family History Library is open to the public, and the microfilm records there are available for consultation by anyone. Copies of the microfilm records can also be ordered through LDS stakes (ecclesiastical units—there are more than one thousand located in major cities throughout the United States, Canada, and the rest of the world), each of which has at least one microfilm reader.

The Family History Library began copying Napoleonic civil records more than twenty years ago in the regional state archive at Florence. Because state civil records from the town offices are supposedly available through correspondence, and because many towns have refused permission to microfilm these records, the Napoleonic records received priority. The work has required several years for each archive, but most of the Napoleonic records held by state archives in the south and central areas of Italy have been microfilmed. The birth, marriage, and death records dating from 1809 to 1865 for most towns that were in the Kingdom of the Two Sicilies have been microfilmed, and in some archives work has begun on the notary and conscription records. Parish records for the dioceses of Trento, Bolzano, Vercelli, and Ivrea and the Waldensian parishes in Piedmont have also been microfilmed. A complete and current list of the available microfilmed records can be obtained by writing to the Family History Library, 35 North West Temple, Salt Lake City, Utah 84150. When writing, specify the areas in which you are interested.

In those areas, particularly in the north of Italy, where the records have not been microfilmed, or if you want to pursue research using records that predate 1809, research must be conducted personally or by correspondence, as described in chapter 11. This is also true for records dating from around 1865 to the time of a person's emigration in most areas. In some regions, microfilming of civil vital records dating from 1865 to 1920 has begun, but these efforts are still in the initial stages.

RESEARCH IN ITALY

If you decide to visit Italy to perform genealogical research, or if you hire someone to conduct research who may be unfamiliar with Italian records, there are some norms and procedures that will aid in this endeavor. The first steps are to locate the records and then obtain permission to consult them.

Because there are no national archives and few regional archives in Italy, research must be performed at the town (commune) level in the individual town office, in the state (provincial) archive, or in the local parish (or all three). The civil vital records are the responsibility of the civil vital records office of each commune and, in theory, only the town officials are allowed to consult them. The normal procedure requires that you submit the name and as much information as possible about the person to be researched; the town officials will then perform the research. Of course, it may be weeks before they have the time, and often they research only the person named, requiring further requests for parents and siblings and so on. A fee, presently up to L10,000, is charged for each name and date researched. Also, though most officials are very conscientious, if there are difficulties in establishing the correct family line, the clerk will not always investigate all of the possibilities; in many large cities, the officials will simply refuse to perform the research because they do not have time. For these reasons, when possible, it is preferable to perform the research yourself.

Accessing Civil Records at the Local (Commune) Level

In small communes, officials of the *ufficio di stato civile*—the town civil vital records office—sometimes allow outside researchers to consult the older civil records (preceding 1900) so that they do not have to do the research themselves. This is especially true if the person has come all the way from the United States. All you need to do is explain the research you wish to conduct and request to consult the records personally. Usually, however, record clerks will not take the responsibility for allowing research—particularly because it is not legal! Often, in these cases, a simple written request to the town mayor explaining why you want to consult the records and what records you will examine is sufficient to allow access. Such a request, however, may not

be viewed and approved by the mayor for several days, so do not expect immediate entry to the archive. You can prepare for a research trip to the civil office by writing to the town mayor and *ufficio di stato civile*, stating when you plan to arrive, why it is important to perform the research, and requesting permission to consult the records.

In larger cities, however, even a letter to the mayor will not be sufficient. It is necessary to submit a written request on "legal paper"—paper with a special stamp sold in the *tabacchi* (shops that sell tobacco products and stamps) throughout Italy (presently the stamp costs L15,000)—to the *procura della repubblica*, an organization similar to a U.S. county court (see chapter 5). (This is, in fact, the proper legal procedure for all civil records offices.) Again, the written request, in Italian, will state who you are, why it is necessary to examine the civil records, and what records you need to consult. (See chapter 11 for a discussion and examples of written requests.) Such a request is rarely denied, but the response may take anywhere from a few days to several weeks, so the delay needs to be planned for. A written request can be sent by mail before your arrival, but it must be made on legal paper.

When you have gained access to the *ufficio di stato civile*, you will usually find that the records are well preserved and easy to consult. For most towns there are one or two record volumes for each year for each type of record. Thus, there would be one volume of birth records for 1865, a volume of marriage records for 1865, and a volume of death records for the same year. Each volume has an alphabetically arranged surname index. Usually, too, there is a ten-year index for each decade: one for the 1860s, one for the 1870s, and so on. In larger cities there will be more than one volume per year, and there may be many volumes for each type of record, so research becomes much more time consuming. In a metropolis, such as Naples, Rome, or Palermo, the records are divided by neighborhood as though each neighborhood were a different city, each with its own set of records and indexes. If you do not know what neighborhood an ancestor came from, you could spend days trying to find the right person!

You will not be permitted to photograph or make photocopies of civil records. However, for a fee (which should not exceed L1,000 for each certificate, since the officials did not perform the research) the town officials can make out certificates for each ancestor. In most cities, the civil vital records office is open in the morning until 1:00 p.m. In a small commune, the office may be open for only a few hours a day. Examining all of the necessary records may take several days or weeks, depending on the size of the town and the records that are available.

Accessing the Parish Records

Because of these difficulties, even though the state civil records, at least back to 1865, are the principal sources of information, it is often faster and easier to use the parish records. There are obstacles to gaining access to the parish records as well, however. The parish records are under the direct jurisdiction of the parish priests, and the priests always have the last word in allowing consultation of the records. Except in the Trentino and Alto Adige regions of Italy, where the priests also served as civil vital records officers when the regions were under Austrian rule until 1919 (see chapter 5), parish priests have no obligation to perform or to allow research. In fact, for the priest it is only a nuisance! Priests are very busy and have many commitments, and many are aged. Also, unfortunately, unscrupulous researchers have been known to ruin records by removing acts and have even stolen entire volumes of records. Therefore, many priests are justifiably suspicious, and many dioceses discourage priests from allowing research, usually requiring priests to supervise researchers personally or provide someone to supervise the researcher. Nevertheless, many priests graciously allow research to be performed.

Although a telephone call to the priest before beginning a long and perhaps expensive trip to the parish might seem logical, this tactic almost always fails! It is too easy for the priest to say "no" or to make excuses—and once he has said "no," you cannot then appear at his door and request to enter. On the other hand, traveling halfway across Italy or coming from America to have him say "no" in person would be equally impractical. The best approach, therefore, is to write a courteous letter, again stating why you wish to perform the research and when you plan a trip to the parish (see chapter 11). It is quite appropriate to include an offering to the parish; the amount will depend on how much time the research will take but should not be less than L20,000. In the letter, you might ask the priest to either write or telephone if the planned trip interferes with his plans. If the priest does not contact you, he is then somewhat obliged to allow research.

Some priests will not allow research unless you have obtained permission from the diocese's *curia vescovile* (bishop's office). Some dioceses, such as those of Lucca and Pordenone, will not allow the priest to let researchers in without permission from the *curia vescovile*. In these cases, but also as a rule, it is wise to write or visit the *curia* before going to the parish (see chapter 11). The curia can also be very helpful in indicating whether the parish is still active, whether it still has the records of interest, and, if so, who the priest is. The boundaries of dioceses in Italy follow to some extent the political divisions of the provinces, so most *curie* are found in the major city of each province. There are exceptions, of course; you should search for the *curia* that has jurisdiction over the parish of interest. (Appendix B contains a list of *curie*.) Normally, a request should be addressed to the "Vicario Generale," and you should include a list of the parishes that you intend to visit. Of course, an explanation of who will be performing the research and why is important as well, and, if you are Catholic, a letter of recommendation from your priest would be helpful. Rarely will the *curia* deny permission and, although writing there is an extra effort for the researcher, this effort usually insures access to the parish records.

The parish records are usually more compact than those of the town (civil vital records), usually containing twenty to fifty years of records in one volume depending on the size of the parish. Usually, the more recent records, dating back to around 1830, are indexed and therefore are as easy to consult as the civil records. Many records in this later period were made out on standardized, preprinted forms and are therefore easy to read. Records from earlier periods were rarely indexed, and the handwriting and physical condition of the records is noticeably worse. Parish records remain, however, the most important source of genealogical information in Italy.

Entering the State Archives

The only other archive that will normally be visited by a genealogical researcher is the *archivio di stato*—the state archive, which is usually found in the major city of each province. State archives contain many sources of genealogical and historical information, among them conscription and military service records, notary records, census and tax assessments, university records, and others pertaining to the provinces (see chapter 9). These archives have been created expressly for researchers, so no special permission is required to enter them. You must complete a special form, however, each time you visit, and you must present legal identification, such as a passport, on the first day. The form requests anagraphical information, the purpose of the research, and what documents need to be consulted. You should always state that the research is for personal reasons; otherwise, if it is for done for monetary gain, the archive will require payment for the consultation.

The archives are normally open from 8:00 a.m. to 1:00 p.m., but these hours may vary from one province to another. Most archives close in August for summer vacation. The major drawback of these archives is that most allow consultation of only three volumes of documents per day. Daily access to three volumes of notary records is usually more than sufficient, as it can take several hours or days to consult one volume. However, if you were examining the Napoleonic civil records of one town, for example, and could consult only three years of birth records each day, covering the birth, marriage, and death records for the period of 1809 to 1865 would take fifty-six days! Most archives will make an exception to this rule for people from out of town, but rarely will you be able to consult as many records as you would like.

Gaining entry to any of the archives is the first important step to research, and these hints should enable you to accomplish this. The next step is to find the ancestor and perform the research.

PERFORMING RESEARCH

There are many different ways of performing genealogical research that depend on what you are interested in achieving. Some people are interested only in completing pedigree charts of their family lines with their direct ancestors (figure 10-1). Others may desire to complete the paternal line to establish a claim of nobility (figure 10-2). Still others want to complete all family units for all lines. Most researchers begin with the most recent ancestor, or with themselves, and work backward, but it is possible to create a reverse pedigree chart in which you find the earliest ancestor, usually of the paternal line, and then work forward, following all the male children and their children, including everyone of a particular surname found in a particular location. I will use as an example here the most common and also the most thorough and detailed type of genealogical research: completing each family unit with all siblings.

All research using Italian sources must begin with the ancestor who left Italy. Sometimes this ancestor's history is well known based on passport records, immigration records, or other sources; however, often only an approximate birth date is known. In either case, you must confirm the known information before searching for more. Often you will find that the name, birth date, or other information from U.S. sources is wrong! Immigration in-processing at the turn of the century was rarely based on personal documents but rather was based on what the immigrant stated and what the immigration officer understood. Some immigrants took the opportunity to "become" younger or older or to change their names. Many who desired no such change nevertheless found their names radically altered through misunderstanding and decided to keep the American form. Others changed their names later to avoid persecution for being Italian. Thus, not only should you confirm all known data in the civil and parish records, but you should not be

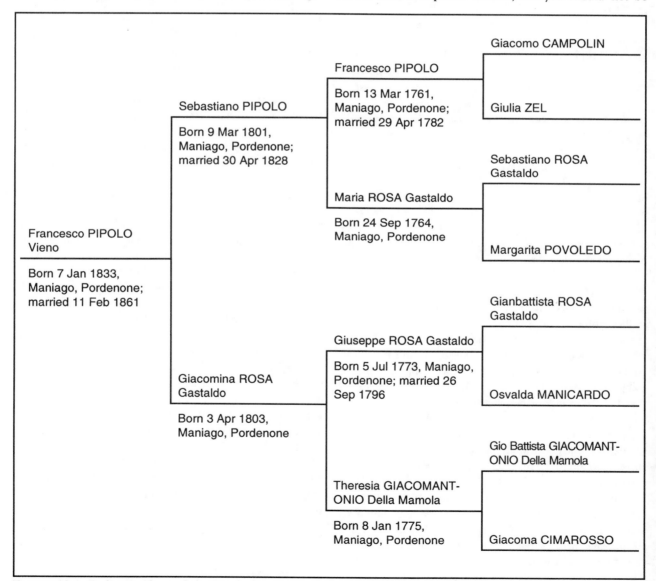

FIGURE 10-1. Pedigree Chart of the Pipolo Family Line, Showing All Ancestral Lines

FIGURE 10-2. Pedigree Chart Showing Certain Male Lines From a Common Ancestor; Used Often to Show the Primogeniture Lineage in Noble Families

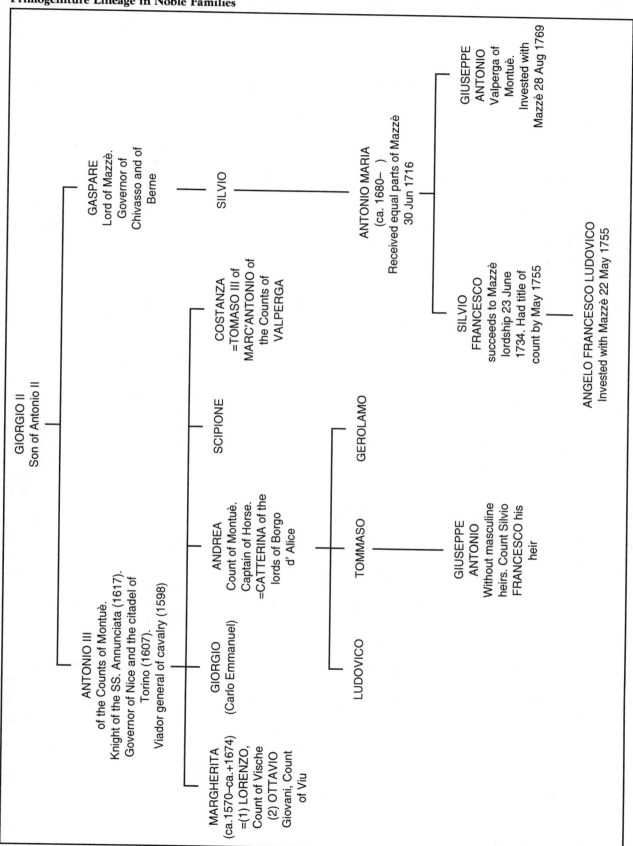

surprised to find variations in the names and dates. Because such variations are likely, you need all available information to establish the identity of the correct ancestor and his or her family—even more so if the research is being performed by a professional or someone else.

Genealogy is not an exact science; much of it is logical deduction based on available information. Therefore, in all phases of research, obtaining all available information about each ancestor is a primary goal (figure 10-3). If, for example, all you know is that Giovanni Transano was born on 15 June 1876 at Caluso, in the province of Torino, but you find no Giovanni Transano born on that date, it would be difficult to establish that a Vincenzo Giovanni Battista Tronzano born on 17 June 1878 is the direct ancestor. If, instead, it is known that Giovanni's father was also named Giovanni, or that he had two older brothers, Carlo and Giuseppe, who emigrated with him, it becomes easier to establish that the Giovanni Battista born in 1878 *is* the direct ancestor because that information would likely apply to only one family. Any detail about an ancestor, no matter how insignificant, can make the difference in identifying him or her. Nazzaro Reno, discussed in chapter 3, had deliberately changed his surname, so no identification could ever have been established if it had not been known that his mother's name was Gioconda and that he was in San Francisco during the 1906 earthquake. Gioconda is a very unusual name, and it was a deciding factor in determining that Nazzareno Paindelli, whose mother was named Gioconda, was the correct ancestor. This conclusion was corroborated by an annotation in Nazzareno's military act that mentioned his appearance at the San Francisco consulate in 1908.

Because of the need to constantly compare information, a personal search of the records is always best. In the case of Giovanni Transano, a written request to the town office or parish might very well have brought a response stating that no 1876 birth record was found for him. Because usually only the first name of each person appears in the indexes of the civil records, the searcher would not have noticed that Vincenzo Giovanni was born in 1878 and could be the correct ancestor. Therefore, the researcher might never have known that the ancestor originated in Caluso and that the line could be pursued there. For the same reason it is best to research entire family units rather than direct ancestors only and to search all records, not just the birth records. Often, for example, there were several children with the same name in the same family. This is normally an indication that the first children of that name died in infancy; only the last child by that name will have survived and could be the correct ancestor. If you did not research the whole family, you might not learn that there were several children with that name; and unless you consulted the death records, the assumption that the last child is the direct ancestor could not be established. What if that child too were found in the death records, having died in infancy?

Once you have established the correct ancestor, fruitful research can begin. In most areas of Italy, families with five, six, or more children were quite common—one reason being that nearly half of them died early in life. The average couple had a child every two years for a ten-to-fifteen-year period. Toward the end of that period, the time span between one child's birth and another often increased to four or five years. Thus, the average family covered about a twenty-year period. Obviously there are many exceptions. Often two children were born within the same year, even at eight- or nine-month intervals! Sometimes only two or three children were born at ten-year intervals. The possibilities are numerous, and special attention should be dedicated to the exceptions. If only one or two children were born, did the father or mother die soon after? Was there a second marriage? If there was a long interval between children, was it because the father was away at war, or did the spelling of the surname change, resulting in some children being missed? If two children were born in the same year, is it possible that there were two families whose parents shared the same names—for example, two separate families with a father named Giovanni Maria Transano and wife named Margarita? (This, by the way, occurs quite often.) Obviously, not all exceptions are due to unusual events or careless research, but certainly these are factors that must be investigated.

How to go about research is much a question of choice. You might first search for the marriage record of each couple and then proceed to find all of the children. The drawback with this approach is that you may waste much time searching for a marriage that is not in the records. It also presumes that there were no children before marriage; or the first child may not appear because he or she was born only a few months after marriage. Previous marriages may be ignored as well. The other solution is to examine the birth or baptismal records, starting with the ancestor's marriage and working backward. For example: Giulia Pipolo married Luigi Cozzarini in 1892. In Giulia's marriage act, not only were both her parents' names stated, but her birth date was included as well. The first step in this case could be to go directly to Giulia's baptismal act to see if there was additional information about her parents. If you were interested only in the direct ancestors, you might then search for the marriage act of the parents and continue on. What if, however, as often occurs, the birth date of the direct ancestor, in this case Giulia, is not known? You might go back about fifteen or sixteen years from her marriage date and start searching for her. If a Giulia is found in 1868, can you be sure that she is the direct ancestor and not perhaps a sibling who died at birth? Even if the death record is consulted and no Giulia is found, does this confirm that she is not a sibling? This kind of uncertainty makes it better, in my opinion, to search entire family units; and, of course, they provide a wealth of additional family history.

Therefore, ideally, you might start from 1892, the year of Giulia's marriage, and search backward through the records for any other children of her parents, Francesco Pipolo Vieno and Giuseffa Mazzoli Segat. This method is more time consuming but certainly is more thorough, and you can search several lines at the same time—for example, not only the Pipolo family but the Cozzarini family as well. Because records of this period are indexed, you probably would not have to search every page, but in earlier records every annotation on each page must be examined. When all the children of Francesco and Giuseffa have been found, it is fairly easy to find their marriage date—in their case it was ten months before their first child was born. Again, in Francesco's marriage record, both of his parents were named, so a search beginning in 1860 and working backward could be begun for the children of Sebastiano Pipolo Vieno and Giacomina Rosa Gastaldo. At the same time, the Mazzoli family and branches of the Cozzarini family could be searched for as well.

Potential Problems in Research

This process can continue as far back as the records exist, and each family can be completed. If you know how to read the records, can identify the necessary information, and are thorough, you won't overlook any children. In the case outlined above, enough information was found to clearly establish the family lines, so the results are fairly certain. Genealogy, however, is not always so simple! Take, for example, the Transano research again. Vincenzo Giovanni Battista was established as the direct ancestor, son of Joannes Baptista Antonius Tronzano (notice the change in surname), who, in turn, was the son of Joseph Tronzano. Joseph, it was found from his children's baptismal record, was the son of Antonius, but his marriage, which took place in approximately 1833, was not found at Caluso, and the name of his mother was unknown. Going back in the records, I found that between 1801 and 1816 four Joseph Tronzanos were born—three of them sons of Antonius. There were two different families headed by an Antonius Tronzano: one Antonius, son of Joseph, was married to Margarita Monte; and one, son of Joannes, was married to Marianna Bretti. Which was the direct ancestor? Two children, Joseph Mattheus, born in 1801, and Joseph

Husband:	Joannes Baptista Antonius TRONZANO
Born:	3 March 1835, Caluso, Torino
Married:	17 March 1857, Caluso, Torino
Died:	16 March 1881, Caluso, Torino
Father:	Joseph TRONZANO
Mother:	Maria Margarita GUGLIELMO
Wife:	Maria Margarita Aloysia SCAPINO
Born:	5 March 1836, Caluso, Torino
Father:	Francesco SCAPINO
Mother:	Catarina CAPIRONE

Children:

1. Pietro Giacinto TRONZANO
M   Born 19 June 1858, Caluso, Torino

2. Francesco Giacomo TRONZANO
M   Born 23 September 1860, Caluso, Torino

3. Giuseppe Michele TRONZANO
M   Born 20 June 1863, Caluso, Torino

4. Teresa TRONZANO
F   Born 29 March 1869, Caluso, Torino

5. Clemente Gioanni Battista TRONZANO
M   Born 1 April 1869, Caluso, Torino

6. Carlo Luigi TRONZANO
M   Born 7 June 1875, Caluso, Torino

7. Vincenzo Giovanni Battista TRONZANO
M   Born 17 June 1878, Caluso, Torino
    Married 7 October 1905 to Maria Luigia BOERO
    Died 31 December 1967

FIGURE 10-3. Family Group Sheet of the Family of Joannes Baptista Antonius Tronzano Showing the Birth, Marriage, and Death Dates of Vincenzo Giovanni Battista Tronzano

Laurentius, born in 1809, were brothers, but either could have been the ancestor. The other, Joseph Michael, was born in 1809 as well, just five months apart from Joseph Laurentius. This case was resolved because it was known from family stories that the ancestor in question died in 1895 at Caluso, and only one of these two died in that year at age eighty-six. The death records clearly stated that it was Giuseppe (Giuseppe and Joseph are the same name), son of Antonio and Margherita Monte, so Joseph Laurentius was the ancestor. However, what if that clue had been missing?

A similar problem would occur if you had an ancestor, say Pietro Rossi, and had found all of his children, but neither the children's baptismal records nor Pietro's own marriage record included the name of his father (or perhaps no marriage record was found). How could you find the correct family line? It would be easy if you found just one Pietro Rossi in earlier records (and sometimes this will happen, especially with ancestors with unusual names, such as Ermenegildo), but usually there will be several possibilities. Can you continue? The answer is "yes," but the research becomes much less certain.

The first step, in any case, is to search for the death record of the ancestor. Even if the names of the father or both parents are not given, it may be possible to determine which of the alternatives is the ancestor from the age provided in the death record. The age cited in a death record is not always precise, and the possible range may span several years. It may be necessary, for example, to search for the future marriage dates and death dates for all the Pietro Rossis found within a certain period and try to map out the lives of each. This would give a much more precise and reliable idea of who was the direct ancestor. For the Transano research, to solve the question of the two Josephs and of other, earlier ancestors with similar uncertainties, all the Transanos appearing in the baptismal, marriage, and death records, from the beginning of the records, were noted and then all family units were established. Normally, such in-depth research is not necessary, but it usually achieves the purpose of establishing reliable family connections.

Another determinant that will help in the evaluation is the average age at the time of marriage. Despite popular myth, it was very rare for either men or women in earlier periods to be married as teenagers. I have found only a few instances in which a woman married before the age of eighteen, and even fewer in which men did. Most women married between the ages of eighteen and twenty-five, and men between twenty and twenty-seven, but many waited until they were thirty or older. Woman were far more likely to marry at thirty than at sixteen. Therefore, if there was a Pietro Rossi in earlier records who would have been seventeen at the time of marriage or eighteen at the birth of his first child, and another Pietro Rossi who would have been twenty-four and twenty-five at the times of those events, this second person is far more likely to be the ancestor.

A final consideration is the use of similar names within a family. It was traditional in many areas of Italy to name the first male child for the paternal grandfather and the second male for the maternal grandfather. Although the practice was not as strongly established as tradition, often the first female was named for the paternal grandmother and the second for the maternal grandmother. In many cases you may complete family group sheets for many generations and find the repetition of the same names over and over again. For example, in the Pipolo research, the names Giacomo and Francesco were found in this family line in almost every generation. Such a tradition becomes an additional aid for determining family connections. Assume, in the previous situation of finding the correct Pietro Rossi, that Pietro's first son was named Giovanni and his first daughter Maria. If a Pietro Rossi born to a Giovanni and

Maria Rossi in the right time period was found, all other things being equal, such as age and lack of death in infancy, this would be the likely family.

It is obvious that research at this point is no longer certain, but rather is a result of evaluation of the probabilities. Realize, however, that when research extends back to the seventeenth and eighteenth centuries, less information is available in the records; either the research terminates or it must continue based on the best information available. Often, the first lines to be lost are the maternal lines. If a marriage record can't be found, it is probable that the wife originated elsewhere, but often no mention will be made of her town of origin. Searching the marriage records of all the nearby villages and parishes may turn up some lines to continue. Also, in many records of the 1700s, only the given name of the mother is mentioned and not her surname. If no marriage record is found, the line cannot be continued; even if the marriage record is found, there may be some doubts. For example, there could be two married couples named Joannes and Maria Caputo in the same period. Which children belong to one family and which to the other? If only one married couple named Joannes and Maria is found, is it the correct one? Again, additional information, such as the typical span between one child and another and the use of the same family names in each family line, is necessary to make the decision. It is advisable that you record the information for both families, however, because the likelihood of errors based on this method is considerably increased.

In some cases, where it is impossible to choose correctly between two lines, you may wish to follow both lines back. Sometimes the direct ancestor just cannot be found. Perhaps a likely family is found, but no one of that ancestor's name is in the records. An obvious conclusion is that the ancestor was not born in that village or baptized in that parish. Although certainly not the rule, some families were mobile, particularly in the plains areas, where they might have had to change locations at the behest of an employer. In such a case, a family might change parishes more than once within one generation; from one generation to another there might be several changes. Usually, however, if the family remained in the same parish and there is no indication that it arrived from somewhere else, it is more probable that this ancestor was simply overlooked by the parish priest. Usually the priests were very conscientious, but occasionally there are notes at the end of a volume or out of sequence in a volume concerning a baptism or other event that had occurred but was not recorded at the time. It is reasonable to assume that there were other events that were never recorded. These omissions, of course, are the exception rather than the rule.

Another possibility, which occurs rather frequently, is that the person became known by a different name than that given at baptism. That is, a person baptised as Giovanni might have been known by his family and village as Gio Battista because he resembled his uncle, Gio Battista. Or the parish priest may have imposed a name the family didn't want or mistakenly written one name when the child was baptized with another. Therefore, later in life the person might be recorded in the marriage, death, and his children's baptismal records as Gio Battista; on searching for his baptismal record, there would be no Gio Battista—just a Giovanni. The difference could easily be greater, the name having changed from Giovanni to Pietro or Antonio, and it is usually impossible to find out. In more recent records and in comparison between civil and parish records, some of these incongruencies have been documented, suggesting that they occurred in earlier records as well. These discrepancies are almost impossible to prove, but it may be worthwhile to continue researching the apparently correct family and to continue the family line. As will be seen, such unsolved problems may be one of the best indications of a good professional researcher, since complex research projects are rarely without them.

There are other reasons why an ancestor might not be found. It could be that the father's name in a marriage record is incorrect and that the ancestor belongs to another family; it would be worthwhile to record all of the people with the same given name and surname who are found in the records within the most likely period and to search for indications that they might belong to another family. Finally, an ancestor might be not be found simply because the researcher was not thorough or careful enough and skipped the ancestor in the records by reading the surname incorrectly or by erroneously reading another surname in the record. Careful research sometimes means searching records repeatedly to make sure no mistakes have been made!

Another problem that can occur is a change in the spelling or form of a surname or a change of the name itself. Many records were written in Latin until Italian began to be used commonly in the 1800s. If you have been following the Rossi family, the surname may appear as Rossi in Latin records, or it may be Latinized as De Rubeis or a similar spelling variation. If you were not aware of this, you might find that the surname Rossi has disappeared and discontinue your research. Sometimes, depending upon the priest's familiarity with Latin (not many wrote in correct Latin), he might use De Rubeis and sometimes Rossi or De Rossi; therefore, you might note only the Rossis and skip the others, thinking that they were different surnames. What if the whole surname changed?

In the Venetian and Piedmont areas, the use of double surnames was common, and sometimes they were used interchangeably. The Pipolo family is a good example. For three generations, back to around 1800, the family's only surname form was Pipolo detto (called) Vieno. There was only one Pipolo line, and all of its members had the second name Vieno; it was apparently the only family line that had this second family name. Then, in the fourth generation, in the family of Francesco, there was a major change (figure 10-4). Pipolo was the name used in the marriage act of Francesco and for most of his children. However, because the couple had been married in 1782 but the first child found with the surname Pipolo was not born until 1791, the records were searched again to see if earlier children had been missed. Only by chance was a child found, born in 1783, with the name Ludovico Campolin detto Vieno, the son of Francesco Campolin and Maria Rosa Gastaldo. Another child, Maria Anna, was found with the same surname and the same parents. The surname Campolin was not found in the records searched back to this time period. Since the second surname was the same and the names of both parents were the same, this represented a second, similar family—or these were components of the family of Francesco Pipolo. With further research, another son was found in the gap in the children born between 1791 and 1796. His given name was Giacomo Atanasio, and his surname was Campolin detto Pipolo. He, too, was the son of Francesco and Maria Rosa Gastaldo; this, the fact that the children were born in the right time period, that there were no other children named Campolin, and that there was no marriage of a Campolin seemed to confirm that it was the same family. The previous generation had the surname Pipolo, although Vieno was no longer used; in the earlier generation still (figure 10-5), the surname Pipolo did not appear at all, but the surname Campolin was common. The baptismal annotation of one child, Maddalena, gave the surname as Campolin detto Pipolo; for all the others it was just Campolin. However, in the marriage record of the father, Giacomo, the surname was again stated as Campolin detto Pipolo, confirming this connection; his wife's name was Maddalena del Pipolo (which, in earlier generations, was del Pippo), making the beginning of the Campolin del Pipolo name combination. Here was a new family name that, in recent records, was matched by neither of the two family names, but for which there is evidence that it is, indeed, the correct original surname of the family. Only very careful research and attentiveness to every detail could have established such a line; otherwise, research would have ended in the mid–1700s because no one of the surname Pipolo appeared in the records. These conclusions could never have been reached by searching only for the direct ancestor and not his or her siblings. It is necessary to research the entire family unit and even alternative family units to make the necessary comparisons and arrive at the proper conclusions. By researching carefully, examining all available sources of information, and reading each act carefully, most of these research problems can be overcome, and research can proceed on all lines back to the beginning of the records.

RECORDING THE DATA

Many different types of forms can be used for recording data. Any family group sheet and pedigree chart is appropri-

```
Husband:   Francesco PIPOLO
  Born:      13 March 1761, Maniago, Pordenone
  Married:   29 April 1782, Maniogo, Pordenone
  Father:    Giacomo CAMPOLIN
  Mother:    Giulia ZEL

Wife:      Maria ROSA Gastaldo
  Born:      24 September 1764, Maniago, Pordenone
  Father:    Sebastiano ROSA Gastaldo
  Mother:    Margarita POVOLEDO

Children:

  1.        Ludovico CAMPOLIN Vieno
  M         Born 24 August 1783, Maniago, Pordenone

  2.        Maria Anna CAMPOLIN Vieno
  F         Born 9 May 1786, Maniago, Pordenone

  3.        Rosa PIPOLO
  F         Born 30 August 1791, Maniago, Pordenone

  4.        Rosa CAMPOLIN Pipolo
  F         Born 19 December 1796, Maniago, Pordenone

  5.        Osvaldo PIPOLO
  M         Born 9 February 1798, Maniago, Pordenone

  6.        Sebastiano PIPOLO
  M         Born 9 March 1801, Maniago, Pordenone
            First married 30 April 1828

  7.        Rosa PIPOLO
  F         Born 23 January 1804, Maniago, Pordenone
```

FIGURE 10-4. Family Group Sheet of Francesco Pipolo Showing the Initial Change in the Surname to Campolin Pipolo or Campolin Vieno in the Baptismal Acts of Some of His Children

ate; however, there should be space for additional comments and information.

Write down all of the details found in an act—not just names and dates. Even the way in which you record names and dates is important. As the example above demonstrates, it is very important that you record all given names and surnames found in each act and that you record the name exactly as it appears in the act, without variation. Thus, if a name appears as Joannes Baptista De Rubeis, do not Italianize it as Giovanni Battista Rossi. Even if the name appears to have been misspelled, record it as found; this allows for later comparison, evaluation, and cross-referencing.

In the last few years, one of the most significant developments in the field of genealogy has been the pooling of information into large databases that enable researchers to find other, heretofore unknown, relatives who are researching the same family line. Dr. Thomas Militello's organization, P.O.I.N.T. (see chapter 1), has several thousand Italian

family names in its database and has enabled a number of people to find new relatives. The Everton Publishers of Logan, Utah, has tens of thousands of surnames in its database, and the LDS church database has millions of surnames from all over the world. These databases will undoubtedly expand rapidly in the coming years as more and more people enter information about their families. Eventually, you may be able to find much of your family research already completed through these databases. To allow cross-referencing of the data, however, all researchers should abide by the same basic rules for compiling the data. If one researcher finds a name written as Mariae De Polettis in the records and Italianizes it to Maria Poletti when recording it, but the next researcher records it as found in the act, the two may not be cross-referenced even if the same birthplace and birth date are given, since two different surnames will result in the computer records.

Unfortunately, some researchers attempt to estimate birth dates. If the date of baptism is the principal date given in a baptismal record, it should be recorded as a baptismal date; the birth date should not be calculated from it but rather recorded as stated—for example, "born this morning." If a baptismal record gives the baptismal date as 6 July 1796 and then states "born last night," the researcher might conclude that the birth date was 5 July 1796 and record that as the principal date. However, that could be incorrect, because "last night" could have been two o'clock that morning. Furthermore, that date will not be cross-referenced to the baptismal date recorded by another researcher.

Therefore, it is standard practice to record all names and dates as found in the documents. The same is true for death records. Some parishes have burial records, and in them the principal date given is that of the burial. In other records the death date is stated and should be recorded as such. If both dates are specifically stated, either or both can be used.

The same rule applies to names and surnames. For each child in a family, the name and surname should be written exactly as found. Particularly in older records, there may be considerable variety in the spelling of the surname within one family, but this is to be expected. The problem of recording names, however, is more complicated than that of dates. In researching a direct ancestor, you will often find one name in the death records, a variation of the name in the marriage records, and still another variation in the baptismal records. For example, you might find a Pietro Rizzotti in the death records, Pietro Antonino Rizzoti in the marriage records, and Petrus Antoninus De Rizzotis in the baptismal records. Which name should be used? Most genealogical organizations request that the name in the birth or baptismal record be used when variations are encountered. On the other hand, if the spelling differences are found in both civil records and parish records, civil records are the preferred source. It might be wise, particularly when entering information into a database, and certainly for your own family history, to include the other spelling variations found in the records.

Another problem you may encounter is the constant use of abbreviations, particularly in the parish records. If you find P.tro Ant.o (for Pietro Antonio) or M.a Mag.na (for Maria Magdalena), should you record the abbreviated form or the full name? In this case the most correct method would be to write the name as written in its abbreviated form, followed by the full name in parentheses. Often, however, a researcher will record the name as Pietro Antonio or Maria Magdalena, excluding the abbreviation. The danger here lies in misreading the abbreviation; and what appears to be an abbreviation can actually be the name itself. For example, Gio Batta is an abbreviation for Giovanni Battista, but it is also a name. The same is true for Fran.co (for Francesco); Franco is also a popular name. The correct procedure eliminates this chance for error.

Many people wonder what an ancestor's "real name" was. Though an ancestor's name appears as the Latin Aloysius Maria De Ferraris in the records, you might think that the person certainly could not have been known by this name in daily life. The answer is not so simple. Just as many people now have a given name and surname on their birth certificates but are known by a nickname, the same has been true in the past. An official act, whether in Latin or Italian, was a legal document bearing the legal and historically recognized name, but most people were known by an entirely different name during their lives—usually the dialectic name; even families had nicknames. Thus, Aloysius Maria De Ferraris might have been called "Gigi the Fabro" all his life. Unfortunately, you might only be able to guess at what a person was called through a knowledge of local dialects and common regional nicknames (see the list of common names in chapter 12).

Husband:	Osvaldo CAMPOLIN Pipolo
Born:	19 August 1704, Maniago, Pordenone
Married:	3 February 1734, Maniago, Pordenone
Father:	Giacomo CAMPOLIN
Mother:	Maddalena DEL PIPOLO
Husband's other wives:	
	Domenega CANDIDO Brusian
Wife:	Gratia BRANDOLISIO Campanaro
Born:	9 June 1712, Maniago, Pordenone
Father:	Domenico BRANDOLISIO Campanaro
Mother:	Valentina DEL TIN

Children:

1. M	Giacomo CAMPOLIN Born 24 December 1734, Maniago, Pordenone
2. M	Angelo CAMPOLIN Born 11 July 1737, Maniago, Pordenone
3. F	Angiola CAMPOLIN Born 12 November 1739, Maniago, Pordenone
4. F	Domenica CAMPOLIN Born 24 December 1742, Maniago, Pordenone
5. F	Domenica CAMPOLIN Born 17 January 1745, Maniago, Pordenone
6. F	Maddalena CAMPOLIN Pipolo Born 3 September 1749, Maniago, Pordenone

FIGURE 10-5. Family Group Sheet of Osvaldo Campolin Pipolo Showing Further Variations in the Change of the Family Name to Campolin

HIRING A PROFESSIONAL RESEARCHER

Many people are satisfied with the research they accomplish by mail or with microfilm copies of the records available through the LDS church. However, others do not feel capable or are not able to access even the microfilm copies themselves, so the question eventually arises: "If I can't do it myself, how can I find someone reliable to do it for me?"

Research in the United States

Probably the easiest course is hiring someone to search U.S., Canadian, or local sources or microfilm copies of the Italian records available in the United States and Canada. Many professional genealogists and record searchers advertise their services in genealogy periodicals that can be found in local libraries, such as *Everton's Genealogical Helper* (published by The Everton Publishers, P.O. Box 368, Logan, Utah 84323-0368), *The New England Historical and Genealogical*

Register (published by the New England Historic Genealogical Society, 101 Newbury St., Boston, Mass. 02116), *The National Genealogical Society Quarterly* (published by the National Genealogical Society, 4527 Seventeenth St. North, Arlington, Va. 22207), and others. Many professional researchers are located in the Salt Lake City, Utah, area, where the Family History Library is located. Because there are many researchers in the area and the records are readily available, the expenses involved are reduced and a fairly precise estimate of the total cost can usually be made.

For sources created in the United States, such as naturalization records, usually there are few problems associated with hiring a researcher because many researchers have accumulated expertise in this area. If you want someone to research microfilmed Italian records, however, you should be much more cautious. Few researchers are expert in Italian genealogy, and fewer still are familiar with the Italian language—an attribute which, if not absolutely necessary, would certainly be worthwhile since the researcher is being paid as an expert and professional.

Research in Italy

Research in Italy presents a number of possibilities. When writing to a parish priest, if you indicate that you are willing to pay someone to continue research in the parish archive, the priest may recommend someone whom he trusts or may even offer to perform the research himself. You may even have a relative in Italy who is willing to conduct research. Most Italian state archives have affiliated researchers who will perform research for a fee—usually graduate students or recently graduated persons who specialize in archival work. They are familiar with the archival records and are competent researchers, but few specialize in genealogical research and so may not be aware of the nuances of this kind of research. Nonetheless, they can be very helpful if properly guided in their efforts.

These researchers, however, present potential problems that you should be aware of. While any of these people would probably speak Italian well, they might not be familiar with genealogical research or with paleography (the study of ancient handwriting) and might not know how to read the earlier records. Even parish priests, unless they have a passion for research and some experience, often have considerable difficulty in reading older records, and usually they know little about genealogical procedures or how to solve the research problems they encounter. Relatives are often the worst choice because, while they may feel obliged to do their "American cousin" a favor and will likely refuse payment, they usually have neither the expertise nor the desire to pursue long research projects.

These problems can be overcome if you can properly guide the researcher by explaining exactly what information you desire and what procedures you want the researcher to use. If you can locate someone from an ancestor's town of origin and establish a good working relationship, this solution has two advantages: one is that the person in Italy has access to the records and is able to consult them; gaining entrance to the archive can be a formidable obstacle to any research. The second advantage is that he or she lives in the locale of the research and therefore has none of the travel and lodging expenses that would exist for you or a professional genealogist. Often, too, the cost per hour will be less than that charged by a professional genealogist. On the other hand, of course, the reliability of the research might be questionable. In any case, this is certainly a route worth investigating, and through it many people have had much of their family researched for a relatively modest sum.

The last alternative is to hire a professional genealogist, but even if you do so there are several options. The first is to go through a genealogy company or institute that performs research internationally. There are several of these in the United States, most of them concentrated in Salt Lake City and Washington, D.C. There are others elsewhere, such as Debretts of London, that have an international reputation. An advantage of using these companies is that they can perform all forms of research, beginning with U.S. sources and continuing research in Italy with record sources there. Another advantage is that, if you have family lines originating in several different countries, as many Americans do, the company can conduct research in all of the countries. These companies usually carefully control the quality of their research and have a reputation to maintain. A disadvantage is that usually their services are more expensive than those of an independent professional genealogist or record searcher. Often these companies rely on the services of genealogists in each country where research takes place; these genealogists then rely on record searchers to do the actual research. The person who commissions the research often is paying the overhead for all of those involved.

There are companies located in Italy that perform genealogical research. Most of them specialize in heraldry research, establishing nobility, and searching for noble titles, but they are also capable of performing genealogy research. The best known of them are located in Florence and Rome. Certainly for those who want to establish a noble title or to obtain a coat of arms, these companies or their equivalents in the United States are the best choice.

Another option is to hire a genealogist who specializes in Italian genealogy. Such a genealogist should have a knowledge of Italian, Latin, dialectic forms, and Italian history and culture. Other services that may be offered are translations, heraldic information, and written reports of research results.

Guidelines for Hiring a Researcher

A distinction should be made between a professional genealogist and a record searcher (or record agent), although the difference may be slight. A record searcher often is the person who actually views the records, much like those who advertise for U.S. record sources and microfilm. A genealogist may not perform the actual research, but certainly should direct the record searcher's work. The genealogist solves the research problems, selects the best sources of records to consult, and should counsel the patron on how to go ahead with research for better results. He or she should also control the quality of research done by the record searcher and is responsible for the results.

A professional genealogist should be affiliated with some professional organization or have some other credentials. Because only Brigham Young University in Provo, Utah, offers an associate degree in genealogy research and family history (to my knowledge), many genealogists are self taught and do not have degrees. They should, however, be able to display evidence of their experience and expertise. Two organizations in the United States have established written and oral exams to certify genealogists in their areas of expertise. One is the Board for Certification of Genealogists, P.O. Box 5816, Falmouth, Va. 22403-5816. This organization tests and certifies U.S. researchers in various categories of expertise. The other is the Genealogical Society of Utah, 35 North West Temple, Salt Lake City, Utah 84150, which tests and accredits genealogists who specialize in particular geographic areas. Both organizations will provide a list of certified or accredited genealogists on request. The Association of Professional Genealogists, 3421 M St. NW, Suite 236, Washington, D.C. 20007, has a directory of professional genealogists who belong to that organization, and The Everton Publishers prints a yearly directory in *Everton's Genealogical Helper* (cited earlier in this chapter). (Those listed by the Association of Professional Genealogists and in the *Genealogical Helper* are not necessarily certified or accredited genealogists.)

A professional genealogy researcher should have some credentials and be a member of an accrediting organization; this is your best assurance for the honesty and accuracy of the researcher's work. Difficulties that have arisen between clients and genealogists have led the Association of Professional Genealogists and the Genealogical Society of Utah to publish pamphlets that describe how to select a genealogist. These pamphlets suggest some of the following guidelines to follow when hiring a professional genealogist:

1. Determine your research needs. In Italian genealogy this means knowing whether you want U.S. or local sources researched or if research can begin in Italy. It also means knowing what type of research you desire—i.e., the paternal line only, direct ancestors only, a reverse pedigree, all lines with complete family units, etc. The funds available for research should be taken into account as well.
2. Obtain a list of genealogists. Names of potential researchers can be obtained from sources of advertisement or from the organizations listed above.

3. Contact appropriate candidates.
4. Determine which candidate is best for your needs.
5. Make an agreement before work begins. The better this agreement, the better the professional relationship will be. The agreement should include the research goal, frequency of reports, content of reports, forms used for presenting data, time limits for research, an understanding of fees and expenses, and what happens if you or the researcher cannot maintain the agreement.
6. Provide information and fees to begin research. All known information should be provided to the researcher at the beginning to aid research.

All of these guidelines are valid, whether you are hiring a professional genealogist, a record searcher, a genealogy research company, or someone in Italy. Clearly established ground rules at the beginning of the relationship will lead to fewer problems in the long run. The leading causes of discord are the understandable but sometimes unrealistic expectations of the client regarding costs and results in Italian research, and the researcher's failing to correspond frequently and discuss problems as they arise.

Most research in the United States can be performed by mail or with locally available microfilmed sources. As a result, most researchers will provide results on a regular basis, without additional expenses, at a modest price for each report. In fact, it is often recommended that transactions that require research using U.S. sources be limited to no more than one or two hundred dollars at a time, particularly at the beginning of the research process.

However, research is not so simple in Italy. Research there means, in most cases, traveling directly to the town or parish and thus becomes quite expensive. The cost of living in Italy and most of Europe is considerably higher than in the United States. In Italy, for example, gasoline costs from four to five dollars per gallon, depending on the dollar exchange. The road system in Italy is good, but some are toll roads and they are expensive. Hotels, too, particularly in the larger cities, are expensive. Such expenses mean that a research foray to a town may cost several hundred dollars. Someone who is used to research using U.S. sources may have unrealistic expectations about what can be accomplished in Italy.

It is difficult to be precise about costs; they vary from one genealogist to another. According to the Family History Library pamphlet *Hiring a Professional Genealogist*, published in January 1993, rates range from $10.00 to $75.00 per hour, the average rate being from $15.00 to $35.00 per hour. It is important that the rates be clearly stated and agreed upon. For example, what is included as one hour of research? I know of a genealogist who had apparently low rates; however, he charged for all time from when he left home for a research trip to when he returned, whether he was traveling, eating, sleeping, waiting for a priest, or actually working! Most researchers will charge for preparation time, time spent researching the actual records, and time spent compiling and reporting the results. Many will also include travel time, since it may be considerable; some have a separate rate for travel time. Travel, hotel, and postage expenses will always be charged separately, and often the price of meals as well. Time spent on the search but not actually consulting records—waiting for a priest to return, waiting for records to arrive at an archive, searching for the parish, etc.—often will justly be counted as research time or possibly as travel time with a reduced rate. These details should be specified in the calculation of the rates.

Because conditions vary so greatly, no researcher can provide beforehand an exact idea of the costs that will be involved or the amount of research that may be accomplished, at least before an initial visit to a parish or town. Sometimes the town is easily accessible, the parish priest is very hospitable, and the records are in perfect condition, so several families can be researched for just a few hundred dollars. Usually, however, the town is far away, many expenses are involved, several days are required to consult the civil records, the priest will allow only a few hours of research each day, and the records are illegible and can only be read with time-consuming difficulty. Under these circumstances, research on the same number of families may cost two or three times the amount of the first example.

After the first research foray, the researcher can communicate a more precise idea of research conditions and costs to the client. In the research agreement, not only should the rates be clearly communicated; the obligations of the researcher should be stated as well: how often he or she will write, when the first report will be made, what will be included with the report, etc. Many researchers use contracts in which these items are stated.

Because relatively large amounts of money can be spent in researching Italian genealogy, a client wants to guarantee the investment and be sure that the research is reliable. Unfortunately, Italy has had a poor reputation among genealogists because of some unscrupulous researchers. You, as a client, can take some steps to reduce the risk of research fraud. The first, of course, is to use a genealogist who is well known and accredited or who belongs to a professional organization with a code of ethics. If need be, a complaint can be made to the organization, which can then help the client to clarify any misunderstanding or to investigate the reliability of the research. The organizations mentioned above can be helpful in this regard (except The Everton Publishers, whose list is merely informative). It is not improper to ask a researcher for references from present or former clients, and most are happy to provide them. Another guarantee is a signed contract that clearly states the research agreement. Most researchers will request a deposit to cover their expenses; this may amount to several hundred dollars for Italian research. A deposit is appropriate, but the research should not be paid for in full without some evidence that it has been performed. You should keep some documentation of the payment in your records.

A request for postcards of the ancestor's town of origin is both a guarantee that the researcher visited the area and an enhancement of your family history. Most towns and villages in Italy have printed postcards that are available only in the particular town. Some small villages and *frazioni* do not have postcards, but communes usually do. You might also request books on the history and customs of the area, but these will usually be written in Italian. You should request certificates from the town office or, if possible, photocopies or photographs of parish records. This allows you to participate in the research by viewing some of the documents; it also enhances your family history, and it is certainly a check on the accuracy of the research. Civil records cannot be photographed, but parish records can with the permission of the parish priest (sometimes the *curia vescovile* requests copies of the photographs or even the negatives). Photographs can be expensive but, when available, they are well worth the expense. You probably don't need photographs of all the documents found; those concerning direct ancestors or direct ancestors in the paternal line would be sufficient.

A final check is the research itself. Was it performed according to the standards outlined in this book? Were the names recorded as found in the records? Do the dates correspond to the availability of the types of record being used? Above all, is the research too perfect? Particularly for research in the early 1700s and earlier, it is rare that no problems, such as missing ancestors, missing maternal lines, family lines that are lost or can't be established with certainty, etc., are encountered. If the research is too complete—all large families in correct sequence—its validity is worth investigating.

Needless to say, most researchers are honest; a genealogist cannot stay in business very long today if he or she is not qualified and honest. Misunderstandings can usually be resolved through a letter. Before you turn to the referring organization, you should first contact the researcher with your doubts and worries; only if this communication is ignored or not satisfactorily answered should you turn to the professional organization.

Chapter 11

RESEARCH BY CORRESPONDENCE

I F YOU ARE INTERESTED IN YOUR ITALIAN HERITAGE BUT, AS IS MOST likely, you live outside Italy, it may be difficult for you to know how to begin the process of using record sources in Italy for genealogical research. Many people become discouraged at this point and fail to pursue the search for their family histories, but this chapter will enable you to begin consulting Italian record sources immediately.

You can consult the civil vital records and obtain copies of them only through town civil records offices, so it is quite appropriate to request information and copies from them. It is also important, however, to recognize some considerations inherent in their work. In Italy it is necessary to have a certificate for just about any official act. Certificates of residency, family certificates, vaccination certificates, and birth certificates are necessary to enroll children in school, to obtain a driver's license, to apply for a job, to marry, to receive retirement pay, and for just about any other dealing with the state. The *anagrafe* offices of most towns have up-to-date vital statistics of living residents in electronic files, so obtaining certificates for such people is relatively easy. However, most of a town clerk's time is occupied with this service and with registering new births, marriages, deaths, changes in residency, etc. Civil vital records more than seventy or eighty years old, which most genealogists are interested in, are not in electronic databases; in many large towns they are kept in separate archives. As a result, even though it is the duty of town officials to release records, including older documents, often they are reluctant to perform time-consuming searches for them.

In a city of several million inhabitants, such as Naples or Palermo, the records are organized by neighborhood. In Naples there are twelve separate sets of records for each year, according to the divisions of the city. Each has its own set of indexes, and there are multiple volumes of birth records for each year. It is a formidable task to understand how the records are organized, much less to find anything! Thus, even though it is the town officials' duty to release certificates for these acts, such tasks often go beyond their normal routines and duties; therefore, officials tend to feel that they are doing favors in making searches. The difficulty of performing a record search and the officials' natural reluctance are increased when they receive letters written in English. Requests for many certificates, perhaps with little

identifying information, further complicate the matter. Say, for example, that you were requesting information about a Pasquale Esposito of Naples, born between 1876 and 1879. There may have been twenty people of that name in that city in those years. It would take hours, if not days, to find them all. Officials of many large cities will perform the search for a record only if the date and name are specified. Officials of smaller towns, however, are more accommodating, but basic rules should be followed. If a letter-writer is perceived as being rude, demanding, or presenting too difficult a task, the request may very well be thrown out.

The same considerations are true of research in the parishes. Parish priests are usually very busy and have little time to search their records, and, unlike town officials, they have absolutely no obligation to do so. Some priests very kindly take the time to perform research, but most are too busy and have little reason to do so. The following suggestions apply for requests to both town officials and parish priests.

WRITING TO SOURCES IN ITALY

Many Italians understand English, but not all do, and there are many differences between the English they study in school and American English. Also, American and European handwriting styles are considerably different. Thus, it is advisable to write in Italian using a typewriter or word processor instead of sending a handwritten letter.

When writing, it is always better to request one or two items of information at a time; do not send an extensive list. This makes the task easier for the town official or parish priest, and there is more likelihood of a reply. Often, the civil document that is most useful for genealogy research is the *stato di famiglia storico* (historical state of the family) certificate (see chapter 5), which lists parents and children, usually with complete birth, marriage, and death information. Realize, however, that such a document often has to be constructed by a town official using separate birth, marriage, and death records, since they are rarely complete for periods before the 1900s. It usually takes much research and effort to complete such a certificate, and it may not be a good idea for you to request anything else. You can always write later for an additional item or two. On the other hand, for example, if you were researching two families from the same time period and town, perhaps those of both your great-grandmother and great-grandfather, it would be better to request both family certificates together so that research of the same records would have to be done only once.

Most important when writing, provide all available information when making your request. If you requested a birth certificate for Giovanni Canton, born sometime after 1872, and gave no other information, there is little likelihood that the correct ancestor would be identified. The clerk or parish priest might very well stop at the first Giovanni Canton found, when, in fact, several males with the same name may have been born in the same time period. Thus, including a more exact time frame (between 1872 and 1877) and the name of the father or future wife or the name and birth date of a later child might hasten the research and would help to establish the correct family connection.

It is also important to mention the purpose of the request. More urgency will be given, and justly so, to a request for a document that will serve an official purpose, such as for requesting Italian citizenship or for requesting a retirement pension, than to a general request for information. However, a priest or clerk will be curious about your quest for knowledge of your Italian heritage and will be more likely to help in the search if you indicate the purpose for the request. Unless there is some official purpose for the request and a deadline is involved (which should be explained in the letter), no deadline should be given. A deadline imposed without an apparent reason is another annoyance that reduces the chances of receiving a reply.

Finally, include the return address in your letter (not just on the envelope); or, better, include a self-addressed envelope. It may sound obvious but, in my experience, many people forget to clearly write their address, even on the envelope, making a reply impossible. Envelopes are easily lost or torn, so, if the return address is not included in the letter itself, again, there may be no possibility of an answer. A self-addressed envelope is an additional courtesy and always makes a good impression, even if it is not used. Do not place stamps on the envelope; Italian postal rates vary considerably, and U.S. stamps are worthless in Italy. International postal coupons are much more appropriate and they are an additional courtesy.

Sample Letter Requesting Civil Vital Records

Figure 11-1 is an example of a letter to be used for requesting a civil record. (With a few modifications, however, the letter can be used as a model for just about any request.) The letter should be addressed to the *ufficio di stato civile*, the town office concerned with births, marriages, and deaths. This office is always in the commune; there is none for the *frazione*. If you don't know the town's "zip code," you may omit it; the letter will arrive but will be delayed. If you don't include the zip code, however, you should include the name or abbreviated name of the province in parentheses following the name of the town. PD stands for Padova, the province in which the town of Albignasego is located. It would be equally correct to write "(Padova)." Omission of the province or the zip code may cause confusion because there are many towns of the same names in different provinces. (All of the provinces and their abbreviations are listed in chapter 5.)

It is correct to begin a business letter with "Egregi signori," as in the English "Dear sirs," and to end it with "Distinti saluti," the equivalent of "Sincerely yours." The first part of the letter indicates who is making the request and the purpose of the request. Translated, the letter in figure 11-1 reads:

> My name is [Joseph Travolta], and I live in the United States at the above-stated address. I am searching for information regarding my ancestor, [Antonio Travolta], who was born at [S. Giacomo] in the commune of [Albignasego]. I am requesting this information to find out more about my family, and to find my relatives who remained in Italy.

Instead of stating *antenato* (ancestor), you might want to state the specific relationship: *nonno/nonna* or *paterno/paterna* (paternal grandfather or grandmother), *nonno/a* or *materno/a* (maternal grandfather or grandmother), *padre* (father), *madre* (mother), *bisnonno/a* (great grandfather or great grandmother), *zio* (uncle), *zia* (aunt), *prozio/a* (great uncle or great aunt). All that is necessary is to substitute the most appropriate term for the word *antenato*. (Remember that if the person in question is female, the word will end with an "a," as in *nata, bisnonna,* or *materna*; if a male, it will end with an "o.")

The sample letter first states the name of the village or *frazione* and then of the commune. If you know the *frazione* or even the neighborhood or parish of a large city, it is always better to be specific and include this information; otherwise, you can simply state "nato a . . ." and name the town or city. You can also substitute the following words for *nato* as necessary: *sposato/a* (married), *morto/a* (died), *sepolto/a* (buried), *residente* (resided).

The next paragraph is the request for information, and there may be considerable variation in the text according to the information desired. The sample letter is translated as:

> I would be very grateful if you could mail me the [state of the family] certificate for [Antonio

Travolta] on non-legal paper. I don't know his date of birth, which I suppose was around [1870]; but I do know that he married [Lucia Fracasso] in [1893] or [1894] at [Padova], and their first child, my [grandfather, Giuseppe Travolta], was born at [S. Giacomo] on [23 June 1895].

The important principle is that you provide as much pertinent information as possible to the town official so that the right ancestor and his or her family can be located. As discussed in chapter 5, the *certificato di famiglia storico* (sometimes *originario* instead of *storico*) is a very complete history of the family, with birth and marriage dates for the parents, and birth dates and sometimes even marriage and death dates for all of their children. For ancestors who were born before 1870, this certificate will probably not be available, and a town official may not wish to compile one because it would have to be constructed from the original birth and marriage records. As a result, your request may be refused, or the certificate you receive may be only partially complete. Even so, this certificate is a good place to start; if it is available, one whole family group will be complete.

Other certificates that may be requested are: *estratto dell'atto di nascita* (birth certificate), *estratto dell'atto di matrimonio* (marriage certificate), *estratto dell'atto di morte*, (death certificate), and *certificato di residenza*, (certificate of residency—available only for a living relative still residing in a town). As discussed in chapter 5, the certificate of birth or marriage will provide much less information than the extract of the birth act or marriage act; therefore, it is always better to request the extract of the act, not the certificate.

The next point of interest (also discussed in chapter 5) is the difference between "legal" and free or "non-legal" paper. For most official acts in Italy, such as receiving a pension, getting married, or applying for a driver's license, it is necessary to present documents on "legal" paper, which means that an official stamp has been placed on each certificate. Presently this stamp costs L15,000, but the cost rises every year or so. Rarely, for a family history, is there a need for a legal copy of a certificate, so you should write *in carta libera* (on non-legal paper) or *in carta semplice* on the request to avoid any misunderstanding and additional expense. If, however, you need the certificate to apply for Italian citizenship or to receive an Italian pension, you will need to specify *in carta legale* in your request.

[Return Address]

[Date]

Ufficio di Stato Civile
Comune di [Albignasego]
[35020 Albignasego (PD)]
Italy

Egregi Signori,

Mi chiamo [Joseph Travolta], ed abito negli Stati Uniti, all'indirizzo sopraddetto. Cerco informazioni sul mio antenato, [Antonio Travolta], nato a [S. Giacomo] nel comune di [Albignasego]. Cerco questi dati per conoscere meglio la mia famiglia, e per trovare i miei parenti rimasti in Italia.

Vi sarei molto grato se poteste spedirmi il certificato di stato di famiglia storico di [Antonio Travolta], in carta libera. Non conosco la sua data di nascita, ma suppongo sia intorno al [1870]. So che ha sposato [Lucia Fracasso] nel [1893] o [1894] a [Padova], e il loro primo figlio fu mio nonno [Giuseppe Travolta] nato a [S. Giacomo] il [23 giugno 1895].

Vi ringrazio in anticipo per la vostra gentilezza e premura, e vi prego di addebitarmi tutte le spese postali e dei certificati.

Distinti saluti,

FIGURE 11-1. Sample Letter Requesting Civil Vital Records

Of course, you should include the name of the ancestor and state all available information about him or her. If you already know the date and place of birth, marriage, or death, state them clearly. The sample letter states *non conosco la sua data di nascita* (I don't know his date of birth), *ma suppongo sia intorno al 1870* (but I suppose that it was around 1870). You could state simply *nato nel 1870 circa* (born in approximately 1870); this is more direct but also implies some knowledge that 1870 is the exact year. Most town offices have ten-year indexes for each decade; the years from 1867, or whenever the records begin, to 1869 or 1870 comprise one index, from 1870 to 1879 another, and so on. If the ancestor could have been born in one decade or the other, it is wise to either state this, *nato/a nel 1868–1871 circa*, or, as in the sample letter, express considerable doubt regarding the date or explain how you arrived at that date. Then the official will be more likely to examine the indexes for both decades.

If the marriage date isn't known but the date of death is, that date can be included; if the age is known, certainly include that as well. Therefore, you can write:

... nato nel [1868–1871] circa, perchè è morto a [Colorado] il [17 marzo 1932] all' età di [63] anni circa.

Or:

... born in [1868–1871] approximately, because he died in [Colorado] on [17 March 1932] at about [63] years old.

The important principle is that a "frame of reference" be provided and a purpose stated so that a town official can properly make a complete search. If you include only the year and nothing more, the official may very well search that year, find nothing, and send a negative reply; or, worse, may find someone of that name and search no further, when perhaps the correct ancestor was born a couple of years earlier. For example, in a recent search, I found that approximately one-third of the inhabitants of the town of Caltrano in the Vicenza province had the surname Dal Santo. The search was for a Maria Dal Santo born around 1850. In a five-year period, twelve different Maria Dal Santos had been born in nine different families! Without further information to properly identify the ancestor, it was impossible to continue research. Therefore, it is always necessary to provide as much specific information as possible.

The best information is usually the name of the ancestor's father; this readily identifies the family and thereby narrows the search. The father's name is often mentioned in the yearly index of the records, greatly facilitating the work of the researcher. Often, however, the father himself is the object of the search and nothing is known of his parents. If you knew the name of the father of our sample ancestor, Antonio Travolta, to be Francesco, you could simply insert "di" (of) after the name to indicate this: *Antonio Travolta di Francesco*. If you knew the mother's name as well, the conjunction "e" (and) and "di" would be sufficient: *Antonio Travolta di Francesco e di Anna Marchione*. Obviously, the more information you provide, the better.

If you don't know the names of the ancestor's father or mother, the name and birth date of one or more of the ancestor's children can be very useful. The town official may first look up the child's birth act, which could provide useful information for identifying the father. Often the child's paternal grandfather will be mentioned in the act, and sometimes the couple's marriage date will be indicated.

If you are requesting a marriage certificate but don't know the date of marriage, obviously the years of birth of the first children will be very important in determining when the couple was married. Death dates are more difficult to arrive at, but the ancestor's birth date, the birth date of his or her last child, and the last known year that the ancestor was alive are all indications. Even if the

emigration date, *data di emigrazione dall'Italia*, is the only date known, it should be included as well.

If your request is quite complicated, you can resort to writing in English; you may or may not get a response. A better option would be to have the letter translated into Italian. However, most requests can be made using the sample letters in this chapter. Even a letter with some mistakes in Italian may be more legible than a similar letter in English and will probably receive a speedier reply.

The last paragraph states:

I thank you beforehand for your kindness and efficiency, and I ask you to charge me for the postal expenses and for the certificates.

This brings us to the important issue of costs. Most towns will very graciously send the certificates free of charge to foreigners. However, they have the right to charge for postal expenses, the certificates, and the research. A 1984 law established the right of each town to charge up to L10,000 for each name and date researched outside the normal *anagrafe* records. Therefore, compiling a "state of the family" certificate with five children included could cost L70,000 just for the birth dates of the parents and children, and up to L150,000 (more than $100 at 1994 exchange rates) for death dates and the parents' marriage date as well. Each printed certificate is L1,000 (L15,000 extra if on "legal paper"). The amount charged is at the discretion of the town office.

When writing the town office, include a self-addressed (unstamped) envelope, but, as in the last paragraph of the sample letter above, indicate that you are willing to pay for the postage and certificates. If the town official sends the information free of charge, so much the better. If there is a charge it will be indicated in the response; it should be paid with a cashier's check in Italian lire. (Most major banks are capable of making payment in foreign currencies.) If you pay directly in dollars, you should still use a cashier's check; take into account that the dollar exchange in Italy is lower than in the United States and that bank commissions will be charged the receiver of the money, so you should overestimate rather than try to save a dollar or two. Underestimating these expenses will make it more difficult to obtain further information from that town for you and for anyone else who writes later. (This procedure is not the same for the parish, as will be discussed.) U.S. postal money orders may be accepted, but they are more difficult for the receiver to cash.

After one letter has had success, you can request more information and certificates. However, if a town office receives new requests every three or four months, the officials may become annoyed and cease to respond. It may be wise to wait some time before writing again or to write, in the meantime, to other town offices where information about the same or other ancestors can be found. You may even want to alternate between writing the town office and the parish priest. The fact is that genealogical research requires patience; if you want all the information right away, you risk antagonizing those who can supply the data. There is an appropriate Italian saying: *Chi troppo vuole, nulla stringe*—"Those who want too much will be left empty-handed!"

If you plan to travel to Italy to personally search for civil records, the first paragraph of the letter above is applicable for requesting permission from the town mayor (*sindaco*) or the *procura della repubblica*. (The town mayor is in charge of the town's civil vital records, and permission should first be requested from him or her. The *procura della repubblica* [see chapter 5] is responsible for the civil vital records throughout the province and is the final authority for all vital statistics; if the mayor does not respond, or if you are researching in several towns in the same province, direct your request to the *procura*.) A request to the mayor can be written on non-legal paper, but a request to the *procura* should be on legal paper. If writing to the mayor, address your letter to

Sig. Sindaco
Comune di [Albignasego]

and begin with the salutation "Egregio Sig. Sindaco."

If you are writing to the *procura*, address your letter to the "Procura della Repubblica," followed by the name of the provincial seat (usually the largest city in the province) and its zip code. For example, such a letter would not be adressed to the town of Albignasego, but rather to "35100 Padova, Italy." Begin with the salutation "Egregio Procuratore."

Sample Letter Requesting to Personally Consult Civil Vital Records

Translated, this sample letter (figure 11-2) reads:

My name is [Joseph Travolta], and I live in the United States at the above-stated address. I am searching for information regarding my ancestor, [Antonio Travolta], who was born at [S. Giacome] in the commune of [Albignasego]. I am requesting this information to find out more about my family, and to find my relatives who remained in Italy.

I am planning a trip to Italy and, if possible, I would like to personally consult the civil birth, marriage,

[Return Address]

[Date]

Procura della Repubblica
[35100 Padova]
Italy

Egrego Procuratore,

Mi chiamo [Joseph Travolta], ed abito negli Stati Uniti, all'indirizzo sopraddetto. Cerco informazioni sul mio antenato, [Antonio Travolta], nato a [S. Giacomo] nel comune di [Albignasego]. Cerco questi dati per conoscere meglio la mia famiglia, e per trovare i miei parenti rimasti in Italia.

Sto programmando un viaggio in Italia e se è possibile vorrei svolgere la ricerca personalmente consultando i registri civili di nascita, matrimonio e morte che riguardano i miei avi. Quindi vorrei chiedere a Lei, come responsabile dello stato civile, il permesso di poter consultare nel comune di [Albignasego] i registri dal 1865 al [1895]. Vorrei dedicare due o tre giorni a questa ricerca dal [19 maggio] al [24 maggio] nell' orario di apertura dell' ufficio di stato civile.

In attesa di cortese riscontro porgo distinti saluti,

FIGURE 11-2. Sample Letter Requesting to Personally Consult Civil Vital Records

and death records that concern my ancestors. Therefore, I would like to ask you, as the head of the civil vital records, for permission to consult in the town of [Albignasego] the records from [1865] to [1895]. I would like to dedicate two or three days to this research, from [19 May] to [24 May] during the hours that the civil records office is open.

Waiting for your courteous reply, I send my best regards,

It is important to indicate that you will be searching *only* the records of *your* ancestors and that you will be using older civil records (from before 1915)—because more recent records cannot be searched for any reason by unauthorized persons, due to the privacy laws which protect records of the last seventy-five years; and because earlier records can be consulted only by persons who are directly related. It is always best to be as specific as possible regarding when you will be searching the records and, if writing to the *procura*, to specify the town or towns where you will be searching. This letter should assure you access to the civil records, but permission is always at the discretion of the mayor or *procura*.

Sample Letter Requesting Additional Civil Vital Records Information

Figure 11-3 is an example of a second letter that could be written to a town office. The heading and much of the letter remain the same as in the first sample. The first paragraph is translated as follows:

> I would like to thank you for your kindness in sending me the family certificate of [Antonio Travolta] last year. Now I have another request to make of you, and I hope that you will be equally thoughtful in answering me. I would like the extracts of the birth acts of all of the brothers of [Antonio Travolta], son of [Francesco] and of [Anna Marchione], who was born on [14 April 1869].

Do not assume that your previous requests will be remembered. Large towns receive many requests each month from within Italy and from all over the world. Thus, this paragraph states all of the necessary information that was provided in the certificate sent in response to the previous request. The word *fratelli*, which literally means "brothers," actually refers to all siblings, both brothers and sisters, so it is not necessary to specify both. In this case, since the names of both parents are known, they should be included to facilitate research. Because this letter requests birth dates for a whole family, it would not be prudent to ask for more information. Instead of the siblings of Antonio, you might have asked for the extracts of the death acts of Francesco and Anna—"L'estratto degli atti di morte di Francesco Travolta e di Anna Marchione." Since nothing is known of them, it would be proper to include Antonio's birth date and to indicate that he was their son. The marriage date of the couple could be requested as well—"l'estratto dell'atto di matrimonio"—although it is very possible that they were married before the civil records were begun. Any of these different requests can be inserted into the same form letter.

The last paragraph restates sentiments from the first letter (figure 11-1). It reads:

> As always, I am grateful for your kindness, and I ask you to charge the postal expenses and the cost of the certificates to me. I send you my best regards.

Even if payment for the certificates was not requested the first time, it is still proper to offer payment because, in fact, it is due.

Many people become discouraged after writing a town office or parish priest without receiving a reply, which is not unusual. Following the guidelines stated here should increase the probability of receiving an answer but, even so, a prompt reply is not always forthcoming. As stated, both for the town official and the parish priest this type of research is beyond normal duties and can be delayed and forgotten. However, there are steps that can be followed to better assure an answer. Allow a couple of months for a reply; the mail requires ten days or so each way (and few offices have fax machines). If no reply comes after this period, send another copy of the original letter by registered mail with a return receipt. This costs more, but it provides the sender with proof that the letter was received at a particular date. There is no need for a cover letter, but you may add a few lines. For example, you might begin your follow-up letter with the following:

> Rimando la mia lettera del [17 giugno] in cui richiedo il [certificato di famiglia] di [Antonio Travolta]. Temo che la prima lettera sia andata smarrita, ed avrei bisogno di una risposta appena vi sara' possibile.

This is translated as:

> I am re-sending my letter of [17 June], in which I requested the [state of the family certificate] for [Antonio Travolta]. I fear that my letter was

---

[Return address]

[Date]

Ufficio di Stato Civile
Comune di [Albignasego]
[35020 Albignasego (PD)]
Italy

Egregi signori,

Vorrei ringraziarvi per la vostra cortesia nell'inviarmi, l'anno scorso, il certificato di stato di famiglia del mio antenato [Antonio Travolta]. Ora ho un'altra richiesta da farvi, e spero che sarete altrettanto premurosi nel rispondermi. Vorrei, se è possibile, l'estratto dell'atto di nascita di tutti i fratelli di [Antonio Travolta] di [Francesco] e di [Anna Marchione] che risulta nato il [14 aprile 1869].

Come sempre vi sono riconoscente per la vostra gentilezza, e vi prego di addebitarmi sia le spese postali che le spese dei certificati. Vi porgo i miei piu' distinti saluti.

FIGURE 11-3. Sample Letter Requesting Additional Civil Vital Records Information

lost, and I need an answer as soon as would be convenient for you.

This will keep the tone polite and does not place blame for the lack of communication. At the same time, it reminds the town official that you are waiting for an answer.

Sample Letter to the Town Mayor Requesting Action

If there is still no reply within the next few months, a final letter, as in the sample below, can be sent. This letter should be addressed to the town mayor, who is responsible for the performance of the civil records office. The letter should be firm but polite, and it too should be sent by registered mail with return receipt. The letter, figure 11-4, reads, in English:

> I sent a letter to the civil vital records office on [17 June], and I again sent the same letter by registered mail on [23 August]. It was received on [30 August]. After almost another three months, I still have received no reply. As may be seen from the enclosed letter, I requested the [family certificate] for my ancestor, [Antonio Travolta].
>
> I know that it takes time to complete research, but I fear that my letter has been lost under other papers or forgotten. I would like to ask you to look into this case, so that I may receive a reply.
>
> Thank you for your kindness, and I trust to hear from you soon.
>
> Best regards,

Such a letter, directed to the town mayor, will rarely go without a reply. The answer may be that the town office does not have the records or is incapable of performing the research, but at least you will not be waiting helplessly for an answer that will never arrive.

A recent law established the right of the public to receive a reply from a public office within thirty days of a request. Although many public offices have not yet put this law into practice, the bureaucratic process has been gradually expedited. You can cite this law, number 241 of 7 August 1990, in your letter to the mayor by changing the last sentence in the second paragraph to:

> Vorrei chiederLe, ai sensi della legge 241/1990 sul diritto d'accesso ai documenti amministrativi, se puo'

[Return address]

[Date]

Egregio Sindaco
Comune di [Albignasego]
[35020 Albignasego (PD)]
Italy

Egregio signor Sindaco,

Ho scritto all'ufficio di stato civile di [Albignasego] il [17 giugno] scorso, ed ho rimandato la stessa lettera per raccomandata il [23 agosto]. E' stata ricevuta il [30 agosto] ed ora, dopo quasi tre mesi, non ho ancora ricevuto alcuna risposta. Come puo' vedere dalla lettera qui allegata, ho richiesto il certificato di [famiglia storico] del mio antenato [Antonio Travolta].

Capisco che ci vuole tempo per svolgere le ricerche e compilare il certificato, però temo che la mia lettera sia finita sotto altre carte, o altrimenti persa o dimenticata. Vorrei chiederLe se puo' gentilmente interessarsi a questo caso, affinche' io possa ottenere una risposta.

La ringrazio per la sua gentilezza, e attendo con fiducia una risposta.

Distinti saluti,

FIGURE 11-4. Sample Letter to the Town Mayor Requesting Action

gentilmente interessarsi a questo caso, affinche' io possa ottenere una risposta entro un tempo ragionevole.

This is translated as:

> I would like to ask you if you could kindly intervene in this case, according to law 241 of 1990 regarding access to public documents, so that I may receive a reply within a reasonable time.

Rarely will money sent through the mail expedite the process, unless it has been specifically requested as payment for the certificates. However, this is not necessarily true for the parish, which will be examined next in detail.

WRITING THE PARISH PRIEST

There are advantages and disadvantages in writing to the parish priest rather than the town office, and much depends on the individual priest. In the last fifty years in Italy, there has been a dramatic decrease in the number of men who join

[Return address]

[Date]

Rev. Vicario Generale
Curia Vescovile di [Trento]
[38100 Trento]
Italy

Rev. Vicario,

Sono [John Zon], nipote di [Antonio Zon] di [Lundo] nella diocesi di [Trento], e cerco informazioni riguardo ai miei antenati. So che mio [nonno] e' nato a [Lundo], e vorrei scrivere al parroco per ottenere altri dati. Purtroppo non conosco nè il suo nome nè l'indirizzo, e non so nemmeno se [Lundo] sia una parrocchia indipendente.

Le sarei veramente grato se potesse indicarmi a chi posso scrivere per avere quest'informazione.

Distinti saluti,

FIGURE 11-5. Sample Letter to the Curia Vescovile Requesting the Name of a Parish Priest

the clergy. As a result, in many parishes where several priests once presided, today there may be only one. Also, many parishes and churches have been closed, leaving one priest to preside over several villages. In the Tuscany region, for example, in the Apennine Mountains, are hundreds of small villages and hamlets, each of which has a parish church. Not long ago each hamlet, or perhaps two together, formed a separate parish and had a presiding priest. Today, in many cases, only elderly people on pensions still live in these villages; the churches are closed, and one priest has to travel and visit up to ten or fifteen villages. Even in the cities, churches have been closed and parishes combined because there are not enough priests. Many of the priests are elderly themselves and have less energy for their many tasks. Also, while priests once lived on the contributions of their parishioners, today many work to support themselves, usually as teachers. Therefore, priests are very busy. Usually they will take the time to answer letters requesting information, but the principles cited for requests of the town office are true for priests as well: make your letter clear, do not request too much information, and be courteous.

There are several advantages in writing to a priest. If you are searching for a living relative, the parish priest is more likely to know the person and be willing to put you in contact than a town official because, usually, the priest has more personal contact with his parishioners. Also, many priests are scholars; some have personally written local histories or know of them, so they are sometimes more

willing to send books or give historical information than other sources. Some priests even send church bulletins or newsletters to emigrant families. They are a rich source of local customs, traditions, and town news. (The parish priest of one town in the Belluno province found that there were more people who were originally from that town living at Buenos Aires, Argentina, than still living in Italy. The priest was constantly in contact with these and other emigrants and had even visited his "flock" in Argentina.) Finally, because many priests are scholars, some are very interested in genealogy and may be very willing to help in your research or may know others who can assist you.

There are also disadvantages and difficulties in writing to parish priests. The first is in directing requests to them. Some large cities have hundreds of parishes; obviously, if you do not know from which parish the object of your research originated, little can be done. In the same way, a large commune with many *frazioni* may have fifteen or twenty parishes within the commune limits, one in each village. Even smaller towns, particularly in the south, may have several parishes. Agnone, in the province of Isernia, today is a town of only eight thousand inhabitants, but there are still five active parishes. This is one reason why it is important to request the extract of the act of birth or marriage from the town office: usually the name of the parish or the *frazione* will appear, enabling you to continue research in the parish. In the north of Italy there is commonly only one parish in each town—even in large towns, such as Agliè in the province of Torino and Camposampiero in the Padova province, both of which have more than 20,000 inhabitants—but in most of Italy this is not true. Thus, if you address a letter to the parish of Albignasego, it may not reach the correct destination because there are nine parishes in Albignasego: one for each *frazione* of the commune and three in the town of Albignasego itself. Further complicating the matter is the fact that the parish may now be closed, or the priest may live in another town and visit the parish only occasionally. In such a case, usually the letter will arrive, but it will be delayed.

To avoid these problems, you should know the exact name of the parish. If it is impossible to obtain the name of the parish from the extracts of the acts in the civil records, you should write to the *curia vescovile* of the appropriate diocese. The *curia vescovile* is the bishop's office in each diocese; it has administrative control over the parishes (see chapter 8). If you know the name of the commune or *frazione* or the address or neighborhood in the city where your ancestor lived, from the *curia* you can learn the correct parish for that address and the name and address of the parish priest. The *curia* staff can also state whether the parish has been closed and where the records are presently kept. Most *curie* are in the major town of each province, so addressing your letter there will usually bring success. Remember, too, that often the *curie* have copies of parish records and keep the records of parishes that have been closed. Therefore, if you have a simple request for a record of a recent period, the *curia* itself may be able to accomplish the research. If not, by writing first to the *curia* you gain a good reference when later writing to the parish priest, so your letter of request will probably receive attention.

A sample letter that can serve as a model when writing to the *curia* follows. As always, the letter begins with a personal presentation and the letter's purpose. It should be addressed to the *vicario generale*, who is the bishop's executive secretary and is in charge of administrative work, or to the *archivista*, the clerk in charge of records.

Sample Letter to the Curia Vescovile Requesting the Name of a Parish Priest

The sample letter, figure 11-5, is translated as:

I am [John Zon], grandson of [Antonio Zon], who was born at [Lundo] in the diocese of [Trento], and I desire information about my ancestors. I would like to write to the parish priest of [Lundo] for more information, but I don't know his name or address, or even if [Lundo] is a parish.

I would be very thankful if you could provide this information.

Best regards,

This example is used because Lundo, even though a parish today, is a *frazione* of Lamaso and does not have records dating back more than fifty years. If you merely asked for the address of the priest at Lundo, without stating the purpose of the request or including any other information, the address would have been forthcoming but would be useless since the research cannot be performed there. The sample letter that follows is appropriate for a more general request.

As previously stated, it is best to obtain the extract of a birth act or marriage act for an ancestor because it will contain an exact address or the name of the parish. This is particularly important in a large city, where research can continue only through the parish. What do you do, however, if these can't be found or if the ancestor was born before the civil vital records began? If you were to search the telephone book of a large city, you would find dozens or even hundreds of parishes; the research would seem overwhelming. Usually, however, even in large cities there were fewer active parishes one hundred years ago than exist now. Torino, which now has several million inhabitants and more than one hundred parishes, had only around twenty active parishes before 1870.

The sample letter below addresses such an issue because the source that can tell you what parishes were active at an early date is, again, the *curia*. The letter reads:

Sample Letter to the Curia Vescovile Requesting Information About Parishes

Translated, the sample letter, figure 11-6, reads:

I am [Philip Mansell], and my ancestor [Pasquale Manzella] was born at [Benevento] in [1856], but I don't know in which parish. I would like to know more about my ancestors and to follow my genealogy, but I don't know where to begin. I would be very thankful if you could help me by indicating which parishes existed in the city of Benevento in that epoch and who I could write to for this information.

Best regards,

After identifying the parish, you can write the parish priest for information, much like the town office. There are, however, some differences. For one, as said, the parish priest

---

[Return address]

[Date]

Rev. Vicario Generale
Curia Vescovile di [Benevento]
[82100 Benevento]
Italy

Rev. Vicario,

Sono [Philip Mansell] e il mio antenato [Pasquale Manzella] e' nato a [Benevento] nel [1856], ma non so in quale parrocchia. Vorrei conoscere di più sui miei antenati e seguire la mia genealogia, ma non so da dove iniziare. Le sarei molto riconoscente se potesse aiutarmi, indicandomi a quali parrocchie, che esistevano nella città di Benevento in quell'epoca, posso scrivere per quest'informazione.

Distinti saluti,

FIGURE 11-6. Sample Letter to the Curia Vescovile Requesting Information About Parishes

has no obligation to respond. Therefore, you should make every effort to express your gratitude for this favor and to facilitate the priest's research by providing as much information as possible. While it is not appropriate to send money to the town office unless requested, the opposite is true for the parish. It is quite appropriate to include an offering to the parish with the original request or at least to promise to send an offering after the research has been performed. The amount of the offering depends considerably on how much research is requested; at least L20,000 to L25,000 ($15 to $20 at 1994 exchange rates) is advisable. Some parishes have fixed rates for each certificate, but most do not, and the priest may not ask anything—but an offering should be made in the form of a cashier's check made out to the name of the parish.

While a town office will always send standard certificates, a priest may write down and send only the pertinent information. Therefore, it is very important that you specify exactly what information you desire. Certificates certainly look better in a family history, but they may not contain all the essential information desired in genealogical research. Therefore, you should indicate, for example, that the names of a child's parents are important or that you desire both the baptismal date and the birth date. A transcript of the entire act would be ideal, but this takes longer for the priest to execute. A photocopy of the act is an excellent solution, but many parishes, particularly in the poorer areas of Italy, do not have copy machines, so such a request can be difficult to satisfy. A request for photocopies is included in the sample letter below, but it should be included only as a special request.

While the town records are usually well ordered, written on standardized forms, and indexed by decade and by volume, the parish records may have none of these attributes. Therefore, it will be more time consuming for the priest to search for the information, and he may not be able to read the handwriting any better than an inexperienced researcher. A parish priest may be even more likely than a town clerk to stop at the first name similar to that requested without examining all of the alternative possibilities, so it is even more important that you provide all of the information known about the ancestor in question. On the other hand, some parish priests have a passion for research and will continue researching for you, usually for a fee but at a lower cost than a professional researcher. This possibility should not be overlooked when writing the priest. The following sample letter provides several phrases that you can add or withhold as you consider appropriate.

Sample Letter to a Parish Priest

A priest is generally addressed as *reverendo* (reverend). If you happen to know, perhaps from previous letters or from the *curia*, his exact position in the church, such as *monsignore* or *arciprete* (archpriest), such a title can be used, but *reverendo* is still appropriate.

The letter is addressed to the specific parish by the name of the parish. It is always best to use the name of the parish, but if you do not know it and are writing to a town that has only one parish, it can just as easily be written "Parrocchia di" (parish of) followed by the name of the town; in this case it would be "Parrocchia di Austis." As stated earlier, if you do not know the town's "zip code," the name of the town followed by the name of the province in parentheses is sufficient.

Any of the introductions used in the previous sample letters could be used here as well. To allow you a variety of phrases, however, each letter differs. The first paragraph of the sample letter, shown in figure 11-7, reads:

I am [John P. Slusky] and my [maternal great-grandmother] came from the town of [Austis] in [Sardinia]. I have already received information from the town office, but they told me to write to you for information from before [1872]. I would like to ask you a favor.

Sometimes the parish priest will respond by telling you to write to the town office, so, if you've already done that, indicate so in your letter. It also lets him know that the town office has helped you—the priest won't want to lose face by doing less! The letter continues:

I am searching for the [marriage date] and the [birth dates] of the [parents of my great-grandmother]. All I know is that she, [Maria Concetta Cuccuru], daughter of [Pietro] and of [Maria Rosa Virdis], was born on [24 May 1876] at [Austis] and had an older brother, [Giuseppe Cuccuru], born on [10 November 1873]. There may be other siblings who were born before 1872, when the civil records began.

The important principle is that you supply all of the information possible to identify the ancestor for whom you are requesting information. Obviously, the information you supply will differ according to your needs. There may be no older brother, but you may know of a younger one (*fratello minore*) or an older sister (*sorella maggiore*). By providing this information, not only do you facilitate the search; you also make clear that your search is serious—that precise information has been collected already, and the same is expected of the priest.

The next part translates as:

I would like to ask you if you could be so kind as to please search for these dates and transcribe onto parish certificates the birth and marriage acts in their entirety; or, if possible and more convenient, to photocopy each act.

This paragraph requests the transcription of the entire act onto parish certificates. This may not be possible because the certificates usually do not have space for all the information, but it certainly communicates the idea that you are interested in all relevant information. You could request only the names of the parents and dates, asking: "... ricercare e trascrivermi le date di matrimonio e di nascita, ed includervi i nomi dei genitori di ognuno"; or ask only for the certificates: "... ricercare e spedirmi un certificato parrocchiale per ogni atto di matrimonio e nascita." Of course, if a death date is needed the phrase would be "data di morte" (date of death) or "data di sepoltura" (date of burial). Use any of these phrases to fit the circumstances.

The last paragraph contains another request that can be deleted or used later in a thank-you note. It is a request for the addresses of other families that may be related and are still living in the town. It reads:

> I would also be very interested in knowing if I still have relatives living at Austis so that I could write them and exchange family news. Could you kindly send me the addresses of the Cuccuru families still living in the town?

> I know I am asking a lot, so I would like to thank you already for your kindness and thoughtfulness, and I would like you to accept the enclosed check as an offering for your parish.

> Best regards,

This example allows for an offering to be included. As for the town office, it is best to send a bank check in lira; however, a cashier's check in dollars is acceptable. (Often it is difficult to cash a personal check in foreign currency or to exchange dollars.) You may decide not to send a check immediately but rather to wait for the priest to reply—wise if you are not certain that the letter will arrive at the right parish or if a preliminary letter is being sent to several parishes. In such a case you can include a final paragraph such as this one:

> La ringrazio fin d'ora per la Sua gentilezza e premura. Vorrei mandarLe un piccolo contributo alla parrocchia, ma attendo che Lei mi scriva come posso effettuare questo pagamento. Accetta assegni in dollari?

[Return address]

[Date]

Reverendo Parroco
Parrocchia di [S. Maria Maggiore]
[08030 Austis (Nuoro)]
Italy

Reverendo Parroco,

Sono [Joseph P. Slusky] e la mia [bisnonna materna] provenne da [Austis] in [Sardegna]. Ho già ricevuto delle informazioni dall'ufficio di stato civile del comune, ma mi hanno detto di rivolgermi a Lei per i dati anteriori al [1872]. Vorrei chiederLe un favore.

Cerco la [data di matrimonio], e le [date di nascita] dei [genitori della mia bisnonna]. Tutto ciò che so è che lei, [Maria Concetta Cuccuru] di [Pietro] e di [Maria Rosa Virdis], è nata il [24 maggio 1876] ad [Austis], ed aveva un fratello maggiore [Giuseppe Cuccuru] nato il [10 novembre 1873]. Forse ci sono altri fratelli nati prima del 1872, l'anno d'inizio dei registri comunali.

Vorrei chiederLe se, per favore, puo' essere cosi' gentile da ricercare questi dati e trascriverli per esteso sui certificati parrocchiali di nascita e di matrimonio che cortesemente Le chiedo di inviarmi, oppure, se avesse la possibilità e fosse più conveniente per Lei, vorrei una fotocopia di ogni atto.

Sarei anche molto interessato di sapere se ho ancora parenti ad Austis per poter scrivere e scambiare notizie. Lei potrebbe gentilmente darmi l'indirizzo delle famiglie [Cuccuru] ancora abitanti nel paese?

So che Le chiedo molto, e pertanto La ringrazio fin d'ora per la Sua gentilezza e premura, e Le chiedo di accettare questo assegno quale offerta per la Sua parrocchia.

Distinti saluti,

FIGURE 11-7. Sample Letter to a Parish Priest

This is translated as:

> I would like to thank you for your kindness and thoughtfulness. I would like to send you a small offering for your parish, but I will wait to hear from you so that I will know how to make this offering. Do you accept checks in dollars?

If the priest sends the information but does not mention anything about payment, it is wise to send something anyway. You may need to contact that priest again, and kindness and generosity are always remembered! If you have a more complicated request or wish to correspond regularly with a town office or priest, you should engage the services of a translator. (There is computer software that will execute simple translations as well.)

The final sample letter for the parish is a thank-you note. This note, besides thanking the priest for the information sent, includes two more requests: one for postcards depicting the town and one to find out if the priest knows anyone who would be interested in continuing research in the parish. (Most towns of a certain size or that have historical or artistic artifacts of interest to tourists also have postcards of the town that cost about a dollar each. These make nice additions to a family album and can be requested of the town official or parish priest as a personal favor.) These requests do not necessarily have to be included in the thank-you note; they can be included with any of the other sample letters, but they are appropriate in the thank-you note. Also, while thanking the priest for the information sent, you may want to ask for more information using any of the phrases already demonstrated in earlier letters. Remember, however, not to request too much information at one time!

Sample Thank-you Note to a Parish Priest

This sample letter, figure 11-8, is translated as:

Reverend [Don Sebastiano],

I would like to thank you for sending me the information about the family of my great-grandfather, [Pasquale Giannini]. This has enriched our knowledge of our family and our Italian heritage.

I am enclosing, as promised, a cashier's check for $20 as an offering for your parish, and I have another favor to ask you. Would it be possible to send me some postcards showing Agnone and the surrounding countryside? Also, since we would be very interested in continuing the genealogical research of our family in the parish records, do you know anyone who would be willing to perform this for a fee?

Thank you again for your help.

Best regards,

If you have already been in contact with the parish priest and he has signed a response with his name, it is appropriate to address the letter directly to him. He may even prefer to be addressed by his first name, as in this case.

For additional information about the province of origin and to receive illustrated pamphlets, you can also write to the provincial tourist office. This office is usually in the seat (capital) of each province and is called the *ente provinciale del turismo*. It exists to promote tourism and has maps, hotel information, and usually tourist and historical information about the province. You may write in English; often, the pamphlets can be found in English. It is sufficient to address your request to the office along with the name of the city. For example, for the city of Padua (in Italian, Padova) the address is:

Ente Provinciale del Turismo
[35100 Padova], Italy

The names of the provinces and their zipcodes are the same as those listed for the state archives in appendix A. Many large towns also have a tourist office called the *pro loco*. These local offices can provide more specific details about a town; often, they sponsor historical research that you can request and purchase. The major purpose of

---

[Return address]

[Date]

Reverendo Parroco [Don Sebastiano]
Parrocchia di [S. Antonio Abbate]
[86081 Agnone (IS)]
Italy

Rev. [Don Sebastiano],

Vorrei ringraziarLa per la Sua gentilezza nell' inviarmi i dati sulla famiglia del mio bisnonno [Pasquale Giannini]. Questo ha arricchito la nostra conoscenza della famiglia, e del nostro retaggio italiano.

Allego alla presente un assegno circolare, come promesso, per $20, quale offerta per la Sua parrocchia. Vorrei chiederLe poi, un altro favore: sarebbe possibile spedirmi delle cartoline che raffigurano Agnone e la campagna circostante? Infine, siccome sarei molto interessato a continuare la ricerca genealogica della mia famiglia nei registri parrocchiali, desidero sapere se Lei conosce qualcuno che sia disposto, dietro compenso, a ricercare questi dati per me.

La ringrazio ancora per il Suo aiuto.

Distinti saluti,

FIGURE 11-8. Sample Thank-you Note to a Parish Priest

both the provincial and local offices is to promote tourism and to provide hotel and lodging information, so, if you indicate that you are interested in visiting the town or province and are fascinated by the history and culture of the region, much of this information will be sent free of charge. Special requests to purchase books in English or Italian concerning local traditions, culture, and history can be addressed to these offices as well.

If a parish priest does not reply to your letter, you can use a procedure similar to that suggested for the town office: send a second letter by registered mail to the parish priest, and, if you get no response, send a final letter to the *curia vescovile*. Before doing so, however, allow more time for a priest to reply. He is under no obligation to answer you, and if he does it is from good will. There should never be a demanding or accusing tone to followup letters.

WRITING TO THE STATE ARCHIVE

Most documents and interesting information will be obtained by writing the town office or the parish priest, but the other important record source, the state archive (*archivio di stato*), will also reply to written inquiries. Although the state archive will not make out certificates for birth, marriage, or death acts, you may want to inquire there concerning any of the alternative records discussed in chapter 9. The archive contains the records of the entire province, so the problems encountered by town office staff are increased a hundredfold in the archive. Most of the work of the archive is to preserve the existing documents, to file and catalogue them, and to assist the researchers who go there to consult them. Most archives are understaffed and cannot conduct extensive research for anyone.

On the other hand, I have usually found the directors and archivists very cordial and willing to help in a research project, and they will reply to letters. Again, the secret of obtaining information by mail is knowing exactly what types of records are found in the archive and requesting precise information. Chapters 6 and 9, which are concerned with the Napoleonic records and alternative record sources, should provide a good understanding of what records are contained in the archive and of what to request. It would be inappropriate to request a search for your family genealogy among the Napoleonic civil records because that would require long and involved research and would exceed the resources of the staff. However, it is reasonable to ask them to check one or two names and dates. The most common request to the archive is for a search of the conscription records; such a request is shown in the sample letter below.

Sample Letter Requesting Conscription Records

This letter (figure 11-9) is addressed to the director of the archive because he or she is responsible for all work done there. A director must have at least a master's degree in history or the humanities and usually has had special training in archival work and research. Most have worked for years in archives before becoming directors, so they are expert in their work and have a thorough knowledge of archive holdings. They often act as consultants for research projects, and they are almost always willing to help.

As in most situations, the more information the archive staff has about both the purpose of the research and the person being researched, the better they can assist in finding information. They may suggest other research sources peculiar to a region that are not even mentioned in this book, so your letter should take this into consideration; that is, you should seek their help and provide ample information with just a suggestion of what documents should be researched.

This letter begins with a presentation of the writer and an explanation of the purpose for writing:

> Dear Director,
>
> I am [Giulia Luciani] from [Colorado], and I am writing to ask you a favor. I am searching for my great-grandfather, [Giovanni Luciani], who I believe was born in the province of [Ascoli Piceno], but I don't know from which town. Since I would like to pursue the genealogy of my Italian family, I need to find the town and parish of my ancestor.

This introduction provides the director with a clear idea of the purpose of the request. If you know only the general region of origin of your ancestor, you could send similar letters to the state archives of all the provinces in the region, including the name of the appropriate province in each letter. The letter continues with the known information.

> For this reason I would like to ask you if you could please have the conscription records for the province of Ascoli searched to find [Giovanni]. From the immigration records in the U.S.A. in [1883] and from his death act of [February 1932], where his age is given as [63] years old, it would seem that he was born in [1868 or 69]. I know I am asking a lot, but I don't know who else to turn to.
>
> Also, if I could have a photocopy of the document, if it is found, I would be very grateful. If the conscription records don't exist for that period, or if you know of other sources, I would be grateful if you could suggest how the research could be pursued.

You can delete or change the phrases in these paragraphs as fits each case. If the immigration date is unknown it would be left out, and if the age was given from a marriage act it could be cited instead of the death act. If none of this is known, you might include the birth date of the first child born in America: "So solo che il suo primo figlio/a nacque nel 1892" (I only know that his first

[Return address]

[Date]

Direttore
Archivio di Stato di [Ascoli Piceno]
[Via S. Serafino 8c]
[63100 Ascoli Piceno]
Italy

Egregio Direttore,

Sono [Giulia Luciani] da [Colorado] e scrivo per chiederLe un favore. Sto cercando il luogo di provenienza del mio bisnonno, [Giovanni Luciani], che presumo sia nato nella provincia di [Ascoli Piceno], ma non so in quale comune. Vorrei svolgere una ricerca genealogica sui miei antenati italiani, ma prima devo conoscere il comune e la parrocchia di nascita.

A questo fine, vorrei chiederLe se, per favore, puo' far consultare le liste di leva per la provincia di [Ascoli], e cercare [Giovanni]. Dai documenti di immigrazione negli U.S.A. nel [1883], e dall'atto di morte di [febbraio 1932], risulta che [Giovanni] e' nato nel [1868 o 69] in quanto aveva [63] anni all sua morte nel [febbraio 1932]. So che Le chiedo molto, ma non so a chi altro rivolgermi.

Inoltre, Le sarei veramente grata se potessi avere una fotocopia del suo documento, nel caso venisse trovato. Se i registri di leva non ci sono per quel periodo, o se Lei conosce altre fonti, Le sarei grata se potesse suggerirmi come proseguire la ricerca.

La ringrazio in anticipo per la Sua gentilezza e premura, e chiedo che qualsiasi spesa inerente alla ricerca mi sia addebitata.

Distinti saluti,

FIGURE 11-9. Sample Letter Requesting Conscription Records

son/daughter was born in [1892]). This statement is not as specific, but it still gives a partial time frame for the search.

All state archives can photocopy documents. Although the fee is quite high (almost $2 per copy), it is worthwhile to have such a copy of the record because information may be gleaned from it that might otherwise be missed.

The letter ends with the usual thanks and the request that the expenses be charged to whoever is making the request:

I thank you beforehand for your kindness and timeliness, and I ask that all expenses regarding the research and photocopying be charged to me.

Best regards,

As for the town office, the archive usually will not charge for research time, but it will charge for photocopies. Usually the staff will respond first by stating the total cost for the documents and then will send them on receipt of payment.

Researchers are affiliated with some of the large archives, such as those at Florence and Rome. When dealing with these archives, you will first be put into contact with a researcher, and a fee will be established for the research performed. Often the researchers are students working on their degrees, and usually the fee, particularly for small requests such as this, is not exorbitant. In these archives, extensive research among records such as the Napoleonic or notary records can be commissioned that is not possible in other, smaller archives.

Other types of special requests can certainly be made of the archive director, and he or she may often be a good consultant for any research problem, particularly when looking for alternative record sources and historical information. These requests, however, cannot be synthesized into a sample letter; they are best made in English or with the help of a translator.

With these form letters, you can begin research in Italy through correspondence; you may be able to complete several generations of your family history. Those who are searching for ancestors from the area of the former Kingdom of the Two Sicilies (which occupied the area from Naples southward) will find the Napoleonic civil records on microfilm from 1865 back to 1809 (in Sicily back to 1822). These microfilmed records are available for consultation at the LDS church's Family History Library in Salt Lake City and at the church's family history centers located throughout North and South America (see chapter 10). Through mail and by personal consultation of the microfilmed records, genealogy can sometimes be pursued back to 1809 and five or six generations of family history completed through the civil vital records.

Chapter 12

READING THE RECORDS

C HAPTER 11 DESCRIBED HOW YOU CAN BEGIN RESEARCH BY writing to town offices, parishes, or state archives in Italy. Anyone who desires to explore his or her family's genealogy, however, will eventually arrive at a point where research must be pursued by reading the documents themselves. Whether you do this research personally, have it performed by a friend or relative, or engage a professional to do it, it is still wise to understand how to read the records. If you learn to decipher the handwriting in the records and to read the acts, you will be more satisfied with the research and can personally verify the validity of the work.

It is not possible to provide a comprehensive understanding of paleography (the study of ancient handwriting), much less a language course in Italian and Latin, in one chapter, but some vital clues are provided here so that you can glean essential information from the records. This chapter provides examples and translations of civil and parish records to indicate what you should look for and to provide examples of handwriting styles.

CIVIL AND NAPOLEONIC CIVIL RECORDS

Although a birth or marriage act written in a foreign language may seem incomprehensible initially, the essential information is fairly easily extracted; it is not necessary to be able to read the entire act. (Chapters 4 and 5 include many examples of these acts and provide entire translations to enable you to understand the format of each act and where to look for the information.) For genealogical purposes, in any act, essentially you need to know four items: the date of the event, the location of its origin, the names of the ancestor or ancestors, and the names of their parents. Any other information, although interesting, usually is not needed to complete a genealogy. Thus, it is important to know how to identify at least this much information in the document and to distinguish it from the remainder. Several examples are shown on the following pages.

Civil Birth Records

The first two examples are a birth certificate from the commune of Salcedo (figure 12-1) and an extract of a birth act from the commune of Avigliana (figure 12-2). The most evident information, printed at the top of each document, is the name of the commune and province where the act originated. The place of the act's origin is therefore the most

readily identifiable information. This item usually appears in the heading; if not, it appears at the bottom of the certificate, but it is always present. An important item to look for is the *frazione* of origin. In figure 12-1 is stated *è NATO in*, or "was born in," Mure di Salcedo. Mure is the small village outside of Salcedo where the ancestor was actually born. (It is important to know the *frazione* so that you can pursue research in the right parish when consulting parish records.) The extract (figure 12-2) does not indicate the *frazione*, so only the name of the commune is known. Thus, it is important to look not only at the heading of the document but also where it indicates, usually at the beginning, *nato/a in* or *nato/a a*. The same is true of any other type of certificate: *battezzato/a a* (baptized at), *sposato/a a* (married at), *morto/a a* (died at), or *sepolto/a a* (buried at).

The next important item of information is the date of the act. This usually appears at the beginning of the act and is clearly indicated. The date often appears both spelled out and in numeral form. (If the date is in numeral form—for example, 11/06/1887—contrary to the U.S. system, in Italy and Europe the day is placed first; this example would be the eleventh of June and not the sixth of November.) In these two examples, however, the date is spelled out, so it is important to be able to count in Italian and to know the names of the months (see tables below). *Il giorno* always refers to the day of the month. (Sometimes this is also written *il dì*, but the meaning is the same.) Month, in Italian, is *mese*, so in both these certificates it is written *del mese di*, or "the month of," followed by the name of the month. "Year" is *anno*, and it is written either *L'anno* or *dell'anno*, both with the same meaning. The extract of the birth certificate will also include the hour (*ore*) and minute (*minuti*) of birth. In modern Italy the twenty-four-hour clock is used, so, in the case of the act from Avigliana, 19:20 is actually 7:20 p.m. Tables 12-1 and 12-2 list the numbers, the months, the days of the week, and their Italian equiva-

FIGURE 12-1. Civil Birth Certificate of Giovanni Nepumuceno Maccagnan, 1874, Salcedo, Vicenza

COMUNE DI SALCEDO
PROVINCIA DI VICENZA

CERTIFICATO DI NASCITA

L'Ufficiale dello Stato Civile
(artt. 1 e 3 della legge 31-10-1955, n. 1064 - G.U. 297)

certifica

che (1) .... MACCAGNAN GIOVANNI NEPOMUCENO -------

è NATO in .... MURE DI SALCEDO -- .... (Prov. di .... Vicenza ....)

il giorno .... VENTOTTO --

del mese di .... agosto -----

dell'anno .... Milleottocentosettantaquattro ---

come risulta all'atto N. 52 Parte I^ Serie .... dell'anno 1874

Si rilascia per uso .... amministrativo --

li 07.12.1990

L'UFFICIALE DELLO STATO CIVILE

(1) Scrivere semplicemente cognome e nome.

FIGURE 12-2. Extract of the Civil Birth Act of Giuseppe Secondo Borla, 1895, Avigliana, Torino

COMUNE DI AVIGLIANA

PROVINCIA DI TORINO

UFFICIO DELLO STATO CIVILE

ESTRATTO PER RIASSUNTO DELL'ATTO DI NASCITA

Anno 1895 *Atto n.* 94 *Parte* I *Serie* 2

Si certifica che dai Registri degli atti di Nascita esistenti presso questo Comune, anno, parte, serie e numero sopraindicati, risulta che

l'anno 1895

il giorno TRENTA del mese di GIUGNO

alle ore 19 e minuti 20

in AVIGLIANA è nato un bambino di sesso maschile

col cognome BORLA

al quale venne dati i nomi: GIUSEPPE SECONDO

pat. GIOVANNI mat. SENORE TERESA

Annotazioni marginali: nessuna

Rilasciato ai sensi art. 3 del D.P.R. n. 432 del 2-5-1957.

Si rilascia il presente estratto per uso USI PER I QUALI NON E' PREVISTO IL BOLLO

Avigliana, li 29/7/1987

L'UFFICIALE DELLO STATO CIVILE

CITTA' DI AVIGLIANA Stato Civile

maggioli MODULGRAFICA

lents. The ordinal numbers are included as well; they may be very useful because often the date is written, rather than "one May" (*uno maggio*), as "the first of May" (*il primo maggio*) or "the last day of April" (*l'ultimo di aprile*). Counting in Italian is much the same as in English: "twenty-one" is *ventuno*, "twenty-two" is *ventidue*, and so on. In the same way, "two hundred" is *duecento*, "three hundred" is *trecento*, and so on to one thousand. When written, years are spelled in their entirety: *milleottocentosettantaquattro* (one thousand eight-hundred seventy-four), as in figure 12-1. In the extract (figure 12-2) the year is in numeral form; if it had been written out, it would be *milleottocento-novantacinque*.

Napoleonic Birth Act

The major difficulty usually is not in reading the date in an act but in locating the correct date. Neither of the certificates above from the town office causes confusion but, as discussed in chapter 6, two dates, and sometimes three, are usually found in the Napoleonic civil acts. The next example (figure 12-3), which is from the Napoleonic birth records, begins with a date: *L'anno mille Ottocento cinquanta il dì Undici del mese di Luglio*. Tables 12-1 and 12-2 should enable you to readily translate this as 11 July 1850—however, that is not the birth date! Birth acts (and death acts as well) actually begin with the date on which the birth (or death) was declared to the town mayor. Only below, in the handwritten midsection of the document, is the actual birth date of the child stated. It reads: *ed a' dichiarato che la stessa* <u>*nacque*</u> *il giorno nove detto mese ed anno ad ore sedici . . .*, or "and declared that the same was born on the day (*giorno*) nine, of said month (*mese*) and year (*anno*) at the hour (*ore*) sixteen (4:00 p.m.)." The words *nacque, nato, è nata, natus,* and *natam* all mean "was born" and will precede the actual birth date, just as *morto, è morta, morì, quondam,* and *è deceduta* all mean "died"; *sepolta, tumulato, sepellita,* and *interrata* will be found for the word "buried." In the same act the baptismal date (stated in the margin at right) also appears: thirteen (*tredici*) July (*luglio*) 1850. The word *detto* or *suddetto* means, literally, "said" or "above stated" and appears often in documents referring to a date already

referred to previously in the act. Thus, *detto mese ed anno* means "above stated month and year"—July 1850, as indicated previously in the act.

The next two items of information needed for genealogical research are the name of the ancestor and the names of his or her parents. In the civil birth certificate (figure 12-1) locating that information was easy—the ancestor's is the only name that appears, in this case Giovanni Nepomuceno Maccagnan. The difficulty, if any, is in determining which is the surname, because the entire name appears in capital letters and because Nepomuceno is a rarely encountered name and could just as easily be a surname! In this example, which represents the norm, the surname, Maccagnan, is given first, so Maccagnan is the surname and Nepomuceno

Table 12-1. Numbers and Ordinals

Italian	Italian Ordinal	Latin	Latin Ordinal	English	English Ordinal
uno	primo	unus	primus	one	first
due	secondo	duo	secundus	two	second
tre	terzo	tres	tertius	three	third
quattro	quarto	quattuor	quartus	four	fourth
cinque	quinto	quinque	quintus	five	fifth
sei	sesto	sex	sextus	six	sixth
sette	settimo	septem	septimus	seven	seventh
otto	ottavo	octo	octavus	eight	eighth
nove	nono	novem	nonus	nine	ninth
dieci	decimo	decem	decimus	ten	tenth
	ultimo		ultimus		last
	penultimo		proximus ab ultimo		second to last
undici		undecim		eleven	
dodici		duodecim		twelve	
tredici		tredecim		thirteen	
quattordici		quattuordecim		fourteen	
quindici		quindecim		fifteen	
sedici		sedecim		sixteen	
diciassette		septemdecim		seventeen	
diciotto		duodeviginti		eighteen	
diciannove		undeviginti		nineteen	
venti		viginti		twenty	
ventuno, etc.		unus et viginti, etc.		twenty-one, etc.	
trenta		triginta		thirty	
quaranta		quadraginta		forty	
cinquanta		quinquaginta		fifty	
sessanta		sexaginta		sixty	
settanta		septuaginta		seventy	
ottanta		octaginta		eighty	
novanta		nonaginta		ninety	
cento		centum		one hundred	
duecento		ducenti		two hundred	
trecento, etc.		trecenti, etc.		three hundred, etc.	
mille		mille		one thousand	

FIGURE 12-3. Napoleonic Birth Act of Angela Vaggoccio, 1850, Rosolì, Reggio Calabria

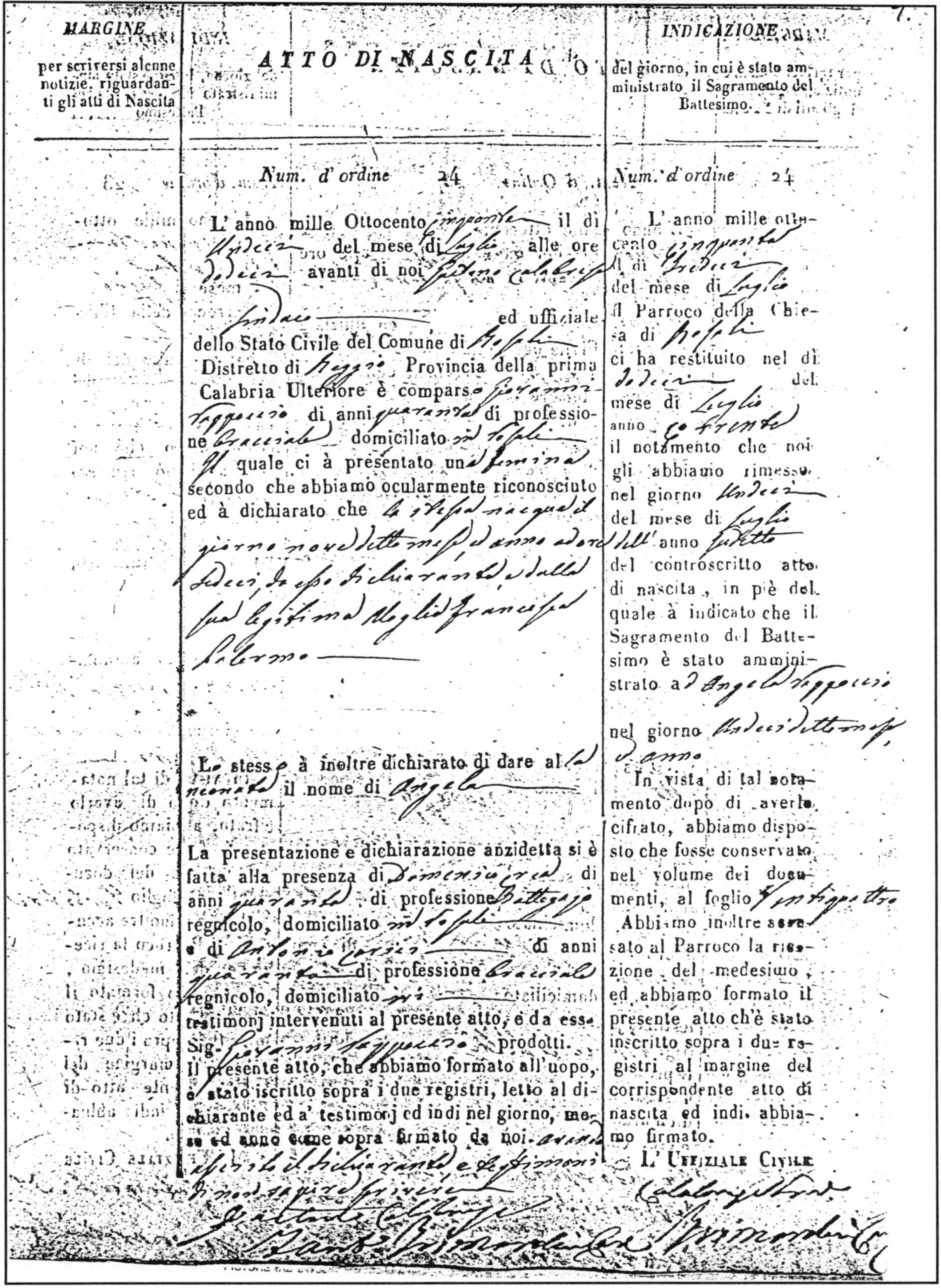

MARGINE

per scriversi alcune notizie riguardanti gli atti di Nascita

ATTO DI NASCITA

Num. d'ordine 24

L'anno mille Ottocento cinquanta il dì Undici del mese di Luglio alle ore dodici avanti di noi Gaetano Calabrese Sindaco ed uffiziale dello Stato Civile del Comune di Rosolì Distretto di Reggio Provincia della prima Calabria Ulteriore è comparso Giovanni Vaggoccio di anni quaranta di professione bracciale domiciliato in Rosolì Il quale ci à presentato una femina secondo che abbiamo ocularmente riconosciuto ed à dichiarato che la stessa nacque il giorno nove detto mese ed anno a ore dodici, da esso dichiarante, e dalla sua legittima moglie Francesca Palermo

La stessa à inoltre dichiarato di dare alla neonata il nome di Angela

La presentazione e dichiarazione anzidetta si è fatta alla presenza di Domenico Greco di anni quaranta di professione Bottegajo regnicolo, domiciliato in Rosolì e di Antonio Iorio di anni quaranta di professione bracciale regnicolo, domiciliato ivi testimonj intervenuti al presente atto, e da esso Sig. Giovanni Vaggoccio prodotti. Il presente atto, che abbiamo formato all'uopo, è stato iscritto sopra i due registri, letto al dichiarante ed a' testimonj ed indi nel giorno, mese ed anno come sopra firmato da noi avendo asserito il dichiarante e testimoni di non saper scrivere

Gaetano Calabrese

INDICAZIONE

del giorno, in cui è stato amministrato il Sagramento del Battesimo.

Num. d'ordine 24

L'anno mille ottocento cinquanta il dì tredici del mese di Luglio il Parroco della Chiesa di Rosolì ci ha restituito nel dì dodici del mese di Luglio anno corrente il notamento che noi gli abbiamo rimesso nel giorno Undici del mese di Luglio dell'anno suddetto del controscritto atto di nascita, in piè del quale à indicato che il Sagramento del Battesimo è stato amministrato ad Angela Vaggoccio nel giorno Undici detto mese, ed anno

In vista di tal notamento dopo di averlo cifrato, abbiamo disposto che fosse conservato nel volume dei documenti, al foglio Ventiquattro Abbiamo inoltre rimesso al Parroco la ricezione del medesimo, ed abbiamo formato il presente atto ch'è stato inscritto sopra i due registri al margine del corrispondente atto di nascita ed indi abbiamo firmato.

L'UFFIZIALE CIVILE

Calabrese Sindaco

Table 12-2. Months and Days of the Week

Italian	Italian Abbrev.	Latin	Latin Abbrev.	English
gennaio	gen.o	januarius	jan.s	January
febbraio	feb.o	februarius	feb.s	February
marzo	mar.o	martius	marti	March
aprile	apr.	aprilis	apr.is	April
maggio	mag.o	maius	mays	May
giugno	g.no	junius	jun.s	June
luglio	l.o	julius	jul.s	July
agosto	a.sto/ag.o	augustus	aug.s	August
settembre	7bre	septembris	7bris	September
ottobre	8bre	octobris	8bris	October
novembre	9bre	novembris	9bris	November
dicembre	Xbre	decembris	Xbris	December
domenica		solis		Sunday
lunedì		lunae		Monday
martedì		martis		Tuesday
mercoledì		mercuri		Wednesday
giovedì		jovis		Thursday
venerdì		veneris		Friday
sabato		saturni		Saturday
anno		annus		year
mese		mensis		month
giorno/dì		dies		day

is just an unusual middle name. Usually given names, such as Giovanni, are readily distinguishable from surnames. In the civil birth extract (figure 12-2), as is more common, a separate line exists for the surname (*cognome*), Borla, and the given name or names (*nome* or *nomi*), Giuseppe Secondo. The parents' names are listed underneath: *pat.*, an abbreviation of *paternità*, which means "father," and *mat.*, for *maternità*, which means "mother." Many certificates would read this way: *Borla Giovanni Secondo di* (of) *Giovanni e di* (and of) *Teresa Senore*. The father's surname is almost never stated because it is assumed to be the same as that of the child. In civil records and recent parish records, however, both the given name and maiden name of the mother will be included in the document.

In the birth certificate from the Napoleonic records of Rosolì, Reggio Calabria (figure 12-3), it is not as readily apparent where to find the name of the child, nor is it clear which are the names of the parents. The first name that appears in the act is usually that of the town mayor. The child's name appears approximately halfway down after the phrase *il nome di*, or "the name of." The person's name appears similarly in the death and burial acts as well. The problem, then, is in identifying the mother and father of the child or the parents of the deceased. In the birth records,

the person who declared the birth was almost invariably the father. Thus, in this format, the second name shown in the record is that of the person who appeared before (*è comparso*) the town official to declare the birth—in this case the father, Giovanni Vaggoccio. Below, it then indicates the name of his "legitimate" wife (*sua legittima moglie*, or sometimes *sua consorte*, which means the same), in this act Francesca Palermo. If a midwife (*ostetrica*) or relative declared the birth, the name of the father and mother will appear after the date of birth of the child, and the act will usually contain an explanation of the father's absence (often this was due to the death of the father; if so, the death date will be indicated). Sometimes one or both of the parents were unknown, as for an illegitimate child or a foundling. Then one or both parents will be listed as NN (*nescio nomen*, or "unknown").

Napoleonic Marriage Act

The marriage act (figure 12-4) is harder to decipher because most of it is handwritten and it includes many different names. If all documents regarding the marriage are available for examination, there will be little confusion because the birth acts of both the bride and groom will include the names of their parents, and acts such as the solemn promise to marry (see chapter 6) are usually very easy to read. Sometimes, however, the only available source is the marriage act itself.

The act comprises two pages, but the important information is found on the first page. The act begins with the date, *milleottocento diciasette* [1817] *a dì ventuno del mese di Ottobre* [21 October]. It then states the name of the town and province: Santo Stefano, L'Aquila. Then comes a long portion containing many names that, to the untrained eye, may be difficult to differentiate. The first name written in the document, Stanislao Florio, appears on many documents that precede and follow this act, so we can infer that he is a town official (the fact is also stated in the document: he is the *ufficio di stato civile*, or "civil vital records officer"). In this example, the person who appeared before the town official was the groom, the ancestor of interest. The phrase to look for, as in the birth records, is: *è comparso* (appeared before). The name that appears directly after will be that of the groom—in this case, Michelangelo Rusciolelli.

Usually, the groom's name is followed by the names of his parents. In fact, the last printed word in the first section of the document is *figlio* (son). Usually, *di* (of) is followed by the name, age, and profession of the father; then the words *e di* (and of) and the name of the mother with her age and profession. However, this document is more complicated (which is why it was chosen as an example). In this case Michelangelo's father is dead, so, instead of *di* we find *del fu*: "of the deceased"; the Latin *quondam*, abbreviated as *q* or *qm*, was also used in the same sense. The father's name, Saverio, and his profession, *pastore di pecore* (shepherd), are also given, together with the date and place of his death, Foggia. The next name mentioned is that of Isidoro Rusciolelli—not Michelangelo's mother, since Isidoro is a male's name and it is not preceded by the conjunction and proposition: *e di* or *e della fu*. Indeed, the document states that Isidoro is the uncle (*zio*) and guardian. A couple of lines below is the important phrase *e della fu* (and of the deceased . . .), followed by the mother's name, Pasqua Cocco, her profession, and date of death.

Only after the groom's parents have been named and all relevant information appears will the bride be mentioned. Invariably her name will be preceded by the conjunction *e* (and). Then her name, age, and profession will be listed with the names of her parents. Therefore, two lines below Pasqua Cocco's name we find *e Maria Francesca Colajezzi d'anni ventisei anche maggiora, filatrice* (age twenty-six, of legal age and a weaver). Both of her parents were alive, as indicated by the phrases used: *figlia di Sabbato* (daughter of Sabbato) and, further on in the act, *e di Innocenza Chiarelli* (and of Innocenza Chiarelli).

Normally, in Italian, all names that end with "a" are female, and all names ending with "o," "i," or "e" are male. Thus, Maria is female, Mario male; Antonia is female, Antonio male; Raffaele is male, Raffaella female; Michele is male, Michela female. Exceptions are the names Andrea and Mattia, which are both male; the female equivalent of the first is Andreina, and there is none for the second. There are also names that are used for both, such as Nicola; the male version can also be written Nicolò, and Nicoletta is commonly used for females to avoid ambiguity. Also, the sex of the name can be determined by other words that refer to the person, such as *figlio* (son) or *figlia* (daughter), *nato* or *nata*, *morto* or *morta*, *battezzato* or *battezzata*, and so on. These can assist you in determining who is being referred to in the document.

All other names mentioned in the act, particularly on the second page, are those of the witnesses to the marriage and the town official (again). These people are usually not related and, although their roles are interesting to know for a family history, they are of little relevance in genealogy research. (The witnesses for birth and death acts were often people who worked in the town office or were casual acquaintances. In fact, the same names often appear on successive civil acts as witnesses. The witnesses for marriages, however, were carefully chosen. They—one or more for the bride and one or more for the groom—were considered responsible for assisting the couple to have a stable and fruitful marriage throughout life. Thus, they were usually the best friends of the couple but were seldom direct relatives.) The dates mentioned at the bottom of the first page and the top of the second refer to when the banns were posted.

This document represents a particularly difficult example, the added names and dates because of the previous deaths of the groom's parents being a complicating element. It serves to demonstrate that, when you know what to look for, even a complex document will begin to take form and become legible.

The profession or occupation of a named person is indicated in the civil records but rarely in the parish records. Although not strictly essential for genealogy, this information certainly adds to a family history. (Occasionally the occupation can be important in distinguishing an ancestor from someone else of the same name on passenger lists or census records in the United States; an Antonino Bellomo listed as a tailor [*sarto*] could be identified as different from an Antonio Bellomo listed as a farmer [*contadino*].) The occupation is always noted in the Napoleonic records, and often it can be found in extracts of birth, marriage, and death in the civil records as well. Many of the occupation titles are in archaic Italian and will not be found in a current dictionary.

The terms *villico, bracciante, bifolco, contadino, agricolo,* and *mezzadro* all mean "farmer," but there are subtle differences among them. A *villico* was normally a farmer who owned his land; a *bracciante* was a farm worker who worked for others. The first term is much more common in the north, and the next two are commonly found in the south. *Bifolco, contadino,* and *agricolo* are terms for "farmer" that make no clear distinction as to ownership of property. The *mezzadri* were workers whose families lived on the property of large landowners and worked their farms, often for generations. Usually, besides houses, they were entitled to a certain percentage of the crop, but they provided the seeds and the labor. Many of these families lived quite comfortably. The *mezzadri* gained the most from the land reforms that followed World War II by becoming owners of the land their families had worked for centuries. Table 12-3 is a list of other more common occupations.

In much of southern Italy and in the mountainous regions, water was and still is very scarce, and in the past houses did not have running water. If the town had a public fountain or a spring close by, families supplied themselves with water. If the source was far away, the *vaticale*, or "waterman," would fill large vats with water and sell the water from house to house, usually from a cart drawn by a donkey. In fact, there were a number of occupations that provided door-to-door services. There were those who collected rags or oil, who sold wood or blocks of carbon for cooking and heating, or who sold household items or fruits and vegetables from door to door. Often, while the men worked in the fields, the women took their wares to market

FIGURE 12-4. Napoleonic Marriage Act of Michelangelo Rusciolelli and Maria Francesca Colajezzi, 1817, S. Stefano, Aquila; Left-Hand (below) and Right-Hand (right) Facing Pages

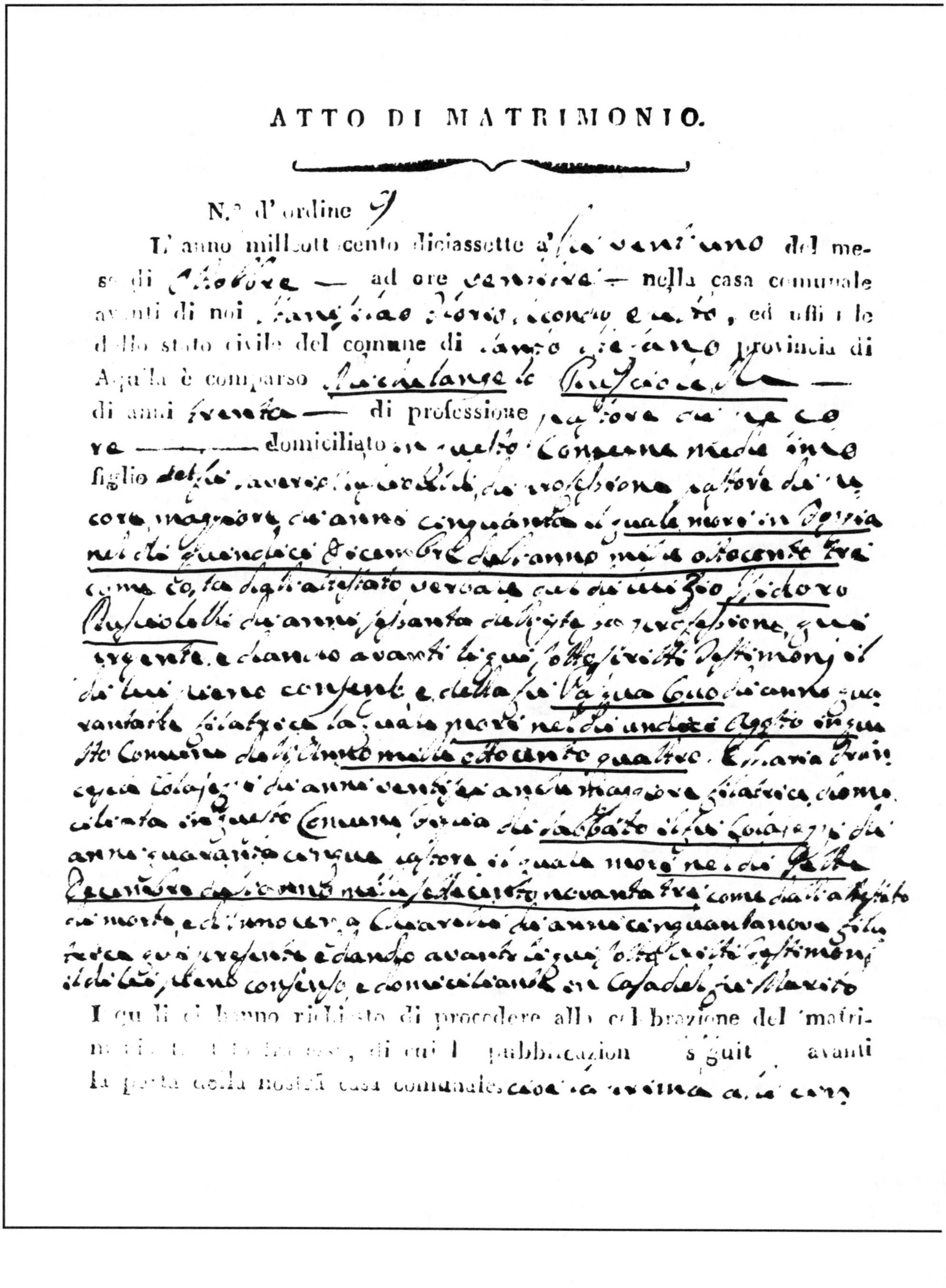

ATTO DI MATRIMONIO.

N.° d'ordine 9

L'anno milleottocento diciassette a' [illegible] del mese di Ottobre — ad ore [illegible] — nella casa comunale avanti di noi [illegible], ed uffiziale dello stato civile del comune di Santo Stefano provincia di Aquila è comparso Michelangelo Rusciolelli — di anni trenta — di professione [illegible] domiciliato [illegible] figlio [illegible]

[illegible]

I quali ci hanno richiesto di procedere alla celebrazione del matrimonio [illegible], di cui le pubblicazioni [illegible] seguite avanti la porta della nostra casa comunale, [illegible] que del corrente Mese di Ottobre giorno di Domenica alle ore dodici di questo corrente Anno e la seconda alle diodici di detto Mese di ore giorno di Domenica alle ore venti di questo corrente Anno mille ottocento decias sette ————————— secondando le loro domande, dopo d'aver letto tutti i documenti, ed il capitolo sesto del codice civile sotto il titolo del matrimonio, abbiamo domandato a' futuri sposi se vogliono prendersi per marito e moglie; ciascun di essi avendo ri sposto separatamente, ed affermativamente, noi li abbiamo avverti ti di presentarsi al Paroco per esser congiunti in matrimonio, se condo le forme prescritte dal Concilio di Trento; a qual effetto abbiamo loro dato un certificato a norma del Real decreto dei 16 Giugno 1815.

Di tuttociò ne abbiamo formato il presente atto in presenza di Domenico di Majo Leone ————— d'anni Trenta ora e di professione l'avocato ————— domiciliato in questo Co mune di Simone Cicci ————— d'anni cinquan cin ——— di professione l'artigale, ————— domiciliato in questo Comune di Felice Sontavellu ————— d'anni ottottadeci di professione sagristano ————— dymiciliato in questo Comune di Federe di Ago i ————— d'anni quarantaquattro di professione Parjol lo ————— domiciliato egualmente in quello Comune il su detto atto è stato letto tanto a' testimoni, che a' contraenti; s' e ..... trmato da noi e ....

.... testimonio, ...

Firma del Giudice delegato
dal Presidente del Tribunale di prima Istanza.
Lica

Sposati dal Paroco delle .... nov. Marco il di 9 Novembre 1817

come da l' attestato in serito negli atti.

Firma
....
T. Ciquoccas

Table 12-3. Occupations

Common Occupations

Arcari	constructed arches
Arrotino	knife sharpener
Artigiano	craftsman
Beccaro/macellaio	butcher
Boscaiolo	lumberjack
Bovaro	cattle herder
Callegaro	repaired shoes and sold wooden slippers
Calzolaio	cobbler
Canaparo	made and sold ropes, nets, etc.
Capraro	goat herder
Carbonaro	delivered carbon blocks and wood for heating
Carniel	weaver from Friuli area
Carraro	made carriages and carts
Castagnaro	gathered and sold chestnuts
Coltellinaio	knife craftsman
Fabbro	smith or craftsman of metals
Falegname	carpenter
Fattore	administrated large farms
Fattorino	handyman
Gelataio	ice cream maker
Lattoniere	maker of sheet metal gutters for houses
Maniscalco	shoed horses and donkeys
Marinaio	sailor
Muratore	bricklayer
Negoziante	storekeeper
Olivaro	delivered olive oil and picked up used oil
Ortolano	sold vegetables at market
Oste	innkeeper
Pagliaro	made and sold wicker and straw products
Panettiere/ fornaro	made bread
Pasticciere	made pastries
Pastore	shepherd
Pescatore	fisherman
Pignataro	sold pots and pans
Rais	boatswain
Saponaro	made and sold soap
Sarto	tailor
Scalpellino	mason
Soldato	soldier
Spadaro	made swords and weapons
Stagnino	soldered and repaired pots and pans
Straccivendolo	ragman
Tabacchino	treated and sold tobacco
Tagliapietra	stone cutter
Vaticale	waterman
Venditori ambulanti	traveling salesman
Vetraio	glass maker (usually for windows)

Prestigious Occupations

Avvocato	lawyer
Maestro	professor
Medico/dottore	medical doctor
Mercante	merchant
Notaio	notary
Prete/sacerdote	priest

Common Female Occupations

Agricola	farmer
Commessa	store clerk
Contadina	farmer
Filatrice	spinner
Infermiera	nurse
Insegnante	teacher
Magliaia	knitter of wool articles
Mistra	sewed shoes together
Mondina	worked in the rice paddies
Ostetrica/levatrice	midwife
Tessitrice	weaver
Villica	farmer

in a nearby town or city. Some of these occupations had specific titles; others had dialectic names that varied from one region to another. They can perhaps best be characterized as traveling salesmen and women.

For an *artigiano* or *fabbro*, often the act will specify the person's specialty; there were many different crafts—glassblowing in the Venice region, furniture making in Veneto and Piedmont, leather crafting in Tuscany, porcelain making in the world-famous works of Capo di Monte near Naples. There were craftsmen of bronze, copper, and iron throughout Italy. Some professions were occupied seasonally by farmers. This work was often done during the winter, the off season from work in the fields. Men from the Belluno province in Veneto were famous for their *gelato* and *storti*, or ice cream cones, and they traveled throughout the north during the off season selling their wares. *Arrotini* were men who traveled with stone wheels from house to house, sharpening knives and other implements. Many worked as painters or bricklayers. Rarely did a man have just one occupation; although he might have been listed as a farmer in documents, he likely was capable of performing several jobs.

In an agricultural society, work was a family affair, and the women worked as hard as the men. Children also worked in the fields as early as age five or six, first at light tasks and then at steadily harder work.

There were occupations other than those listed in table 12-3, of course, but these certainly are the most frequently listed in the records. Because, until this century, more than ninety-five percent of the people lived from agriculture or the sea, related occupations are most frequently mentioned.

PARISH RECORDS

The parish documents generally were handwritten, often in Latin (so names differ from their Italian and dialectic forms), and they were not standardized in form as the civil and Napoleonic records were. Therefore, it can be difficult to identify the essential information you need. (See chapter 7 for other examples of parish records.)

In the parish records, rarely is the name of the parish or of the town or village repeated in each separate act. The name may be mentioned at the beginning of each volume, or sometimes not at all. Normally, if you have found the record, you will know what parish you are dealing with–but not always. For example, in the northern regions, a common ecclesiastical unit was the *pieve*. This was a parish that had jurisdiction over several smaller parishes in the area, much like the relationship between the commune and the *frazione*. All baptisms, marriages, and deaths were recorded only at the *pieve*. For example, in the Val di Non in Trento, the Revò pieve had jurisdiction over all the records for Revò, Cagnò, Tregiovo, and Romallo. Thus, if you were researching the De Prettis family from Cagnò, the records would be in the parish of Revò. In the more recent records, each family's village of origin is indicated clearly in each act, but before around 1780 this distinction was not made, so it is impossible to know the ancestor's exact location, except to assume that he or she stayed within the same village. In such a case the source would be cited as Revò parish, and you would know that the act came from somewhere within the *pieve*. In most areas of Italy, however, this situation does not occur, and the location can be clearly established.

The next item of information necessary for research is the date of the event. Much as in the civil records, the date is usually found at the beginning of the act. In the parish records, however, it is necessary to distinguish between the birth date and the baptismal date. Usually, the two were within a few days of each other because children were baptized as soon as possible to avoid the risk of their dying before baptism. The first date in the act is usually the baptismal date. Later in the act the birth date may be stated, but usually the birth date is indicated by a statement such as *nata ieri* (born yesterday) or *nacque l'altro ieri* (born the day before yesterday).

Parish Baptismal Act

The first parish baptismal act shown (figure 12-5) begins *Die viges.ma octava ms. 8bris 1799*, as does the next act. Because these are christening or baptismal records, the date stated at the beginning of the act will be the baptismal date. On the second line of the act the child's birth date is indicated: *infantem <u>natem</u> die 25 d.o* (infant <u>born</u> the 25th of said month). In the second example of parish baptismal acts (figure 12-6), in the fourth act (third line), the birth date is simply indicated as <u>nato</u> hoggi, or, "born today" (*hoggi* is a misspelling of *oggi*). In some cases, particularly in the Piedmont and Aosta regions, which were influenced by the French, the opposite occurs: the baptismal records list first the birth date and indicate later in the act the baptismal date. *Nacque, nato, nata, natem, natus,* and *natum* are Italian and Latin variations of the verb *nascere,* which means "to be born." A date that follows any of these words will be the birth date.

The baptismal date indicated in figure 12-5, *Die viges.ma octava ms. 8bris 1799*, exemplifies two problems commonly encountered in reading parish records: the date is in Latin, and abbreviations are used. Both of these practices complicate understanding of the record. Latin numbers are spelled very similarly to those of Italian. For example, in this case the Latin *vigesima octava* corresponds to the Italian *venti otto,* or "twenty-eight." The months, too, are similar to Italian and English forms. The names of the months are listed in table 12-2 in their Italian and Latin versions and with common abbreviations.

The use of numbers in the abbreviated forms of the last four months of the year was a very common practice; it can

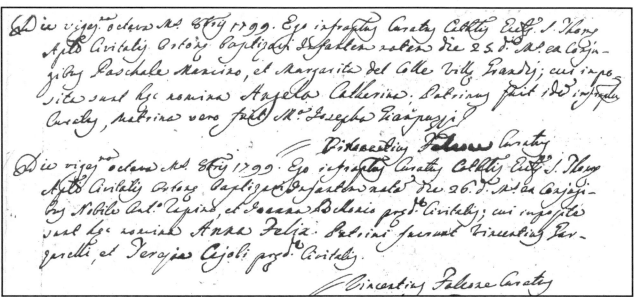

FIGURE 12-5. Parish Baptismal Acts, 1799, Ortona, Chieti

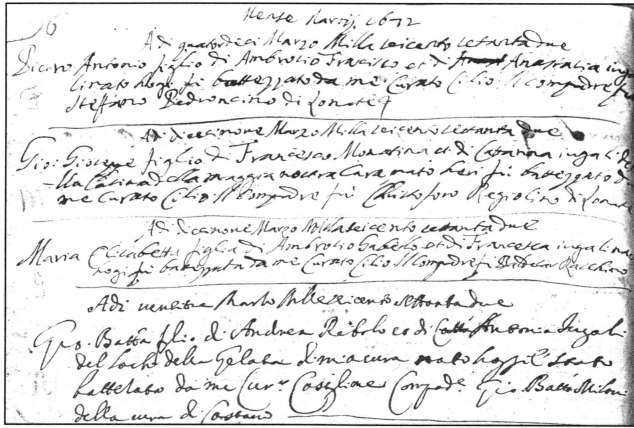

FIGURE 12-6. Parish Baptismal Acts, 1672, Lonate Pozzolo, Varese

lead the unwary to make mistakes in recording the date. Numerals simply replace the corresponding spelled part of the month's name: *7bre* for *settembre, 8bre* for *ottobre*, etc. (Note that these do not correspond to the seventh and eighth months. This discrepancy derives from the old Roman calendar. First established in the seventh century B.C., it had 304 days and ten months, starting with March. The months were martius, aprilis, maius, junius, quintilis [fifth], sestilis [sixth], settembris [seventh], ottobris [eighth], novembris [ninth], and decembris [tenth]. In 46 B.C., Julius Caesar reformed the calendar to better match the Muslim calendar and astronomical calculations by using 365 days with a leap year every four years. He added the months januarius and februarius, and he renamed the months quintilis and sestilis; they became julius [for himself] and augustus [for his title]. As a result of this change, the months named for seventh to tenth became out of order. Pope Gregorio XIII incorporated further minor changes; his Gregorian calendar was adopted in Italy and most of Catholic Europe in 1582, and it was adopted in America in 1782.) The numbers are listed in table 12-1.

A common phrase at the beginning of a date is *Anno Domini* (year of our Lord), abbreviated as *D.ni* or *A.D.* If the date is not found at the beginning of the act, it will usually be within the act itself toward the end. Very common in parish records are acts that begin with the word

suddetto, (usually abbreviated *sud.o*) or *detto* (abbreviated *d.o*). The first means "above stated"; *detto* means "stated." There may be a partial date, perhaps the day or the day and month, followed by *d.o*—meaning that, in the first case, the date is the same as that in the act above; or, when part of the date is left out, meaning that it is the same year, or month and year, as the act above. This can be rather confusing, and sometimes it is necessary to go back several acts to find the right date. In parish record volumes, the year may be indicated only once at the beginning of the year in January; or it might be noted in the first act at the top of each page. Take great care not to skip the beginning of a new month or year and record the wrong one!

After you've established a date, the next item of information is the ancestor's name. Here things become even more complicated. The name can appear in several different parts of the record and, again, Latin forms and abbreviations are frequently present. There are two basic formats for the baptismal and death records. The most common begins, after the date, with the name of the ancestor who was baptized or who died. As in the second example of parish baptismal acts (figure 12-6), each act includes the name of the child who was born and baptized, so the first in that example is for *Pietro Antonio figlio di* (Peter Anthony, son of . . .); then the parents' names are stated. This is certainly the most comprehensible format; both the child's name and those of his parents are provided in the first line or two without confusing, extraneous information. The other common format for these records is shown in the first act of figure 12-5, in which the parish priest began the act with his own name: *Ego infrascriptus Curatus Cathiis* (I, the here-written Parish Priest Cathiis). The act may go on to cite the name of the parish, as this example does, and it will certainly mention the parents and sometimes even the godparents before stating the child's name. Almost always the child's name is preceded by the words *cui impostem fuit nomen*, or, as in the example, *cui impostem sunt hec nomina* (the correct Latin would be *haec nomina*, once again demonstrating that priests did not always use the correct form), both of which mean "to whom was given the name." This phrase will be followed by the name or names of the child, sometimes written in larger characters or otherwise emphasized, but often not. The surname will not be given with the child's name; it is always assumed to be the same as the father's surname. The words *nome* and *nomen* mean "name," and *nomen* is the plural, "names"; they indicate that the child's name(s) will follow.

In some parish records, the parish priest will have written the name and surname of each individual in the margin near the appropriate act. This aid greatly facilitates your search, as you need not read each act; you can simply scan the page margins for the family of interest. You should not rely completely on these marginal annotations, however; sometimes the name and even the surname may not match what is in the act. If there is a difference between the name in the margin and that in the act—for example, if the name in the act is in Latin and that in the margin is in Italian—the act is the official document, so the spelling or version of the name contained therein is preferred.

Once you know where a name is typically found in an act, the remaining problem is understanding what is written. The spelling variations for some names are numerous, and they are sometimes rendered more complicated by the use of Latin and abbreviations. In table 12-4 are listed the most commonly used Italian names, their abbreviations, and Latin and English equivalents.

There are thousands of other names, but those above are the most frequently encountered in the records. In many areas, a dozen or so common names were used repeatedly. Many names were created by combining two others. For males this was often done with the name Giovanni—as in Giovanni Battista, Gian Luca, Giovanni Maria, Gian Pietro, Gian Francesco, and so on. Similar compositions for females were almost invariably formed with the name Maria: Maria Grazia, Maria Elena, Maria Maddalena, Maria Teresa, Maria Anna, etc. Maria was also a popular middle name, particularly as Anna Maria. Maria was often used as a middle name for males, particularly in the south, where Giovanni Maria, Francesco Maria, Pasquale Maria, and others are found. The sex of the child can be determined by the first name and by other indications in the act.

There is much less variation between the Italian and Latin forms of female names than with male names. Although the most common abbreviations are listed above, each parish priest added his own variations. Giovanni, the most common male name, could also be found as Gio, Giovan, Gian, Gioanni, or just G; and similarly in the Latin form, with J, Jo, Joes, Joan, Johan, Johan.es, or Jon.es. In addition, of course, are the many dialectic variations!

Latin itself has many spelling variations. In Latin there are five different declensions and six cases for each name or noun according to its use in a sentence. In other words, a name's spelling changes according to how the name is used in the phrase. The spellings in table 12-4 are in the nominative case, which is most commonly found in the records. However, there can be a different spelling for each declension and each case, creating many spelling variations for each name. For example, when used in the accusative case (as a direct or indirect object), an "m" was often added to the name. Joannes would be written as Joannem, Josephus as Josephem; and Maria as Mariam, Angela as Angelam, etc. In the genitive case, denoting possession, a male name such as Joannes becomes Joannis and Georgius becomes Georgi, and most female names gain an "e," as in Maria, Mariae. This case is important in a document because it often denotes the parents' names. For example, you might find a phrase such as *Joannes Josephi De Casati* or *Maria Antonii De Rosettis*. Neither of these represents the first, second, and last names of one person. Rather, the first name in each example is in the nominative case and the second is in the genitive case. Thus, the first phrase would translate as "Joannes son of Josephus De Casati" and the other as "Maria daughter of Antonius De Rosettis." Always record the name the way it is found in the record, but realize that all of these variations, including the different abbreviations, can refer to the same person.

The name of an ancestor may very well change from one record to another. Thus, in christening records the father's name might appear as ZPiero, in his marriage record as Gio Pietro, and in the baptismal records (written in Latin) as Johannes Petrus or even abbreviated as Jo.nes P.us. These all refer to the same person, but if you were not aware of these variations, you might not find the correct act and would not be able to continue the research. In addition, in one act he might appear as Piero and in the other as Joannes, when in fact his full name was Giovanni Pietro.

When the ancestor's name has been identified, even in its abbreviated form, the last step is to identify his or her parents. When the act begins with the name of the newborn child, as in figure 12-6, the name is followed immediately by *figlio di* (son of), *figlia di* (daughter of), or just *di* and the name of the father. In this example only the father is mentioned but, often, in more recent parish records, his name will also be followed by *di* and the name of his father (the paternal grandfather). This would be very important in identifying the correct family lines and should always be recorded when mentioned in the record. This name will then be followed by the now-familiar phrase *e di* (and of) or, in this case, *et di*, and then the name and usually the surname of the child's mother and, if followed by *di*, her father as well. Generally, in the older records, as this example from 1672 shows, less information is provided: only the given name of the mother is included in this case, not her surname. Also, her name is followed by the word *jugali* (married) to indicate that the parents are married. This was sometimes abbreviated as *jug* and often will be written *sua legittima moglie* or *sua legittima consorte* (his legitimate wife). These phrases, too, can be abbreviated as *s.l.m* or *s.l.c.*

Another variation often found in the parish records occurs when the names of the father and the mother are given, but the family surname appears after *jugali*. Thus, you might find a sentence such as: Carlo Pietro Ant.o *figlio di* Hieronimo *e di* Lucia *jugali* Porcione; Porcione is the surname.

A final item to focus on in the baptismal act, again following the mother's name or following *jugali*, is the place of origin of the family or of the mother. Usually this will be the same parish, and it will be written *huius* or *hic loci* or *huius parochialis* or, as found in figure 12-5, *pre.do civitalis* or *huius civitalis*; all of these essentially mean "this place" or "this town." Otherwise, the name of the town will be indicated. For example, in the third line of the first act in figure 12-5, the mother appears as Margarita del Colle Villa Grandi, which translates as "Margarita Del Colle from Villa Grandi." This is very important because, if the mother is from another parish, the couple's marriage record will be found only in her home parish; research on the maternal line would have to be continued there. This could be the only indication as to where the mother or even both parents originated, so it is necessary to note this information.

Parish Death Act

The parish death records are somewhat similar to baptismal records. For exam-

Table 12-4. Common Names

Common Male Names

Italian	Italian Abbr.	Latin	Latin Abbr.	English	Dialect or Nickname
Alessandro	Ales.ro	Alexius	Alex.s	Alexander	Sandro
Andrea	An.a	Andreas	And.s	Andree	
Angelo	Ang.o	Angelus	Ang.s	Angelo	Nino
Antonio	Ant.o	Antonius	Ant.s	Anthony	Toni
Bartolomeo	Bart.o	Bartholomeus	Barth.us	Bartholomew	Bartolo
Battista	Batta	Baptista	Bapta	Baptist	Batta
Carlo		Carolus	Car.us	Charles	
Carmelo	Carm.o	Carmelus	Carm.us	Carl	Meluccio
Carmine	Carm.e	Carminus	Car.nus	Carmine	
Cristiano	Crist.o	Christianus	Chris.us	Christian	Chris
Daniele	Dan.le	Daniel	Dan.l	Daniel	Lele
Domenico	Dom.co	Dominicus	Dom.cus	Dominique	Mimmo/Mino
Filippo	Fil.po	Philippus	Phil.pus	Philip	Pippo
Francesco	Fran.co	Franciscus	Fran.cus	Frank	Franco
Gabriele	Gab.le	Gabrielis	Gab.lis	Gabriel	Lele
Giacomo	Giac.o	Jacobus	Jac.s	James	
Giorgio	Gior.o	Georgius	Geor.us	George	Zorzi
Giovanni	Gio/Gian	Joannes	Jo./Jo.es	John	Zuanne
Giuseppe	Gius.e	Josephus	Joseph	Joseph	Beppe/Pino
Gregorio	Greg.o	Gregorius	Greg.us	Gregory	
Leonardo	L.do	Lunardus	Lun.s	Leonard	Nardo
Lorenzo	Lor.zo	Laurentius	Laur.s	Lawrence	Renzo
Luca		Lucas		Luke	Luca
Luigi	L.gi	Aloysius	Aloy.s	Louis	Gigi
Marco	M.co	Marcus	M.cus	Mark	
Mario	M.o	Marius	Mar.s	Mario	
Martino	Mar.o	Martinus	Mart.us	Martin	Tino
Matteo	Mat.o	Mattheus	Math.s	Matthew	Teo
Mattia	Mat.a	Matthias	Math.s	Matthew	
Michele	Mich.e	Michael	Mich.is	Michael	Michelino
Natale	Nat.e	Natale	Nat.lis	Natale	
Nicola	Nic.a	Nicolaus	Nic.s	Nicholas	Cola
Nicolò	Nic.o	Nicolaus	Nic.s	Nicholas	
Osvaldo	Osv.o	Osvaldus	Osv.s	Osvald	
Paolo	P.lo	Paulus	Pa.lus	Paul	
Pasquale	Pasq.le	Paschalis	Pasch.is	Pasquale	Lino
Pietro	P.tro	Petrus	P.s/Pet.s	Peter	Piero
Raffaele	Raf.le	Raphaele	Raph.e	Raphael	Lele
Renato	Ren.to	Renatus	Ren.tus	Renato	
Roberto	Rob.to	Robertus	Rob.tus	Robert	Berto
Salvatore	Salv.re	Salvatoris	Sal.is	Salvator	Totò
Sante	S.te	Sanctus	Sanc.s	Saint	Santino
Simone	Sim.e	Simeone	Sim.ne	Simon	
Stefano	Stef.o	Stephanus	Steph.us	Stephen	
Tommaso	Tom.so	Thomas	Thoma	Thomas	Tomi
Ugo		Ugus		Hugh	
Vittorio	Vit.rio	Victorius	Vic.us	Victor	

Table 12-4. Common Names (continued)

Common Female Names

Italian	Italian Abbr.	Latin	Latin Abbr.	English	Dialect or Nickname
Agata	Agata	Agata	Agata	Agata	Tina
Alba	Alba	Alba	Alba	Dawn	
Angela	Ang.a	Angela	Ang.a	Angelique	Lina
Anna	Ana	Anna	Anna	Ann	
Annunziata	Ann.ta	Annuntiata	Ann.ta	Announced	Nunzia
Antonia	Ant.a	Antonia	Ant.a	Antonia	Tonia
Antonietta	Ant.a	Antonietta	Ant.a	Antonietta	Tonina
Assunta	As.ta	Assunta	As.ta	Assunta	Assuntina
Barbara	Bar.a	Barbara	Bar.a	Barbara	Barbi
Bartolomea	Bart.a	Bartholomea	Barth.a	Bartholomea	Bortola
Carmela	Car.a	Carmela	Car.la	Carmela	Carmelina
Catterina	Catt.a	Catharina	Cath.a	Katherine	Rina
Diana	Diana	Diana	Diana	Diane	
Domenica	Dom.ca	Dominica	Dom.ca	Domenique	Mimma
Elisabetta	Elis.ta	Elizabeta	Eliz.a	Elizabeth	Elisa
Filomena	Fil.a	Philomena	Phil.a	Philomene	
Francesca	Fran.ca	Francisca	Fran.ca	Francis	Franca
Giovanna	Giov.na	Joanna	Jo.na	Joanne	Zuanna
Giuseppina	Gius.pa	Josepha	J.pha	Giuseppa	Pina
Grazia	Gr.zia	Gratia	Gr.tia	Grace	
Letizia	Let.a	Letitia	Let.a	Letizia	
Lorenza	Lor.za	Laurentia	Laur.tia	Lorenza	
Lucia		L.cia	Lucia	L.cia	Lucy
Luigia	Lu.gia	Aloysia	Aloy.a	Gina	Gina
Maddalena	Mad.a	Magdalena	Mag.a	Magdalena	Nena
Margherita	Mar.ta	Margarita	Mar.ta	Margaret	Rita
Maria	M.a	Maria	M.a	Mary	
Marta	Mar.a	Martha	Mar.a	Martha	
Nicoletta	Nic.a	Nicola	Nic.a	Nicole	
Osvalda	Osv.a	Osvalda	Osv.a	Osvalda	
Paola	Pa.la	Paula	Pau.a	Paula	Paolina
Raffaella	Raf.a	Raphaela	Raph.a	Raphael	Lella
Regina	Reg.a	Regina	Reg.a	Regina	Gina
Rosa	Rosa	Rosa	Rosa	Rose	Rosina
Rosalia	Ros.a	Rosalia	Ros.ia	Rosaline	Lia
Santa	San.a	Sancta	Sanc.a	Santa	Santina
Teresa	Ter.sa	Theresia	Ther.a	Theresa	Teresina
Valeria	Val.a	Valeria	Val.a	Valery	Valli
Vittoria	Vit.ia	Victoria	Vic.a	Victoria	Rina

ple, normally they begin much as do the baptismal records: first with the date and then the name of the deceased. As seen in the example from the parish of Lonate Pozzolo in the Varese province (figure 12-7), however, there are variations worth noting. For deceased adults, as in both of these acts, the names of the deceased's parents were not mentioned. This omission is not universal—in some parishes at least the name of the father was usually indicated—but it is common. For deceased children, however, the name of the father (or of both parents) was normally stated. The name of the spouse of a deceased person who had been married or widowed was usually stated, particularly if the spouse was still living. Thus, in the second act, that of Gerolama Gavato, her father's name is not included, but it states that she was *vidova x la morte Giovanni Gavato* (widow of the deceased Giovanni Gavato—x means "per" or "for"). (Women were always referred to by maiden name in documents, so both must originally have had the surname Gavato.) In the last act, that of Antonia Aubiini, the names of both the deceased's father, g. Carlo, and of the husband—she is *moglie di* (wife of) Gerolamo Soldavini—are given.

The other item that is important to ascertain from a death record is the age of the deceased, which is usually written immediately after the names of the parents or spouse. In the first act, Maria Zarra is *in età* (age) *d'anni sessantotto* (sixty-eight); in the second, Gerolama is *in età d'anni sessanta incirca* (age approximately sixty); both are good examples of how the age is written. Usually the term *d'anni* (of years) or *d'età* (of age), or both, is used. Often found as well is the word *circa* or *incirca* or the abbreviation *cir.*, *c.a*, or *cir.a*, meaning "approximately." Age was usually calculated by the parish priest or determined based on what relatives said, and, very often, the result was several years off the mark. In any case, it is important to record the age along with the other data because the age is necessary to properly identify the person as the ancestor in question.

FIGURE 12-7. Parish Death and Burial Records, 1751, Lonate Pozzolo, Varese

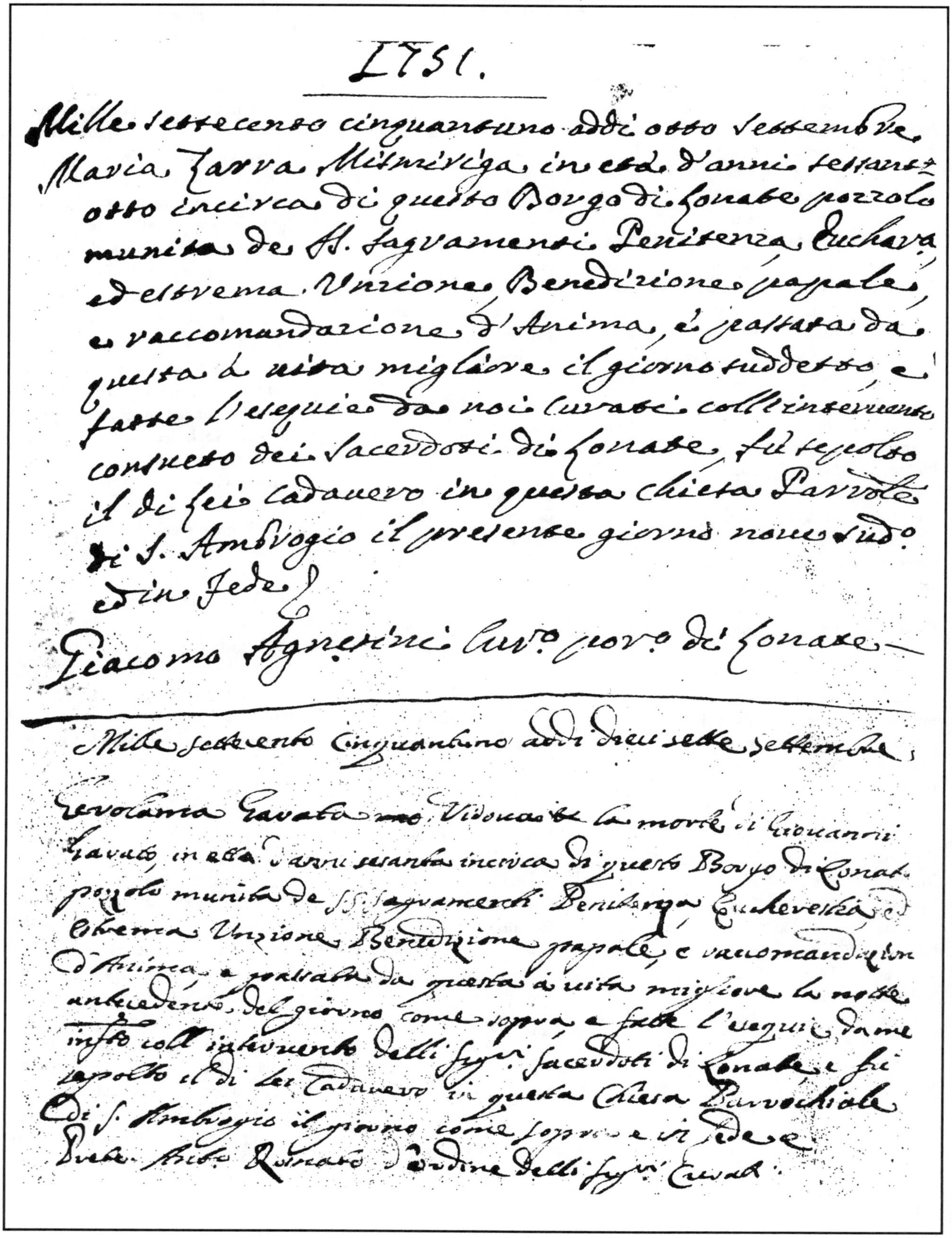
1751.

Mille settecento cinquantuno addì otto settembre
Maria Zarra Mismiriga in età d'anni settanta
otto incirca di questo Borgo di Lonate pozzolo
munita de SS. Sagramenti Penitenza, Euchara
ed estrema Unzione, Benedizione papale,
e raccomandazione d'Anima, è passata da
questa a vita migliore il giorno suddetto, e
fatte l'esequie da noi Curati coll'intervento
consueto dei Sacerdoti di Lonate, fu sepolto
il di lei cadavero in questa Chiesa Parrochle
di S. Ambrogio il presente giorno nove sud.o
ed in Fede
Giacomo Agnesini Cur.o Coad.o di Lonate

Mille settecento cinquantuno addì dieci sette settembre
Gerolama Gavata mo. Vidoua per la morte di Giovanni
Gavato, in età d'anni sessanta incirca di questo Borgo di Lonate
pozzolo munita de SS. Sagramenti Penitenza, Eucharestia ed
Estrema Unzione Benedizione papale, e raccomandazione
d'Anima, è passata da questa a vita migliore la notte
antecedente del giorno come sopra, e fatte l'esequie da me
infra coll'intervento delli Sig.ri Sacerdoti di Lonate e fu
sepolto il di lei cadavero in questa Chiesa Parrochiale
di S. Ambrogio il giorno come sopra e in fede
Prete Ant.o Rossaro d'ordine delli Sig.ri Curati.

Parish Marriage Act

Parish marriage records are typically lengthier than birth and death records, and usually the names of the spouses are not placed conspicuously at the beginning of the act. In figure 12-8, the year is indicated in Roman numerals at the top of the page: *MDLXX (1570)*. Each act begins with the day and the month; for the first act it is 28 September. Then follow the publication of the banns and the date on which each was declared in the parish church. These dates should not be confused with the wedding date, which is at the beginning or the end of the act.

Occasionally, the names of the bride and groom appear at the beginning of the act. Much more often, however, the act contains the name of the parish priest in the first part with the name of the parish or the chapel where the marriage was performed. The name of the parish priest will appear in most of the acts, so he can be readily identified. If a priest from another parish or some other ecclesiastical officer performed the marriage, that fact will be noted too. Usually such persons can be identified by the title used, the most common being *reverendo*, usually abbreviated as *Rev.* Other common titles include *don, parroco, curato, arciprete, pievano, capellano,* and *sacerdote*. In the example shown the title *curato* was used; it appears toward the end of the act. The act normally ends with the names of the two official witnesses to the marriage.

The names of the groom and bride are usually located in the middle of the act. The groom is always mentioned first, and the names of his parents or, at least, his father are included. If the groom is from another town or parish, this too will be noted after the names of his parents and before the name of the bride. You may find the name of the bride after the conjunction *e* (or, in Latin, *et*), and her father's name or the names of both parents will be mentioned as well. The middle act (figure 12-8) documents the marriage of *Gio Maria De Tosi di Busto che habit al molin di Ferno et Anzola fig.a di Andrea Buonalanza*. This could be rather confusing because the preposition *di* (of), which normally precedes the father's name, might also precede the place of birth. You might be led to believe that Busto was the name of Gio Maria's father when, instead, it was Gio Maria's birthplace. The only way to determine whether it refers to the birthplace or the father's name is by the name itself. Since Busto is not a commonly found name, you would consult a gazetteer to determine if it was actually the name of a nearby town. So this phrase reads: ". . . Gio Maria De Tosi of (from) Busto, who lives at the mill at Ferno, and Anzola daughter of Andrea Buonalanza." (Note that the groom's father was not mentioned, while the bride's father was. This is just the opposite of what is normally found. Usually, less information was given about the bride; often, in that time period, even her surname was not mentioned, much less the name of her father.)

INTERPRETING THE HANDWRITING

This brief survey of the different civil and parish records should have provided you with a good idea of what information to look for, where to find it in each act, how to identify and record the necessary names, and how to read the dates. However, the task of finding the information and reading the records can still be hindered by the handwriting you encounter. As is probably obvious from the many examples given, European handwriting differs in style from American handwriting, ancient handwriting even more so. These differences often make reading an act like deciphering hieroglyphics! The study of ancient handwriting and how to interpret it is called paleography. A volume such as this one cannot cover this field of study in depth, but I have provided some examples that might aid the serious researcher in interpreting the handwriting.

If you return to the Napoleonic marriage act in this chapter (figure 12-4) and examine the name of the groom, you will find a good example of why it is important to interpret the handwriting correctly. Even knowing where to look for the name in the act and properly identifying the ancestor is of little help if you can't read the name! The illustration is from a photocopy of the original and, like the original, portions are faded or smudged—as was the entire record volume. The groom's given name can be read as Michelangelo (fifth line), even though the "M" is faded, but the surname is very difficult to read. How do you go about trying to decipher what the surname is?

The first steps in the research process normally begin with more recent civil or parish records. (Normally, research is begun with recent records, gradually working back in time.) Fortunately, most recent records are more legibly written—some are on preprinted forms—and have not been ruined by humidity or insects. You should examine and record not just the names in your own family tree but also the other names in the record. This will provide you with a guide for comparison when these different surnames appear in earlier records of your own family line. Even though many names undergo spelling changes, they still can be recognized and identified in earlier records. Thus, the surname in this example, Rusciolelli, would probably be recognizable because you would already be familiar with the surname from other, more recent records.

If you encounter an unfamiliar name or some other indecipherable word, the first step is to compare the name or word with a similar one in the same document that is recognizable. For example, in this act the surname seems to begin with a "P." There is no continuity between the P and the vertical line underneath, so it could be a "Pi," with the next letter definitely a "u." Farther down in the same act, however, the name appears again after Isidoro (eleventh and twelfth lines), and what had seemed to be P and i are attached, forming an "R." Thus, the name begins with "Ru,"

FIGURE 12-8. Parish Marriage Records, 1570, Lonate Pozzolo, Varese

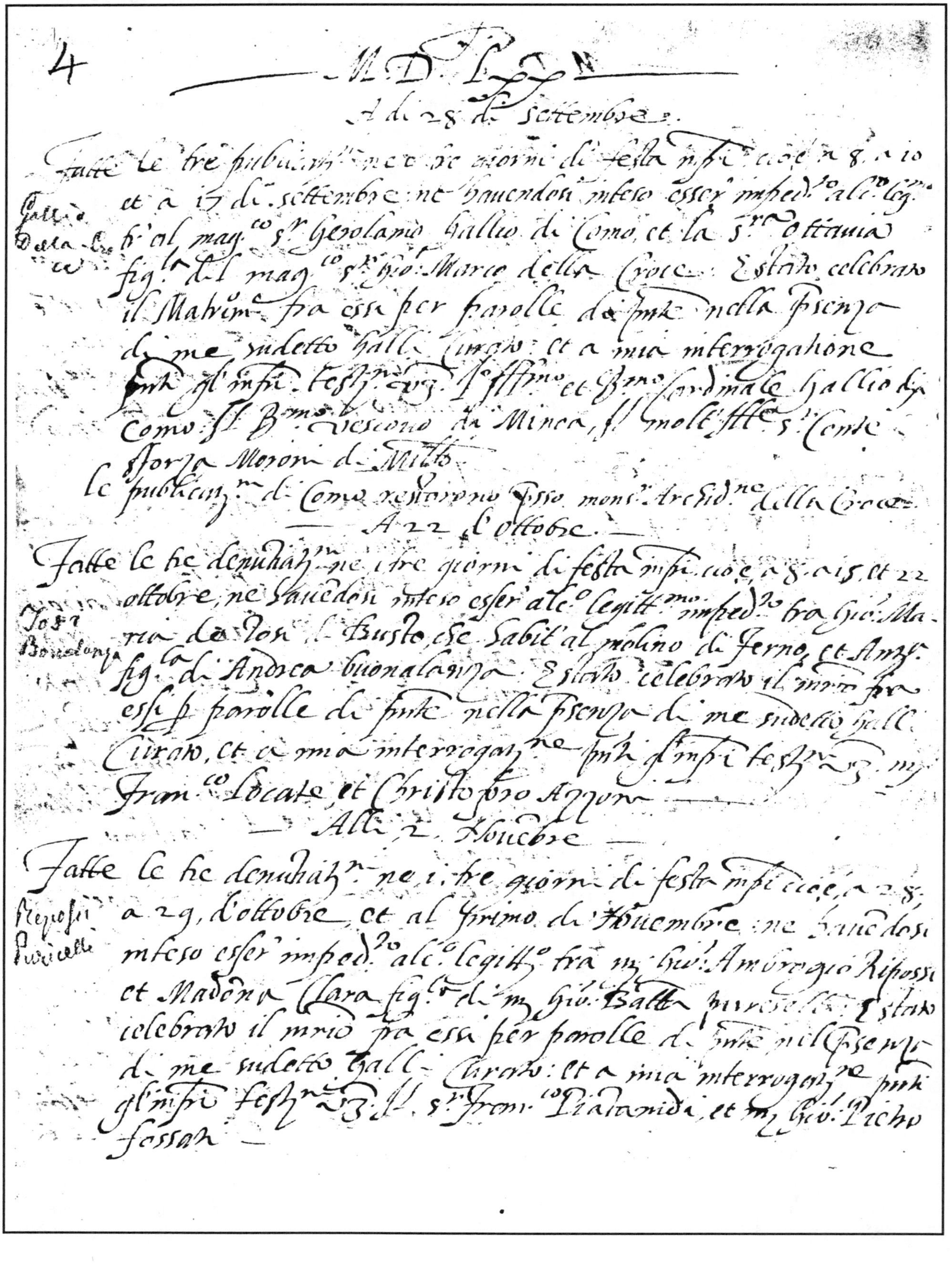

4

M.D.LXX

A di 28 di settembre

Fatte le tre publicationi ne tre giorni di festa infrascritti cioè a 8, a 10 et a 17 di settembre: ne havendosi inteso esser impedimento alcuno legitimo fra il mag.co s.r Gerolamo Gallio di Como, et la s.ra Ottavia fig.la del mag.co s.r Gio: Marco della Croce: E stato celebrato il Matrim.o fra essi per parolle di presente nella presenza di me sudetto Gall. Curato: et a mia interrogatione presenti gl'infrascritti testimonii cioè l'Ill.mo et R.mo Cardinale Gallio di Como, il R.mo Vescovo di Minca, il molto Ill.e s.r Conte Sforza Moroni di Milano

le publicationi di Como restorono presso mons.r Arcid.no della Croce.

Gallio Della Croce

A 22 d'ottobre

Fatte le tre denuntiationi ne i tre giorni di festa infrascritti cioè a 8, a 15, et 22 ottobre, ne havendosi inteso esser alcuno legittimo impedimento fra Gio: Maria da Pon di Busto, che habita al molino di Ferno, et Ang. fig.la di Andrea buonalanza: E stato celebrato il matrimonio fra essi per parolle di presente nella presenza di me sudetto Gall. Curato, et a mia interrogatione presenti gl'infrascritti testimonii m. Fran.co Locate, et Christoforo Appon

Josi Bonalanza

Alli 2 Novembre

Fatte le tre denuntiationi ne i tre giorni di festa infrascritti cioè a 28, a 29, d'ottobre, et al primo di Novembre: ne havendosi inteso esser impedimento alcuno legittimo fra m. Gio: Ambrogio Riposso et Madonna Clara fig.la di m. Gio: Batta Purcello: E stato celebrato il matrimonio fra essi per parolle di presente nella presenza di me sudetto Gall. Curato: et a mia interrogatione presenti gl'infrascritti testimonii il s.r Fran.co Piatanida, et m. Gio: Pietro Fossati

Riposso Purcelli

not "Piu." The next letter would seem to be an "f," but if you compare it with other written f's, you will see that an f was usually crossed in the middle and that the loop turns to the left, somewhat like an English "g." Figure 12-9 provides examples of how capital and lowercase letters may appear in early records (note that the Italian language has no J, K, W, or Y and that Latin has no K or W). By comparing the document with figure 12-9, you can see that the next letter is not an "f" but an "s." This would also be obvious to someone who knows Italian, because in that language there are never more than two consonants in a row; an "fc" combination would never occur, but "sc" followed by a vowel is common. The next letter has to be a vowel, and it is dotted, so it would be an "i." The next letter is clearly an "o." The ending, "-lelli," is quite legible in the second example of the name, so the whole surname can be read as "Rusciolelli."

Very often, researchers use magnifying glasses to aid in reading the letters, and considerable time is often necessary to discern the important names and other words in documents. When researching the records of a town, a detailed map or gazetteer of the area can help you to distinguish the names of other localities mentioned as the place of origin.

Successful interpretation of handwriting is largely a matter of practice. The more you pursue your genealogy and study the parish records, the easier it will be to understand what is written and to find the essential information. Most of the names and surnames in each parish are specific to that parish and are repeated frequently. Therefore, the more you research them the more familiar they will become and the easier it will be to read them. Examining the documents is often one of the most rewarding aspects of researching family history; these examples should assist you in locating and reading the essential information from Italian documents and to verify information found by other researchers.

FIGURE 12-9. Handwriting Variations of Alphabet Characters as Found in Handwritten Documents From the 1500s to the Early 1900s

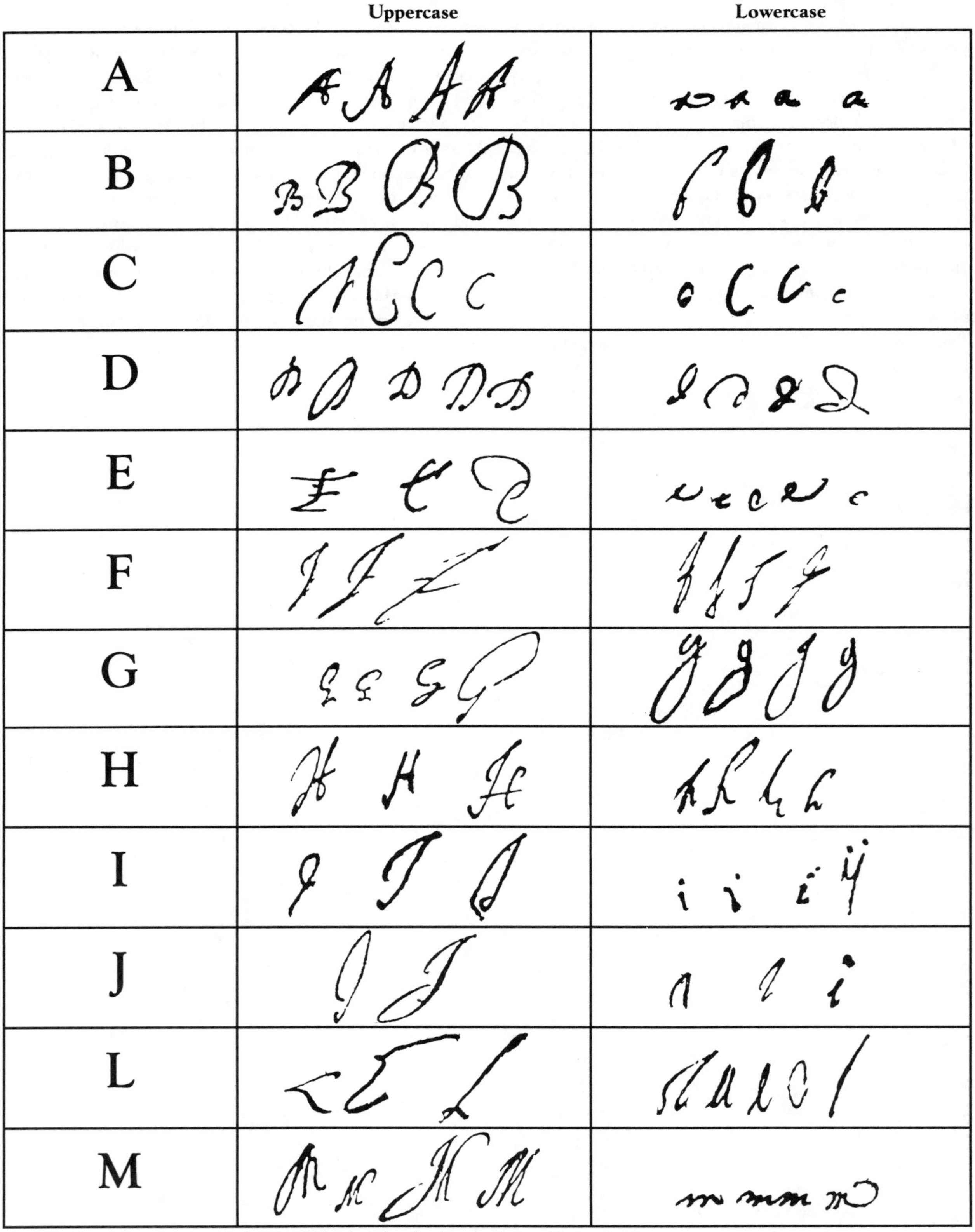

	Uppercase	Lowercase
A		
B		
C		
D		
E		
F		
G		
H		
I		
J		
L		
M		

Reprinted by permission. Copyright © 1995 by the Church of Jesus Christ of Latter-day Saints.

	Uppercase	Lowercase
N		
O		
P		
Q		
R		
S		
T		
U		
V		
X		
Z		

ADDRESSES OF THE ITALIAN STATE ARCHIVES

Addresses of the Italian state archives (*archivio di stato*) are listed alphabetically by province below.

Archivio di Stato
Provincia di Agrigento
Per. Aragona 189
92100 Agrigento, Italy

Archivio di Stato
Provincia di Alessandria
Via Solero 43
15100 Alessandria, Italy

Archivio di Stato
Provincia di Ancona
Via Maggini 80
60100 Ancona, Italy

Archivio di Stato
Provincia di Aosta
Via de Sales 3
11100 Aosta, Italy

Archivio di Stato
Provincia di Arezzo
Via Albergotti 1
52100 Arezzo, Italy

Archivio di Stato
Provincia di Ascoli Piceno
Via S. Serafino da Montegrao 8/c
63100 Ascoli Piceno, Italy

Archivio di Stato
Provincia di Asti
Piazzetta Dell'Archivio 1
14100 Asti, Italy

Archivio di Stato
Provincia di Avellino
Via Soldi 9
83100 Avellino, Italy

Archivio di Stato
Provincia di Bari
Via Pasubio
70100 Bari, Italy

Archivio di Stato
Provincia di Belluno
Via S. Maria dei Battuti 3
32100 Belluno, Italy

Archivio di Stato
Provincia di Benevento
Via Mulini
82100 Benevento, Italy

Archivio di Stato
Provincia di Bergamo
Via Tasso 84
24100 Bergamo, Italy

Archivio di Stato
Provincia di Bologna
Piazza Celestini 4
40100 Bologna, Italy

Archivio di Stato
Provincia di Bolzano
Via Diaz 8
39100 Bolzano, Italy

Archivio di Stato
Provincia di Brescia
Via Galilei 44
25100 Brescia, Italy

Archivio di Stato
Provincia di Brindisi
Via S. Teresa
72100 Brindisi, Italy

Archivio di Stato
Provincia di Cagliari
Via Gallura 2
09100 Cagliari, Italy

Archivio di Stato
Provincia di Caltanissetta
Via Libertà 2
93100 Caltanissetta, Italy

Archivio di Stato
Provincia di Campobasso
Via Orefici 43
86100 Campobasso, Italy

Archivio di Stato
Provincia di Caserta
Via Nazionale Appia 1
81100 Caserta, Italy

Archivio di Stato
Provincia di Catania
Via Vittorio Emanuele 156
95100 Catania, Italy

Archivio di Stato
Provincia di Catanzaro
Piazza Rosario 6
88100 Catanzaro, Italy

Archivio di Stato
Provincia di Chieti
Via Ferri 25
66100 Chieti, Italy

Archivio di Stato
Provincia di Como
Via Briantea 8
22100 Como, Italy

Archivio di Stato
Provincia di Cosenza
Via Miceli 67
87100 Cosenza, Italy

Archivio di Stato
Provincia di Cremona
Via Antica Porta Tintoria 2
26100 Cremona, Italy

Archivio di Stato
Provincia di Cuneo
Via Monte Lovetto 28
12100 Cuneo, Italy

Archivio di Stato
Provincia di Enna
Contrada Scifitello 1
94100 Enna, Italy

Archivio di Stato
Provincia di Ferrara
Corso Giovecca 146
44100 Ferrara, Italy

Archivio di Stato
Provincia di Firenze
Viale Giovine Italia
50100 Firenze, Italy

Archivio di Stato
Provincia di Foggia
Piazza XX Settembre 70
71100 Foggia, Italy

Archivio di Stato
Provincia di Forlì
Via Gerolimini 6
47100 Forlì, Italy

Archivio di Stato
Provincia di Frosinone
Grattacielo L'Edera
03100 Frosinone, Italy

Archivio di Stato
Provincia di Genova
Via T. Reggio 14
16100 Genova, Italy

Archivio di Stato
Provincia di Gorizia
Via Ospitale
34170 Gorizia, Italy

Archivio di Stato
Provincia di Grosseto
Piazza Socci 3
58100 Grosseto, Italy

Archivio di Stato
Provincia di Imperia
Viale Matteotti 105
18100 Imperia, Italy

Archivio di Stato
Provincia di Isernia
Via Testa 27
86170 Isernia, Italy

Archivio di Stato
Provincia di L'Aquila
Piazza Prefettura
67100 L'Aquila, Italy

Archivio di Stato
Provincia di La Spezia
Via Galvani 21
19100 La Spezia, Italy

Archivio di Stato
Provincia di Latina
Via Piceni
04100 Latina, Italy

Archivio di Stato
Provincia di Lecce
Via Jozy Carafa 15
73100 Lecce, Italy

Archivio di Stato
Provincia di Livorno
Via Fiume 40
57100 Livorno, Italy

Archivio di Stato
Provincia di Lucca
Piazza Giudiccioni 8
55100 Lucca, Italy

Archivio di Stato
Provincia di Macerata
Corso F.lli Cairoli 175
62100 Macerata, Italy

Archivio di Stato
Provincia di Mantova
Via Ardigò 11
46100 Mantova, Italy

Archivio di Stato
Provincia di Massa Carrara
Via Sforza
54100 Massa Carrara, Italy

Archivio di Stato
Provincia di Matera
Via Stigliani 25
75100 Matera, Italy

Archivio di Stato
Provincia di Messina
Via XXIV Maggio
98100 Messina, Italy

Archivio di Stato
Provincia di Milano
Via Senato 10
20100 Milano, Italy

Archivio di Stato
Provincia di Modena
Corso Cavour 21
41100 Modena, Italy

Archivio di Stato
Provincia di Napoli
Piazzetta Grande Archivio 5
80100 Napoli, Italy

Archivio di Stato
Provincia di Novara
Via Archivio
28100 Novara, Italy

Archivio di Stato
Provincia di Nuoro
Via Mastino
08100 Nuoro, Italy

Archivio di Stato
Provincia di Oristano
Via Ciuso 2
09170 Oristano, Italy

Archivio di Stato
Provincia di Padova
Via dei Colli 24
35100 Padova, Italy

Archivio di Stato
Provincia di Palermo
Via Vittorio Emanuele 31
90100 Palermo, Italy

Archivio di Stato
Provincia di Parma
Via M. D'Azeglio 43/e
43100 Parma, Italy

Archivio di Stato
Provincia di Pavia
Via Cardano 45
27100 Pavia, Italy

Archivio di Stato
Provincia di Perugia
Piazza G. Bruno 10
06100 Perugia, Italy

Archivio di Stato
Provincia di Pesaro
Via Neviera
61100 Pesaro, Italy

Archivio di Stato
Provincia di Pescara
Piazza della Marina 2/4
65100 Pescara, Italy

Archivio di Stato
Provincia di Piacenza
Piazza Cittadella 29
29500 Piacenza, Italy

Archivio di Stato
Provincia di Pisa
Largo Arno Mediceo 30
56100 Pisa, Italy

Archivio di Stato
Provincia di Pistoia
Piazza Scuole Normali 2
51100 Pistoia, Italy

Archivio di Stato
Provincia di Pordenone
Via Monreale 7
33170 Pordenone, Italy

Archivio di Stato
Provincia di Potenza
Via Due Torri 33
85100 Potenza, Italy

Archivio di Stato
Provincia di Ragusa
Vicolo Fante
97100 Ragusa, Italy

Archivio di Stato
Provincia di Ravenna
Via Guaccimanni 51
48100 Ravenna, Italy

Archivio di Stato
Provincia di Reggio Calabria
Argine Destro Annunziata 59/61
89100 Reggio Calabria, Italy

Archivio di Stato
Provincia di Reggio Emilia
Via Benedetto Cairoli 6
42100 Reggio Emilia, Italy

Archivio di Stato
Provincia di Rieti
Via Monte Di Gaio 7
02100 Rieti, Italy

Archivio di Stato
Provincia di Roma
Corso Rinascimento 40
00100 Roma, Italy

Archivio di Stato
Provincia di Rovigo
Via Sichirello 23
45100 Rovigo, Italy

Archivio di Stato
Provincia di Salerno
Largo Abate Conforti 7
84100 Salerno, Italy

Archivio di Stato
Provincia di Sassari
Corso Angioi 1/a
07100 Sassari, Italy

Archivio di Stato
Provincia di Savona
Via Quarda Superiore 7
17100 Savona, Italy

Archivio di Stato
Provincia di Siena
Via Banchi di Sotto 52
53100 Siena, Italy

Archivio di Stato
Provincia di Siracusa
Via Crispi 66
96100 Siracusa, Italy

Archivio di Stato
Provincia di Sondrio
Largo Mallero Cadorna
23100 Sondrio, Italy

Archivio di Stato
Provincia di Taranto
Via Di Polonia 4
74100 Taranto, Italy

Archivio di Stato
Provincia di Teramo
Via Delfico
64100 Teramo, Italy

Archivio di Stato
Provincia di Terni
Via Pozzo 2
05100 Terni, Italy

Archivio di Stato
Provincia di Torino
Via S. Chiara 40
10100 Torino, Italy

Archivio di Stato
Provincia di Trapani
Via Libertà 31
91100 Trapani, Italy

Archivio di Stato
Provincia di Trento
Via Maccani 161
38100 Trento, Italy

Archivio di Stato
Provincia di Treviso
Via Marchesan 11/a
31100 Treviso, Italy

Archivio di Stato
Provincia di Trieste
Via Lamarmora 17
34100 Trieste, Italy

Archivio di Stato
Provincia di Udine
Via Urbanis 1
33100 Udine, Italy

Archivio di Stato
Provincia di Varese
Via Col di Lana 5
21100 Varese, Italy

Archivio di Stato
Provincia di Venezia
3005 Contrada S. Polo
30100 Venezia, Italy

Archivio di Stato
Provincia di Vercelli
Via A. Manzoni 11
13100 Vercelli, Italy

Archivio di Stato
Provincia di Verona
Via Franceschine 2
37100 Verona, Italy

Archivio di Stato
Provincia di Vicenza
Via G. Casale 91
36100 Vicenza, Italy

Archivio di Stato
Provincia di Viterbo
Via Romiti
01100 Viterbo, Italy

ADDRESSES OF THE DIOCESE SEATS

Addresses of the Italian Catholic diocese seats (*curie vescovili*) are listed alphabetically by region below.

ABRUZZO

Curia Vescovile
Diocese di Avezzano
Corso Libertà 114
67051 Avezzano (AQ), Italy

Curia Vescovile
Diocese di Chieti
Piazza Volignoni 4
66100 Chieti, Italy

Curia Vescovile
Diocese di Lanciano
Via Finamore
66034 Lanciano (CH)

Curia Vescovile
Diocese di L'Aquila
Piazza Duomo 33
67100 L'Aquila, Italy

Curia Vescovile
Diocese di Pescara
Piazza S. Spirito 5
65100 Pescara, Italy

Curia Vescovile
Diocese di Sulmona
Viale Roosevelt 7
67039 Sulmona (AQ), Italy

BASILICATA

Curia Vescovile
Diocese di Lagonegro
Piazza Trieste e Trento
85042 Lago Negro (PZ), Italy

Curia Vescovile
Diocese di Matera
Via Riscotto 11
75100 Matera, Italy

Curia Vescovile
Diocese di Melfi
Piazza Vescovile
85025 Melfi (PZ), Italy

Curia Vescovile
Diocese di Muro Lucano
Piazza Minzoni
85052 Muro Lucano (PZ), Italy

Curia Vescovile
Diocese di Potenza
Via Pretoria 41
85100 Potenza, Italy

CALABRIA

Curia Vescovile
Diocese di Catanzaro
Via Borrelli
88100 Catanzaro, Italy

Curia Vescovile
Diocese di Cosenza
Piazza Arcivescovado 16
87100 Cosenza, Italy

Curia Vescovile
Diocese di Locri
Corso Garibaldi 104
89044 Locri (RC), Italy

Curia Vescovile
Diocese di Reggio Calabria
Via Cimino 24
89100 Reggio Calabria, Italy

CAMPANIA

Curia Vescovile
Diocese di Avellino
Via Nappi 11
83100 Avellino, Italy

Curia Vescovile
Diocese di Battipaglia
Via Gen. Gonzaga 94
84091 Battipaglia (SA), Italy

Curia Vescovile
Diocese di Benevento
Piazza Orsini
82100 Benevento, Italy

Curia Vescovile
Diocese di Caserta
Piazza Vescovado
81100 Caserta, Italy

Curia Vescovile
Diocese di Castellammare di Stabia
Vicolo S. Anna 2/3
80053 Castellammare di Stabia (NA),
Italy

Curia Vescovile
Diocese di Napoli
Largo Donna Regina 22
80100 Napoli, Italy

EMILIA-ROMAGNA

Curia Vescovile
Diocese di Bologna
Via Altobella 6
40100 Bologna, Italy

Curia Vescovile
Diocese di Carpi
Via Don Loschi 2
41012 Carpi (MO), Italy

Curia Vescovile
Diocese di Cesena
Via Giovanni XXIII 13
47023 Cesena, Italy

Curia Vescovile
Diocese di Faenza
Piazza XI Febbraio 3
48018 Faenza (RA), Italy

Curia Vescovile
Diocese di Ferrara
Corso Martiri Libertà 77
44100 Ferrara, Italy

Curia Vescovile
Diocese di Fidenza
Piazza A. Grandi 15
43046 Fidenza (PR), Italy

Curia Vescovile
Diocese di Modena
Piazza Duomo 34
41100 Modena, Italy

Curia Vescovile
Diocese di Piacenza
Piazza Duomo 33
29100 Piacenza, Italy

Curia Vescovile
Diocese di Ravenna
Via Canneti 3
48100 Ravenna, Italy

Curia Vescovile
Diocese di Reggio Emilia
Via Vittorio Veneto 6
42100 Reggio Emilia, Italy

Curia Vescovile
Diocese di Rimini
Corso IV Novembre 35
47037 Rimini, Italy

FRIULI-VENEZIA-GIULIA

Curia Vescovile
Diocese di Gorizia
Via Vescovado 2
34170 Gorizia, Italy

Curia Vescovile
Diocese di Pordenone
Via Revedole 1
33170 Pordenone, Italy

Curia Vescovile
Diocese di Trieste
Via Cavana 16
34100 Trieste, Italy

Curia Vescovile
Diocese di Udine
Via Treppo 7
33100 Udine, Italy

LAZIO

Curia Vescovile
Diocese di Civitavecchia
Piazza Vittorio Emanuele 21
00053 Civitavecchia (Roma), Italy

Curia Vescovile
Diocese di Frosinone
Via Monti Lepini
03100 Frosinone, Italy

Curia Vescovile
Diocese di Latina
Via Sezze 16
04100 Latina, Italy

Curia Vescovile
Diocese di Pontecorvo
Via Di Sopra
03037 Pontecorvo (FR), Italy

Curia Vescovile
Diocese di Rieti
Via Cinta
02100 Rieti, Italy

Curia Vescovile
Diocese di Roma, Porto S. Rufino
Via Del Cenacolo
00100 Roma, Italy

Curia Vescovile
Diocese di Roma
Via S. Cenacolo
00100 Roma, Italy

Curia Provinciali Padre Gesuiti
Diocese di Roma
Via Astalli 16
00100 Roma, Italy

Curia Vescovile
Diocese di Tivoli
Via S. Anna 1
00019 Tivoli (Roma), Italy

Curia Vescovile
Diocese di Viterbo
Piazza S. Lorenzo 10
01100 Viterbo, Italy

LIGURIA

Curia Vescovile
Diocese di Chiavari
Piazza Nostra Signore, dell'Orto 7
16043 Chiavari (GE), Italy

Curia Vescovile
Diocese di Genova
Piazza Matteotti 4
16100 Genova, Italy

Curia Vescovile
Diocese di Imperia
Via Unione 7
18100 Imperia, Italy

Curia Vescovile
Diocese di La Spezia
Via Minzoni 64
19100 La Spezia, Italy

Curia Vescovile
Diocese di Savona
Piazza Vescovado 13/rp
17100 Savona, Italy

LOMBARDIA

Curia Vescovile
Diocese di Bergamo
Piazza Duomo 5
24100 Bergamo, Italy

Curia Vescovile
Diocese di Crema
Piazza Duomo 27
26013 Crema (CR), Italy

Curia Vescovile
Diocese di Cremona
Piazza Zaccaria 5
26100 Cremona, Italy

Curia Vescovile
Diocese di Como
Piazza Grimaldi 5
22100 Como, Italy

Curia Vescovile
Diocese di Lodi
Via Cavour 31
20075 Lodi, Italy

Curia Vescovile
Diocese di Mantova
Piazza Sordello 15
46100 Mantova, Italy

Curia Vescovile
Diocese di Milano
Via Signora 1
20100 Milano, Italy

Curia Vescovile
Diocese di Vigevano
Piazza S. Ambrogio 1
27029 Vigevano (PV), Italy

LE MARCHE

Curia Vescovile
Diocese di Ancona
Via Ferretti 11
60100 Ancona, Italy

Curia Vescovile
Diocese di Ascoli Piceno
Piazza Arringo 27
63100 Ascoli, Italy

Curia Vescovile
Diocese di Fabriano
Piazza Cattedrale 2
60044 Fabriano (AN), Italy

Curia Vescovile
Diocese di Macerata
Piazza S. Vincenzo
62100 Macerata, Italy

Curia Vescovile
Diocese di Pesaro
Via Rossini 62
61100 Pesaro, Italy

Curia Vescovile
Diocese di S. Benedetto del Tronto
Piazza Sacconi 1
63039 S. Benedetto del Tronto (AP),
Italy

Curia Vescovile
Diocese di Urbino
Piazza Pascoli 4
61029 Urbino, (PS), Italy

MOLISE

Curia Vescovile
Diocese di Campobasso
Via Mazzini 36
86100 Campobasso, Italy

Curia Vescovile
Diocese di Isernia
Piazza A. D'Isernia 2
86170 Isernia, Italy

Curia Vescovile
Diocese di Termoli
Piazza S. Antonio
86039 Termoli (CB), Italy

PIEMONTE

Curia Vescovile
Diocese di Alba
Piazza Grassi 9
12051 Alba (CN), Italy

Curia Vescovile
Diocese di Asti
Via Carducci 50
14100 Asti, Italy

Curia Vescovile
Diocese di Biella
Via Vescovado 10
13051 Biella, Italy

Curia Vescovile
Diocese di Casale Monferrato
Via Liutprando 1
15033 Casale Monferrato (AL), Italy

Curia Vescovile
Diocese di Cuneo
Via Roma 7
12100 Cuneo, Italy

Curia Vescovile
Diocese di Ivrea
Piazza Castello 3
10015 Ivrea (TO), Italy

Curia Vescovile
Diocese di Novara
Via Puccini 11
28100 Novara, Italy

Curia Vescovile
Diocese di Pinerolo
Via Vescovado 1
10064 Pinerolo (TO), Italy

Curia Vescovile
Diocese di Saluzzo
Corso Piemonte 56
12037 Saluzzo (CN), Italy

Curia Vescovile
Diocese di Torino
Via S. Antonio da Padova 7
10100 Torino, Italy

Curia Vescovile
Diocese di Vercelli
Piazza D'Angennes 6
13100 Vercelli, Italy

PUGLIA

Curia Vescovile
Diocese di Bari
Via Bellomo 94
70100 Bari, Italy

Curia Vescovile
Diocese di Brindisi
Piazza Duomo 17
72100 Brindisi, Italy

Curia Vescovile
Diocese di Foggia
Piazza Immacolata
71100 Foggia, Italy

Curia Vescovile
Diocese di Gallipoli
Piazza Duomo 2
73014 Gallipoli, Italy

Curia Vescovile
Diocese di Lecce
Piazza Duomo
73100 Lecce, Italy

Curia Vescovile
Diocese di Taranto
Via Arcivescovado 11
74100 Taranto, Italy

SARDEGNA

Curia Vescovile
Diocese di Cagliari
D. Palazzo 4
09100 Cagliari, Italy

Curia Vescovile
Diocese di Nuoro
Piazza S. Maria della Neve 19
08100 Nuoro, Italy

Curia Vescovile
Diocese di Oristano
Via Duomo 5
09170 Oristano, Italy

Curia Vescovile
Diocese di Sassari
Via Arcivescovado 1
07100 Sassari, Italy

SICILY

Curia Vescovile
Diocese di Acireale
Piazza Duomo 52
95024 Acireale (CT), Italy

Curia Vescovile
Diocese di Agrigento
Via Duomo 96
92100 Agrigento, Italy

Curia Vescovile
Diocese di Catania
Via Vittorio Emanuele 159
95100 Catania, Italy

Curia Vescovile
Diocese di Cefalù
Piazza Duomo 12
90015 Cefalù (PA), Italy

Curia Vescovile
Diocese di Messina
Via S. F. Bianchi 12
98100 Messina, Italy

Curia Vescovile
Diocese di Monreale
Via Arcivescovado 3
90046 Monreale (PA)

Curia Vescovile
Diocese di Palermo
Piazza S. F. D'Assisi
90100 Palermo, Italy

Curia Vescovile
Diocese di Patti
Piazza Cattedrale
98066 Patti (ME), Italy

Curia Vescovile
Diocese di Ragusa
Via Roma 109
97100 Ragusa, Italy

Curia Vescovile
Diocese di Siracusa
Piazza Duomo 5
96100 Siracusa, Italy

Curia Vescovile
Diocese di Trapani
Corso Vittorio Emanuele 42
91100 Trapani, Italy

TOSCANA

Curia Vescovile
Diocese di Arezzo
Via Ricasoli 3
52100 Arezzo, Italy

Curia Vescovile
Diocese di Firenze
Piazza S. Giovanni 3
50100 Firenze, Italy

Curia Frati Minori
Via Giacomini 3/m
50100 Firenze, Italy

Curia Vescovile
Diocese di Grosseto
Via Garibaldi 8
58100 Grosseto, Italy

Curia Vescovile
Diocese di Livorno
Via Seminario 61
57100 Livorno, Italy

Curia Vescovile
Diocese di Lucca
Via S. Nicolao 81
55100 Lucca, Italy

Curia Vescovile
Diocese di Massa Carrara
Via Zoppi 14
54100 Massa, Italy

Curia Vescovile
Diocese di Pisa
Piazza Arcivescovado
56100 Pisa, Italy

Curia Vescovile
Diocese di Pistoia
Via Nicolò Puccini 36
51100 Pistoia, Italy

Curia Vescovile
Diocese di Prato
Piazza Duomo 48
50047 Prato (FI), Italy

Curia Vescovile
Diocese di Siena
Piazza Duomo 6
53100 Siena, Italy

Curia Vescovile
Diocese di Viareggio
Via Bonaparte 214
55049 Viareggio (LU), Italy

TRENTINO-ALTO ADIGE

Curia Vescovile
Diocese di Bolzano & Bressanone
Via Marconi 9
39100 Bolzano, Italy

Curia Vescovile
Diocese di Trento
Piazza Fiera 1
38100 Trento, Italy

UMBRIA

Curia Vescovile
Diocese di Assisi
Piazza Vescovado 3
06081 Assisi (PG), Italy

Curia Vescovile
Diocese di Foligno
Piazza Faloci Pulignani 3
06034 Foligno (PG), Italy

Curia Vescovile
Diocese di Perugia
Piazza IV Novembre 6
06100 Perugia, Italy

Curia Vescovile
Diocese di Spoleto
Corso Garibaldi 75
06049 Spoleto (PG), Italy

Curia Vescovile
Diocese di Terni
Via XI Febbraio 4
05100 Terni, Italy

VAL D'AOSTA

Curia Vescovile
Diocese di Aosta
Via Hotel D'Etats 15
11100 Aosta, Italy

VENETO

Curia Vescovile
Diocese di Belluno & Feltre
Piazza Duomo 3
32100 Belluno, Italy

Curia Vescovile
Diocese di Chioggia
Via del Vescovado
30015 Chiogia (VE), Italy

Curia Vescovile
Diocese di Padova
Via Vescovado
35100 Padova, Italy

Curia Vescovile
Diocese di Rovigo
Via S. Sichirello18
45100 Rovigo, Italy

Curia Vescovile
Diocese di Treviso
Piazza Duomo
31100 Treviso, Italy

Curia Vescovile
Diocese di Venezia
Parr. S. Marco 320/a
30100 Venezia, Italy

Curia Vescovile
Diocese di Verona
Piazza Vescovado 7
37100 Verona, Italy

Curia Vescovile
Diocese di Vicenza
Piazza Duomo 10/12
36100 Vicenza, Italy

Curia Vescovile
Diocese di Vittorio Veneto
Via De Ponte 21
31029 Vittorio Veneto (TV), Italy

Glossary of Italian Terms

The following terms are some of those most commonly found in Italian records. Note that many Italian words have gender inflections: the ending of the word denotes the gender of the person to whom it refers. For example, *bisnonno* means "great-grandfather"; *bisnonna* means "great-grandmother."

Italian	English	Italian	English
d'anni	age	Italia	Italy
anno	year	legittimo/a	legitimate
antenato	ancestor	levatrice	midwife
arciprete	archpriest	luogo	place
atto	act	madre	mother
battesimo	baptism	mammana	midwife
battezzato/a	baptised	marito	husband
bisnonno/a	great-grandfather/mother	maschile	male
bocca	mouth	matrimonio	marriage
capelli	hair	matrina/madrina	godmother
capo	family head	mese	month
casa	house	mezzadri	farm workers
catasto	tax record	minuti	minute
celibe	unmarried male	moglie	wife
censimento	census records	morte	death
certificato	certificate	morto/a	died
cimitero	cemetery	municipio	town hall
città	city	NN	abbreviation for the Latin *nescio nomen:* of "unknown name"
cittadinanza	citizenship		
cittadino/a	citizen		
cognome	surname	nascita	birth
colorito	skin color	naso	nose
comune	commune (the smallest civil administrative unit within a province)	nato/a	born
		nobile	noble
		nome	given name
cresima	confirmation	nonno/a	grandfather/mother
cugino/a	cousin	nubile	unmarried female
data	date of birth	numero	number
divorziato/a	divorced	occhi	eyes
donna	woman/lady	ore	hour
estratto	extract	ostetrica	midwife
età	age	padre	father
famiglia	family	parrocchia	parish
fanciullo/a	young boy/girl	parroco	parish priest
femminile	female	patrino/padrino	godfather
figlio/a	son/daughter	pieve	group of parishes
foglio	page	prete	priest
fratello	brother	professione	profession
frazione	small village within a *comune*	provincia	province
fronte	forehead	prozio/a	great uncle/aunt
genitori	parents	religione	religion
giorno	day	residente	residence
illegittimo/a	illegitimate	sacerdote	priest
indice	index	sepoloto/a	buried

Italian	English		Italian	English
sepultura	burial		statura	height
sesso	sex		tempo	time
sindaco	mayor		testimoni	witnesses
sorella	sister		ufficio	office
sposa	bride		vedovo/a	widower/widow
sposo	groom		vescovo	bishop
stato civile	marriage status		viso	face
			zio/a	uncle/aunt

Beltrami, Daniele. *Forze di lavoro e proprietà fondiarianelle campagne Venete dei secoli XVII e XVIII.* Venice, Italy: Istituto per la Collaborazione Culturale, 1961.

Berengo, Marino. *L'agricoltura Veneta dalla caduta della repubblica all'unità.* Milan, Italy: Banca Commerciale Italiana, 1963.

Bolognani, Bonifacio. *A Courageous People From the Dolomites.* Trent, Italy: T.E.M.I., 1981.

Callovini, Carlo Giuseppe. *Guida storica e turistica dell'anaunia* Tip. Anaune, Fondo, (TN), Italy, 1971.

Camera, A., and R. Fabietti. *Il medioevo.* Vol. 1 in *Elementi di storia.* Bologna, Italy: Zanichelli, 1968.

Chabod, Federico. *L'Italia contemporanea (1918–1948).* Edited by Giulio Einaudi. Torino, Italy: 1961.

Conrad, J. "Freedom and Commitment: Families, Youth, and Social Change." *American Psychologist* 36 (1981): 1475–84.

The Church of Jesus Christ of Latter-day Saints. *Genealogical Records in the United States.* Genealogical Dept. Series B No. 1 Revised. Salt Lake City: 1977.

_____. *Major Genealogical Sources for Italy.* Salt Lake City: 1977.

_____. *From You To Your Ancestors.* Salt Lake City: 1978.

_____. *Hiring a Professional Genealogist.* Salt Lake City: 1993.

Cole, Trafford R. "Italian Genealogical Record Sources." *The Genealogical Helper* Sep–Oct 1980: 9–13. Logan, Utah: The Everton Publishers.

_____. "The Origin, Meaning and Changes in Major Italian Surnames." *The Genealogical Helper* Mar-Apr 1982: 11–14. Logan, Utah: The Everton Publishers.

_____. "Italian Emigration: A Tale of Hardship." *The Genealogical Helper* Sep–Oct 1984: 11–13. Logan, Utah: The Everton Publishers.

_____. "Only the Province in Italy Was Known" in *How to Trace Your Ancestors to Europe.* Edited by Hugh Law. Salt Lake City: Cottonwood Books, 1984.

_____. "Born in Italy Near the Swiss Border" in *How to Trace Your Ancestors to Europe.* Edited by Hugh Law. Salt Lake City: Cottonwood Books, 1984.

_____. "Overcoming False Information" in *How to Trace Your Ancestors to Europe.* Edited by Hugh Law. Salt Lake City: Cottonwood Books, 1984.

_____. "Tracing the Family of an Eminent Scholar" in *How to Trace Your Ancestors to Europe.* Edited by Hugh Law. Salt Lake City: Cottonwood Books, 1984.

_____. "Researching Your Italian Ancestors." *Genealogy Digest* 18(1): 25–29. Bountiful, Utah.

_____. "Do Not Procrastinate Your Research." *Ancestry Newsletter* 8(6): 11–12. Salt Lake City: Ancestry.

Colletta, John. *Finding Italian Roots: The Complete Guide for Americans.* Baltimore: Genealogical Publishing Co., 1993.

Colletti, Joseph. "Query #89-0001." *POINTers* 3(1). Palos Verdes, California.

Corsini, Umberto. *Tavola Clesian, dalla romanità al risorgimento.* Trent, Italy: Saturnia, 1977.

De Felice, Emidio. *Dizionario dei cognomi Italiani.* Milan, Italy: Mondadori, 1978.

_____. *Dizionario dei nomi Italiani.* Milan, Italy: Mondadori, 1981.

Di Benedetto, D., A. Greco, and F. Del Vecchio. *Guida bibliografica di cripte ipogei e insediamenti rupestri della.* Edited by Puglia Levante. Bari, Italy: 1990.

Eakle, Arlene, and Johni Cerny. *The Source: A Guidebook of American Genealogy.* Salt Lake City: Ancestry, 1984.

Folkel, Ferruccio. *La risiera di San Sabba.* Verona, Italy: Mondadori, 1979.

Gorfer, Aldo. *Le Valli del Trentino, Trentino occidentale.* 2nd ed. Calliano (TN), Italy: Manfrini, 1975.

Heimberg, Marilyn Markham. *Finding Your Roots.* New York: Dell Publishing Co., 1978.

Kogan, Norman. *A Political History of Italy: The Postwar Years.* New York: Praeger, 1983.

Konrad, J. *Italian Family Research.* Rev. ed. Munroe Falls, Ohio: Summit Publications, 1990.

Lane, Fredric C. *I mercanti di Venezia.* Turin, Italy: 1982.

Law, Hugh T. "Italy and the Astro-Hungarian Empire" in *How to Trace Your Ancestors to Europe.* Salt Lake City: Cottonwood Books, 1984.

Leonardi, Enzo. *Cles, capoluogo storico dell'anaunia editrice.* Trent, Italy: Editrice T.E.M.I., 1982.

Levi, Primo. *Se questo è un uomo.* Turin, Italy: Giulio Einaudi, 1976.

Luzzatto, Gino. *Breve storia economica dell'Italia medievale.* Edited by Giulio Einaudi. Turin, Italy: 1958.

Maspoli, Carlo. *Stemmario quattrocentesco delle famiglie nobili della città e antica diocesi di Como.* Como, Italy: 1661.

Masur, Jenny. "The Society and Its Environment" In *Italy, a Country Study.* 2nd ed. Area Handbook Series, edited by Rinn S. Shinn. U.S. Government, 1985.

Mendola, Louis. Correspondence. 1993.

Mezzetti, Giulio. *Geografia, Atlante di Lavoro.* Florence, Italy: La Nuova Italia, 1981.

Militello, Thomas. "Growth." *POINTers* 7 (4). Palos Verdes, California: 1993

Moore, Rita. "Historical Setting." In *Italy, a Country Study.* 2nd ed. Area Handbook Series, edited by Rinn S. Shinn. U.S. Government, 1985.

Negro, Carlo. *Il mondo contemporaneo.* Vol. 3, *L'umana conquista.* Turin, Italy: 1963.

Nilo, Mario, et al. *Maximus: dizionario enciclopedico.* Novara, Italy: Istituto Geographico De Agostini, 1992.

Norwich, John Julius, ed. *The Italians: History, Art, and the Genius of a People.* New York: Abrams, 1983.

Preto, Paolo. *Peste e società a Venezia, 1576.* Edited by Neri Pozzi. Vicenza, Italy: 1978.

Preece, P.P., and F.S. Preece. *Handy Guide to Italian Genealogical Records.* Logan, Utah: The Everton Publishers, 1978.

Pullan, Brian. *Gli ebrei d'Europa e l'inquisizione a Venezia dal 1550 al 1670.* Rome: Il Veltro, 1985.

Repubblica Italiana. "Disposizioni relative alle generalità in estratti, atti e documenti e modificazioni all'ordinamento dello stato civile." Legge n.1064, Gazzetta Ufficiale n. 267, 19 Nov. 1955, 1857–1859.

_____. "Regolamento di attuazione recante disposizioni relative alle generalità in estratti, atti e documenti e modificazioni all'ordinamento dello stato civile." Decreto del Presidente della Repubblica n.432, Gazzetta Ufficiale n.156, 24 June 1957, 981–983.

_____. "Disciplina dei casi di scioglimento del matrimonio." Legge n.898, Gazzetta Ufficiale n.306, 3 December 1970, 2365–2369.

_____. "Disciplina dell'importo di registro." Decreto del Presidente della Repubblica n.634; Gazzetta Ufficiale n.292, 11 Nov. 1972, 2109–2143.

_____. "Disciplina dell'importo di bollo." Decreto del Presidente della Repubblica n.634; Gazzetta Ufficiale n.292, 11 Nov. 1972, 2331–2339.

_____. "Ordinamento delle autonomie locali." Legge n.142, Gazzetta Ufficiale n.135, 12 June 1990, 1100–1129.

_____. "Nuove norme in materia di procedimento amministrativo e di diritto di accesso ai documenti amministrativi." Legge n.241, Gazzetta Ufficiale n.192, 18 August 1990, 1564–1571.

Sacchi, Paolo. *Storia del mondo giudaico.* Turin, Italy: SEI, 1976.

Soldani, A., et al. *Calendario Atlante De Agostini 1994.* Novara, Italy: Istituto Geografico De Agostini, 1994.

Smith, Denis Mack. "Italian Fascism" in *Fascism: A Reader's Guide.* Edited by Walter Lacquerer. Berkeley: University of California Press, 1976.

_____. *Italy: A Modern History*. Valori Press, 1969.

_____. *Storia d'Italia 1861–1969*. Vols. 1, 2, and 3. Rome: Laterza, 1973.

Tamburin, Vincenzo Menegus. *S. Vito, Borca, Vodo e Venas nella storia cadorina*. Bologna, Italy: Tamari, 1975.

_____. *Al pan de i morte*. Belluno, Italy: Tarantola Libraio, 1974.

Tourn, Giorgio. *I Valdesi, la singolare vicenda di un popolo-chiesa*. Turin, Italy: Claudiana, 1977.

Wonk, Dalt. "Sons of Contessa Entellina." *Dixie*. 16 October 1983.

C